MACK INNON

CASES IN MARKETING RESEARCH

MACKINNON

CASES IN MARKETING RESEARCH

F. Stewart DeBruicker

University of Pennsylvania

David J. Reibstein

University of Pennsylvania

Prentice-Hall, Inc., Englewood Cliffs, N.J. 07632

Library of Congress Cataloging in Publication Data

DeBruicker, F. Stewart.
Cases in marketing research.

Includes bibliographical references.
1. Marketing research—Case Studies. I. Reibstein, David J. II. Title.
HF5415.2.D37 658.8:3 82-277
ISBN 0-13-118927-1 AACR2

Editorial/production supervision and interior design by Richard C. Laveglia
Cover design by Ray Lundgren
Manufacturing buyer: Ed O'Dougherty

Printed in the United States of America

10 9 8 7 6 5 4 3 2 1

Case material of the Harvard Graduate School of Business Administration is made possible by the cooperation of business firms who may wish to remain anonymous by having names, quantities and other identifying details disguised while maintaining basic relationships. Cases are prepared as the basis for class discussion rather than to illustrate either effective or ineffective handling of administrative situations.

ISBN 0-13-118927-1

Prentice-Hall International, Inc., *London*
Prentice-Hall of Australia Pty. Limited, *Sydney*
Prentice-Hall Canada, Inc., *Toronto*
Prentice-Hall of India Private Limited, *New Delhi*
Prentice-Hall of Japan, Inc., *Tokyo*
Prentice-Hall of Southeast Asia Pte. Ltd., *Singapore*
Whitehall Books Limited, *Wellington, New Zealand*

Our most personal thanks go to our wives, Shelby and Karen.

Contents

Preface

A case study has much in common with a photograph. Both capture moments in time so that they may be observed. Both can stop processes that are inherently dynamic so that the viewer may better understand the steps within. Both offer the person that views them the chance to learn without firsthand experience. Both can become a part of the viewer's cumulative history of experience. And both can contribute valuable lessons to those viewers who intend to one day participate in the process and to those who wish only to become better observers.

This casebook is like an album of photographs. Like many albums, it was prepared with a strong sense of who would be in its primary audience. In this instance, that audience consists of upper-level students of marketing research at university business schools. Most of those students study marketing research not to become researchers per se but rather to acquire the confidence of knowing the differences between good and bad research. As future managers, they seek this confidence so they can *use* research and make decisions accordingly. Many are to serve roles comparable to orchestra conductors. Whereas orchestra conductors do not need to know how to play each of the instruments, they do need to know how to identify sour notes. Further, if they intend to make good music, they must know how the pieces all fit together.

A significant minority of students study marketing research because of their ambition to one day *do* research. Like future users, they are welcome members of this book's primary audience, for at the crucial moment of the manager's decision, or the researcher's recommendation, or the conductor's downbeat, we believe that there are only scant differences between successful users and doers.

Like many photograph albums, this casebook was prepared over a long period of time, yet is unfinished. It is unfinished because the subject matter continues to grow, challenge, and excite. As with any collection of photographs, the cases in this book only describe processes of the past, however recent they may be. To our intended audience, we hope that is a basis for inspiration.

Finally, like many photograph albums, this casebook was prepared with the help of many contributors. Casewriters, like photographers, must have subjects, points of view, and skills to present them to an observer. They must inform and stimulate. On rare occasions, photographers and casewriters create unique masterpieces that are both eloquent and succinct. More often, they must display a series of apparently mundane images to convey their personal visions. We are proud to present herein examples of both, since masterpieces are always in rather short supply.

Our professional respect and gratitude are given to Claudine Malone and Steven Star for allowing their work to be reproduced in this book. Their contributions have added greatly to the technical and practical content of the "Analysis for Marketing Decisions" sections of the book. Former students have made substantial creative contributions to those cases for which we claim authorship, and our debts must be acknowledged to Mark Chussil, Beth Burnam Fink, Jan-Erik Modig, John O'Donnell, Harvey Singer, Elizabeth Webster, and George Yip. These students have gone on to academic or managerial careers, and we wish them the same high levels of assistance that they rendered us.

Our own academic careers benefited from the inspiration and instruction of Professors Frank M. Bass and Edgar A. Pessemier of Purdue University, supervisors of our doctoral theses and fine "photographers" in their own rights.

At the institutional level, we must acknowledge the support of the Harvard Business School where we equally divided the years 1972 through 1980 as course head for Marketing Research and Information Systems. The cumulative development of that course is reflected in these case studies. That work continues with the support of our colleagues in the Marketing Department of the Wharton School.

We are sincerely grateful for the investment of time and information made by all of the companies and organizations who agreed to serve as sites for these case studies.

F. Stewart DeBruicker
David J. Reibstein

Philadelphia

CASES IN MARKETING RESEARCH

Introduction and Overview

This is a casebook about marketing decision makers and their marketing research suppliers. The cases are developed from a managerial point of view. They tell of managers who dealt with the need to develop information to identify, clarify, and support their choices of marketing actions. They tell also of techniques for defining problems, obtaining relevant data, and conducting analytical inquiries. And they illustrate solutions to the problem of balancing the always scarce resources of time and money with the desire for precise marketing information. But at its core, each case is a personal one. Each describes the personal career risk that every manager assumes in the process of decision making. This book was written so that future managers might learn from those of the past, and by making their own applications of marketing research methods, make their future career-risking decisions with confidence and success.

Marketing managers and their marketing research suppliers work together to solve problems and to develop opportunities using their best individual talents: the decision-making skills of managers, and the analytical skills of research suppliers.[1] These are separate skills and they do not easily converge. Evidence of their separateness is found in several areas. First, in the organization structures of modern corporations, the research function may be centralized or not, but it is nearly always held separate from the management groups which are its internal clients. Second, there is a thriving independent research industry made up of firms that never implement the strategies they recommend, though their existence is based on the information needs of managers in dozens of client industries. Finally, the fact that marketing research is taught in business schools as a separate (and usually) elective course is based on more than simple pedagogical convenience—it is based on the recognition that the underlying concepts of marketing management and marketing research are drawn from quite different scholarly traditions.

[1]In more than a few of the cases in this book, as in real life, the manager and the research supplier are one and the same person. The same dual-identity is presumed for all users of this book.

Thus, whether it might be a dotted line or a gulf, there is indeed a separation between the functions of marketing management and marketing research. And though marketing research is derived from, and supportive of, marketing management, effective relationships between managers and their research suppliers are neither established nor sustained with ease. This book is intended to be a bridge between the functions of management and research.

EVALUATING MARKETING SITUATIONS

Just as one may build a bridge by starting on either side of a gap, one may attempt to link the separate disciplines of marketing management and marketing research by beginning on either side. But given the practical domination of research by management issues, and given the fact that the study of marketing management usually precedes the study of marketing research, it seems advisable to first build where the intellectual terrain is most familiar.

Marketing managers are charged with the responsibility of implementing marketing strategy for a business. Theirs are the decisions that affect the basic choices that a firm must make: which products to offer, which market segments to serve, and which competitors to rival. Based on these fundamental choices, operating marketing programs are designed, implemented, and maintained in the areas of the marketing mix: product line management; pricing; promotion; advertising and sales management; physical distribution; and marketing research. All of these programs are founded on knowledge or assumptions about the customers in a market, and their purchasing behaviors.

Table 1-1 lists the types of knowledge that all marketing managers might be expected to possess regarding their businesses. Where this knowledge is incomplete, out of date, or based on untested assumptions, there exists the opportunity for practical marketing research. When evaluating a new marketing situation, or reviewing an old one, the listed types of information make up the foundation of marketing plans and programs. The items in Table 1-1 can be thought of as a series of questions that marketing managers should be able to answer with ease about their businesses. Any element in the list could serve as a starting point for inquiry, but eventually all the answers should be complete and consistent among themselves. Marketing research can often aid in the search for those answers.

Table 1-1

Sizing Up Marketing Situations

What is the Product-Market Fit?
Product Analysis
Benefits to Users
Stage in the Product Life Cycle
Bases for Product Differentiation
Market Analysis
Size of the Market, Dollars and Units
Growth Rate of the Market
Bases for Market Segmentation
Customer Analysis
Decision-Making Units
Decision-Making Processes
Marketing Mix Decisions
Product Line
Pricing
Promotion and Communication
Physical Distribution
Marketing Research
Evaluation of Competitors' Strategies
Stack-Rated Issues
Problems
Opportunities

Product-Market Fit information refers to the overall matching of specific products to specific market segments. It represents a statement of which technologies a firm will employ in order to serve selected types of customers. The choices of products and markets are fundamental to the strategy of the business, and until those choices have been made and ratified by top management, operating decisions will be impossible in any supporting management function. When the product-market fit of a business is unclear, or the subject of critical review, it is useful to decompose the product and market components of this decision into three areas.

Product Analysis information answers three sets of questions: what are the product's benefits to its users, what is the product's position in its life cycle, and what are the bases for differentiating the product from potential substitutes?

Market Analysis information answers three questions also: what is the size of the market in units and dollars, what is the growth rate of the market, and what are the potential bases by which the market might be segmented?

Customer Analysis information describes in depth the major segments identified in the business's overall strategy. For each segment, knowledge of the number and type of individuals making up the decision-making unit (DMU) and their decision-making processes (DMPs) is at the very core of the marketing concept.

There is a great deal of interaction and overlapping among the types of information needed for DMU/DMP analysis, market segmentation analysis, and product differentiation analysis. Though these interactions can become quite complex, there is usually some value in separating the customer, market, and product issues in a marketing information bank since each can contribute contrasting implications to the strategy decision-making process.

Marketing Mix Decisions require specialized types of information, each addressing issues unique to a particular marketing program. Just as the marketing management task is often organized into functions such as product management, sales management, advertising, and distribution, so are types of marketing information organized according to these separate but related tasks.

Evaluation of Competitors' Strategies raises the same questions as an internal marketing evaluation, but directs them to the strategies of the business's major competitors. In common practice, analyses of competitors' strategies tend to be more subjective than internal strategy analyses, but in view of the increased attention given to formal strategic marketing planning systems, it is expected that more attention will be directed to developing competitive strategy evaluations that are as empirically supported as those conducted internally.

Stack-Rated analyses can be conducted following any phase of the sizing-up process. Stack-rating is simply the process of sorting sets of problems and opportunities by levels of priority. Highest priority problems and opportunities are the ones which should be addressed first. They should receive the greatest share of management time and resources. They provide a fast track, visibility, and career advancement potential for the managers and the research suppliers who manage and study them.

The situation size-up of Table 1-1, then, is a summary of the types of information that most marketing managers need, based upon the tasks of marketing management. It is not an end, rather it is a means for identifying the types of information that managers find helpful in furthering their strategy decision processes.

The marketing situation size-up can be conducted quickly or with deliberate slowness. It offers a clear separation of strategic and tactical information required by marketing managers, and it identifies a relatively thorough inventory of facts that any manager, consultant, or competitor would require before developing more specific types of diagnostic analysis. Almost always, alternative strategy choices flow from sizing up a marketing situation—and the analysis of stated alternatives is precisely the type of problem where marketing research methods can be applied with greatest effectiveness.

If managers are certain of all the

aforementioned information, then the role of research is very limited. But without research, managers must make strategy decisions solely on the basis of accumulated experience and intuitive judgments. These may be imperfect for three reasons: the manager's recall may not be correct, competitive environments may have changed, and intuitions may not always be reliable. All three make past experiences questionable guides for present actions, and intuitive judgments often bear high costs of error.

One frequent argument against market research is that it only confirms what is already known. This is only partially true, and is in fact an argument for, not against, the role of marketing research. For example, a package-goods company may be confident that a new product will be successful. But it would still proceed with concept testing, prototype testing, test marketing, advertising research, and other research studies to reduce the cost and risk of a new product introduction. The research may in fact confirm management's early judgments, but it will also provide useful quantitative information such as the likely rate of acceptance of the product and the price customers are willing to pay, or qualitative information such as how the product should be positioned, and what its advertising should say. Research, therefore, can not only confirm expectations, it can make them more precise and provide new information that is useful for marketing program management. The resulting program efficiencies can create tremendous competitive advantages for the research-driven firm.

MANAGING AT THE INTERFACE BETWEEN MANAGERS AND RESEARCHERS

Users and doers of marketing research must interact in the context of marketing decision making. There, managers' abilities for moving a business into areas of opportunity merge with marketing researchers' abilities to collect and analyze data. Merging these different skills can be difficult. Managers may not appreciate the time requirements or the financial necessities of those research methods that are best suited to the decisions at hand, and they may avoid discussions of research processes or of full findings in preference for presentations of top-line or "flash" summary results. These are classic mistakes.

Researchers may object that they are not fully informed of the marketing decisions for which their studies are intended, or they may complain that their studies are used to justify decisions that were not explicitly included in the research design. They may protest that they are asked to conduct too many studies that are trivial or repetitive, thereby wasting their resources for studies that are truly strategic. And they are almost certain to complain that there are very few managers who know how to use them to best competitive advantage. These are classic complaints.

There is a way to avoid many of these classic difficulties by focusing on the research management process. Figure 1-1 is a flow chart illustrating the relationships between managers and researchers, showing their areas of respective expertise and the area of most productive interaction: the definition of management's information needs.

The function of a manager is to make and implement strategic marketing decisions. These decisions are the driving force behind the remainder of the marketing research process, for if research has no decision consequences, it can be of little value to the firm.

Marketing researchers' functions, as indicated in Figure 1-1, are to create information useful to the management decision process. Information is created by the separate but related processes of data collection and data analysis.

The interface that joins the management

Figure 1-1

Managing the Relationships Between Users and Doers of Marketing Research

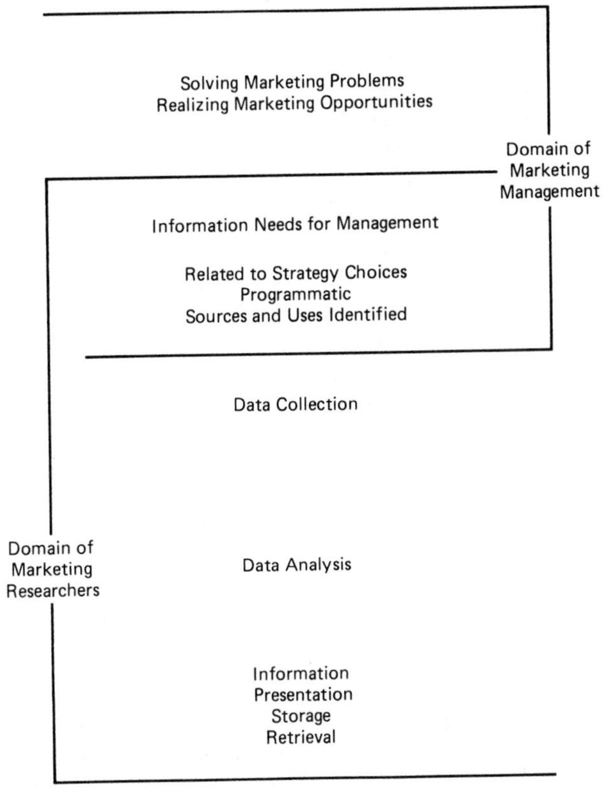

process and the marketing research process is the set of information needs specified by management, and agreed to by research suppliers. Like any area of negotiated agreement between parties of differing objectives and skills, the information needs area can be a source of frustration and disappointment. This need not be so. To overcome the expected difficulties, each party to the negotiation needs an understanding of the interests and capabilities of the other, and both need to commit themselves to a process of frequent discussion. Ultimately, there must be a basis for identifying what needs to be known. There are three guidelines that can help.

First, the information required by management should be explicitly related to strategy choices. Though obvious in retrospect, the case studies that follow will occasionally illustrate situations in which neither managers nor research suppliers devoted sufficient thought to the types of marketing program decisions that might be made as the result of a particular program of research. A common danger sign that an information needs statement is not tied to management action is the justification of a study because it is "exploratory," "baseline," or "fundamental." Such justifications are disguises for fishing expeditions, and though they may be the best way to catch fish, they often result in studies that are expensive, lengthy, and inconsequential. Such studies can undercut management's enthusiasm for future research projects, especially if few new marketing programs have emerged from earlier "exploratory" studies.

Second, the information needs specification should be programmatic. Being programmatic means that research programs are conducted in a series of relatively small, discrete phases, each reviewed before the next is undertaken. Being programmatic tends to avoid the complications of large exploratory studies. Management is more frequently involved in the research process. Later research steps can be adapted to the findings of earlier steps. Questions can be focussed on selected marketing strategy questions in a linked series—avoiding the problem of studying too much with too few resources and with consequently shallow analysis. Being programmatic does not mean avoiding large-scale research projects, but it does mean that even large projects should be uncoupled into discrete phases that have realistic expectations.

Third, and as a consequence of the needs to be decision-oriented and programmatic, the information needs identification process should include a statement of the sources and the uses of information. By decomposing the data collection process into sources and uses, both managers and researchers will have a basis for negotiating the issues of timing, precision, and cost of the information that is to be developed. Sources are the units of analysis where the necessary data can be obtained, and uses are the management decisions that are to be made once the information is available. Since there are usually several sources for a particular type of information—industry sales, for example, could be measured at the user, retailer, warehouse, or factory level—choosing the ones that are most cost-effective in the context of a particular set of management decisions is an activity worth doing well.

The sources of information can range among any and all of the following

1. Users of the product
2. Non-using advisors in the DMU
3. Selected segments of a market
4. Various members of a distribution channel
5. Competitors
6. Major suppliers to the industry
7. Secondary sources (government and industry associations, for example)
8. Proprietary in-house sources

The types of information that can be obtained from each source is virtually unlimited, though all sources will have relative strengths and weaknesses in their ability to yield information on specific issues. Reviewing the list of marketing information required for a situation size-up in Table 1-1 indicates the wealth of possible questions that could be directed to any information source. Clearly, planning and selectivity are requirements for efficient information gathering.

Selectivity can be increased by organizing the types of desired information according to the types of marketing decisions that are to be made. For example, pricing decisions require different types of inputs than advertising decisions, new product positioning studies require data different from that required for measuring the performance of a sales force, and so on. By sequencing the types of decisions that have to be made as part of the management process, it is usually possible to rank the steps in an information gathering process and to identify those information sources that will be of greatest overall value to the research program.

Combining the sources and uses of information ideas makes it possible to dissect any research program into a series of source and use statements of needed information, each related to contingent management decisions. Figure 1-2 is a grid representing the interaction of information sources and uses. The individual cells are left empty since it is difficult to generalize further about all types of research projects. It is safe, however, to assert that projects dealing with developing major new strat-

Figure 1-2

Information Sources and Information Uses

	Uses of Information: Strategy Decisions			
Sources of Information	Product Decisions	Pricing Decisions	Promotion Decisions	Physical Distribution Decisions
Users of the Product				
Non-using Advisors in the DMU				
Selected Segments of the Market				
Members of the Distribution Channel				
Suppliers				
Secondary Sources				
In-house Sources				

egies for a business usually involve information in the upper left of the matrix, and that projects dealing with the fine-tuning of existing marketing decisions usually involve projects located in the lower rows and the rightmost columns of the matrix. Even if the matrix is not formally used as part of an information needs identification process, its informal use stimulates disciplined thinking of where data might be obtained and for what purpose. This can clarify discussions among managers and research suppliers, which is a significant contribution to a difficult user-doer problem solving process.

Against the background of information source-and-use analysis, it is much easier for managers to make their remaining decisions that affect the marketing research process:

1. Deciding when to initiate research.
2. Identifying the need for specialized assistance.
3. Deciding how much to spend at each step in the process.
4. Reviewing and critiquing proposed research designs.
5. Choosing formats for presenting research results to their management colleagues.

NARROWING THE MANAGER-RESEARCHER GAP

The tasks of managing the marketing function and of doing marketing research have been discussed to this point as independent tasks whose interaction is more often a point of friction than enlightenment. There are signs that give rise to the expectation that in the future the gap, and the friction, may soon be significantly reduced. The changes in the knowledge industry—data analysis and data telecommunications—are the basis of this expectation.

The fields of data collection and data analysis have benefited from generations of cumulative experience in the uses of sampling procedures, various questionnaire designs, many secondary data sources, and increasingly sophisticated computer programs for data analysis. The interaction among various methods of data collection and data analysis has made possible new types of information that can be relevant to management decisions.[2] Future evolutions in telecommunications technology coupled with the steady decline in the real cost of data analysis hardware and software have brought steady advancement in the contributions of the social and information sciences to the marketing research management process.

The resulting low-cost computer technology and marketing research software are changing the manager's job. Some advanced firms have already placed computer terminals at product managers' desks and require empirical evidence to support each recommended marketing change. Without supporting analysis, managers find it is extremely difficult to get approval of suggested changes. The managers are expected to act as their own researcher suppliers. They have data available and are called upon to create their own marketing research information. There are many similar systems that only hint at the future of manager-operated research tools, and all managers of the future are sure to be more active in interpreting and directing the research they receive.

ORGANIZATION OF THIS BOOK

The case studies included here have been selected to complement many contemporary marketing research textbooks.[3] Students will find that the parallel study of one of those texts, along with these case studies, offers a rewarding interaction between theory and practice, concept and application, and ideas and their implementation. Each of the case studies is drawn from real events involving real companies. Though certain disguises have been employed when requested by some of these companies, the decision context of each case is true.

There are three sets of case studies within the book. The first includes cases which address the tasks of defining information needs and managing the relationship between research users and research suppliers. These cases are rather more managerial than technical in their content and are designed to help make explicit the process of research administration from the manager's point of view.

The second set of case studies deals with data collection issues. Sample design, measurement, and data reduction issues are brought out in case studies that are written in serial fashion. Each member of the series deals with an explicit set of data collection issues.

The third, and largest, set of case studies is organized according to types of marketing strategy decisions. Topics include quantifying and forecasting demand, product positioning, communications management, and market testing of comprehensive marketing programs.

[2]Many established methods such as perceptual mapping, cluster analysis, multiple discriminant analysis, factor analysis, multiple regression analysis, and econometric modeling are demonstrated in the following case studies.

[3]Many of the case studies in the "Analysis for Marketing Decisions" section of this book demonstrate the use of advanced research methods which are not discussed in many of the more basic marketing research texts.

Given the breadth of subject matter in most of the cases, there are several ways to sequence them in a course of study. Figure 1-3 suggests the way that the cases in this book fit the chapter outlines of some current marketing research texts, but because of the rich management content of many of the cases, it is possible for cases to be used effectively in many ways. Within each section, cases involving multivariate data analyses tend to follow cases involving less complex methods of data analysis.

ANALYZING A MARKETING RESEARCH CASE STUDY

Cases are used in classroom discussions to demonstrate alternative ways of thinking about marketing management problems. A case places those problems in situations where the management context is revealed in some detail. The reader is asked to define problems, suggest solutions, and evaluate alternatives. Members of the class are asked to tell what they would do in a variety of case-dependent situations and why. As discussions of the cases proceed, the instructor will provide summaries to the discussions so that the general lessons suggested by the specific situations drawn in the case studies can be identified.

Effective use of the case method requires a certain suspension of disbelief on the reader's part. Obviously the case is only a summary of a particular situation and must necessarily omit a great deal of information that might have been available to management in the real situation. Usually, great care is taken to make sure that most of the omitted information is extraneous and to make sure that most of the included information is relevant. The cases are also designed, however, to help readers develop the skill of deciding what is, and is not, relevant.

Your task is to define the problems and opportunities presented in the case, not from the viewpoint of the casewriter or the managers described in the case, but from a personal point of view using personal experiences and problem-solving skills as your guide. You should then analyze why those problems and opportunities exist, and try to identify both their surface and underlying causes. Long- and short-range time frames can be imposed, and questions involving research techniques and management decisions can be raised. You should then consider a set of alternative solutions, and choose one solution that you would be prepared to present and defend in class. In class, as alternative decisions are presented and discussed, you will have the opportunity to learn from your classmates by comparing and evaluating different approaches to solving different kinds of problems.

You should prepare in the following way: first, read through the case as quickly as you can, forming a general impression of the types of problems and data that are presented in the case. Then re-read the case selectively, spending more time on those sections and data which you think are most relevant. Follow this stepwise procedure, if you find it helpful:

1. Problem definitions
2. Opportunity definitions
3. Analysis
4. Alternative decisions
5. Recommended decision
6. Defense of recommendation

For the cases in this book, with their emphasis on marketing research applications, you should try to apply your knowledge of the techniques of marketing research as well as your skills as a marketing manager. Begin by identifying and critiquing the apparent objectives of the research project. Evaluate the extent to which management decisions are likely to be affected by the research. Identify which possible outcomes of the study would influence management to new courses of action.

Figure 1-3

Case Study and Chapter Correlations

	Aaker and Day[1]	*Boyd, Westfall and Stasch*[2]	*Churchill*[3]	*Green and Tull*[4]	*Lehmann*[5]	*Kinnear and Taylor*[6]	*Luck, Wales, Taylor and Rubin*[7]	*Tull and Hawkins*[8]
Western Electric (A)	1, 2, 3	1	1, 2	1, 2, 3	1, 2, 3, 7, 20	1-4	1, 2, 3	1, 2, 3
Kendall-VETMAT	1, 2, 3	1, 18	1, 2, 16	1, 2, 3	1, 2, 3, 11	1-4	1, 2, 3	1, 2, 3, 19
L'eggs Products, Inc. (A)	1, 2, 3	1, 2, 7	1, 2, 17	1, 2, 3	1, 2, 3	1-4	1, 2, 3	1, 2, 3
Daisy (A)	1, 2, 3	1, 2, 7	1, 2	1, 2, 3	1, 2, 3	1-4	1, 2, 3	1, 2, 3
MassNORML (A)	10, 11	4, 10, 11	8, 9, 10	7	9	8-11	7, 8	11
MassNORML (B)	10, 11	4, 10, 11	8, 9, 10	4, 5, 7	5, 9, 11	8-11	7, 8, 9	7, 8, 11, 12
MassNORML (C)	10, 11	4, 10, 11	8, 9, 10, 12, 13	4, 5, 7	9, 11	8-11	7, 8, 9	7, 8, 11
Olympia Brewing Company (A)	6, 7, 8, 9	4	5	4, 5	10	12, 13		4, 5
Olympia Brewing Company (B)	6, 7, 8, 9	4, 8	5, 6, 10	4, 5	6, 9	5, 6, 7, 13, 19	4, 9	5, 7, 15
Strategic Planning Institute (A)	6, 7, 8, 9	4, 7, 8	3, 4, 6, 7	3, 4, 5	5, 6	5, 6, 18, 19	4, 9	8
Strategic Planning Institute (B)	6, 7, 8, 9, 13	10, 11, 13, 14	11	3, 4, 5, 8	6, 10	5, 6	9, 10	8, 9, 12, 17

Ocean Spray Cranberries, Inc. (A)	16, 17, 20	7, 8, 9, 16	3, 4, 6, 7, 11, 14, 15	8, 9, 10	5, 6, 16	12, 13, 23, 25	5	5, 8, 9, 17
Daisy (B)	13, 14, 15	5, 13, 14	5, 11, 12, 13	8	4, 6, 8, 11	21, 22	12	14
Olympia Brewing Company (C)	18, 20	15, 22	5, 14	10, 15	14, 18	26	15	4, 15, 16
Franklin Corporation (A)	18	15, 22	5, 14	10, 15	14, 18	7, 26	6, 15	15, 16
Franklin Corporation (B)	18	15, 22	5, 14	10, 15	14, 18	7, 26	6, 15	15, 16
Daisy (C)	5, 20	9		4	7			10
Strategic Planning Institute (C)	15	15	14	13, 14	15			17
Ocean Spray Cranberries, Inc. (B)	17, 19, 20	10, 11, 12, 16	10, 15	12, 13, 14	5, 11, 15, 17	11, 20, 25		5
AdTel, Ltd.	12, 14	3, 21	3, 4	11	4, 8			18
Tang Instant Breakfast Drink (A)	18	15, 21	14	10, 16	14			18
Tang Instant Breakfast Drink (B)	14	3, 9, 13, 14, 21	7, 12, 13	5, 11	4, 8			6, 18
Daisy (D)	23	13, 14, 22	12, 13, 16	8, 17	19	14-17	12	6, 14, 17
Daisy (E)	23	13, 14, 22	12, 13, 16	8, 17	19	14-17	12	6, 14, 17
L'eggs Products, Inc. (B)	14, 23	3, 9, 22	12, 13	8, 15, 17	19	14-17	12	6

See whether the study has been designed to let the data speak to those decisions.

Then turn your attention to the research design. Begin with the data collection phase and examine the sampling and measurement issues that were anticipated. Consider the way that the study sought to minimize problems of bias and error. Then evaluate the methods of data analysis used. Try to trace the procedures by which the variables were transformed and the way in which they were fitted into data analysis models. Note whether the assumptions of the models were met by the data.

Examine the results of the analysis. Try to determine the range of error inherent in the results, and determine the degree of statistical significance of the findings. Practice the art of anticipating "null" results, those results which would have been observed if the assumed relationships among sales, marketing mix elements, or customer phenomena in fact did not exist as hypothesized. Compare the findings of the study to the null, and decide whether they constitute a basis for managerial action. Occasionally, it may be possible for you to reanalyze some of the data. Do so, and test ideas that may have been overlooked by the managers and researchers in the case.

Resist the temptation to categorize the research as either being all good, and worthy of action, or all bad, and therefore worthless for decision-making purposes. Marketing research findings are rarely at either extreme. Even if methodological problems are severe, strive to find what is useful. For example, if data were gathered without a control group, or if there might be some reason to suspect that samples were improperly obtained, ask: "Does the lack of a control group or a precisely proper sample matter? How? What results would be affected in what way? How can I interpret the data to correct, judgmentally, for the problem?"

Marketing research *is* imperfect, but your challenge is to understand the imperfections so you can feel confident using existing data. No research design is faultless, so it is incumbent upon you to assess the bias in the results, and to make operational decisions in the context of the existing situation.

Finally, draw conclusions for administrative action from the research. What management decisions are justified by the study, and which decisions should be advised against? Use the evidence of the study in support of your decisions, and anticipate how other analysts might interpret the same evidence in a contrary fashion. If there is potential for further marketing research, identify the appropriate information needs and suggest the sources and uses of the data you require. Tell what procedures might be used to develop the information, and identify any other advantages that might accrue if your recommended project were to be fielded.

After coming to your personal decision, arrange to meet with a study group. Discuss the issues that you thought were important but do not try to achieve consensus among yourselves.

In class your instructor will ask members of the class to present personal evaluations of the case. Your instructor will probably adopt a nondirective policy through much of the class, putting the responsibility for problem solving directly on you and your classmates. Your instructor will draw out alternative points of view and will invite members of the class to comment on the strengths and limitations of what has been suggested at different points in the discussion. Your instructor will summarize the discussion near the end of the class period, but may not tell what actually happened in the real situation. There are many possible successful solutions to a problem, and the one which management used is not necessarily the most correct one.

At the end of each class you should have a better appreciation of different ways of managing a marketing process, and with a few basic concepts for dealing with similar situations in the context of your own present, or future, management environment.

SUMMARY AND REVIEW POINTS

1. Marketing research activities are driven by strategic management information needs. Marketing managers must provide the decision context in which research is conducted.
2. Marketing management decisions require a knowledge base that includes product, market, customer, marketing mix, and competitive factors. Dated, incomplete, or erroneous knowledge are all justifications for marketing research programs.
3. Research users and research suppliers have specialized skills which are often difficult to coordinate in a problem-solving context. The process of defining management's information needs can be an effective process for forcing convergence between the information that management requires, and the abilities of research suppliers to collect and analyze relevant data.
4. Good information specifications are decision-related, programmatic, and clear in the specification of the sources and uses of the information.

BIBLIOGRAPHY

1. Aaker, David A. and George S. Day, *Marketing Research: Private and Public Sector Decisions* (New York: John Wiley & Sons), 1980.

2. Boyd, Harper W., Jr., Ralph Westfall and Stanley F. Stasch, *Marketing Research, Text and Cases* (Homewood, Illinois: Richard D. Irwin), 5th Edition, 1981.

3. Churchill, Gilbert A., *Marketing Research: Methodological Foundations* (New York: The Dryden Press), 1976.

4. Green, Paul E. and Donald S. Tull, *Research for Marketing Decisions* (Englewood Cliffs, New Jersey: Prentice-Hall, Inc.), 4th Edition, 1978.

5. Lehmann, Donald R., *Market Research and Analysis* (Homewood, Illinois: Richard D. Irwin), 1979.

6. Kinnear, Thomas C. and James R. Taylor, *Marketing Research: An Applied Approach* (New York: McGraw-Hill), 1980.

7. Luck, David J., Hugh G. Wales, Donald A. Taylor and Ronald S. Rubin, *Marketing Research* (Englewood Cliffs, New Jersey: Prentice-Hall, Inc.), 5th Edition, 1978.

8. Tull, Donald S. and Del I. Hawkins, *Marketing Research: Measurement and Method* (New York: Macmillan Publishing Co., Inc.) 2nd Edition, 1980.

I

DEFINING INFORMATION NEEDS

1

Asking the Right Questions

Western Electric (A)

In October 1977, the members of the Product Line Planning and Management (PLPM) group for toll switching systems of Western Electric's Switching Equipment Division were beginning their final review of information that they had prepared in response to a request that they fund a substantial product development program. The request, made by the Bell Telephone Laboratories, involved the evolutionary development of known technologies in an overall pattern that was long established.

Specifically, the proposal called for developing a feature package (No. 2BE3) for the 2B ESS switching system which would improve its maintenance and custom-calling features, would increase its call-handling capacity, and would give it the ability to handle toll calls in addition to local calls. This feature package, which would involve the upgrading of software and some minor hardware redesign, was to be offered to operating telephone companies beginning in 1980 if the proposal were funded.

The PLPM group had argued in the last quarter of 1976 that the local/toll features for the No. 2B ESS switch not be developed. They had not been persuasive, and it appeared that the project was feasible in terms of the necessary technology and the development capabilities of the Bell Laboratories. The PLPM group was a relatively new organization within the Switching Equipment Division, having been formed in 1975. Just prior to the submission of this proposal, there had been several controversies between Bell Laboratories and the division's PLPM groups that centered around various technical aspects of proposals. The technical expertise of the laboratories had prevailed in these controversies. The members of the toll switching PLPM group believed it was critical that this case be evaluated on the basis of market assessment.

THE SWITCHING EQUIPMENT DIVISION

Western Electric's Switching Equipment Division (SED) manufactured switching systems used in both the local and toll networks of the Bell System. Depending on the function of the offices in which they were located, switches were normally classified as local switches, which switched calls among users of the telephone system within local calling areas, or as toll switches, which handled the distribution of long-distance calls between widely separated local offices. In 1977 the SED was involved in the continuing process of helping the operating telephone companies of the Bell System convert their switching technologies from electromechanical technologies, which dated as far back as 50 years, to all-electronic technologies, which had first been placed in service in the 1960s. Looking to the future, the division saw the probable introduction of digital switching technology into the local switching area. Currently, digital technology was being used only in the large toll switching centers because the economics were unattractive for the use of digital switching for other purposes. Additionally, the rapid pace of improvements in semiconductor technology and large-scale integration were expected to yield another generation of processors for switching machines. These two prospective developments—digital switching throughout the network and the next evolutionary generation of processors—were considered to act as the closing of the technological window, around 1985, for the division's present electronic switching systems.

The SED was one of five manufacturing divisions of Western Electric. Western Electric's sales reached $8.1 billion in 1977, with earnings of $490 million. Western Electric functioned as the manufacturing and supply unit of the Bell System, serving the needs of 22 principal operating telephone companies (OTCs) and AT&T's Long Lines Department. Together with AT&T, Western Electric owned Bell Laboratories, the research and development organization of the Bell System. During the 1970s, a number of factors, among which was the increasing degree of competition in the telecommunications marketplace, had accelerated the Bell System's progress toward a market-oriented philosophy of management. Western Electric adopted the product management approach in 1975 to better fulfill its responsibilities as interpreter of the equipment and service needs of the OTCs and their customers.

The PLPM concept focused a number of important responsibilities on product management teams, each of which was in charge of recommending strategies for families of products that share common technologies and, on occasion, common customer segments. Each team was headed by a product family manager who was responsible for, according to the job description,

> directing and participating in the development of product strategies that result in the offering of goods and services which meet the needs of our customers while meeting the product line financial objectives. In addition, this position is responsible for gaining commitment from and coordinating the efforts of various corporate resources to implement the developed strategy.

BELL TELEPHONE LABORATORIES

Bell Telephone Laboratories (BTL) separated its development efforts into two major categories. Research and Systems Engineering (R&SE), which was the more basic development, was funded by AT&T. Specific Design and Development (SD&D) was funded by Western Electric. SD&D efforts included the design of hardware and software that was of near-term commercial value and would be manufactured and marketed by Western Electric. AT&T, BTL, and Western Electric coordinated their activities through hierarchies of management councils, the highest of which was the Tri-Company Council, which included the vice presidents of each company and which was chaired by an AT&T representative. At lower operating levels, a series of intercompany forums functioned as advisory councils for the purpose of coordinating AT&T, BTL, and Western Electric efforts at a product specific level.

New Western Electric product ideas were processed into eventual products by passing them through a series of screens that are sketched in Exhibit 1. In the early stages, the ideas would be proposed as a "case" by the Systems Engineering group of BTL, which would provide a study of technical feasibility and a rough financial analysis of the ideas. The findings would be reviewed by an Intercompany Forum of Western Electric, AT&T, and BTL representatives. BTL's Development Engineering group would then propose a second case for the actual design of products that would actually be manufactured by Western Electric for sale to the OTCs. The smooth functioning of this process depended on integrating the technical design capabilities of BTL with Western Electric's manufacturing expertise and its knowledge of OTC needs. SD&D cases were subject to the final approval of Western Electric, since the funds supporting SD&D came ultimately from Western Electric's sale of equipment to the OTCs.

THE SWITCHING NETWORK

The Bell System Network switching machine system was organized according to the size, location, and function of individual switching centers. There were five classes of switching centers. The lowest tier of the hierarchy was the Class 5, which included nearly 10,000 end offices providing local switching services to users of the telephone system. When users originated long-distance calls, the local switching machines, would switch the call to a hierarchy of toll network switching machines, which were designated Class 4 centers at the base of the network, up to the Class 1 centers. The relationships between various classes of switching centers and the paths taken by typical toll calls is described in Exhibit 2. Moving up the hierarchy, each successive level of switching center provided consolidation and distribution services—consolidating calls for efficient transmission to the next higher level switching center in the network and distributing calls to switching centers lower in the network. As described in Exhibit 3, each switching center was planned to "home" on certain other centers higher in the network, thus providing efficient paths for the prevalent patterns of toll calls.

In sparsely populated areas, it was often advantageous to combine the normally separate functions of local call switching (Class 5) and the lowest level of toll call switching (Class 4) within a single office. Such an office was called a "local/toll" office or a Class 4/5 office.

A major change to improve the efficiency and capability of the toll network was underway with the deployment of common channel interoffice signaling (CCIS). CCIS, which was installed on an office-by-office basis, was expected to be complete in the mid-1980s. As described in the May 17, 1976, edition of *Bell Labs News*, as CCIS was installed throughout the country, it would

> reduce the time it takes to complete a coast-to-coast call to two seconds or less, compared with 10 seconds or more today. With the national system, the Bell System also will be able to provide new customized services.
>
> Today, most of the information needed to connect calls travels in musical tones on the same circuit as the customer's voice. With CCIS, the information will be carried on a separate high-speed channel in the form of short electrical pulses. . . . The new system

will not require new route construction; existing facilities will be used to carry the CCIS signals.

As listed in Exhibit 4, step-by-step equipment was an important part of the local network in 1976.[1] Over 60% of the systems were step by step, and one-third of all Bell System lines were served by step-by-step systems. Panel and No. 1 crossbar systems had the highest average number of lines per system, reflecting their design for application in large metropolitan areas. No. 5 crossbar served the greatest number of lines of the systems listed and was second only to the step-by-step community dial offices (CDOs) in number of systems served. In the future, demand for new local switching was expected to grow at a lower rate than the demand for new toll switching, but because the average age of local switching systems was greater than that of most toll switching equipment, many new local installations were expected due to retirements of existing systems. In general, new installations were to be electronic switching systems (ESS), which would allow the introduction of services such as call waiting, call forwarding, and speed calling. The use of ESS would result in more flexible routing and office code usage, savings in floor space, and less maintenance expense.

The 1976 toll switching network is described in Exhibit 5. Seventy-nine percent of the 1976 Bell System toll switching (in hundred-call-seconds per busy hour) was performed through No. 4A crossbar and crossbar tandem switching systems. These were located in major metropolitan areas. The No. 4A crossbar systems switched over 55% of the toll load. Because of their larger capabilities, No. 4A crossbar, No. 1 ESS toll, and No. 4 ESS were expected to handle most of the toll growth. About 20% of toll switching was done by step-by-step and No. 5 crossbar systems. These served less densely populated areas, where demand was too small to warrant a larger capacity No. 4A crossbar or crossbar tandem system.

If the total traffic volume in an area did not justify separate tandem or toll systems, these functions were performed in a portion of a local switching system. For instance, several small local offices often homed on a larger local office. Part of the switching network in the larger office was then equipped for trunk-to-trunk switching in a combined local-tandem-toll operation. The need to consolidate small quantities of toll traffic in sparsely populated areas led to the development of toll functions on the No. 5 crossbar local switching machine. In many instances this postponed the start-up expense of a new toll switch for many years. In early 1976 approximately 800 offices were defined as Class 4/5 local/toll offices.

ELECTRONIC SWITCHING SYSTEMS AND THE EVOLUTION OF LOCAL/TOLL SWITCHING CAPABILITY

At all levels of the toll switching network the Bell System had to plan for modernization and expansion of the network to seek improvements in operating efficiency and in the quality of customer service. For local/toll offices the planning process involved evaluating decisions either to replace older switching equipment with newer technologies or to consolidate the toll switching functions into larger, nearby offices. Though there was a systemwide pattern that tended to favor consolidation rather than replacement of local/toll switching functions, such decisions depended on a number of factors, among which were expected growth in the area and cost of transmitting toll traffic to the nearest logical toll switching office.

[1]Material in this section is excerpted from *Engineering and Operations in the Bell System* (Murray Hill, N.J.: Bell Telephone Laboratories, 1978), pp. 284 ff.

The ESS family of machines represented a major advance in switching technology for the Bell System. Whereas the step-by-step and No. 5 crossbar technologies relied on electromechanical logic to perform switching functions, the ESS technology utilized software rather than hardware to control the switching functions. The use of stored program control greatly increased a switch's flexibility and its ability to meet the future needs of a changed user base. The ESS generation required large investments for the development of program control software. There was constant demand among operating telephone companies for custom calling services and fuller utilization of the capabilities of an electronic network. Often the evolution of basic technologies was impeded by the need for software advances rather than the need for new forms of hardware and circuitry.

The first electronic switching system, introduced in 1965, was the No. 1 ESS. This local switch was intended to serve metropolitan areas and could serve a maximum of 65,000 lines. The 1976 introduction of an improved processor for the switch resulted in the No. 1A ESS, which had double the call-handling capacity.

The No. 2 ESS was introduced in 1970. This was essentially a down-sized No. 1, developed to serve the needs of suburban local switching markets where electronic switching benefits were needed but where there was neither present demand nor expected future growth that would justify the installation of the larger No. 1 ESS. The No. 2 ESS could serve a maximum of about 12,000 lines. As had happened to No. 1, an improved processor was introduced in 1976 resulting in the 2B ESS, which could serve double the amount of lines or about 24,000 lines.

Historically, as tabulated in Exhibit 6, the ability to handle toll switching functions was engineered into local switching systems a few years after their introduction. Step-by-step systems, the No. 5 crossbar switch, and the No. 1 ESS switch had all been designed for local switching purposes but had been modified subsequently to handle the duties of the Class 4/5 office. There were indications in the Bell System that this pattern of product evolution would also apply to the No. 2B ESS switch.

The desirability of building toll features into the No. 2B ESS local switching machine began to emerge as early as 1975. There were occasional requests from the operating telephone companies for toll features in an ESS machine of moderate size, such as one request received by AT&T and Bell Telephone Laboratories managers in 1975. In it, the chief engineer of a midwestern telco argued for placing the highest priority on the development of toll features on No. 2B ESS. Portions of the request are included in Exhibit 7. The engineer concluded the request with an alternate appeal for AT&T's evaluation of small Class 4/5 switches manufactured by two of Western Electric's competitors.

Within BTL, considerable momentum gathered from late 1975 through 1976 for the modifications to the No. 2B ESS. The pattern of evolutionary design of both local and toll switches, primarily via software improvements; the requests of AT&T and BTL for ESS based Class 4/5 toll switching; and the availability of proved technology readily adaptable to the No. 2B ESS combined to make a persuasive argument for modifying the No. 2B ESS.

THE PROPOSAL FOR LOCAL/TOLL FEATURES

In the third quarter of 1976, during the annual BTL budget review and approval cycle, a proposal was included to fund the development of toll features for the No. 2B ESS. The proposal was circulated to the SED product manager for toll switching systems for comment and evaluation. The proposal had some apparent merit, for it was based on OTC stated needs for sparse area ESS switching to replace step-by-step and No. 5 crossbar electromechanical switches in Class 4/5 local/toll switching offices.

Although a No. 1 ESS switch (for which local/toll features had already been developed) could meet the sparse-area replacement needs, the BTL systems engineering drafters of the proposal believed that the No. 2B ESS switch would provide a better alternative. This was based in part on the expressed needs of several OTCs and on the lower price of the No. 2B ESS compared with the No. 1 ESS. The difference in price was about $900,000 in favor of the No. 2B ESS, which was priced at $600,000. The lower base price of the No. 2B ESS made it the preferred switch in areas where the larger capacity of the No. 1 ESS could not be fully utilized. BTL used these arguments in favor of enhancing the No. 2B ESS with local/toll features.

The product manager, after visiting with BTL engineers, determined that the proposal's toll-related features would require development expenditures of about $2.5 million to prepare the toll features and to enlarge the switch's capacity to carry the additional local and toll traffic. The BTL rough estimates included expected demand for the resulting No. 2B ESS with local/toll features to average at least three units per year over the ten-year period beginning in 1980. The present value of the expected savings to the Bell System, based on the $900,000 advantage over either the No. 1 ESS or its successor, the No. 1A ESS, was approximately $20 million.

The development of local/toll features for the No. 2B ESS was only one relevant cost, if the SED decided to support BTL's proposal. The division would also incur costs related to engineering, manufacturing, and service support over the expected life cycle of the equipment, and the division had certain financial objectives that it had to achieve as well. With these factors in mind, and without conducting formal market analysis, the SED product manager believed that the local/toll development request represented a relatively small benefits-to-cost ratio, and he recommended that the development investments not be included in the 1977 BTL budget.

In the early weeks of 1977, however, it became clear that the proposal to include toll features in the No. 2B ESS was going to be pushed by BTL.

BTL presented a formal case in June 1977 for the design of the No. 2B ESS local/toll features. The local/toll feature required about $2.5 million in Western Electric support for the development of new software and hardware for the switch itself and the development of new network hardware necessary to adapt the switch into the toll switching system. The breakdown of local/toll development requests was as follows:

Feature	*BTL Budget Request (000)*
No. 2B ESS local/toll hardware	$ 675
No. 2B ESS local/toll software	550
Network expansion requirements	1,250
	$2,475

The SED PLPM customer analysis included several elements; among them were a review of the economics of toll consolidation versus replacement in sparse areas based on a 1973 study; a review of a 1975 switching network survey, which projected when each of the nearly 10,000 offices would reach its theoretical switching capacity; and a special survey of OTC demand for Class 4/5 local/toll capability for No. 2B ESS.

THE 1973 SPARSE-AREA TOLL MACHINE REPLACEMENT VERSUS CONSOLIDATION STUDY

A study conducted by members of the BTL staff in 1973 had identified the issues that had to be considered as sparse-area toll switching machines might "exhaust" or be utilized to the limits of their call-handling capacity. At the point of exhaustion, a switch either had to be replaced or the switching functions had to be performed by transmitting them to a distant switching office with available switching capacity, thereby consolidating the network. The costs of replacement versus the costs of consolidation were significantly correlated with the distance between an exhausted machine and that larger machine to which toll switching functions could be transferred.

Using costs that were typical in 1973, the report estimated that on a Bell Systemwide basis, sparse-area machines that were less than 60 miles from a logical consolidation point were candidates for consolidation and machines farther than 60 miles from a consolidation point were candidates for replacement. The study indicated that approximately three-quarters of the sparse-area local/toll machines would exhaust sometime between 1970 and 1990 and about one-third of the exhausted machines would be candidates for replacement while the remaining two-thirds would be candidates for consolidation, using the 60-mile critical distance rule. As technology advances might reduce the costs of transmission versus the cost of switching, the critical distance was expected to increase.

The study noted that at the time of the 1970 switching network survey (SNS), about 60% of the 760 sparse-area local/toll machines were step-by-step switches and the remainder were No. 5 crossbar switches.

THE 1975 SWITCHING NETWORK SURVEY

Using the 1975 SNS as a data source, a PLPM staff member conducted a series of screening operations on the data to determine the approximate number of switching machines that might exhaust between 1980 and 1985. These boundary dates were selected because local/toll capability would not be available for use by the OTCs until 1980, and by 1985 it was believed that the next generation of switching processors would be available. The screens were set in the following sequence:

1. Only offices that were using electromechanical local/toll switches were considered.
2. Only offices of 10,000 lines or less were chosen to limit the data to suburban and rural offices.
3. Only those offices that passed through the first two screens *and* that were expected to exhaust between 1980 and 1985 were retained.

The stepwise screening proceeded through the 10,000 Bell System offices and found about 800 offices with fewer than 10,000 lines that were using electromechanical equipment in Class 4/5 operation. Of those offices, 67 were expected to exhaust inside the boundary time period. Analysis of the distance from each office to its logical homing office in the event of consolidation revealed the following breakdown:

Distance to Nearest Homing Office, If Consolidated	*Number of Offices*
Up to 60 miles	41
61 to 140 miles	24
More than 140 miles	4
	69

THE 1977 ACCOUNT MANAGEMENT TEAM SURVEY

The PLPM group also conducted some primary market research by surveying the 22 Western Electric account managers, each of whom represented Western Electric to one OTC. Each account manager headed a team of Western Electric personnel forming an account group representing expertise in both the client OTC's needs and in Western Electric's products and services. The survey included seven basic questions, listed in Exhibit 8.

By April 1977, all the account teams had responded to the survey. Only 7 of the 22 operating telephone companies indicated an interest in this equipment. Most companies were not interested in the No. 2B ESS with local/toll; instead they indicated that they were planning to consolidate their toll systems and utilize either No. 1/1A ESS or No. 4 ESS processors. This study forecast the demand for No. 2B ESS with local/toll capability to be

Availability in	*Companies Interested*
Years 1 and 2	20
Years 3 to 5	17
Years 6 to 10	17
Years 11 and beyond	8
Total	62

The account managers indicated that some of their OTCs would require the installation of the equipment as early as 1978. Furthermore, they indicated that new machines had to be compatible with CCIS developments while providing comprehensive local/toll features. The account managers indicated that most OTCs would be price-oriented in their purchasing decisions and would likely purchase the cheapest switching equipment which would fit their needs in the 1980 to 1985 time frame. Specifically, there was a weak consensus that the OTCs would consider $100,000 to be an appropriate price for local/toll capability reflected as a right-to-use (RTU) fee per machine.

The RTU was Western Electric's method of charging OTCs for the software included in its products. It included the recovery of not only the BTL development expense, but also the associated Western Electric development and engineering costs and overhead. The RTU was determined by dividing the division's resulting total revenue requirement for a product by the expected unit demand. Development costs and the resulting revenue requirements for local/toll features and CCIS for the No. 2B ESS are listed in Exhibit 9.

Subsequent follow-up to the survey results was focused on the seven OTCs indicating an interest in the No. 2B ESS with toll features. Because the "willingness to pay" question in the survey had not generated useful results, in the follow-up contracts the OTCs were informed that the RTU fees for the toll features would be in the range of $450,000 to $850,000. Further, they were told that the No. 2B ESS local/toll features could not be available until 1980. These additional pieces of information caused the seven telcos to reduce their estimates of need for the No. 2B ESS downward to a new total of approximately 27 machines over the ten-year period beginning in 1980.

VISIT TO AN OTC

One OTC had conducted an unusually thorough analysis of its needs in the Class 4/5 office area. The members of the PLPM team visited that telco in mid-May 1977 to further discuss the issues surrounding the decision process to adopt or reject the No. 2B ESS feature package. The telco staff indicated that in their area, the critical distance identified in the 1973 study had been extended from 61 miles to 140 miles. This meant that many of the 69 switching offices identified by the 1975 SNS as exhausting between 1980 and 1985 were probably candidates for consolidation rather than for replacement.

SUMMARY OF THE MARKET ANALYSIS PROGRAM

The accumulated evidence in the summer of 1977 seemed to indicate that the No. 2B ESS toll feature would not be popular among the OTCs. Depending on the data source, it was too small, too expensive, or too late to be of service at the time present equipment exhausted. Follow-up discussions with OTCs revealed that much of the indicated interest in the switch was based on unrealistic assumptions about the product and its potential price. In a written summary of the account manager survey, the PLPM group concluded that "[we are led] to the conclusion that the 69 potential applications for small toll applications may be reasonably accurate, but No. 2B ESS toll, due to the constraints caused by timing and RTU fees, will not fill those needs."

Although the prospects for toll features on the No. 2B ESS did not seem promising to the PLPM group, its members felt obliged to keep the option alive at least until preferred alternatives could be identified. Late in the summer of 1977, the following alternatives were being given active consideration for local/toll offices for which consolidation was not viable:

1. Use the No. 1A ESS, with local/toll features, which was presently available.
2. Reuse older No. 1 ESS processors as they might be taken out of service.
3. Agree to the development of local/toll features on the No. 2B ESS as was proposed nearly one year earlier by BTL.

The use of the No. 1A ESS was unattractive because of its cost and its large size (130,000 lines' capacity) though it had the advantages of being presently available with local/toll capabilities.

Reusing older No. 1 ESS processors was an option because many metropolitan offices were replacing No. 1 ESS equipment with newer No. 1A ESS processors that had double the call-handling capacity of the No. 1 ESS processors. It was expected that from 30 to 50 No. 1 ESS processors would be retired each year for the foreseeable future. Although they were too small for metropolitan offices, these No. 1 ESS processors were still serviceable. The No. 1 ESS had over 500 switching features, including 30 toll features and all the necessary local features. Modifying any No. 1 ESS to perform rural local/toll tasks was expected to require no significant development expense. In addition, the development of CCIS for use on the No. 1 ESS was already underway and would be complete by mid-1978.

The 2B ESS, designed for local switching applications, lacked CCIS, a toll switching network feature. CCIS was being adopted into the toll switching network on an office-by-office basis and was expected to be systemwide in the mid-1980s. Development of CCIS capability for the No. 2B ESS was feasible at a development cost of about $2.0 million.

Exhibit 1
Western Electric (A)

New Product Development Process for Western Electric Manufactured Products System

Step	*Activity*
1	Input of source idea from OTC, AT&T market information, BTL technical breakthroughs and state-of-the-art applications, and outside sources
2	Development of the idea by its "champion"
3	BTL research and system engineering case (funded by AT&T)
	Feasibility testing Technical analysis First-cut economic analysis
4	Intercompany forum review (BTL, AT&T, and Western Electric)
	Advisory council format employed
5	BTL specific design and development case (funded by Western Electric)
	Analysis of fit between Western Electric and the proposed business Western Electric analysis of market, cost, and competitive factors Systems engineering technical analysis and analysis of Bell System benefits
6	Intercompany forum review (BTL, AT&T, and Western Electric)
7	Western Electric commences manufacturing

Exhibit 2
Western Electric (A)

Nominal Toll Switching Network Pattern

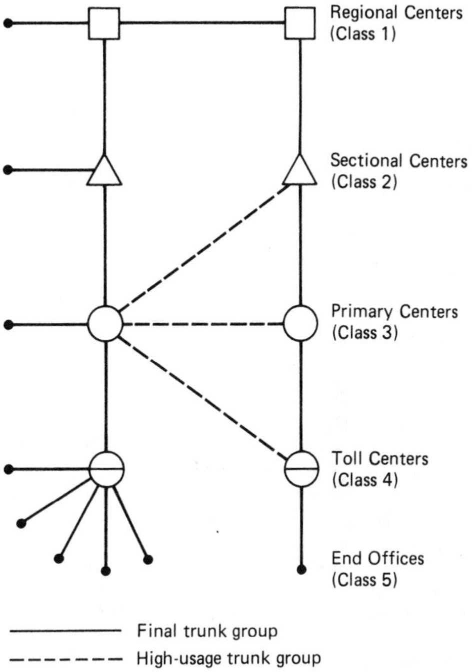

Exhibit 3
Western Electric (A)

Hierarchy of U.S. Bell System Switching Centers, 1976

Class	*No. of Locations*	*Name*	*Type of Service*	*Homes on*
1	10	Regional centers	Toll	Other Class 1 centers
2	67	Sectional centers	Toll	Class 1 centers
3	230	Primary centers	Toll	Class 2 centers
4	800	Toll centers	Toll	Class 3 centers
5	9,994	End offices	Local and local/toll	Class 4 centers

Exhibit 4
Western Electric (A)

Census of Local Switching Systems, January 1, 1976

Type of Switching Machine	*No. of Systems*	*% of Total*	*Total Lines (000,000)*	*% of Total Lines*	*Average Lines per System*
SXS	1,669	16.8%	18.3	27.0%	10,950
CDO SXS	4,388	44.0	4.7	6.9	1,070
Panel	55	0.6	0.9	1.3	16,300
No. 1 crossbar	310	3.1	6.7	9.9	21,600
No. 5 crossbar	2,700	27.2	26.5	39.2	9,300
No. 1 ESS	637	6.4	9.8	14.5	15,400
No. 2 ESS	185	1.9	0.8	1.2	4,330
Total	9,994	100.0%	67.7	100.0%	6,800

Exhibit 5
Western Electric (A)

Census of Toll Switching Systems, January 1, 1976[1]

Type of Switching Machine	*Class of Office* 1	2	3	4	*Total*	*Switched CCS/BH*[2] *(000,000)*	*% of Total CCS/BH*	*Avg. Utilization per Installation CCS/BH (000)*
No. 4A crossbar	10	63	86	18	177	14.4	55.6%	81
Crossbar tandem	0	4	101	105	210	6.1	23.5	29
No. 1 ESS	0	0	2	21	23	0.2	0.8	9
No. 5 crossbar	0	0	41	300	341	2.5	9.7	7
Step-by-step	0	0	3	358	361	2.7	10.4	8
Total	10	67	233	802	1,112	25.9	100.0%	23

[1]In mid-January 1976, a new large-capacity toll switch, No. 4 ESS, was added to the family of products serving the toll switching function.
[2]Hundred call seconds per busy hour.

Exhibit 6
Western Electric (A)

Characteristics of Major Switching Machines

Type	*Year of Introduction* *Local Use*	*Toll Use*	*Primary Applications* *Local Use*	*Toll Use*	*Size Range* *Local Use Lines (000)*	*Toll Use CCS (000)*
Step-by-step	1919	1926	Rural, suburban	Terminating toll	Up to 40	Average 4
No. 5 crossbar	1948	1953	Rural, suburban	Sparse areas	1 to 35	Up to 4
No. 1 ESS	1965	1970	Metropolitan	Sparse areas	10 to 65	Up to 140
No. 2 ESS	1970	—	Suburban	—	4 to 12	—
No. 1A ESS	1976	—	Metropolitan	—	10 to 128	—
No. 2B ESS	1976	—	Suburban	—	4 to 24	—

Exhibit 7
Western Electric (A)

Excerpts from OTC Chief Engineeer to AT&T Product Development Officer

Mr. John Doe One
Chief Engineer

Midwest Telco
Anytown USA

April 18, 1975

Mr. John Doe Two
Product Development Department Head
American Telephone & Telegraph Company
1180 Raymond Boulevard
Newark, New Jersey 07102

Dear Mr. Doe Two:

(omission of early analytical sections of letter)

From the above profiles it is obvious that these locations are not candidates for 4 ESS or even No. 1 ESS. Our economic preference would be to replace the present SXS local, CAMA, and intertoll machines at these locations with a combined local/toll ESS machine. The basic No. 2 ESS with its relatively low getting-started cost and anticipated capacity with the 2B processor comes close to our requirements. *However, the No. 2 ESS does not have the basic toll machine features of CAMA toll terminating and compatibility to serve RTA equipment.* We do not need operator tandem features at these locations since they will all be Class 4P offices.

A recent *general letter* (GL75-01-237), "Analysis of Toll Switching Today and Its Evolution," was disappointing in that it ignores the sparse-population toll center requirement. The letter recognizes the imminent phasing out of the use of 5XB as a replacing machine for a combined Class 4/5 switcher at sparse toll centers. However, it goes on to state "if toll features are developed for No. 2 ESS," etc. Our conclusion is that there will be no effort made to provide a modernized replacement. It is difficult to comprehend why we in the Midwest would be one of the few companies that would have the requirement. There are probably many toll centers throughout the system with profiles similar to those we have listed. *If the development of toll features on No. 2 ESS is indefinite, we would appreciate your evaluation of the following general trades supplier's machines which fill the requirements of a small Class 4/5 switcher:*

Mr. John Doe Two
April 18, 1975
page two

Stromberg Carlson ESC-1
North Electric NX1e

Assuming that we must formulate plans for sparse toll centers based on the present constraints, we see the following as alternative long-range options:

1. Install a No. 1 ESS at these locations and incur the overengineered switching and space penalties for the life of the machine.
2. Discontinue the toll centers listed and incur the facility penalties of trunking to adjacent toll centers.
3. Purchase a suitable switching machine from a general trades supplier.
4. Sell the offices in question to an independent company.

We again request you give urgent attention to the development of toll features on No. 2 ESS so that we and other companies have an economical, viable alternative for serving sparse toll center areas.

Sincerely,

Mr. John Doe One

cc: John Doe Three, AT&T
John Doe Four, BTL
John Doe Five, AT&T

Exhibit 8
Western Electric (A)

January 1977 Account Manager Survey for No. 2B ESS Demand

1. How does your telco plan to modernize toll service in sparsely populated areas?
2. How much do you estimate your operating company would pay for toll capability for a No. 2B ESS office (that is, the incremental price of toll capability above the price of a standard No. 2B ESS office)?
3. Is the expected use based on
   a. One-for-one replacement of existing toll centers YES NO
   b. Area replacement plans, including consolidation YES NO
4. What percentage of expected applications will be in each of these size ranges?
   a. Under 500 trunks
   b. 500 to 1,000 trunks
   c. 1,000 to 2,000 trunks
   d. 2,000 to 4,000 trunks
   e. More than 4,000 trunks
5. What is your telco's toll switching preference?
   a. Two-wire YES NO
   b. Four-wire YES NO
   c. No preference YES NO
6. What is the *latest* date that toll for No. 2B ESS can be made available and still meet your telco's needs?
   a. 1978
   b. 1979
   c. 1980
   d. 1981
   e. 1982
   f. Later than 1982
7. What is the potential demand for No. 2B ESS machines with toll in your telco?
   a. In years 1 and 2 of availability ________
   b. In years 3 through 5 of availability ________
   c. In years 6 through 10 of availability ________

Exhibit 9
Western Electric (A)

Summary of BTL Development Budgets for No. 2B ESS Features and Western Electric Total Revenue Requirements[1]

BTL SD&D Development Project	*BTL Development Budget (000)*	*Western Electric Total Revenue Requirements*
Local/toll software	$ 550	$ 4,100
Local/toll hardware	675	4,700
Local/toll network expansion	1,350	9,000
CCIS development	2,000	14,000

[1]Data are disguised.

Kendall VETMAT[1]

John Buckingham, product manager for Kendall Veterinary Products, opened the report sitting on his desk and began thumbing through it again. In this report, generated in house by Kendall's market research department, were the long-awaited results of the four-month usage study of his proposed new product, VETMAT. The results were clearly stated in the recommendations section of the executive summary:

1. Do not enter the small cage mat market with the present product.
2. Investigate the feasibility of entering this market with a low-priced disposable cage mat.

These recommendations were perfectly clear, and the findings of the study seemed to support the position. The problem was that Buckingham did not believe the findings. Something felt wrong about this study, either wrong with the basic assumptions or wrong with the conclusions. He was not sure which, but that did not make his situation any easier. It was already May 1979, and if he was going to have this product on the market by January 1, 1980, he had to submit an initial purchase order by midsummer.

And even if he had believed the report's results, he felt he could not recommend abandoning this project now. He knew that a "no go" on VETMAT would be seen as a disaster for the joint venture between Kendall, as the major distributor, and American Enka, the VETMAT manufacturer. That agreement had taken months to arrange and had involved top-level managers in both companies. Those managers were watching the VETMAT project closely, and a great deal hinged on its success.

And to complicate things further, Buckingham needed the sales that he felt confident VETMAT could generate. His $2.0 million budget for 1980 would be tough to meet with his current product line, and the $80,000

 This case was prepared by Elizabeth Webster under the supervision of David J. Reibstein.

[1]Quantitative data not publicly available have been subject to disguise.

he had projected for VETMAT were essential. He was convinced that a market did exist for a quality, premium-priced veterinary cage matting, even if the study did not concur. But how was he going to convince top management to go with his intuition versus the hard data of the usage study?

COMPANY BACKGROUND

The Kendall Company, a $650 million industrial marketing/manufacturing company, had its headquarters in Boston, Massachusetts. Founded in 1905 as a manufacturer of nonwoven cotton products (disposable diaper material), it had evolved into a diversified, multinational corporation. Sales in 1979 were generated by five divisions: Hospital Specialty Products, Fiber Products (of which Veterinary Products was a part), Consumer Infant Wear, Polyken (pipeline tapes), and International. Although the Fiber Division was the original base of the company's expertise, at present the Hospital and International divisions represented the greatest growth and potential and therefore received the greatest attention from upper management.

Acquired in 1972 by Colgate-Palmolive (C-P), Kendall was managed as a wholly owned subsidiary. Under this arrangement, considerable attention was paid to Kendall's growth, and the actions and decisions of Kendall's managers were closely scrutinized by C-P executives. Since acquisition, Kendall's presidency had changed three times, each appointment coming from, and returning to, the upper ranks of C-P. Viewed by the financial community as C-P's most successful acquisition, Kendall was moving away from its conservative, traditional background and preparing for the 1980s. New aggressive managers were rising to positions of responsibility, and their aggressiveness was showing in new marketing techniques and rapid new product introductions.

FIBER DIVISION REORGANIZATION

In 1977, after careful study by Kendall upper management, the Fiber Division was reorganized to form cohesive marketing groups out of miscellaneous product categories. The Agriculture and Veterinary Products group (Ag/Vet) was the result of this reorganization (Exhibit 1). With nonwoven cotton milking machine filters as its core product (1977 filter sales, $15 million), Ag/Vet represented a new direction for Kendall, a commitment to the growing agribusiness industry. For over 50 years, Kendall had purchased and sold milk filters for the U.S. dairy industry. In 1976, as the market leader, Kendall enjoyed a large share of the filter market, a large private-label business, and an established and well-respected name. The problem was that the milk filter market was declining, price competition was intensifying, and with old plants and high fixed costs, filter profits were evaporating. Management saw the need to diversify away from the single product base. Animal health products and surgical veterinary products were the chosen extensions.

Several key criteria supported this strategy:

1. All new Ag/Vet products would be either vended or established Kendall products to avoid additional fixed cost allocation.
2. Sophisticated marketing rather than unique R&D application would be emphasized.
3. Animal health products would be related to the dairy industry to benefit from the already established consumer franchise. Veterinary products, Kendall's commodity hospital products sold to veterinarians through established distributors, would capitalize on Kendall's quality image in the hospital market.
4. Animal health products would be sold by the filter sales force, ten former Fiber salespeople. No increase in personnel was planned to handle the new products. The

veterinary products, distributed through the ethical versus the lay channel, would utilize a manufacturer's representative force.[2]

5. The overall objective for all products would be to increase profits through established distribution systems. Products would fit with established Kendall strengths and would be expected to contribute profits immediately.

In addition to a careful product strategy, young, aggressive managers were chosen for this new product area. Linda Kanner, a 1975 MBA graduate of the Harvard Business School and, at the time, the new products manager for the Fiber Division, was promoted to marketing manager for the Ag/Vet group. Doug Merrill, a manager with ten years of Fiber sales force experience and a recent MBA, was appointed Animal Health product manager. And on June 1, 1978, John Buckingham was hired as veterinary product manager. Buckingham, a 1976 graduate of Purdue with a degree in pharmacy, had been a summer intern from Harvard Business School in 1977 and had written an initial marketing plan for veterinary products. His market plan was accepted by upper management on September 1, 1977, and after receiving his MBA from Harvard in June, he was hired to fill the position of product manager.

This management group quickly developed a reputation with upper management of being a highly motivated and dynamic team. They were viewed by Kendall and C-P executives as achievers, risk takers, "winners." But with this high visibility came conflict between the ambitious product plans of the Ag/Vet group and the organizational credibility that their small revenues received. Against many other Kendall marketing groups, the 1979 projected Ag/Vet sales of $10 million looked insignificant, and the result was little power to demand resources or personnel. Promotional funds, advertising dollars, and market research support were very limited, and therefore prudent, productive use of these funds was crucial. A limited income statement for veterinary products is in Exhibit 2 and an Ag/Vet business summary is in Exhibit 3.

[2]"Ethical channel" refers to distribution of hospital and prescription products through veterinary distributors who sold only to licensed veterinarians and animal clinics. "Lay channel" refers to over-the-counter sales of nonprescription animal health and farm products. Farm stores, milk coops, and equipment dealers were major customers.

THE VETERINARY BUSINESS

Prior to 1978, limited sales to veterinary distributors had been made by Kendall's hospital sales force in their attempts to meet quota. Not seen as a viable market for Kendall's premium-priced surgical products, the hospital sales force did little besides handle requests for large commodity product orders from veterinary distributors. In 1977, these sales amounted to about $300,000. But to Kanner, the veterinary business represented a new channel into the animal health market for the Ag/Vet group, and these sales could form the base of their 1978 market entrance.

The veterinary market was composed of 24,000 practicing DVMs (Doctors of Veterinary Medicine) in the country. Concentrated in the Midwest, South, and large urban areas, their numbers had been shifting over the decade to their 1978 breakdown of 80% small-animal practitioners (dogs and cats) and 20% large-animal doctors, specializing mainly in herd health. All could be easily reached by four major trade journals and 65 veterinary distributors.

Several factors made the veterinary market far different from Kendall's existing human health industry. First, veterinarians were *highly* price sensitive. No third-party insurance payments existed for animal health care, a critical factor in the cost structure of human medical practice. Additionally, pet care was often an early victim of an owner's declining disposable income in periods of high inflation. Yet supply costs for the DVM were rising as rapidly as the costs in the human health field, and the expectations of the pet owner for sophisticated treatment was increasing substantially. The result was that the DVM had to deliver complex and expensive medical services in a highly competitive environment. The increasing glut of DVMs further intensified this price competition.

Among suppliers to the veterinary market, the competition was highly fragmented and relatively unsophisticated. Many single-product companies used veterinary distributors to reach the DVM, while divisions of major companies usually employed their own direct sales force. Kendall had only one major competitor in the veterinary surgical supply market. Recent data available on veterinary surgical products lines, market growth, and shares of market are given in Exhibits 4, 5, and 6.

Unlike Pitman-Moore and 3M, who had developed their own sales forces, Ag/Vet had made the strategic decision to employ manufacturers' representatives to sell their products to veterinary distributors. This was essentially an economic decision, with negotiated 5% commissions keeping selling expenses to a minimum. But it also represented a calculated risk: Ag/Vet believed that SGM Ltd., a well-established six-person manufacturer's representative group based in St. Louis, could motivate the 65 veterinary distributors and their 350 salespeople to promote Kendall products over other commodity surgical products. Prior to signing Kendall, SGM Ltd. had represented five noncompeting veterinary product lines, primarily pharmaceutical. If projected sales were achieved, Kendall would almost immediately become their largest client and their only commodity product line. Said Sam McGrath, president of SGM Ltd.,

> An average distributor handles several thousand products each year, of which only 10% are white goods (surgical supplies). That makes the selling tough. But when they believe that Kendall is committed to the veterinary field and when they realize that Kendall has the best products, then we'll win them over even from Pitman-Moore.

VETMAT

Although the initial Ag/Vet strategy stipulated that commodity hospital products would constitute the major part of the veterinary line, from the outset Buckingham had wanted a limited number of specialized veterinary products that would spark the interest of both the distributor and the DVM. With an almost nonexistent R&D budget, he realized that it was unlikely that Kendall could itself develop a revolutionary product for veterinarians. Thus, in early 1978, when he was directed by upper management to consider the application of a new cage matting material in the DVM market, he jumped at the chance. The product in question was a brown, two-layered PVC cage matting material (Exhibit 7). The top layer was slightly textured to prevent animals from slipping and had drainage holes at four-inch intervals. Attached to this, by a patented process, were hundreds of polyamide "coils." The result was a lightweight, reusable, washable matting material to line animal cages in clinics. The coils acted as cushioning for animals, and the PVC material was thought to be warmer and more comfortable for recuperating patients.

The product had come to Kendall through a joint venture with American Enka, a small U.S. subsidiary of a large Dutch firm. For a number of years the Dutch parent had sold a similar matting material to European farmers as a floor covering for milking stalls. Because of Kendall's contacts in the dairy market, and their convincing arguments that they could promote this product in all possible markets, a joint venture had been signed which gave Kendall "exclusive marketing rights for any product developed for animal confinement systems in the U.S." It was Kendall's view that the potential of this material was extensive: stall matting for dairy cows, farrowing matting for swine, stall matting for horses, and cage matting for small animals were immediate possibilities. Although American Enka had not previously manufactured a product specifically for the DVM, they shared Kendall's optimism for this application and saw veterinary cage matting as an important extension of their matting product concept. Additionally, because Ag/Vet had assured American Enka that multiple markets would be served by Kendall's extensive distribution capability, this product extension was of considerable importance to the success of the joint venture.

When Buckingham was first approached on the subject of cage matting, his gut response was

> The need is definitely there. Most veterinarians today use newspaper, because it's cheap, $3/100 lbs., and there isn't much of anything else. The only real cage matting on the market is the Snyder mat. It's an awful green vinyl product developed by a small cage manufacturer as an add-on product. It's expensive, too, I think about $75 a cage. Distributors buy it through SGM Ltd. (Snyder was one of SGM's oldest clients), and they cut it to whatever size the DVM wants.

Buckingham was convinced that the growing sophistication in the veterinary market would increase the demand for this type of product:

> DVMs spend thousands of dollars on fancy X-ray and diagnostic equipment for their animal clinics. Even the cages they buy cost hundreds apiece. Why shouldn't they be willing to spend a reasonable amount on a cage mat if it will contribute to a faster recovery for their patients?

The result was that in March 1978, Buckingham requested that Kendall's market research department begin to study the potential demand for a Kendall small animal cage mat. His real interest centered on the positioning of his product versus the Snyder mat and "anything else currently being used," and in particular, on learning how to "talk about the product in promotions and advertising." The market research department responded by submitting a proposal for a demand model (Exhibit 8). Quoting Peg Relyea of the market research department,

> The model would define the total potential market and identify the appropriate factors and relationships of those factors in defining demand for this product in the veterinary market.

Though an impressive proposal, it did not address the issues that Buckingham saw as crucial. Thinking back, Buckingham said,

> At this stage I guess I never really thought we might *not* sell the product. Prototypes of VETMAT were already in production. I didn't need information for a go/no-go decision, I needed to know how much I would sell to start and how I should market it! And I needed the information soon. Although VETMAT was not the major factor in the Kendall-American Enka agreement, production of the dairy matting was not moving well, and upper management attention was being diverted to my product. Under this scrutiny, I had to get VETMAT to the market as quickly as possible.

USAGE TEST PROPOSAL

In May, marketing research came back with a second proposal, this one for a use test of VETMAT in the veterinary market. Quotes from this proposal were

Background: At this time, product management feels the most immediate entry of this product would be to the veterinary market as a cage mat for small animals. Market research has been requested to provide information on veterinarians' perceptions of this product.

Purpose: To obtain veterinarians' impressions of VETMAT after use. Perceived advantages and disadvantages of VETMAT compared to currently used products will be obtained. Information on average number of cages per veterinarian and number of cages that matting is used in will also be obtained.

Methodology: A national random sample of 100 veterinarians in exclusively small-animal practice will participate in this test. Preliminary information will be obtained from the veterinarians and four feet of VETMAT will be placed with each DVM (for one standard cage). After two weeks, the veterinarians will be called back to obtain their initial impressions of VETMAT. Another callback will be made after four more weeks to obtain longer impressions.

Limitations: This use test is primarily designed to determine the performance of VETMAT as perceived by the veterinarians. Although questions on price will be included in the survey, a market test will be necessary to determine the effect of price on the amount of matting purchased.

Decision Criteria: [For market research to say this product is a "go"] the VETMAT must be rated "very good" by at least 75% of the participants on overall performance and on at least two of the following attributes: improved insulation, cushioning, improved waste drainage, improved cleanliness of animal.

Cost: The out-of-pocket costs for this project through tabulation of the first follow-up interviews will be $3,500. This cost does not include product or mailing costs. The additional cost for the second follow-up interviews and tabulation will be $1,500.

Buckingham accepted this proposal, but he still had concerns about the role this research would play in the final product introduction. Although time was crucial, the study had to be delayed until October when a sufficient amount of VETMAT samples would be available. A timetable was agreed upon (Exhibit 9).

In September, when Kendall's president asked for an update on the American Enka venture, he was informed in a memo from Doug Merrill, Animal Health product manager and coordinator of the joint venture, that

> The VETMAT will be the first (of many) products to market with a target date of the second quarter of 1979. New samples are in transit to us for a market research study to begin in October, with preliminary results in November and a completion date of January. This study will involve a sample of 100 veterinarians and is designed to help us position this product in the marketplace. We will be seeking to confirm such benefits as: cushioning, cleanliness, insulation and ease of cleaning. Since we do have preliminary pricing from American Enka, we will attempt to measure price sensitivity. There are about 7,000 small animal clinics with an average of 15 cages per clinic. [Based on the prices quoted by American Enka] VETMAT will sell to the veterinarian for $5 to $7.50 per linear foot. If we were able to sell 10% of the clinics four feet each, we would have a market of between $210,000 and $315,000.

This projection was well above the $50,000 minimum first-year projection that was required for a new veterinary product, and upper management was satisfied that the project was on target.

Unfortunately, the target date of second quarter 1979 began to fade as the usage study met delay after delay. Initial samples were late. Many more DVMs had to be contacted than anticipated to find a sufficient number to participate in the study. And soliciting their opinions after usage turned out to be more difficult than expected. The completion date was extended several times. While waiting for the test results, the VETMAT trademark was secured, and Miami was designated as the location for the test market.

USAGE TEST RESULTS

Market research submitted the VETMAT report to Buckingham on April 15, 1979. Napoleon Elortegui, the author of the report, commented to a fellow market researcher:

> You know, John really wants this product, and he's not going to like these results. And, even though I know these findings are right, I bet I will go down to his office with this report, and he'll convince me that he's right and I'm wrong, and he'll be right! The product will sell big!

At the beginning of the report, the study's objectives had been stated:

1. Obtain information as to what is being done for cage matting in small-animal cages.
2. Determine the benefits and liabilities of VETMAT as a small-animal cage mat.
3. Identify the likelihood and volume of purchase of VETMAT by small-animal veterinarians.

The methodology followed the initial usage proposal (Exhibit 10), although only 72 DVMs agreed to participate in the usage test, 64 received the first follow-up call and 59 the second. Although these numbers were smaller than planned for originally, the demographics of the respondents mirrored national statistics and were considered appropriate for meaningful results. The decision criteria remained the same and the lack of information on price elasticity was still listed as a limitation.

The executive summary held the essence of the study's results:

Executive Summary

1. Ninety-two percent (92%) of the veterinarians use newspaper for cage matting.
2. Absorption of urine, providing cushioning and comfort, cleanliness of the cage, and simplifying the cleaning of the cage are the reasons veterinarians use mats.
3. Cushioning/comfort and thermal insulation are the best-liked features of the VETMAT.
4. Hard to clean, entrapment of feces by the coils, and the animals chewing the mat are the most disliked features of VETMAT.
5. Veterinarians do not perceive the VETMAT as a boarding cage mat.
6. At the price range of VETMAT, a reduction in price does not promote sufficient additional demand to justify the loss in margin.
7. The potential market for VETMAT is very small (est. $17K/yr.) [See Exhibit 11.]

Conclusions

1. Cleaning the mat and animals chewing the matting are major problems which need improvement.
2. There was not much excitement from the veterinarians about VETMAT. This excitement would be necessary in order to expect any considerable sales volume for a premium-priced product sold through distributors (i.e., little or no promotion).
3. The potential annual dollar volume for VETMAT under its present form is small. Even if the cleaning and chewing problems are solved, it is likely the volume will continue to be small. The main constraints to a sizeable dollar volume are the high price of VETMAT and its long product life span. The former keeps it from the boarding cage market, the latter decreases the repurchase rate significantly.

Recommendations

1. Do not enter the small cage mat market with the present product.

2. Investigate the feasibilities of entering this market with a low-priced disposable cage mat. [Further information from this study is in Exhibit 12.]

PRODUCT MANAGEMENT'S REACTION

Napoleon Elortegui was correct. These were *not* the results that Buckingham had anticipated or wanted. Although VETMAT was only a small part of the larger arrangement between Kendall and American Enka, it was currently the most visible piece of that joint venture, and its progress was being watched carefully by both executive groups.

When John Buckingham brought the report to Linda Kanner, marketing manager, the following conversation ensued:

John: I just don't like this study, Linda. It's not structured properly for a new concept test, but the recommendations dictate that that is what it was intended to be. It seems to me that by asking up front what their current mat is, and then comparing it to our mat, basically comparing VETMAT to newspaper, it creates tremendous bias in the DVM. And that bias invalidates the results for me.

Linda: Yes, I agree, but isn't that always the risk in comparative market research?

John: But, that's just the point. I don't think this should have been a comparative product study. The essential nature of this product is unique. Ninety percent of the doctors said that cleanliness of the patient was *essential* to them in a cage mat—and they can't get that with newspaper. But the test made them compare it to newspaper! It just confused things.

Linda: But what about the dollar potential? Even if the comparative aspect cut down on some of the DVM's enthusiasm, that estimate isn't going to make it with upper management.

John: I have my own view of the market potential. If you take the 9,000 practices times two recovery cages each, that equals 18,000 potential cages. If we got only 20% of that market, and SGM Ltd. assures me they can, it would equal 3,600 × $22 per mat for Kendall, or $80,000 in the first year. And I expect it to grow each year as well as a replacement market growing. You see, the dollars really are there. The risk at this point is next to nothing and we've already made most of the investment. Besides, what choice do we have?

Linda: I don't know, John. Your numbers seem pretty soft to me. And the fact that SGM currently sells the Snyder mat makes things messy. But I agree with you, this market research doesn't do what we intended. It seems whenever you ask the market research people to help you position a new product, they always feel they should start by justifying the product introduction. I used to have faith in market research as a pure tool. But the instrument design is so tricky . . .

John: That still doesn't say what we should do with this. Just ignore it, retest to get better information, or just use what we have? I need this new product, Linda, and I'm sure we have a good one here.

Exhibit 1
Kendall VETMAT

Fiber Division

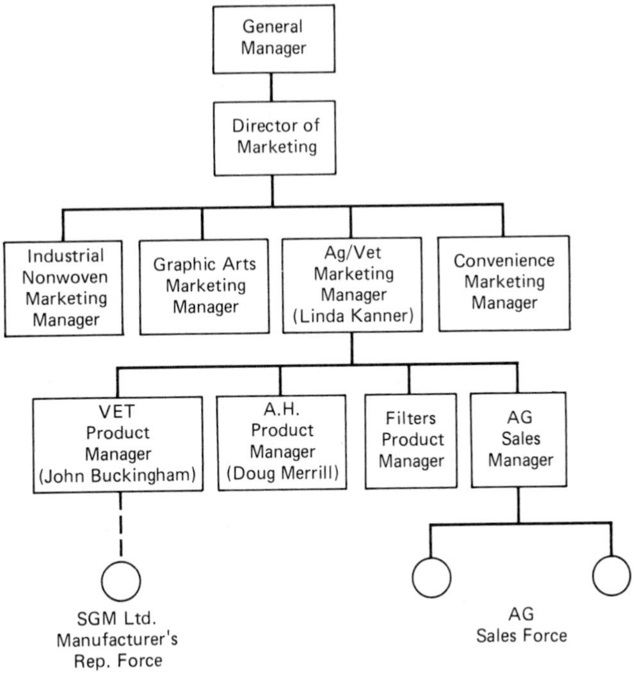

Exhibit 2
Kendall VETMAT

Veterinary Products, 1978–1980

	1978 Actual	*1979 Latest Estimate*	*1980 Objective*
Net sales	$900	$1,500	$2,000
Marginal income[1]	360	608	793
% of sales	40.6%	40.5%	39.6%
Total advertising	128	72	69
% of sales	14.1%	4.8%	3.5%
Total marketing	50	83	85
% of sales	5.5%	5.4%	4.2%
Total R&D	—	30	30
% of sales		2.0%	1.5%
Total fixed costs	48	187	223
% of sales	0.05%	12.5%	13.7%
Profit after tax	70	124	171
% of sales	7.7%	8.3%	8.6%

[1]Gross margin.

Exhibit 3
Kendall VETMAT

Financial Data on Agricultural Department Business, 1977–1979 (000)

	Dairy Filters			*Animal Health*			*Veterinarian*		
	1977 Actual	*1978 Estimate*	*1979 Objective*	*1977 Actual*	*1978 Estimate*	*1979 Objective*	*1977 Actual*	*1978 Estimate*	*1979 Objective*
Sales	$3,981	$5,141	$5,903	$2,066	$2,590	$2,974		$850	$1,392
Gross income after manufacturing expenses	1,438	1,856	2,132	919	1,186	1,362		343	595
Marketing expenses	503	581	641	335	433	498		151	147
Nonvariable expenses	1,019	1,316	1,512	243	314	360		192	217
Profit before taxes	−84	−41	−21	341	439	504		48	231

Exhibit 4
Kendall VETMAT

Total Market Veterinary Surgical Supplies, 1973–1979 (millions)

Year	*Sales*	*% Growth*
1973	$3.5	—
1974	4.33	24%
1975	5.35	24
1976	7.8	46
1977	8.7	12
1978	9.5	9
1979	10.4	9

6-year average rate of growth = 20%/year

Exhibit 5
Kendall VETMAT

Veterinary Market Products: Surgical Supplies and Equipment, 1979

Surgical Supplies ($10.4 million)	*Equipment ($32.2 million)*
Adhesives	Instruments
Sponges	Hypo needles/syringes
Bandages	Catheters/endotracheal tubes
Cotton	Sutures
Other dressings (drapes, etc.)	X-ray equipment
Gloves and sleeves	Cleaners, soaps
Plaster bandages and splints	Other (catheters, masks, swabs, etc.)
Stockinette and wadding	

Exhibit 6
Kendall VETMAT

Market Share Analysis for Veterinary Surgical Supplies 1977–1978

Competitors	*1977*	*1978*
Pitman-Moore (J&J)	60%	60%
3M	9	8
Parke-Davis	7	2
Kendall	5	15
Haver-Lockhart	4	1
Other	15	14

Exhibit 7
Kendall VETMAT

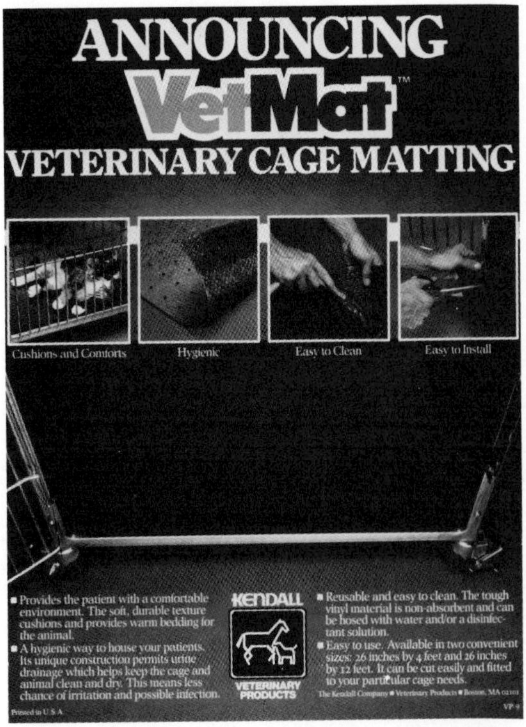

Exhibit 8
Kendall VETMAT
Demand Model

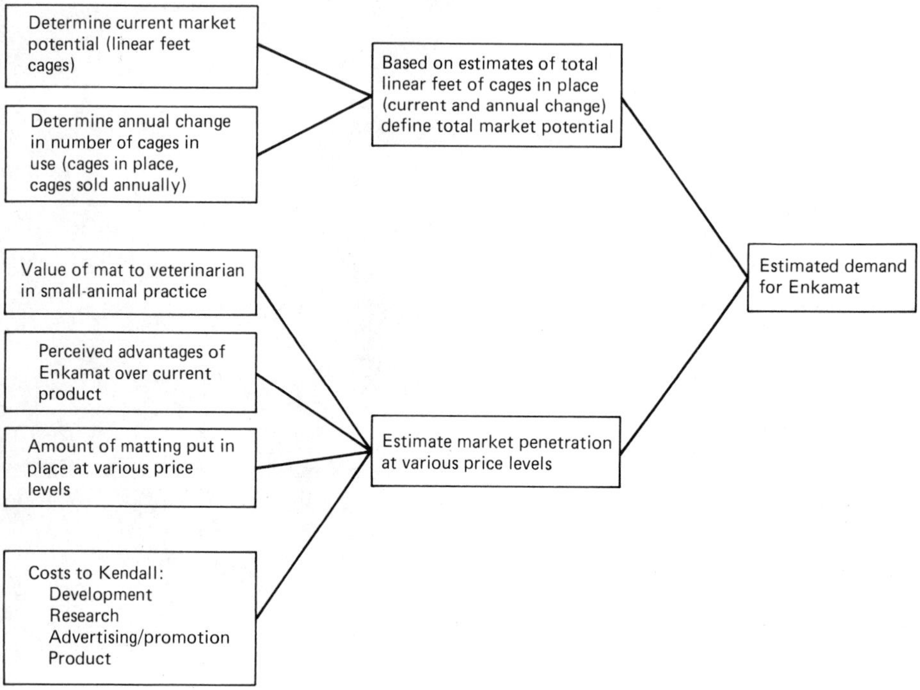

Exhibit 9
Kendall VETMAT
Time Schedule for Testing

Screening	Oct. 16–20
Tabulation of pretrial data	Oct. 23–25
Mail out of VETMAT sample	Oct. 30–Nov. 3
Trial period VETMAT sample	Nov. 20–Dec. 1
First posttrial callback	Dec. 4–15
Tabulation of first callback	Dec. 18–22
Holidays	Dec. 23–Jan. 4
Preliminary report	Middle of Jan. 1979
Second callback	Jan. 15–26
Tabulation of second callback	Jan. 29–Feb. 2
Final report	End of February

Exhibit 10
Kendall VETMAT
Excerpts from Study

Objectives

1. Determine which forms of cage matting are used currently.
2. Determine benefits of cage matting used currently.
3. Determine dislikes of current cage matting.
4. Compare VETMAT with current cage matting.
5. Identify the good features of VETMAT as a cage mat for small animals.
6. Identify the liabilities of VETMAT as a cage mat for small animals.
7. Establish the price sensitivity of the demand for VETMAT (posttrial).
8. Determine whether the veterinarians per-

ceive VETMAT as a boarding mat or as a postoperative mat.

9. Determine the average number of cages in small veterinary practices.

Methodology and Sample

The sample of veterinarians chosen for this study was selected at random from all small-animal veterinarians in the nation. The geographical distribution of the sample is proportional to the distribution of the small-animal veterinarian population in the United States (see Exhibit 11 for details). The original sample size was proposed at 100 veterinarians to obtain a margin of error smaller than ±10%. The sample was later reduced to 72 respondents because of lack of VETMAT samples. After the attrition of three sets of interviews, the sample was reduced to 59 respondents, for a margin of error of ±13%.

The study was conducted in three phases. During the first phase, 72 veterinarians were contacted over the phone. They were asked some general questions about their practice, cages, and cage matting. During this phase, they were asked if they wanted to participate in testing a new product. Those who agreed to participate were sent a piece of VETMAT which they had to cut to fit their cages.

During the second phase, 64 veterinarians from phase 1 were interviewed. The interviews were conducted over the telephone. Three weeks elapsed from the time the veterinarians received the VETMAT mat, and the interviews were conducted. During this second phase, information was gathered on the advantages and disadvantages of the sample mat, its comparison to currently used cage mats, the price elasticity of the VETMAT sample, and intention of purchase. This information was compiled and analyzed to look for areas the interviews should target on during the third phase.

The third and last phase of the study concentrated in the problem areas of the VETMAT and some other areas such as price sensitivity. The third phase was conducted a month after the second phase. Prior to the third phase, cleaning instructions were sent to those interviewed during the second phase (cleaning of the mat was one of the problems detected during phase 2). Fifty-nine veterinarians from the second phase were interviewed during this phase.

The results from all three phases were compiled and tabulated. These data and their analysis are presented in this study.

F. *Decision Criteria*

VETMAT must be rated high (very good) by at least 75% of the participants on overall performance and at least two of the following attributes:

Improved insulation
Cushioning
Improved waste drainage
Improved cleanliness of animal

G. *Limitations*

Due to the final size of the sample, 62 veterinarians, there is a range of error of approximately ±13% (for a 95% sampling tolerance).

The information concerning price elasticity of the VETMAT sample mat should not be regarded as reliable, since it was not tested under an actual purchase situation.

Summary of Findings

A. *Major Findings*

Newspapers Are the Most Commonly Used Form of Cage Matting

Ninety-two percent of the veterinarians were using newspapers as a mat. Their reasons for using newspapers were absorbing the urine, keeping the cage clean, disposability, and inexpensiveness.

Absorption of Urine, Providing Cushioning and Comfort, and Cleanliness of the Cage Are the Main Reasons Veterinarians Use a Cage Mat[3]

Reasons for Using Cage Mat	*% of Total*
Provide absorption of urine	34%
Provide cushioning/comfort	29
Cleanliness of cage	23
Easy to clean cage	19

Absorption of Urine, Easy to Clean, Inexpensive, and Being Disposable Are the Main Re-

[3]See Table 2, page 48, for more details.

quirements Veterinarians Seek in a Cage Mat[4]

Required Cage Mat Features	*% of Total*
Absorbs urine	54%
Easy to clean	27
Reasonable price/inexpensive	23
Disposable	20

Sixty Percent of the Veterinarians Rated the Sample Cage Mat as Being Either Very Good or Good

Cushioning/Comfort and Thermal Insulation Are the Best-Liked Features of the Sample Mat

Over 90% of the veterinarians found the sample mat to be very good or good for cushioning/comfort. More than 70% found the thermal insulation of the sample mat to be either very good or good.

It should be noted that providing thermal insulation is not one of the features required by a significant group of the veterinarians. (See Table 3.)

Over 90% of the veterinarians found the sample mat to be very good or good for cushioning/comfort. Seventy percent of the veterinarians mentioned cushioning/comfort as a particularly liked feature.

More than 70% of the veterinarians found the thermal insulation of the sample mat to be either very good or good. And half of the veterinarians (49%) mentioned thermal insulation as a particularly liked feature. However, thermal insulation is not one of the features required often by veterinarians. Only 9% required this feature in a cage mat.

Being Hard to Clean, the Coils Trapping the Feces, and the Animals Chewing the Mat Are the Most Disliked Features of the Sample Cage Mat

Fifty-eight percent of the respondents disliked the difficulty in cleaning the mat and the feces being entrapped in the coils. Only 27% of the veterinarians rated the ease of cleaning the mat very good or good. The cages and mats are mostly cleaned by kennel assistants (81%).

Twenty-four percent of the respondents complained about the animals chewing the sample mat.

The Veterinarians Were Equally Divided as to Their Preference for Their Current Mat (Newspapers) or the Sample Mat

Being Disposable and Less Work/Easy to Clean Are the Main Reasons for Preferring the Current Mat

Reasons for Preferring Current Mat	*% of Total*
Easier to dispose	61%
Less work/easy to clean	30
Absorbent	13
Inexpensive	13

Cushioning Effect/Comfort, the Elevation of the Mat Keeping the Patient Clean, and Having Good Drainage Are the Main Reasons for Preferring the Sample Cage Mat

Reasons for Preferring Sample Cage Mat	*% of Total*
Cushioning effect/comfort	50%
Elevated bottom kept patient clean	36
Good drainage	27

At the Price Range of the VETMAT Sample Cage Mat, the Increment in Demand Resulting from a Reduction in Price Would Not Warrant the Loss in Margin

At the price range which VETMAT has to start at, $4.50/ft. and above, reductions in price did not increment demand so as to warrant the loss in margin.

The Potential Annual Dollar Volume for the VETMAT Cage Mat Is Small

Under its present form, the dollar volume for VETMAT is estimated at $17,000/year. Even if the product were upgraded, and the cleaning and chewing problems were eliminated, the market would remain small (estimated at about $65,000/year).

[4]See Table 3, for more details.

Exhibit 11
Kendall VETMAT

Geographical Distribution of the Sample

State	*Number of DVMs To Be Interviewed in This State*
1. Alabama	1
2. Arizona	1
3. California	13
4. Colorado	2
5. Connecticut	1
6. Florida	4
7. Georgia	2
8. Iowa	1
9. Illinois	3
10. Indiana	2
11. Kansas	1
12. Kentucky	1
13. Louisiana	1
14. Massachusetts	2
15. Maryland	2
16. Michigan	3
17. Minnesota	1
18. Missouri	2
19. North Carolina	1
20. New Jersey	3
21. New York	4
22. Ohio	4
23. Oklahoma	1
24. Oregon	1
25. Pennsylvania	3
26. South Carolina	1
27. Tennessee	1
28. Texas	4
29. Virginia	2
30. Washington	2
31. Wisconsin	1
Total	70

ESTIMATE OF THE SATURATION LEVEL FOR THE VETMAT MAT MARKET

Known Data/Estimates/Assumptions

1. Veterinary practices tending to small animals = 9,000[a]
2. Estimated percentage of veterinarians expected to purchase the mat for the first time at $4.50/foot = 40%[b]
3. Percentage expected to repurchase the mat at $10.40/foot = 21%[c]
4. Median quantity of mats purchased by each veterinarian at $10.40/foot = 3[d]
5. Assumed average life of the mat = 3 years[e]
6. Estimated average length of cage mats = 3 feet[f]

Saturated VETMAT Volume Potential

9,000 × .4 × .21 × 3 × ⅓ = 756 mats/year

Saturated Dollar Volume Potential at Consumer Level

756 × 3 × $10.40 = $23,587/year (approx. $24,000/year)

Saturated Dollar Volume Potential at Dealer Level

$24,000/year × .70[g] = $16,800/year (approx. $17,000/year)

[a]From data in VM/SAC media profile.

[b]From Table 20, Phase III of this study. This was the percentage of veterinarians who would repurchase the mat at the lowest cost.

[c]From Table 20, Phase III of this study.

[d]From Phase III of this study.

[e]Assumption: no data available.

[f]From data gathered by Peg Relyea on the average length of the cages.

[g]Assuming most dealers will take the customary 30% of sales margin.

Exhibit 12
Kendall VETMAT

General Findings

CURRENT HABITS ON CAGE MATTING

Mats Used Currently

Most veterinarians use newspapers (92%) for cage matting. Newspaper cage mats are used to absorb the urine and keep the cage clean. Newspaper cage mats have the advantage of being disposable, which make them an easy, cheap method of cleaning the mess.

Other forms of cage matting are paper towels, rugs, and blankets.[5]

Cage Matting Used	*% of Total*
Newspapers	92%
Paper towels	20
Rugs	13
Blankets	11

Reasons for Using Mats in the Cages

The reason, mentioned more often, for using mats in the cages is absorption of urine.

Other reasons for using cage mats, mentioned frequently, were providing cushion/comfort, cleanliness of the cage, ease in cleaning the cage, and providing warmth for animals.[6]

Reason for Using Cage Mat	*% of Total*
Provide absorption of urine	34%
Provide cushioning/comfort	29
Cleanliness of cage	23
Ease in cleaning cage	19
Provide warmth for animal (insulation)	17

[5]See Table 1, for more details.
[6]See Table 2, for more details.

Features Required in Cage Mats

Absorption of urine was the feature required most often by the respondents in a cage mat. Other required features mentioned often were ease in cleaning the mat, reasonable price/inexpensive, being disposable, and providing cushion/comfort (base = 22).

Reasons for Preferring Current Mat	*% of Total*
Easier to dispose	61%
Less work/ease of cleaning	30
Absorbent	13
Inexpensive	13
Better	9
Others	4

The reasons given more often for preferring the sample cage mat to the current mat were the cushioning effect/comfort, elevation of the mat kept the patient clean, and good drainage (base = 22).

Reasons for Preferring the Sample	*% of Total*
Cushioning effect/comfort	50%
Elevated bottom kept clean	36
Good drainage	27
Warmth/insulated	9
Fewer problems with ulcers/sores	9
Strong (newspapers are not strong)	9
Others	5

OBSERVATIONS ON THE RELATIONSHIP BETWEEN DEMAND AND PRICE FOR THE SAMPLE CAGE MAT (VETMAT)

To obtain an idea of the price elasticity of the sample cage mat, the respondents were asked their intention to purchase (posttrial) at three widely spread prices.

The results as displayed in Figure 1 (page 47) show that large variations in price affect the demand for the sample mat.

Figure 1
Price Elasticity for VETMAT

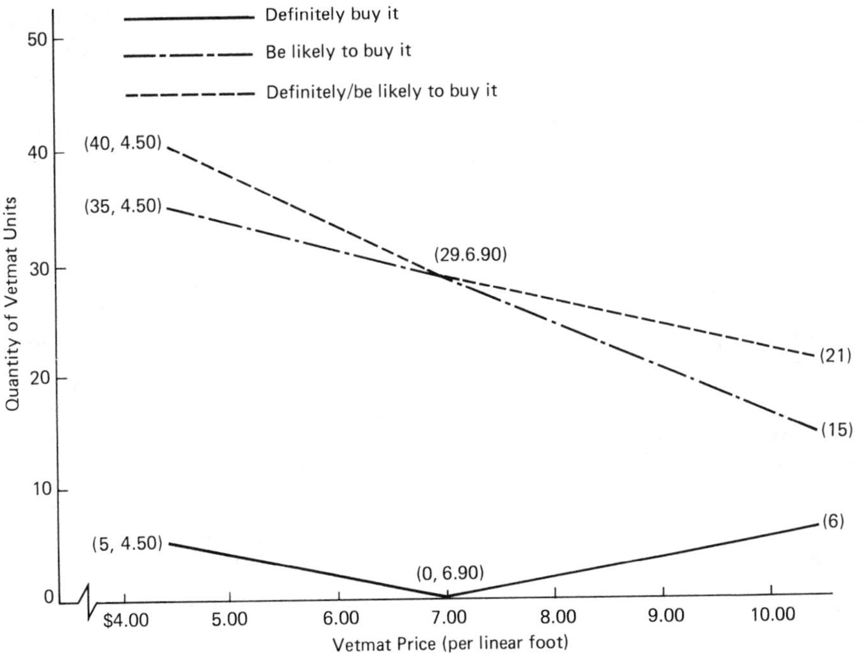

The demand for the product almost doubled when the price was reduced by 60%. At $10.40/foot only 21% of the veterinarians said they would definitely buy it or would be likely to buy it, whereas at $4.50/foot 40% said they would definitely buy it or would be likely to buy it.

Although at first sight, it may appear that it would be desirable to lower the price to increment the demand, analysis of the situation shows this not to be the case, since the increment in demand would not be enough to warrant the loss in margin.

It should be noted that price elasticity can generally not be determined from questions about purchase intention at different prices. It is necessary to sell the product at different prices before price elasticity can be established.

ESTIMATED POTENTIAL MARKET FOR THE VETMAT SAMPLE MAT

The potential market for the VETMAT under its present form is estimated at $17,000/year.

Even if the mat were upgraded and the cleaning and chewing problems were eliminated, the market for the mat would continue to be small. For example, if we upgrade the mat so that 80% of the initial buyers repurchase it, the annual purchase would be $65,000 at the most.

There are two main reasons why the VETMAT cannot be expected to yield large volumes:

1. Due to its large price tag, veterinarians do not consider it for boarding cages.
2. The life span of the product is such that

once a veterinarian buys the product, he is out of the market for a few years.

One could raise an argument that the market could be converted so as to use an upgraded VETMAT (no cleaning and chewing problems) in boarding cages. However, since Kendall will not be selling the product direct, it is unlikely this could be done via distributors.

As for the life span of the product, it would be safe to assume that if a premium-priced product, such as VETMAT, didn't have a long life span, it would have a poor repurchase rate.

Table 1

Matting used currently[1,2]

Matting Type Used	*No. of Users*	*% of Total*
Newspapers	65	92%
Paper towels	14	20
Rugs	9	13
Blankets	8	11
Corrugated cardboard	2	3
Rubber	2	3
Indoor/outdoor carpeting	2	3
Synthetic lambskin products	1	1
Fibers	1	1
Shredded newspapers	1	1
Hot-water bottle	1	1
Picnic table	1	1
Don't use matting	1	1

[1]Multiple answers possible; base = 71.
[2]From phase 1, Q. 6: Which of the following types of matting do you use in your cages?

Table 2

Reasons for using mats in the cages[1,2]

Reasons for Using	*No. of Users*	*% of Total*
Provide absorption of urine	24	34%
Provide cushioning and comfort	20	29
Cleanliness of cage	16	23
Ease in cleaning cage	13	19
Provide warmth for animals	12	17
Protection from animal wastes	5	7
Convenient/easy to use	5	7
Cleanliness of animal	4	6
Insulation purposes	3	4
Disposable protection for cages	3	4
Protect animal from steel cage	2	3
Inexpensive protection	2	3
It is more sanitary	1	1
Security for cats	1	1
Prevent bed sores	1	1

[1]Unsolicited multiple answers; base = 80.
[2]From phase 1, Q. 7: Why do you use mats in your cages?

Table 3

Features required by the veterinarians in a cage mat[1,2]

Required Features	*No. Requiring*	*% of Total*
Absorb urine	38	54%
Ease in cleaning	19	27
Reasonable price/ inexpensive	16	23
Disposable	14	20
Provide cushioning/ comfort	11	16
Convenient/easy to use	7	10
Provide insulation	6	9
Provide warmth for animal	5	7
Durable	5	7
Slip resistant	4	6
Cleanliness of animal	2	3
Prevent bed sores	1	1
Odor free	1	1
Nontoxic to animals if chewed	1	1
Easy drying	1	1
Don't know	2	3

[1]Unsolicited multiple answers; base = 70.
[2]From phase 1, Q. 8: What do you require from a cage mat?

Table 4

Rating of five cage mat features[1,2]

Features	*% Giving This Rating*			
	Essential	*Desired*	*Not Wanted*	*Don't Know, No Answer*
Cleanliness of patient	90%	3%	7%	—
Cleanliness of the cage	79	13	8	—
Fluid drainage	65	20	15	1
Cushioning	32	59	9	—
Thermal insulation	20	65	14	1

[1]Base = 71.
[2]From phase 1, Q. 13: Dr. I am going to read a list of product characteristics. Could you please tell me whether they are (1) essential in a cage mat, (2) desired, (3) not wanted.

Table 5

Unsuggested use of sample mat[1,2]

Use	*No. of Users*	*% of Total*
Recumbent animals	55	86%
Postoperative	50	78
Boarding mat	31	48
Otherwise immobilized	27	42
Broken legs	15	23
Other	14	22

[1]Multiple answers possible; base = 64.
[2]From phase 2, Q. 4: How was the sample cage mat used?

Table 6

Mat preference: sample versus current[1,2]

Preferred Mat	*No. Preferring*	*% of Total*
Sample (VETMAT)	22	34%
Current	23	36
Both	17	27
Neither	2	3

[1]Base = 64.
[2]From phase 2, Q. 8: Which product would you prefer?

Table 7

Reasons for preferring sample cage mat[1,2]

Reasons	*No. Preferring*	*% of Total*
Cushioning effect/ comfort	11	50%
Elevated bottom kept clean	8	36
Good drainage	6	27
Warmth insulated	2	9
Fewer problems with sores/ulcers	2	9
Newspaper is not strong	2	9
Others	1	5

[1]Multiple answers possible; base = 22.
[2]From phase 2, Q. 9: Why did you prefer sample mat?

Table 8

Rating of the sample cage mat for different product features[1,2]

	Rating (%)						
Features Rated	*Very Good*	*Good*	*Sum of Very Good and Good*	*Acceptable*	*Bad*	*Very Bad*	*Don't Know*
Cushioning and comfort	61%	34%	95%	5%	—	—	—
Thermal insulation	34	44	78	3	2%	—	17%
Fluid drainage	25	48	73	13	6	5%	3
Keeping the patient clean	22	39	61	23	8	—	8
Keeping the cage clean	13	37	50	23	16	3	8
Color of the mat	5	20	25	51	11	3	10

[1]Base = 64.
[2]From phase 2, Q. 10: How would you rate the sample for ____________________?

Table 9

Purchase intention at three different prices

Purchase Intention	*$4.50/ft (base = 62)*	*$6.90/ft (base = 31)*	*$10.40/ft (base = 33)*
Definitely buy it	5%	0%	6%
Be likely to buy it	35	29	15
Subtotal	40%	29%	21%
Be unlikely to buy it	41	45	33
Definitely not buy it	19	23	43
Don't know/no answer	0	3	3
Total	100%	100%	100%

Table 10

Rating of different features of sample cage mat when using it with post-operative/recumbent animals[1,2]

Features	*Very Good*	*Good*	*Sum of Very Good and Good*	*Acceptable*	*Bad*	*Very Bad*	*Don't Know*
Cushioning and comfort	53%	37%	90%	8%	2%	—	—
Thermal insulation	38	34	72	22	2	2%	2%
Keeping the patient clean	22	41	63	27	8	2	—
Fluid drainage	14	31	45	41	12	—	2
Keeping the cage clean	5	29	34	46	12	3	5
Color of the mat	5	15	20	60	8	7	5
Ease of cleaning the mat	2	25	27	39	24	8	2
Overall rating	27	34	61	31	5	3	—

[1]Base = 59.
[2]From phase 3, Q. 4: How would you rate the following features of the cage mat when using it with postoperative or otherwise recumbent animals?

L'eggs Products, Inc. (A)

Jack Ward sat down at his desk one day in the summer of 1973 to resolve a problem which required a decision that week. As group product manager of L'eggs Products, Inc., he had to decide what specific alternative—or what combination of specific alternatives—to employ for L'eggs pantyhose's first national promotion during the coming fall season.

L'eggs Products, Inc., was a subsidiary of the Hanes Corporation, producers of hosiery, knitwear, and foundation garments. L'eggs pantyhose was the first major nationally branded and advertised hosiery product distributed through food and drug outlets. It had been remarkably successful since its first test market introduction in 1970, through market-by-market rollout, and now was distributed through grocery and drugstores in 90% of the country. By mid-1973 it accounted for over 25% of the hosiery volume done by food and drug outlets. These outlets represented between 20% and 25% of total U.S. hosiery sales. The resulting 5–6% overall market share made L'eggs pantyhose the largest-selling single brand in the hosiery industry.

 This case was prepared by Harvey N. Singer under the supervision of F. Stewart DeBruicker.

With success, however, had come increased competitive efforts from other major manufacturers and from private-label brands. In response, and in keeping with the L'eggs philosophy of aggressive marketing utilizing packaged-goods techniques to reinforce consumer purchase behavior, L'eggs was planning its fall promotional activities. These would coincide with the back-to-school season and the advent of cooler weather, both traditional stimuli to hosiery sales. The focus of these activities was to be some form of packaging and/or "cents-off" promotional deal to consumers on a national basis.

The prime objective for the promotion was to generate, profitably, the largest number of incremental sales over the next six months. However, there were two other important objectives. In many markets the trial rate for L'eggs pantyhose had peaked at a level considered satisfactory, and the product group felt that promotional vehicles to increase trial would not be necessary or effective. The aim in these markets, therefore, was to find the best promotional alternative to stimulate the repeat rate and to load the consumer with product, thereby reducing her motivation to purchase from competitors. In other markets, however, the trial rate was considerably lower and was judged unsatisfactory. In these markets, the strategy was to utilize the fall promotion for the objective of increasing trial. Absorbing short-term promotional costs would be tolerated here for the purpose of generating increased trial, greater market share, and, it was hoped, sustained long-run volume.

Four alternative promotional vehicles had been developed and screened. Some of the alternatives appeared to be more effective, on a sales basis, in achieving one of the objectives—trial among nonusers. Others seemed to be more effective in generating repeat and loading among current users. In addition, the alternatives had different costs associated with their use. Finally, there were nonquantifiable factors arguing for or against the implementation of each.

Ward knew that he would have to analyze the results and decide whether just one alternative could be utilized—and which one it should be—or whether the efficiency and ease of implementation of having just one promotional vehicle on a national basis should be sacrificed to the effectiveness of using a combination of alternatives targeted to specific areas.

DEVELOPING THE L'EGGS STRATEGY, 1969–1972[1]

L'eggs was the first brand in the hosiery industry to utilize a "packaged-goods" marketing program to advertise, promote, display, and sell hosiery to the consumer through food and drug outlets. This represented a departure from the traditional methods used to merchandise hosiery through any retail outlet.

Before introduction of L'eggs, branded hosiery sales by major industry producers (including Hanes) were made exclusively through department and specialty stores. Starting in 1965, however, sales of private-label hosiery through supermarkets and drugstores had grown dramatically and by 1969 represented a significant share—6% for drugstores and 12% for supermarkets—of the $1.5 billion retail hosiery market.

Noting these trends, Hanes investigated entry into these mass merchandising outlets on a branded basis. Extensive market, consumer, and product research studies were made to determine (1) the actual size, composition, and nature of the market; (2) consumer attitudes and behavior toward hosiery in general and supermarket hosiery in particular; and (3) by means of in-home concept and product-use tests, whether new products developed by Hanes would fulfill planned advertising promises and consumer expectations generated.

Market information received from the A. C. Nielson Co. store audits in 1969 verified the existence of a substantial market, but indicated problems to be overcome if food and drug hosiery sales were to reach full potential (as compared with health and beauty aids products, for example, where mass outlets accounted for 50% of industry volume). Further channel research isolated these problems:

1. A very fragmented market. Over 600 different hosiery brands were sold in mass outlets, and no brand had more than a 4% share.
2. Advertising and promotion to stimulate sales was based on price only—not informing the consumer about product qualities or why she should consider buying in a particular outlet.
3. Stockouts ran as high as 25%—man-

[1]Material in this section is taken from a speech made to the A.M.A. in November 1972 by David E. Harrold, the original marketing director of L'eggs Products, Inc., and now president of Hanes Knitwear Division.

ufacturers did not anticipate needs and keep stocks in balance and did not provide necessary service.

4. Retail turnover lagged the average of all food and drug products—the retailer's return on investment was unattractive.

Consumer research provided answers on what had to be done to establish a permanent branded franchise:

1. The consumer felt that supermarket and drugstore hosiery had a low-quality image.
2. There was no brand loyalty.
3. Products lacked consistency from package to package.
4. Frequent stockouts diluted the consumer's confidence in product availability and drove her back to traditional hosiery outlets where such problems did not exist.

Despite these problems, the research indicated a strong consumer desire to purchase hosiery regularly in convenience outlets if she could develop a lasting confidence in the product.

Hanes concluded that the trade and consumer needed a completely new hosiery product and marketing program for these outlets, which would build consumer loyalty by virtue of unique product benefits: a distinctive name, package, and display; heavy advertising to build awareness of the product, benefits, outlet of availability, and product consistency; and promotional techniques to stimulate trial and repeat, to build the habit of purchasing and repurchasing the product.

The company had developed a new and superior product (preferred over any product tested against it, including the consumer's own brand). It was a one-size, superstretch pantyhose which had no shape until placed on the woman's leg and then shaped itself to conform to her leg structure, thereby providing excellent fit for 70% of all wearers. This product was more expensive to manufacture than conventional pantyhose. However, with one size needed, Hanes could drastically reduce the inventory and display space required at retail and could consider major innovations in packaging and display.

Hanes started to develop an integrated food and drug hosiery program where all elements including name, package design, display configuration, advertising, and promotion would complement each other. The name, package, and display had to focus retail consumer attention in the store. Other objectives were (1) a modular package to distinguish the package from other brands (and to minimize pilferage, of major concern to the trade); (2) a package to make both the consumer selection process as well as replenishing the display convenient; (3) a display of use only to Hanes, to ensure separation from other brands; (4) the display had to provide service and education to the consumer via information panels, literature racks, and so on, to duplicate in these self-service outlets the personalized service available in department stores; (5) a display using a minimum of costly square footage and a maximum of free vertical space; (6) a display capable of holding sufficient inventory to minimize stockouts.

Working with a package design consultant, the Hanes new product group developed the brand name "L'eggs." Within the name was the answer to the package: an actual plastic egg held in color-coded cylinders (for various colors and styles) that was modular and distinctive from competition. They developed a plastic display (called the L'eggs Boutique) that carried through the egg concept. It had only a two-foot diameter, carried 24 dozen pairs, lent itself to island locations in high-traffic locations of the store where consumer exposure was great, and proved to be a most effective point-of-purchase device. Exhibit 1 illustrates the L'eggs Boutique.

The L'eggs program was supported by advertising and promotion spending equal to that of a new cigarette or detergent introduction. Introductory advertising was at the rate of \$10 million nationally, using day and night

TV, magazines, Sunday supplements, and local newspaper media. Harrold reviewed L'eggs advertising and promotion objectives:

> Given the unstructured market, the nonexistent brand awareness of food and drug hosiery, and the need to reinforce brand permanency to the consumer and the trade, we wished to (a) build strong brand awareness and recognition of our logo and package; (b) let the consumer know where L'eggs was available, that it was new and different, and that it would become a permanent grocery and drugstore fixture; (c) stress our major product attribute, that L'eggs fit better than any other hosiery product—our theme was "Our L'eggs fit your legs"; (d) show the display and package in all advertising to make them synonymous with the L'eggs program.

The company launched the largest advertising campaign ever for any hosiery product. Spending was double the amount used previously by the entire hosiery industry for name brands. In L'eggs test market cities, two out of three hosiery commercials seen by consumers were for L'eggs—a brand available only in supermarkets and drugstores.

In addition, a $5 million market-by-market consumer promotion plan was tested, using introductory direct-mail coupons worth 25¢ or 35¢ off the purchase of one pair, as the products were introduced in each test market. This was the hosiery industry's first use of heavy couponing as a strategic trial-generating device to increase consumer awareness and product experience.

The L'eggs marketing strategy also included a major innovation in the distribution system offered to the trade. L'eggs hosiery was delivered through the front door of the store directly to the retail display by L'eggs sales personnel in their own L'eggs trucks. These salespersons saw that styles and colors were always in stock. They ensured attractiveness and cleanliness of the display. They rotated and balanced inventory for each store's display rack to maximize sales velocity at each location. Accordingly, the displays had excellent turnover. The company estimated that L'eggs dollar sales per square foot were more than seven times the retailer's average for all goods and, since the products were consigned, the retailer had no investment. The sales route force also acted as a detail force to implement promotions and other merchandising events at store level.

Another innovation was a computerized, on-line marketing and sales information network to support the distribution system. It tracked product movement for each display, and through its reports L'eggs could assure balanced product availability on every route van, in every warehouse, and along the pipeline from factory to each market. An outside management consulting firm was hired to design and implement this information and control system. In use, it coordinated manufacturing, warehouse distribution, retail inventory balancing, sales and market analysis, and billing and accounts receivable. Each sales call to a display unit provided a body of inventory and sales information to the system. This information was then assembled by display, by account, by route, by market, and by branch warehouse on a weekly basis and provided an excellent and timely data source for analysis of sales performance. In addition, extensive marketing information was routinely gathered in all markets via store audits and diary panels purchased from syndicated information sources. Special field survey research in specific markets conducted by outside research contractors and concept tests and focus group interviews conducted by the company's own market research personnel supplemented the routine syndicated information.

SALES RESULTS THROUGH 1972

Test marketing was conducted from March to October 1970. After the first six months of test market, 40% of all potential women users had tried L'eggs at least once. Over two-thirds of those triers repeated with one or more subsequent purchases. Brand awareness and advertising awareness exceeded 80% after only seven weeks of advertising in the test markets. L'eggs became the leading brand of pantyhose through any outlet in the test markets. At the end of six months, almost 25% of all women listed L'eggs as their regular brand.

Market-by-market rollout commenced in the fall of 1970. At its introduction into each geographical market, L'eggs was accompanied by high levels of advertising, demonstration, introductory coupons, and cents-off deals to induce initial trial. This introductory program was often continued for 13 weeks or more, until the product group felt that the introductory objectives had been met. Additional coupon promotions in specific markets were generally repeated several times per year. The L'eggs brand quickly became the dominant factor influencing the entire industry's approach to consumer marketing of hosiery products. L'eggs quickly established a consumer franchise among a significant proportion of all women.

In 1970, L'eggs retail sales were $9 million, representing only nine months' sales experience in test markets accounting for 3½% of the United States and two months' sales in the first rollout market. In 1971, retail sales were over $54 million. L'eggs became firmly established as the best selling hosiery brand in the country, regardless of outlet, with over a 3% share of the total $1.6 billion market. This level was reached with average 1971 distribution in only 33% of the United States.

The L'eggs program dramatically expanded hosiery sales through food and drug outlets. Prior to the introduction of L'eggs, only one out of four women had purchased hosiery in these outlets. After six months in test markets, over 40% of all women had tried L'eggs, which are available only through food and drug outlets. Nielsen data confirmed that total hosiery sales through convenience outlets had expanded substantially, and so L'eggs sales were primarily "add-on" sales. Trade acceptance and distribution levels in all market areas equaled the penetration that an established marketing company such as Procter & Gamble or General Foods would expect to achieve on a major new product introduction—even though this was Hanes' first exposure to mass merchandising channels.

By the end of 1972, the program had expanded into 75% of all retail markets. Fifty major markets had been opened in the span of 18 months. About 45,000 stores were under contract to display the L'eggs Boutique in prominent, high-traffic locations.

1973: MARKETING ORGANIZATION AND STRATEGY

As of mid-1973, the success of the product detailed in the previous pages had continued. As market-by-market rollout proceeded, and L'eggs attained deeper penetration of each successive market, retail sales climbed to over $110 million in 1972 and were projected to top $150 million for the fiscal year ending December 31, 1973. By mid-1973, L'eggs had achieved distribution in over 90% of the United States and was represented in every major market except New York City. The company's goal was to become fully national by late 1973.

The marketing organization had expanded from an in-house group that in 1969 consisted only of a marketing director, one product manager, an assistant, and one merchandising manager. The present structure included product managers for each of L'eggs major product extensions, assistants and merchandising managers for each, a new product and a market development manager, and a marketing research group. This was in addition to some 700 sales and administrative personnel. An organization chart is shown in Exhibit 2.

Since introducing the original L'eggs pantyhose and stockings, the company introduced several successful product extensions under the L'eggs brand: Sheer From Tummy to Toes pantyhose, Queensize pantyhose, Sheer Energy (a support hosiery product positioned toward nonsupport hose wearers), and L'eggs Knee Highs. All these product extensions cannibalized the original L'eggs brand to some extent, but the majority of sales were true incremental sales, coming at the expense of competitors in the marketplace and expanding the total unit and dollar sales of L'eggs Products, Inc.

The use of packaged-goods marketing techniques received the same emphasis in 1973 as it did during the original test market period. Now that L'eggs was approaching 100% national distribution, the initial test market advertising and promotion spending of $15 million on an equivalent national basis had evolved to an actual spending level of nearly $20 million for advertising, promotion, market research, and new product development.

The sales effectiveness of this strategy was readily apparent, as detailed in the following table:

L'eggs share of total hosiery sold through food and drug outlets, unit basis (pairs), 1972–1973

	Jan.– Feb.	*Mar.– Apr.*	*May– June*	*July– Aug.*	*Sept.– Oct.*	*Nov.– Dec.*
1972	20%	22%	25%	27%	27%	27%
1973	29	30	31	29	—	—

Source: Nationally syndicated retail audit service.

THE INDUSTRY

L'eggs was introduced into a mature, stable industry. After some expansion in the 1960s with the widespread introduction of pantyhose, the industry had stabilized at a dollar volume of about $1.5 billion and was not expected to increase. Unit sales had increased moderately over the last few years, but this increased demand had not expanded dollar volume, since the increased sales had only come in the wake of decreased prices. Many purchases had merely shifted from name-brand department store hosiery at an average price of around $3.00 to discount hosiery sold in food and drug outlets at prices typically ranging from $0.99 to $1.39. Trade publications had estimated that up to 50% of food and drug private-label hosiery pairs sold at prices as low as $0.39.

Grocery and drugstore outlets represented the fastest-growing hosiery channel. Estimates in the trade were that these outlets had accounted for only 5% of the units (pairs) sold in 1968. They accounted for 22.1% of unit sales in 1972 and were expected to account for as much as 50% of unit sales by 1976. L'eggs Products, Inc., had prepared its own estimates of distribution channel changes which are described in Exhibit 3.

The major companies in the industry appeared to be hastening this trend with huge amounts of marketing spending to advertise and promote food and drug hosiery. Estimates of industry spending ran as high as $33 million in each of 1972 and 1973 by three companies alone, although this was probably based on announced intentions and not actual spending.

COMPETITION

Although there were almost 600 different brands of hosiery competing in food and drug outlets, many were private-label and house brands, and the large majority of these were distributed only locally or in a grocery chain's own outlets. L'eggs' only identifiable branded competition in 1972 and 1973 were those products marketed by the Hanes Corporation's major competitors in the hosiery industry: Kayser-Roth Corporation and Burlington Industries. These companies, like Hanes, witnessed the stagnation in department store outlets and, soon after L'eggs appeared, brought out their own heavily advertised and promoted brands for food and drug outlet distribution. Kayser-Roth's entry was called No Nonsense Pantyhose, and Burlington called its product Activ Pantyhose.

These competitors were companies with considerable financial resources in comparison to the Hanes Corp. Hanes' 1972 sales were $245 million, of which women's hosiery accounted for about $140 million. Hanes' other divisions manufactured and marketed men's and women's knit outerwear and underwear, foundation garments, and swimwear. Kayser-Roth had sales of $519 million in 1972, of which women's hosiery was estimated to account for less than 20% of sales. Kayser-Roth also manufactured men's sportswear and clothing, women's sportswear and swim suits, textiles, and Supphose, the industry's leading support hosiery brand. Burlington Industries was even larger, with 1972 sales of $1.8 billion, of which women's hosiery sales were $101 million. Burlington also manufactured many other products, such as fabrics, yarns, hosiery for private-label marketers, carpets, furniture, sheets and pillowcases, and industrial textiles. Additional financial information for the three companies is given in Exhibit 4.

These competitors each utilized a somewhat different marketing strategy for hosiery products sold to food and drug channels. Kayser-Roth marketed its No Nonsense brand through supermarket warehouse distributors, who delivered to the back-door inventory area of the store, a system typical of packaged-goods products. To compensate the store or chain for stocking and cleaning retail displays, No Nonsense offered a retail margin of 42% versus L'eggs' 35%. The No Nonsense retail prices started at $0.99 versus L'eggs from $1.39.

Burlington distributed its Activ brand like L'eggs, using Activ salespersons and vans to deliver via the "front door" to the Activ display in food and drug outlets. In addition, Burlington distributed Activ through the General Cigar Corp., which placed the product in cigar stores and newsstands to achieve a retail base beyond food and drug outlets. Like No Nonsense, Activ's suggested retail price of $1.00 was substantially below that of L'eggs.

L'eggs responded to this price competition neither by direct price-cutting policies of its own nor by permitting the retailers to reduce normal L'eggs prices at the store level. L'eggs was a fair traded item, and indeed the maintenance of the fair trade policy was strictly enforced by the company. Management had not hesitated to drop individual stores or even chains from the retail network when they became aware of discounting and abuse of suggested prices for L'eggs products (via information gathered by the route salespersons during store visits). Retail price maintenance was an important part of L'eggs' overall marketing strategy.

The L'eggs response to competitive price differences was to continue the original strategy of competing in food and drug channels on bases other than price, particularly superior fit. L'eggs management believed that higher prices were necessary and justified because their product was more expensive to produce, due to specially developed high-quality yarn and 100% inspection. L'eggs management preferred over the long run to pursue a strategy of maintaining prices and using the resulting margins toward product improvements and advertising to the consumer. In 1973, L'eggs' gross margin was about $5.00 per dozen pairs. However, L'eggs often built its business in specific geographical markets via promotions, temporary price deals, and special packages.

An additional reaction to branded price competition came in 1971 when L'eggs Products, Inc., test marketed its own 99¢ brand,

First To Last. The First To Last marketing strategy did not utilize price as the primary sales quality differentiating the product—because there were numerous house brands and private-label pantyhose in all retail outlets that sold at prices considerably below 99¢. Rather, the durability and long-lasting qualities of the product were stressed. Advertising and promotion for First To Last made a conscious effort to minimize any linkage in the consumer's mind between First To Last and L'eggs brands, thereby reducing the degree of cannibalization. The First To Last rollout proceeded cautiously, with the objective of profitable penetration before further expansion, and in mid-1973 First To Last was distributed in less than 10% of the United States. The 1973 fall national promotion was concerned only with the L'eggs brand.

Although Activ and No Nonsense each announced at their respective introductions planned advertising and promotion spending levels of $10 million nationally, the actual figures were much less. Industry estimates were that No Nonsense would spend no more than $3 million and Activ no more than $1.5 million in 1973. This was due partially to a slower distribution growth than originally planned. While Kayser-Roth announced that No Nonsense would be distributed in 60% of the United States by the end of 1973 and 100% by 1974, Ward estimated that actual distribution had reached less than 15% of the country by mid-1973 and that the figure would be no more than 40% by the end of the year.

While Burlington planned for Activ to be distributed in 35% of the United States by the end of 1973 and 50% by 1974 or 1975, Ward estimated that actual distribution had reached less than 10% of the country by summer of 1973 and would reach no more than 30% by late fall. Market shares for No Nonsense and Activ reflected this lack of national distribution and penetration in comparison with L'eggs: in late summer 1973, national market shares were 1% for both No Nonsense and Activ, compared with 29% for L'eggs pantyhose. Ward noted, however, that actual spending levels indicated that these competitors could be major factors in geographical markets where they had achieved distribution.

PLANNING THE 1973 FALL NATIONAL PROMOTION

Now that L'eggs had almost completed national rollout, the planning had begun for a national promotion to impact on all markets. The evolution of the desires of major competitors for increased penetration and profitability dictated further marketing efforts at this stage of L'eggs' life cycle. In particular, the product group was looking for a single, high-impact promotional vehicle. They preferred the promotion to be run as an in-store promotion, although the alternative of a coupon mailed to consumers' homes was being considered.

Management's preferences for in-store promotions in this case were due to their feeling that such vehicles were more likely to result in multiple purchases per customer. Experience with coupon promotions during market introductions had shown that coupons rarely led to multiple purchases. In addition, an in-store effort would help to cement relations with the retailers, since L'eggs planned to feature the promotional event in its media advertising that fall and thus would demonstrate their considerable effort to draw customers into retail outlets for other purchases as well.

The goal of having one national promotion across all markets was complicated by the fact that L'eggs seemed to have at least two distinct types of markets in terms of responsiveness to its product. Like many mass marketers, L'eggs used as a measure of this responsiveness a quantity called the BDI (brand development index). For L'eggs, BDI was defined for each geographical market as the number of L'eggs pairs sold per thousand target women per week divided by the national average number of L'eggs pairs sold per thousand target women per week, then multiplied by 100. An area with BDI below 100 was an area where L'eggs lagged in penetration versus its national average. Exhibit 5 presents a listing of markets, their BDIs, and share of L'eggs sales accounted for by each.

In certain regions of the country, BDIs were consistently less than 80. Ward's rationale was that these areas had longer warm seasons that might explain lower pantyhose sales. Consumer surveys and panels conducted frequently by L'eggs market research group, by the advertising agency, and by hired outside research organizations had shown that these low BDI markets almost uniformly had low—and unsatisfactory—L'eggs trial rates. Typical comparisons between markets are shown in Exhibits 5 and 6. Thus, a major objective in low BDI areas was to increase trial rates.

In other areas of the country, trial rates had peaked at around 50% in 6 to 12 months after markets were opened. The brand group did not feel that trial rates in these areas could be increased profitably, or at least would not sustain increases long enough to generate profitable long-run sales. The major problem in high BDI areas, therefore, was to increase the repurchase rate of L'eggs purchasers.

From different sources of research data, Ward inferred that much brand switching was taking place: in consumer market surveys, typically 20–30% of consumers would *say* that L'eggs was their usual brand. However, actual sales figures taken from the company's sales tracking system and from syndicated store audits indicated that L'eggs had achieved around a 10% share of market in these high BDI areas. Therefore, the most important objectives of the promotion in these areas were to change users (even repeaters) from casual users to loyal users, to increase their repurchase rate, and to load users with product to decrease the probability they would switch to competitive brands. Both Activ and No Nonsense were running introductory promotions as part of their rollouts in many market areas that fall.

To summarize, the objective of the fall promotion in poor, or low, BDI markets was offensive—to increase trial. The product group was willing to absorb a certain level of promotional costs to raise trial rates on the theory that this would lead to greater penetration, more market share, and sustained profitable long-run sales increases. In contrast, the objectives of the promotion in high BDI markets were both offensive (increase repeat rates and product loyalty) and defensive (short-run loading). Ward's problem was to decide which one specific promotion, of the alternatives that were now before him, would be most effective against these differing objectives and differing market conditions.

THE ALTERNATIVES

Four alternative promotional vehicles were being evaluated. Each alternative had, in some form, been used with moderate success in specific markets during L'eggs rollouts over the past two years.

The national promotion alternatives in the summer of 1973 were

1. A 40¢-off twin-pack offer (see Exhibit 7).
2. A 25¢-off twin-pack offer.
3. A coupon mailed to homes worth 25¢ off one package (pair) of L'eggs.
4. A 20¢-off single-pack offer (see Exhibit 8).

In choosing these alternatives, the product group had reasoned as follows about their likely effects: the 40¢ twin-pack probably would achieve the objective of loading the consumer in high BDI areas best (for her next pair, the consumer would have the second pair of L'eggs in the twin-pack already and would have no need to go out and purchase, perhaps, a competitive brand). It was hoped that more product use and experience with two pairs rather than one would predispose the consumer more to repurchase L'eggs the next time she needed hosiery. However, Ward thought that the twin-pack might not be effective in low BDI areas because, with low trial and low market share in these areas, sufficient numbers of consumers might not purchase the twin-pack often enough to make the promotion effective. Besides, the consumer, not a L'eggs user anyway, might balk at having to purchase two pairs to try L'eggs.

The 25¢-off twin-pack would presumably produce the same behavior against those objectives and would improve unit contributions considerably. The question in Mr. Ward's mind was whether the offer would be effective enough—whether 25¢ off on two pairs would induce sufficient incremental purchases—to produce desirable results.

The mailed coupon worth 25¢ off on one pair was included as an alternative even though the brand group preferred the fall promotion vehicle to be an in-store offer. The 25¢ mailed coupon had been reasonably effective when used in many rollout markets during introduction. It was expected to induce trial among nonusers. It was to be mailed to all homes, thus coming to the attention of women who were nonusers or who may not have noted an in-store offer because they would not look for, or at, a L'eggs display. The coupon was not expected to be effective in inducing consumer loading or repurchase, however, because it could only be used to purchase one pair.

The 20¢ single-pack seemed to be somewhat effective against both objectives. In low BDI areas, consumer take away for the promotion (the number of consumers purchasing) would presumably be higher because the new trier would not be forced to purchase two pairs. So the single-pack might be more effective in raising trial rates. In high BDI areas the consumer might buy two or more single packs, satisfying the objective of consumer loading and raising repeat rates. On the other hand, there was nothing to encourage the consumer (or force the consumer, as was the case of the twin-pack) to purchase more than one pair. Ward judged the single-pack somewhat less effective as a means of consumer loading and increasing the total number of pairs purchased under the promotion.

For each alternative except the coupon, L'eggs would bear 65% of the cost of the promotion and the retailer would bear 35% of the cost, the same ratio as the retailer's gross margin. For example, for the 20¢-off single-pack, the retailer would absorb 7¢ (35% of 20¢) and L'eggs would absorb 13¢ (65% of 20¢). For the coupon, L'eggs would absorb the full cost and reimburse the retailer upon receipt of the coupon.

IMPLEMENTATION ISSUES IN SELECTING THE PROMOTION

Since L'eggs was a fair traded item, Ward knew that it could not appear in any store under a cents-off deal unless for a limited time only and could not appear in any store under two different prices for the same quantity (such as a regular-priced boutique pair and a 20¢-off promotional single-pack simultaneously). This meant that, to implement the single-pack offer, L'eggs would have to move all existing inventory out of stores at the beginning of the promotion, replace them with special 20¢-off single-packs, remove all special packs at the promotion's end, and move all regular inventory back in.

A possible solution was for L'eggs to make the special single-pack a simple variation of the regular pack. At the promotion's start all existing store packs could have a flag inserted, then removed at the promotion's end. Exhibit 8 actually shows a flag inserted into a regular L'eggs pack. Because the over 600 L'eggs route persons were fully occupied by their normal stocking, accounting, and boutique cleaning operations in over 70,000 outlets, a temporary work force would have to be hired to travel with the route persons to insert flags. Ward estimated each of the 600 L'eggs route persons would need a temporary assistant for one three-week cycle. These temporaries could be hired from well-known agencies at the rate of $30 per day per person. After the promotion was begun, the temporary labor would be replaced by factory labor because flags would be inserted in boutique-destined replacement packs at the factory. For unflagging boutique packs at the promotion's end, it was decided that they could do without the temporaries and use the efforts of route persons only, even though their route schedules could be delayed considerably by the extra work.

To supplement the boutique in the stores during the promotion, the factory would also make up special "shippers"—self-contained cardboard floor displays packed at the factory to minimize setup time at the retail store, but which (if accepted by the retailer) would require allocating additional floor space to L'eggs (see Exhibit 9). Ward estimated the cost of the single-pack shippers, freight, point-of-sale material, and so on would average out to 35¢ per dozen pairs. These shippers could simply be removed at the promotion's conclusion.

The twin-pack required no such expensive field labor to implement. Because the quantity in the twin-pack promotional packs would differ from regular boutique packs (1 pair each), the twin-pack shipper display could be utilized to implement the promotion (see Exhibit 10 for a mock-up of the twin-pack shipper) without boutique flagging. The shipper and promotional packs for it could be completely factory made and placed in the store to co-exist with regular-priced boutique packs, then simply removed at the promotion's conclusion. Fair trade laws would not be violated, since the cents-off promotional twin-packs would hold different quantities than the regular-priced boutique packs. Ward estimated the cost of making up these shippers, freight, point-of-sale material, and twin-packs at 38¢ per dozen hosiery pairs.

He anticipated a bit of increased trade resistance for the twin-pack alternatives since the shippers were absolutely necessary in the case of the twin-packs—and thus the retailer would have to devote roughly six more square feet of selling space to L'eggs during the promotion. In contrast, the 20¢ single-pack alternative could be accomplished solely via flagged boutique packs if the retailer refused the additional single-pack shippers. However, Ward expected this resistance to be minimal because of L'eggs' outstanding sales velocity. In addition, retailer acceptance for the twin-pack alternatives might be greater: the retailer could be shown that, because the boutique packs at regular prices (and margins) were still in his store, consumers could still elect to purchase a single-pack at normal prices and margins instead of the twin-pack with its commensurately lower margins per pair.

ESTIMATING SALES RESPONSE TO PROMOTION

Relying on his personal judgment and his experience gained during the national rollouts, Ward estimated some of the sales response effects of the 20¢ single-pack and the 40¢ twin-pack promotions. For the 20¢ single-pack, he reasoned that, during the four weeks the promotional packs were actually in the stores, about 80% of what would be L'eggs purchases at normal prices would be made instead at the reduced price. The other 20% would represent stores that did not accept the promotion, lost flags, and similar factors. Since normal L'eggs volume was running at 150,000 dozens per week, or 600,000 dozens per four weeks, Ward estimated that normal purchases at reduced prices would thus total 80% of 600,000 or 480,000 dozen.

The hardest factor to estimate was, of course, the effect of the promotion itself on incremental business. Ward made the working assumption that the single-pack promotion would generate a 10–11% net cumulative sales increase over an immediate period of 20 weeks during and following the promotion, plus a 10% long-term (sustained) sales increase.

For the 40¢ twin-pack alternative, Ward judged that, during the four weeks the packs were actually in the stores, about 60% of what would be L'eggs purchases at normal prices would be made instead at the reduced price. This estimate was lower than the 20¢ single-pack figure because

1. Single pairs at regular prices would be co-existing in the stores with promotional packs, and women—even L'eggs users—who did not want two pairs would still have the opportunity to purchase at regular prices.
2. Ward fully expected the twin-pack alternative to have less effect with nonloyal L'eggs users who might resist buying two pairs at a time, but might might pick up one pair, even at regular price.
3. Some stores might not accept the promotion.

Finally, Ward assumed that the twin-pack alternative would generate a 10% net cumulative sales increase over the immediate 20-week period during and following the promotion, but would produce no long-term increase in sales. The 25¢ twin-pack was expected to show the same general sales response pattern as the 40¢ twin-pack, although the magnitude of the expected responses was likely to be considerably smaller. Historical coupon redemption rates had never exceeded 8% and often were much lower.

A MIXED PROMOTION STRATEGIC ALTERNATIVE

Ward did have the option, of course, to select a combination of two (or more) of the alternatives for implementation during the fall promotion rather than just one. One alternative would be chosen which best met the objectives of high BDI markets, whereas a second alternative would be used for low BDI markets. He wanted to resist that option, because L'eggs planned to support the promotion with a heavy schedule of TV and local newspaper advertising. If separate alternatives were used in selected market areas, all national media would have to be switched to local spot media at considerable additional cost. This advertising support was not included in analyzing costs of the promotion because the advertising would substitute for, not supplement, L'eggs' normal advertising over the weeks of the promotion.

In addition, the mechanics of implementing two or more promotions would cause headaches for L'eggs production and warehouse personnel in producing and shipping several different types of point-of-sale materials, special packages, and shipper displays of merchandise. Life would also be more difficult for L'eggs sales account managers trying to explain (and sell) the mechanics of the promotion to national accounts (chain store operators). Ward's example was, "How do you convince Safeway's national buyer to take the promotion when you also have to tell him why Los Angeles stores must take single-packs and Little Rock stores must take twin-packs?"

Exhibit 1
L'eggs Products, Inc.

The classic L'EGGS Boutique.

—A traffic-stopping showpiece.

—Easy to shop.

—Displays 288 of the most attractive packages ever seen in the hosiery industry.

—Stands on a 2-foot circle of floor space.

Exhibit 2
L'eggs Products, Inc.
Organization Chart

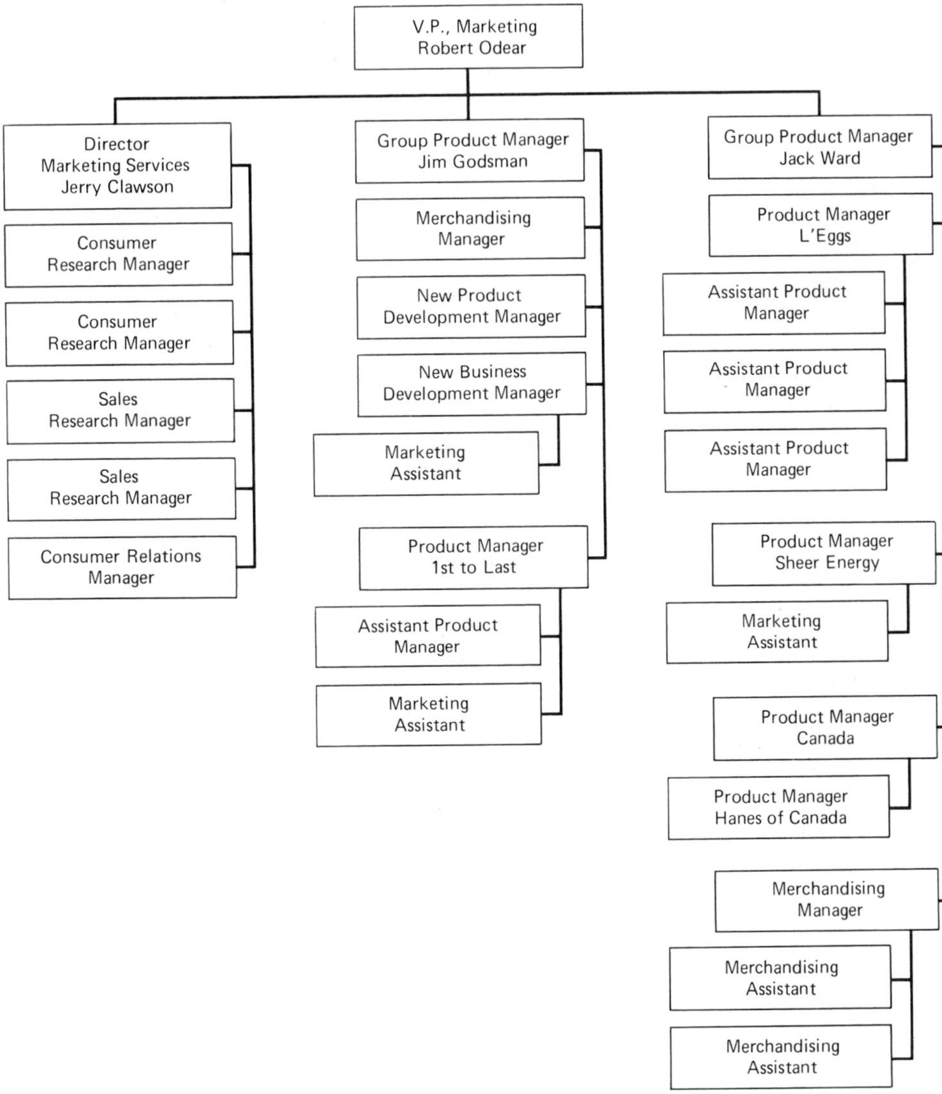

Exhibit 3
L'eggs Products, Inc.

Women's Hosiery Unit Sales, 1971–1974 (millions of dozens of pairs)

	All Hosiery				*Pantyhose*			
Year	*Total Volume*	*% Change*	*In Food and Drug*	*% Change*	*Total Volume*	*% Change*	*In Food and Drug*	*% Change*
1971E	123		28		82		20.8	
1972E	121	−2%	29.5	+5%	92	+12%	24.4	+17%
1973E	114	−6	29.9	+2	85	−8	25.6	+5
1974F	110	−4	30.5	+2	79	−7	25.0	−2

E – Estimated.
F – Forecasted.
Source: Company estimates.

Exhibit 4
L'eggs Products, Inc.

Company Financial Data, 1971–1972

	Hanes	*Kayser-Roth*	*Burlington*
1972 Total sales	$245	$579	$1,816
Women's hosiery sales (est.)	142	80–100	101
Total net income	8.2	11.9	49.6
1971			
Total sales	$176	$467	$1,727
Women's hosiery sales (est.)	88	70–95	115
Total net income	3.5	12.3	40

Source: Company annual reports; corporate 10-K forms filed with the Securities and Exchange commission.

Exhibit 5
L'eggs Products, Inc.

1972 Performance in Markets Opened During 1971 and Earlier

Markets	*BDI*	*Share of Sales*	*Markets*	*BDI*	*Share of Sales*
Portland	80	1%	Binghamton	110	1%
Sacramento	60	1	Springfield	140	1
Milwaukee	90	2	Hartford/New Haven	90	2
Kansas City	70	1	Erie	160	*
Chicago	110	6	Buffalo	100	2
Los Angeles	120	7	Rochester	110	1
Eugene	80	*	Syracuse	150	2
Medford	60	*	Utica	50	*
Klamath Falls	80	*	Columbia/Jefferson City	90	*
St. Joseph	80	*	Macon	60	*
Topeka	60	*	Chattanooga	70	1
Madison	40	*	Grand Junction	170	*
Rockford	70	*	South Bend/Elkhart	100	1
Santa Barbara	70	*	Cincinnati	120	2
Philadelphia	130	9	Dayton	100	2
Reno	80	*	Indianapolis	110	2
Chico/Redding	90	*	Harrisburg/York	120	2
San Francisco	90	6	Green Bay	60	1
Salinas/Monterey	120	1	Terre Haute	60	*
San Diego	90	1	Eureka	130	*
Detroit	140	6	Las Vegas	130	*
Flint/Saginaw	150	2	Grand Rapids/Kalamazoo	150	2
Lansing	180	1	Fort Wayne	100	1
Boston	130	8	Boise	100	*
Providence	100	2	Twin Falls	110	*
Cleveland	110	5	Idaho Falls/Pocatello	130	*
Youngstown	90	1	Fresno	80	1
Atlanta	90	2	Phoenix	100	1
Denver	150	2	Tucson	60	*
Colorado Springs	100	1	Salt Lake City	80	1
Cheyenne	200	*	Miami	50	1
Toledo	90	1	Tampa	80	1
Columbus	150	2	West Palm Beach	60	*
Lima	110	*	Fort Myers	60	*
Zanesville	120	*	Pittsburgh	100	2
				Total	100%

*Less than 0.5%.

Exhibit 6
L'eggs Products, Inc.

Penetration Measures in High and Low BDI Areas

Market	*Kansas City (Low BDI)*			*Philadelphia (High BDI)*		
Time After Introduction	*13 Weeks*	*6 Months*	*12 Months*	*13 Weeks*	*6 Months*	*12 Months*
Brand awareness	90%	90%	90%	100%	100%	100%
Advertising awareness	60	60	60	80	70	70
Trial	20	20	30	30	40	50
Repurchase rate[1]	60	70	70	60	70	80
Product satisfaction	70	70	70	90	90	90
L'eggs is usual pantyhose brand	10	10	10	10	20	20

[1]Defined as percentage of triers who bought more than once in last three months.
Source: Company data.

Exhibit 7
L'eggs Products, Inc.

Twin-Pack Promotion

Exhibit 8
L'eggs Products, Inc.

Single-Pack Promotion

Exhibit 9
L'eggs Products, Inc.

Single-Pack Display

Exhibit 10
L'eggs Products, Inc.

Twin-Pack Display

"Daisy" (A)

THE WOMEN'S SHAVING MARKET

In January 1974, top executives of the Gillette Safety Razor Division (SRD) met to discuss the division's position and possible courses of action with regard to the women's "wet" shaving market. Since the introduction of Lady Gillette in 1931, SRD had held a dominant share of this market. For the most part, its products for women had been essentially style variations of men's razors. Attempts had been made to design shaving products exclusively for women, but these had performed no better than existing products when tested. Nonetheless, in the late 1960s and early 1970s, SRD executives had become increasingly convinced that a substantial market existed for a shaving product designed especially for women. Their belief was strengthened by the performance of Flicker, a shaver designed specifically for women and introduced in mid-1972 by the American Safety Razor Company. Over the last year and a half, Flicker's sales had grown steadily, and it had consistently increased its market share.

Demographic information regarding the women's shaving market was generally gathered by SRD's Marketing Research Department in nationwide triennial surveys. In addition, infrequent ad hoc consumer studies were conducted to test advertising concepts or product performance. Although this information constituted a good base of data, the SRD executives agreed that they needed more thorough, current data about the women's shaving market than they currently had if they were going to make a major effort in that market. Therefore, they asked Mr. Bryan Dwyer, who was then responsible for Lady Trac II and had earlier worked on Lady Sure Touch, both SRD shaving products for women, to coordinate a task force to develop a new shaving product for women. This task force consisted of two components. The technical component had the responsibility to develop and test a variety of new product concepts. It included

 This case was prepared by Nancy J. Davis under the supervision of Steven H. Star.

representatives from SRD's Research and Development, Engineering, Manufacturing, and Finance departments. The second component was to develop data for positioning and advertising the product in the marketplace. Representatives included members of the Marketing Research Department, the Sales Department, and the advertising agency that would handle the product, the J. Walter Thompson Company. In late January 1974, this second group met to determine what they needed to know about the women's shaving market and to develop a consumer survey intended to give them this information.

THE COMPANY

The Gillette Company was founded in 1903 to manufacture and market a safety razor and blade invented by King C. Gillette. Until 1948, the company's product line was limited to safety razors, double-edge blades, and shaving cream. In 1948, Gillette acquired the Toni Company, a leading manufacturer of women's hair preparations. This acquisition was followed by acquisitions of the Paper Mate Corporation (1955), Harris Research Laboratories (1956), the Sterilon Corporation (1962), the Braun Company (1967), Buxton, Incorporated (1971), Welcome Wagon International, Inc. (1971), S. T. Dupont (1972), Jafra Cosmetics (1973), and Hydroponic Chemical Company, Inc. (1973). Each of these acquired companies was operated independently of the Safety Razor Division.

Although Gillette had marketed a brushless shaving cream in a tube for many years, the company's first major thrust in the toiletries business occurred when SRD introduced Foamy Shave Cream (1954) and Right Guard Deodorant for men (1960). This deodorant soon came to be positioned as a product for the entire family and quickly gained a substantial share of the deodorant market. Also during the 1960s, SRD introduced an after shave lotion, a men's cologne, and several hair grooming products for men. These toiletries grew so rapidly that a considerable amount of management time had to be diverted from the highly profitable razor and blade business. Therefore, in 1967, a separate Toiletries Division with its own headquarters, manufacturing plant, and sales force was established.

In 1973 Gillette's worldwide corporate net sales exceeded the billion-dollar mark for the first time, reaching $1,064,427,000. Income before taxes totalled $149,965,000, the highest in the company's history. The approximate contributions of Gillette's most important product lines to its worldwide total sales and profits were as follows:

	Net Sales	*Contribution to Profits*
Blades and razors	31%	66%
Toiletries and grooming aids	32	21
Braun products	22	7
Writing instruments	7	5
All others	8	1
	100%	100%

During 1973 net sales of $519,876,000 and net income of $53,051,000 were attributed to sources outside the United States and Canada. The company had approximately 31,500 employees, 9,400 of which were located in the United States. Over 7 million individual purchases of Gillette products in more than 200 countries and territories were made daily.

The Safety Razor Division (SRD)

SRD was responsible for manufacturing and marketing blades and razors in the United States. Throughout its history, SRD had been a leader in shaving technology. Among its most revolutionary innovations were the Super Blue

Blade, which had a plastic coating applied to the blade edge that significantly reduced the force required to cut beard hair (1958), the super stainless steel blade introduced in 1965, and the Techmatic shaving system introduced in 1966. The super stainless steel blade differed from the regular stainless steel blade in that its metallurgy and plastic coating were marked technological improvements which provided a smoother shave. The Techmatic shaving system consisted of a razor and a replaceable cartridge which contained a tightly wound steel band of continuous shaving edges. When one edge became dull, the user wound a new one into place. When all edges were used up, the user simply clicked on a new Techmatic cartridge. In 1970, partly in response to a bonded blade developed by Wilkinson,[1] SRD test marketed a shaver[2] which it called Sure Touch. Sure Touch was a plastic, disposable shaver which had the Techmatic shaving head permanently attached to the handle. Each head contained a band of five stainless steel shaving edges, and when all five edges became dull, the user simply threw the shaver away. Sure Touch was initially positioned as a razor for men. However, SRD's other products for men continued to be more popular than Sure Touch, so SRD decided to turn Sure Touch into a woman's product by putting a colored handle on it. Lady Sure Touch proved to be only marginally successful, however, and SRD ceased to expect significant volume gains from the brand.

[1]Wilkinson's bonded system consisted of a single blade permanently encased in a plastic shaving cartridge. It was a significant improvement over existing systems in that the angle of the blade was preset at the factory and the plastic casing kept the blade properly aligned. (With existing systems, if the razor were dropped or if the blade were not screwed in tightly, the result was often an uneven shave with frequent nicks and cuts.) Once a Wilkinson bonded blade became dull, the cartridge, but not the entire shaver, was thrown away and a new cartridge was attached.

[2]SRD management used the term "razor" to refer to a shaving instrument that employed replaceable blades of cartridges and the term "shaver" to refer to a shaving instrument the razor and blade of which were sealed together in a single unit. Shavers did not employ replaceable blades or cartridges. When the cutting edge became dull, the whole unit had to be replaced.

In 1971, SRD's Research and Development group explored the possibility of developing for women a reciprocal shaving razor (i.e., where two cutting edges faced each other). The concept was called Atra. To shave with Atra, one used a scrubbing action—the shaver could be moved both upward and downward without the user's changing her grip on it. While Atra apparently gave a close, comfortable shave, in user tests, it, Lady Sure Touch, and virtually any other shaving product lost to another instrument SRD developed in 1971, the Trac II twin blade shaving system. This was a razor which featured two recessed blades locked in a parallel position and encased in a plastic cartridge for extra shaving protection. Lightweight and easy to handle, Trac II was said to have "established a whole new standard in shaving ease and comfort." By 1973 the Atra project had been abandoned, and SRD introduced Lady Trac II, a man's Trac II with a colored handle.

In 1973, SRD, whose products were marketed only in the United States, accounted for about one-sixth of Gillette's worldwide sales and one-third of profits. Its product line included ten razors, twenty-two blades, and Cricket, a disposable lighter originated by a French subsidiary of Gillette. SRD had begun marketing Cricket in the United States in 1972. (See Exhibit 1 for product line.)

SRD's distribution system was one of the most extensive in the United States. In 1973 Gillette razors and blades were sold by more than 450,000 retail outlets in the United States, including 103,000 chain and independent drugstores, 193,000 food stores (of which 20% were classified as supermarkets), and 8,200 discount and variety stores. Convenience stores, liquor stores, tobacco shops, and automotive outlets made up the balance of its distribution outlets.

While SRD sold directly to large drug, food, and discount chains, most of its retail accounts were served by 2,100 independent wholesalers. The latter group included 400 drug wholesalers, 400 food wholesalers, 900 tobacco wholesalers, and 400 toiletry merchandisers. Toiletry merchandisers usually distributed to food and/or discount stores, often on a rack-jobbing[3] basis. SRD management estimated that these wholesalers and toiletry merchandisers together employed approximately 13,200 salespeople and were responsible for about 50% of SRD sales. Gillette exercised no direct control over wholesaler salespeople, but it did offer the wholesalers a variety of incentives such as advertising allowances, off-invoice allowances, and placement money for putting up special displays.

The SRD sales force consisted of a national accounts manager (who was responsible for about 20 large accounts), 4 regional managers, 18 district managers, 90 territory representatives, and 20 sales merchandisers. The territory representatives generally called on buyers at wholesale firms and at the headquarters of small chain and independent retail accounts. They also visited the top 10% to 20% of the retail outlets served by their wholesaler accounts as well as virtually all of the retail outlets of their own accounts. Sales merchandisers called only on retail outlets where they made sure displays were well stocked, tried to obtain special displays and promotions, and left suggested orders for store managers. SRD's sales force was supplemented by about 80 part-time corporate retail merchandisers who performed these functions for all Gillette's products. The total cost of the sales organization normally ran about 5% of sales.

SRD's sales promotion and media advertising were considered exceptionally strong. In working with the trade, SRD often offered 10%-off-invoice allowances for purchase above a certain level, 5% cooperative advertising allowances, and placement money for special displays. Consumer promotions might consist of premium offers, coupons, cents-off deals, on-pack premiums such as a free razor with a cartridge of blades, and so forth. SRD normally ran eight promotional cycles annually. Five or six products were usually promoted in each cycle; four of the cycles usually contained consumer promotions. About 90% of SRD's advertising consisted of sponsorship of prime-time TV programs and various sports events. It did some limited print advertising, primarily in men's magazines. It had done a small amount of TV and magazine advertising for Lady Sure Touch, but by and large its advertising was oriented to the men's market. In 1973 SRD's total advertisng expenditures were estimated to be $17 million.

The standard SRD display consisted of razors and blades in blister packs hanging from hooks on a pegboard. These were almost always located near a cash register or checkout lane, though whenever possible, SRD had multiple displays in a single outlet. For example, in large drugstores or mass merchandise outlets, razors were frequently displayed in the health and beauty aids department, while a limited supply of the best-selling razors was also displayed along with blades at checkout lanes. In food stores, razors and blades were almost always displayed only at checkout lanes.

THE MARKET

In 1973, total U.S. retail sales of blades were about $416,000,000, or 2.372 billion units. The total retail sales of razors were about $52,000,000. At the manufacturer level, blade sales totaled about $226,240,000 and razor sales about $33,280,000. In addition to SRD,

[3]Rack jobbers were essentially wholesalers who set up retail displays and kept them stocked with merchandise. They visited retail outlets frequently to replace defective or worn merchandise, add new items, and set up promotional displays. The retailers usually retained formal authority to determine which products and brands they would carry and how they would be priced, but in practice these functions were often delegated to the rack jobber.

three companies—Schick, Wilkinson, and American Safety Razor—accounted for the major share of the wet shaving market. With about a 1% share, private labels were not considered a major factor.

Schick Safety Razor Company, a division of Warner-Lambert Company, was especially strong in the injector[4] segment of the wet shaving market. (Schick electric shavers were sold by Schick Electric Company, a totally separate company which was not connected with Warner-Lambert.) Schick's share of the injector market was about 78%, and injector blades and razors represented about 17% of the combined markets. Schick's major products for women were Lady Eversharp (an injector razor), Lady Schick Band Razor (a Techmatic-type razor), and Lady Super II. These were all essentially adaptations of men's razors, with the Lady Super II's containing Schick's version of the Trac II shaving system. Schick's share of the wet shaving market was about 21%.

Wilkinson was a division of the British Match Company located in England. Its products were sold and distributed in the United States by the Colgate-Palmolive Company. It was especially strong in the bonded razor segment of the market. It marketed a nondisposable plastic razor for women in England which it was rumored to be considering marketing in the United States. Its share of the U.S. wet shaving market was about 6%.

American Safety Razor Company (ASR), a division of Philip Morris, marketed its products under the brand names Persona, Gem, and Flicker. It held about 12% share of the wet shaving market. With Flicker, it had become the market leader in products designed especially for women. Flicker was thought to account for about 41% of ASR's dollar sales. ASR also manufactured about 80% of the private-label blades sold.

In 1974, in addition to injector, band, and bonded razors, the more conventional double-edge and single-edge razors were still on the market. Double-edge razors, the oldest shaving instruments still being sold in any quantity, used replaceable double-edge blades. The standard double-edge razor held the blade at only one angle, while the adjustable product had a dial with which the user could alter the blade angle and exposure to suit his own preferences. Single-edge razors were those which used replaceable blades with only one shaving edge. Except for injector razors, very few single-edge razors were still on the market in 1974. (See Exhibit 2 for a list of competitive razors in each category.)

Over 20 types of blades were marketed in 1974. Many of these were double-edge blades which were differentiated according to the metal from which they were made. Blades bonded in replaceable plastic cartridges were considered part of this market, as were disposable shavers. (See Exhibit 3 for the major manufacturers' blade lines and Exhibit 4 for illustrations of various shaving products.)

The Women's Shaving Market

According to SRD's Marketing Research Department, the following women's razors had been introduced since the early 1960s:

1962	Lady Gillette (Gillette)[5]
1963	Lady Eversharp (Schick)
1966	Lady Techmatic (Gillette)
1967	Lady Schick Band Razor (Schick)
1971	Lady Sure Touch (Gillette)
1972	Flicker (American Safety Razor)
1973	Lady Trac II (Gillette)
1973	Lady Super II (Schick)

[4]The injector razor was distinguished primarily by the method by which it was loaded. First, the user inserted a stem attached to a small case of blades into a slot on the razor. Next, he pulled a blade loader device back to the end of the case, and a blade moved into a position so that, when the device was pushed toward the razor, the new blade pushed out the old blade. The new blade was then locked into position until removed by the injector. Almost all injector razors used single-edge blades.

[5]While the first razor to carry the name Lady Gillette was introduced in 1931, the name was used for almost every new product for women SRD introduced up through the early 1960s.

With the exception of Flicker, these razors were colored-handle versions of male razors, blister-mounted on a card. (See Exhibit 5 for pictures of these razors.)

Flicker was obviously not a colored-handle version of a man's razor. It was a disposable band razor with a circular shape, except for the even cutting edge. When one cutting edge became dull, the user rotated another into place. Each shaver contained five cutting edges. Using newspaper advertising only, ASR introduced Flicker into seven midwestern markets between June and September 1972. During the fourth quarter of 1972, ASR extended Flicker's distribution to 23 markets, again using only newspaper advertising. In the first quarter of 1973, 8 more markets were opened, and ASR added spot TV ads and ads in magazines and newspaper supplements to Flicker's regular newspaper advertising. During the second quarter of 1973, Flicker's distribution was further extended to 34 more markets, bringing the total to 65. These 65 markets accounted for about 67% of the total U.S. population. In addition to the three types of advertising it had been using, it added both day and night network TV. In each of its markets, it offered liberal terms to the trade.

The SRD market researchers estimated that in 1974 women would purchase for their own use about $75,400,000 in wet razors and blades and that in 1975 the total would reach $83,330,000. They thought these expenditures would break down as follows:

	1974	*1975*
Regular razors	$11,340,000	$12,350,000
Disposable razors (Flicker and Lady Sure Touch)	7,280,000	12,740,000
Blades (excluding Flicker and Lady Sure Touch)	56,810,000	58,240,000
Total	$75,430,000	$83,330,000

In 1972 women had spent $68,250,000 on wet shaving products for their own use, while in 1973 the comparable total had been $70,460,000. The dollar sales of wet shaving equipment for women were substantially larger than sales of other health and beauty aids. For example, it was estimated that, in 1974, women would spend $63,000,000 on eyebrow pencils and eye shadow, $59,000,000 on hair color rinses, $55,000,000 on mascara, and $14,000,000 on rouge. Moreover, it was estimated that women would spend about $42,000,000 on electric shavers in 1974.

SRD products were expected to account for about $8,450,000 of the total $18,620,000 spent solely on wet razors in 1974:

Brands	*Wet Razor Sales*	*% of Total*
Gillette		
Lady Trac II	$ 3,770,000	20.1%
Lady Gillette	650,000	3.5
Lady Sure Touch	520,000	2.8
Lady Techmatic	390,000	2.1
"Male" razors	3,120,000	16.6
	$ 8,450,000	45.1%
Competitors		
Flicker	6,110,000	32.6
All other disposables[1]	650,000	3.5
Lady Super II (Schick)	780,000	4.2
Lady Eversharp Injector (Schick)	520,000	2.8
"Male" razors	2,110,000	11.8
	$10,170,000	54.9%
Total	$18,620,000	100.0%

[1]Several small companies manufactured a wide variety of inexpensive disposable shavers. These were usually convenience items which were sold in places such as airports. Their retail price was often two or three shavers for about $1.00. They were not considered a major factor in the women's shaving market.

Researchers noted that nearly 40% of this $18,620,000 would be spent for disposable razors.

According to SRD's Marketing Research Department, there were 83,600,000 women over 13 years of age in the United States, about

	% of Total Razor Market ($)				% of Total Blade Market ($)	
	Gillette Lady Trac II	Schick Super II for Women	Lady Gillette	Gillette Lady Techmatic	Lady Sure Touch	Flicker
June '72	—	—	2.5%	2.5%	—	0.4%
Jan. '73	—	—	1.1	1.2	0.2%	1.8
June '73	3.7%	1.2%	0.9	1.3	0.9	2.1
Jan. '74	4.6	0.9	0.8	1.4	0.5	2.0
	% of Total Razor Market (units)				% of Total Blade Market (units)	
June '72	—	—	2.9%	2.5%	—	0.2%
Jan. '73	—	—	1.3	1.2	0.1%	1.0
June '73	2.6%	1.0%	0.9	1.1	0.6	1.2
Jan. '74	3.5	0.7	0.9	1.1	0.3	1.3

18,700,000 of whom did not remove hair from their legs or underarms. Of the 64,900,000 remaining, 15,800,000 used electric shavers and 2,600,000 used depilatories. Thus, there were 49,800,000 women who used wet shavers. Thirty million of these currently used Gillette products.

In calculating the share of the total markets which the leading women's products held, SRD researchers felt that Lady Trac II, Schick's Super II for Women, Lady Gillette, and Lady Techmatic should be considered part of the razor market because they were individual units for which new blades or cartridges could be purchased. They felt, however, that since Lady Sure Touch and Flicker were disposable items, they were more comparable to blades and cartridges. Therefore, they felt that Lady Sure Touch and Flicker should be evaluated as part of the blade market. SRD researchers followed the performance of various products in representative food and drug stores in the United States. They were unable to monitor product movement in mass merchandise outlets, so they felt that their data should be considered only a general indicator of product performance. Nevertheless, according to these data, recent market shares of the different products in their respective markets were shown in these tables:[6]

SRD researchers felt that Flicker's success in gaining distribution indicated that the market would, in fact, welcome a razor distinctively designed for women. They provided the following summary of the percentages of food and drugstores through which the major women's shaving products were distributed:

[6]The following market share data are based on the *total* razor and blade markets, not on the market for women's products alone.

	Gillette Lady Trac II		Schick Super II for Women		Lady Gillette		Gillette Lady Techmatic		Lady Sure Touch		Flicker	
	Drug	Food	Drug	Food	Drug	Food	Drug	Food	Drug	Food	Drug	Food
June '72	—	—	—	—	37%	6%	21%	6%	—	—	10%	3%
Jan. '73	—	—	—	—	35	2	21	10	8	8	29	25
June '73	22%	10%	8%	7%	36	2	23	6	32	15	46	35
Jan. '74	25	13	11	5	33	2	19	4	29	14	54	45

In addition to these general market data, SRD's Research and Development department had information about the differences between hair removed by women and that removed by men. Women's hair was generally finer (.0040 inches thick) than men's beard hairs (.0065), and it was fairly uniform, while men's beard hair was very irregular in shape. While the average man's beard shaving area was about 48 square inches, the total average shaving area for a woman was approximately 412 square inches, 400 for legs and 12 for underarms. There were approximately 210 hairs per square inch for underarms and 28 for legs, as opposed to approximately 310 hairs per square inch on a man's face. Thus, on the average, men cut approximately 15,000 hairs during a shave, whereas women cut about 14,000. Both men's and women's hair grew at a rate of about one-sixtieth of an inch a day. On the legs, hairs generally grew downward, with some growing sideways, and under the arms, they grew both up and down. Moreover, the researchers had determined that the amount of force required to produce pain on a woman's leg and underarms was 25% to 40% higher than the force needed to produce pain on a man's face.

FURTHER RESEARCH

In late January 1974, SRD's task force met with Michael Lindroth and Alison Yancy of the J. Walter Thompson Company, the advertising agency which SRD planned to work with if it decided to make a major effort in the women's shaving market. The purpose of this meeting was to determine exactly what further information SRD needed to know about the women's shaving market and to develop a marketing research program which would provide this information.

The group's working assumption was that it would be necessary to use a large-scale (about 2,000 respondents) questionnaire survey to elicit the types of information that they thought they would need. Personal interviews rather than a mail survey were considered necessary to ensure effective communication on a subject likely to be considered "sensitive" by the respondents. Based on previous experience with such surveys, the group estimated that each consumer interview should take no longer than 60 minutes. As was SRD's usual practice, an outside contract research supplier would be responsible for the actual implementation of the survey, at a cost of approximately $15.00 per interview.

Exhibit 1
"Daisy" (A)

SRD Product Line, January 1974

Product Types	*Product Offerings*
Blades	Trac II (5- or 9-cartridge packages) Standard Techmatic band (10 shaving edges) Adjustable Techmatic band (packages contained 5, 10, or 15 shaving edges) Platinum-Plus double edge (packages contained 5, 10, or 15 blades) Super Stainless double edge (packages contained 5, 10, or 15 blades) Platinum-Plus injector (7- or 11-blade packages) Super Blue (10- or 15-blade packages) Regular Blue Blade (5- or 10-blade packages) Thin (4- or 10-blade packages) Valet (10-blade package)
Razors	Trac II Lady Trac II Techmatic Lady Techmatic Trac II Twinjector Super Adjustable double edge Knack Lady Gillette double edge Super Speed double edge Three-Piece double edge Lady Sure Touch
Disposable lighters	Cricket lighters Cricket table lighters

Exhibit 2
"Daisy" (A)

Major Razors on the Market, January 1974

Razor Types	*Razor Offerings*
Double edge	Gillette Standard double edge Gillette Super adjustable Lady Gillette Gillette's Super Speed Gillette three piece Wilkinson double edge, nonadjustable Schick, nonadjustable double edge Assorted private label
Single edge	Gem Contour II (ASR) Assorted private label
Injector	Schick Standard injector Schick Adjustable injector Lady Shick injector
Band	Gillette Techmatic Gillette Lady Techmatic Schick Instamatic Lady Schick Instamatic
Bonded	Gillette Trac II Gillette Lady Trac II Schick Super II Wilkinson Bonded Persona, Double II (ASR)

Exhibit 3
"Daisy" (A)

Blade Lines by Manufacturer, January 1974

Manufacturers	*Blade Lines*
Gillette	Platinum-Plus double edge Stainless Steel double edge Premium double edge Super Blue Blades double edge Blue Blades double edge Thin Blades double edge Carbon Blades double edge Regular Techmatic band Adjustable Techmatic band Gillette Platinum-Plus injector Trac II cartridges Lady Sure Touch
Schick	Platinum/Stainless double edge Plus Platinum double edge Plus Platinum injector Super Chromium double edge Super Chromium injector Super II cartridges Instamatic band
Wilkinson	Wilkinson Sword double edge Stainless Steel double edge Bonded cartridges Sword Master double edge
American Safety Razor	Persona Stainless/Chrome double edge Persona Tungston double edge Persona Face Guard double edge Persona Double II Flicker Gem Super Stainless Steel Blade single edge Persona injector

Exhibit 4
"Daisy" (A)

Razor and Blade Illustrations

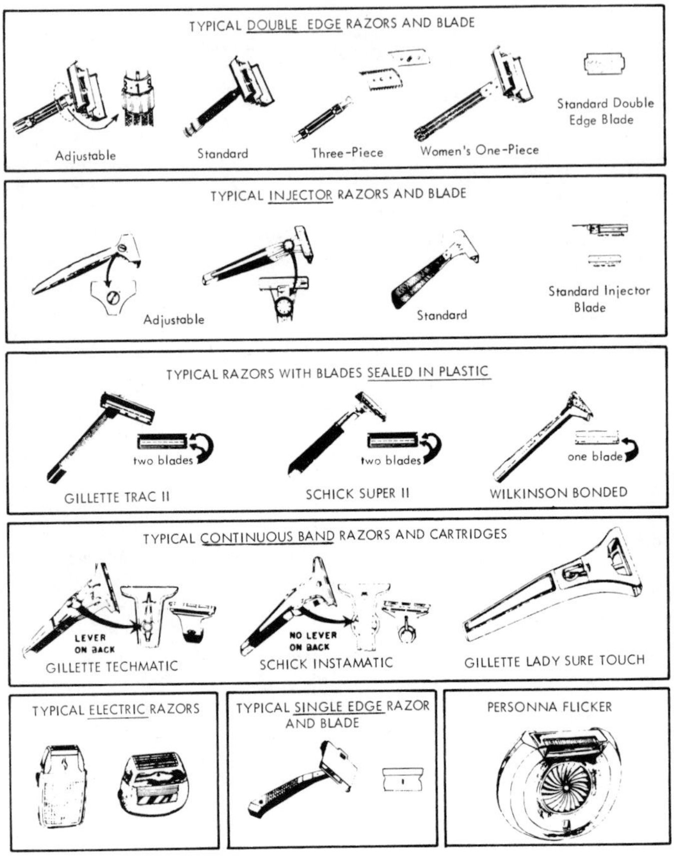

Exhibit 5
"Daisy" (A)

Shaving Products Marketed for Women,
January 1974

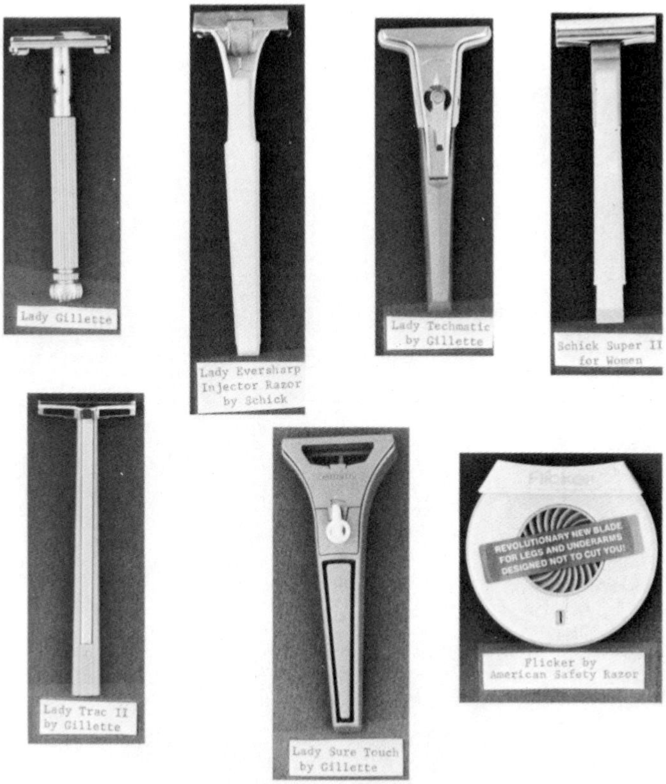

II

DATA COLLECTION

2

Sampling and Measurement

MassNORML (A)

On a rainy day at the end of March 1977, John Cassidy and Steve Dimitry were reviewing the work they had performed for MassNORML, the Massachusetts branch of the National Organization for the Reform of Marijuana Laws (NORML). With public hearings on a marijuana decriminalization bill to be held by the Massachusetts state legislature in the middle of April, a successful culmination of their work might be close at hand; however, much work remained to be done before the hearings. The two men wondered if their past marketing strategy had been the most appropriate, or if not, how it might best be revised for the future.

HISTORY OF NORML

NORML was founded in 1970 by a Washington, D.C., lawyer named Keith Stroup, who was then working in the Product Safety Commission of the federal government. With marijuana arrests topping 400,000 annually, Stroup decided that it was time to represent the marijuana-smoking population of America (estimated at 13 to 15 million regular users) as a legitimate political force. He worked with former Attorney General Ramsey Clark to arrange funding and was able to get a grant from the Playboy Foundation to set up shop. Currently, approximately 28% of NORML's $200,000 annual budget is provided by grants from *Playboy* and *High Times*, while 46% results from membership contributions and 26% from sale of NORML T-shirts, buttons, and stickers.

NORML collects and disseminates research results in the areas of health, medicine, sociology, and other social areas affected by the marijuana issue. It uses these research results to argue for decriminalizing the private possession and use of marijuana.

Decriminalization would replace a criminal offense status with a civil offense status, meaning that the user would no longer be arrested and jailed for possession of marijuana

 This case was prepared by David J. Reibstein.

for personal use, but would only be subject to a civil fine similar to a parking ticket. Offenders would not incur a criminal record and therefore bear no stigma for the offense as they would if they were arrested and jailed.

The group's initial major success came in 1973, when the state legislature of Oregon passed the country's first state decriminalization law. In 1975, California, Colorado, Maine, and Ohio passed similar laws, while the Alaskan State Supreme Court, in the landmark *Ravin* v. *State of Alaska* case, declared the Alaskan marijuana laws unconstitutional on a right-to-privacy basis. As a result, unlimited amounts of marijuana may be possessed in Alaska homes for personal use. The state legislature then decriminalized public possession of smaller amounts.

In 1976, South Dakota and Minnesota joined the decriminalization group, making a total of eight states which no longer arrested and incarcerated people for simple possession of small amounts of marijuana (Exhibit 1).

NORML has 38 affiliate organizations working on the state level and one national headquarters which coordinates the state groups and pursues decriminalization on the federal level. Its board of advisors includes such notables as Ramsey Clark, former senator Jacob Javits, Dr. Benjamin Spock, and several nationally recognized medical experts on marijuana from the Harvard Medical School faculty. NORML believes in a traditional "within the establishment" approach to legislative reforms and shuns all countercultural or radical associations, believing that a respectable, middle-class image is necessary for successful political action.

HISTORY OF MASSACHUSETTS NORML

In June 1976, Cassidy went to Washington, D.C., to organize a management information system and study marketing possibilities for NORML. At the end of the project, Stroup asked him to spend the following year organizing a state chapter in Massachusetts and to assume the title and responsibilities of state coordinator to facilitate the task. Cassidy agreed to Stroup's proposal, and returned to Boston in July to begin laying the groundwork for the project.

His first task was to clarify the objectives of the state project. Between July 1976 and January 1977, Cassidy and his partner, Steve Dimitry, were confident that they could develop the grass roots support necessary to finance a concerted lobbying effort beginning in early 1977 when the legislature opened. They therefore set as the objectives of the project the following:

- Set up a viable, self-financing state chapter;
- Use this chapter's financial and human resources to push for a decriminalization bill in the legislature.
- Train the members of the chapter to continue the NORML effort the following year, should the bill fail to pass.

The organizational structure established for handling these objectives is shown in Exhibit 2.

MASSACHUSETTS NORML'S STRATEGY

MassNORML's ultimate objective was to pass a marijuana decriminalization bill through the state legislature. To accomplish this, several steps needed to be taken. One of the greatest tasks was to educate the state's populus on (1) recent medical findings discounting health hazards of marijuana, (2) legislative reports from decriminalization states praising the change, and (3) cost savings estimates for the Commonwealth of Massachusetts should it decriminalize marijuana. To accomplish this educational task, speakers were provided for college groups, church teen groups, and radio talk shows. In addition, a NORML advisory board member, Dr. Norman Zinberg of the Harvard Medical School, wrote about marijuana frequently in his weekly "Forum" column in the Sunday *Boston Globe*. Through these activities, MassNORML hoped to be able to destigmatize the concept of marijuana reform by providing a clear medical foundation, cogent economic reasons, and a rational, rather than radical or countercultural, image to the question.

To finance the educational program, numerous fund-raising activities were undertaken. Presuming that current users of marijuana were more likely to donate funds to the decriminalization cause, pleas for donations (MassNORML membership) focused on this group. To identify this group, a "smoker analysis" (Exhibit 3) was constructed for Massachusetts based on national survey data collected over the past several years. The results of this analysis were used to determine the demographic structure of the target audience.

To give the decriminalization issue greater public exposure, MassNORML worked in coordination with Bob Downing of the Mayor's Coordinating Council on Drug Abuse in Boston. Together, they were able to solicit a public statement from the governor of Massachusetts in favor of a decriminalization bill. MassNORML felt that the credibility of this approval would do much to allay the fears of the nonsmoking population concerning the bill. In addition, MassNORML provided the city council of Provincetown, Mass., a city which was felt to be favorably disposed to decriminalization, with materials which led to that council's vote to request the state legislature to pass a reform bill. Again, MassNORML felt that the media coverage of these events did much to lay the groundwork for a general public acceptance of the bill.

Approaching the Lawmaking Process

Before beginning any lobbying activities in the state legislature, MassNORML prepared a history of previous reform attempts in the legislature to determine the most effective lobbying strategy. After the election results of November 1976 came in, MassNORML immediately surveyed the new members of the legislature to determine their attitudes concerning marijuana reform bills. This was accomplished by NORML volunteers who stalked the corridors and offices of the State House, tracking down each of the legislators to ask them their position. The interview took the form of free-flowing conversations based around the following guiding questions:

1. If you voted previously on the decriminalization issue, will you vote the same this time? Why? What factors were important to you in making your decision?
2. If you haven't voted before, how will you vote this time? Why? What factors are important in making up your mind?

The prime focus here was to determine which factors were most important in causing a negative vote: fear of voter reprisals, fear of health hazards, dangers to society, and so on.

With this information in hand, MassNORML prepared an information pamphlet to be handed out to the members of the legislature to ensure that accurate, up-to-date information on marijuana reform was available. Interviews were conducted with pro-reform representatives to assist in forming a strategy aimed at applying maximum pressure to the most critical elements in the legislative process.

Based on the surveys, the interviews, and the historical analysis, it was determined that Rep. Mike Flaherty of South Boston, Chairman of the Committee on the Judiciary, was the most important link in the process. It was said that Flaherty's actions could influence as many as 100 votes;[1] if the bill were to come out of his committee with an unfavorable reading, it would be doomed; with a favorable reading, it would have an excellent chance of passing. The Committee on the Judiciary was thus singled out to be the major focus of MassNORML's lobbying, with secondary pressure being applied to less important representatives.

It was believed that a primary reason Flaherty opposed the bill was fear of voter reprisal in his home district. Thus, it was decided to poll Flaherty's district to get an accurate feel for South Boston's attitude toward marijuana reform.

South Boston has a reputation for being one of the most conservative districts in the state. Thus, it was felt that the findings would serve as a base case, and legislators from more liberal districts could assume their constituents to be more favorable toward the decriminalization issue.

Since MassNORML could be accused of a bias by opponents if the survey came up favorably, it was determined to do the survey under the aegis of an independent, nonpolitical research organization.

Voter Attitude Survey, South Boston

The survey was designed to elicit the following specific information:

1. How dangerous people thought marijuana was, to both the individual and to society at large.
2. What legal penalties did people think most appropriate for
   a. possession for personal use,
   b. personal cultivation, or
   c. casual sale to adults.
3. Whether people thought records of marijuana arrests should be maintained.
4. What voter reactions would be toward a representative who voted in favor of various forms of decriminalization bills.
5. Demographic information concerning respondents.
6. Other comments the respondents might care to make (this was included to provide a feel for the flavor of the responses).

MassNORML expected to find the following results from the survey:

1. A response rate of 13–15% as is normally expected for a mail survey.
2. A higher response rate from the younger age groups, corresponding to higher usage patterns.
3. More favorable responses from the younger age groups.
4. A high correlation between those opposed to decriminalization and those who felt marijuana was dangerous.

Methodology

MassNORML's first task was to determine the type of survey to implement. It was felt that a phone survey might cause paranoia as well as provide too short a time for adequate presentation of the questionnaire. Door-to-door sampling was ruled out as outsiders sometimes provoked adverse reactions on the part of inhabitants of an area. A mail questionnaire, thus, seemed to be the best format and is shown with results in Exhibit 4. Since MassNORML was concerned only with voters, as opposed to all citizens of the district, voter registration lists, which provide the name and address of each registered voter in the district, seemed to be the most feasible way of defining the target population.

MassNORML then had to perform several tasks to implement the survey:

[1]Interview with legislative aide to Rep. Backman, cosponsor of one reform bill.

1. Obtain voter registration lists: these were procured from the voter registration office, South Boston, by Bob Downing.
2. Determine a sample size: the voter population was approximately 16,000 (determined by counting the names on the registration lists). MassNORML had \$350 to spend on the survey. Printing costs estimated at \$35 and envelope costs of \$50 left \$265 for postage. Business response envelopes cost 25¢ each to redeem at the post office. MassNORML assumed the response rate would be between 10% and 20%, and it guessed 15%. With this information it set up the following equation:

$$.13x + .15(.25x) = 265$$

$$x = 1{,}582$$

Since 1600 questionnaires would provide a sample size of 10% of the entire population, MassNORML decided on that figure as an appropriate sample size.
3. Determine a random sampling technique: since the sample size was 10% of the entire population, MassNORML chose every tenth name on the voter registration lists as an addressee. This was expected to provide a random sample whose demographics matched those of the district as a whole. Thus, any variation in respondents' demographics from that of the district could be attributed to a response bias rather than to a sampling bias.
4. Mail the questionnaires: MassNORML assembled a team of volunteers who formed an assembly line to fold the questionnaire and response envelope, stuff them into another envelope, stamp the envelope, and address the envelopes. This work took about 60 person hours.
5. Tabulate the results: the results were tabulated after 212 responses had gathered in the post office box. Two weeks later, 38 more responses were picked up and tabulated. The changes caused by the addition of the further responses were minimal, usually on the order of less than 1% (for total figures). This provided a good check to Cassidy and Dimitry that the responses gathered earlier were fundamentally valid.

RESULTS

The results show that

1. 73.3% of respondents believe that possession of small amounts of marijuana for personal use should not be punishable by law, and of the remaining 26.7%, only 7.3% believe it should be punishable by a jail sentence (question 3).
2. 69.4% believe that private cultivation of marijuana should be allowed (question 5).
3. 60.5% believe that nonprofit sale of small amounts of marijuana should not be punishable by law, and of the remainder, 11.3% believe that it should be punishable by a jail sentence (question 6).
4. 56.1% would respond favorably to their representative's voting for a bill removing jail sentences for personal use of marijuana but maintaining punishment by fine (question 8-1).
5. 64.9% would respond favorably to a bill removing all penalties for possession for personal use (question 8-3).
6. 58.3% would respond favorably to a bill allowing cultivation of small amounts of marijuana plants for personal use (question 8-4).

COMMENTS

1. Confidence intervals of 95% were calculated for the percentage numbers given in 1–6 above. This interval indicatesa range over which there is 95% confidence that the actual percentage does lie. The intervals are

Result	*Percentage (Mean)*	*95% Confidence Interval (in %)*
1	73.3%	67.6–79.0%
2	69.4	63.5–75.3
3	60.5	54.3–66.7
4	56.1	49.6–62.6
5	64.9	58.8–68.0
6	58.3	51.9–64.7

2. Of the 100 people who responded either "no effect" or "unfavorably" to question

8-1 (see Exhibit 4), 43 responded favorably to question 8-3, which is effectively no more than a stronger statement of 8-1. These 43 people would appear to be unsatisfied by a weaker form of the bill, that is, one maintaining punishment by fine. If these 43 are added back to the "favorably" for 8-1, the 56.1% becomes 75.3%.

3. Some 70.4% of the people who believe that possession of small amounts of marijuana should be punishable by a jail sentence also believe that marijuana, in small amounts, is more dangerous than alcohol and tobacco.

RESPONDENT ANALYSIS

Because of the random sampling technique used, MassNORML reasoned that the 1,600 questionnaires would be received by the various age subgroups in approximate proportion to their relative sizes. Under this assumption, and using the population subgroup percentage for Massachusetts as a proxy, response rates for each age group were calculated and are shown in Exhibit 5.

The response rate, 15% in total, showed a definite negative correlation with age, varying from as high as 40% for the 18–23 age group to as low as 2½% for the 35+ age group. As mentioned before, MassNORML had expected this result as being due to higher usage patterns in the younger age groups. The high response rates of the younger age groups suggest a high level of concern on their part over the marijuana reform process. Cassidy interpreted the low response rates of the older age groups as suggesting a general lack of concern over the issue.

Of the 232 respondents who gave their sex, 124 (or 53.4%) were men and 108 (or 46.6%) were women. Also, 136 out of 207 (65.2%) gave their occupation as student, professional, or managerial. These results, indicating a male, higher-educated respondent, are also consistent with MassNORML's knowledge of the marijuana smoker as presented in Exhibit 3.

From the perspective of MassNORML, the overall results of the survey were excellent. To them, the high number of responses indicated the magnitude of the concern over marijuana reform, and their favorable nature showed its direction. It was hoped that Flaherty could be persuaded not only that he need not fear any repercussions from his constituents if he assumed a positive stance on the issue but also that, based on their wishes, it was the desirable stance to take.

MassNORML intended to publicize the findings through news releases to the major state newspapers two weeks before the public hearings on the bill. In the meantime, it would commence personal lobbying toward the members of the Judiciary Committee, distributing individualized information packets to the members depending on their attitudes toward the bill.

CONCLUSION

As the two men finished reviewing their past year's efforts, they felt they had done much to accomplish the goals they had given themselves the previous year. The organization they had established was viable, self-financing, and seemed likely to continue after their departure. The marketing work they had done had brought MassNORML much visibility, many volunteers, and had paved the way to successfully passing a decriminalization bill in the legislature.

As the time approached for the state Judiciary Committee to consider the decriminalization bill, Cassidy and Dimitry wondered whether their survey results were believable. They felt the survey was unbiased and that their sample selection was appropriate, but they wondered if it would be convincing to Flaherty and the other state legislators. One fear was that their results were even more favorable than expected. Were people's attitudes toward decriminalization that positive? It appeared to Cassidy and Dimitry that their research approach was correct, but would the state legislators see it that way?

Exhibit 1
MassNORML (A)

Summary of Marijuana Citation Laws

State	*Max. Fine Imposed*	*Max. Amount Possessed*	*Criminal or Civil Violation*	*Effective Date*
Oregon	\$100.00	1 oz.	Civil	Oct. 5, 1973
Alaska	\$100.00	Any amount in private for personal use or 1 oz. in public	Civil	Mar. 1, 1976
Maine	\$200.00	Any amount[1] for personal use	Civil	Mar. 1, 1976
Colorado[2]	\$100.00	1 oz.	Class 2 petty offense, no criminal record	July 1, 1975
California[2]	\$100.00	1 oz.	Misdemeanor, no permanent criminal record	Jan. 1, 1976
Ohio[2]	\$100.00	100 gr. (aprox. 3½ oz.)	Minor misdemeanor, no criminal record	Nov. 22, 1975
South Dakota	\$ 20.00	1 oz.	Civil	Apr. 1, 1977
Minnesota[2]	\$100.00[a]	1½ oz.	Civil	Apr. 10, 1976

[1]There is a rebuttable presumption that possession of less than 1½ oz. is for personal use and possession of more than 1½ oz. is with an intent to distribute.
[2]Distribution of marijuana by gift, or for no remuneration, is treated the same as possession in four states: California (for up to 1 oz.), Colorado (up to 1 oz.), Ohio (up to 20 gr.), and Minnesota (up to 1½ oz.).
[a]Only Minnesota provides for increased penalties for second offense: 0–90 days in jail and/or a \$300 fine for second offense within a two-year period.
Source: NORML records.

Exhibit 2

MassNORML (A)

Organization Chart
Massachusetts Chapter of NORML

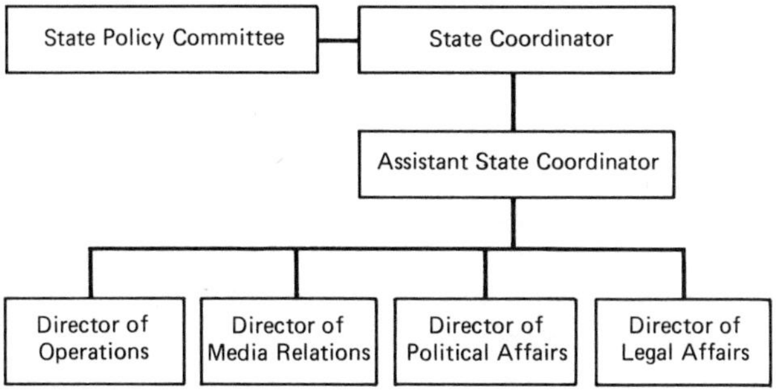

Responsibilities of Directors

Operations: Coordination of campus representatives, local organizers. Fund-raising activities: membership sales, "street begging", film and party benefits.

Media Relations: Newspapers: editorials, advertisements. Radio: news releases, public service announcements. Interviews: radio, with church groups, PTAs, etc.

Political Affairs: Direct lobbying, voter additude research, legislative research.

Legal Affairs: Preparation of test cases, legal counseling.

Exhibit 3
MassNORML (A)

The Marijuana Smoker

In early 1976, the National Institute on Drug Abuse (NIDA) conducted its latest nationwide study on marijuana use and related attitudes. The study revealed that, of the population aged 12 years and over, 21%, or 37 million, had tried marijuana at least once, and 9%, or 16 million, were current users of the drug.

Of these 37 million people, 21 million were 25 years old or younger. Some 52% of the 18–25 age group had tried marijuana, whereas only 6% of those 35 and over had done so. The prevalence of use, broken down by age group, is shown below.

Prevalence (ever used) of use of marijuana among subgroups of U.S. population

Age	% of Subgroup Population	Subgroup Population (millions)	No. of Ever Users (millions)
12–17	22[a]	24.2[b]	5.4[c]
18–21	52	16.3	8.5
22–25	53	14.1	7.5
26–34	36	27.7	10.0
35+	6	88.7	5.3
Total	21	171.2	36.7

[a]Statistics taken from the 1976 report by the National Institute on Drug Abuse entitled, *Nonmedical Use of Psychoactive Substances*.
[b]January 1, 1976 population estimates by the U.S. Bureau of the Census.
[c]Column 1 × column 2.

The "current[2] users/ever used" ratio has increased from 33% in 1971 to 43% in 1976. A breakdown of the ratio by age shows it to be as high as 52% for the 12–17 age group, dropping at 16% for the 35 and over age group.

Marijuana used is also related to sex. Males are more likely than females to have tried marijuana. Some 29% of male adults (18 years of age and over) have ever used marijuana compared with 14% for female adults.

Marijuana use depends on educational attainment. Among adults, only 12% of those who are not high school graduates have tried it, whereas 30% of those with some college education have done so. Among current college students, prevalence jumps to 48%. The average marijuana smoker appears then to be a young collegiate male.

Based on age and the NIDA study, the distribution of users in the Commonwealth of Massachusetts is as follows:

Prevalence of use of marijuana among subgroups of Massachusetts population

Age	% of Subgroup Population	Subgroup Population (000)	No. of Ever Users (000)
12–17	21[a]	670[b]	140[c]
18–21	59	400	240
22–25	60	480	290
26–34	41	710	290
35+	7	2,560	180
Total 12+	26	4,820	1,140

[a]Nationwide statistics taken from 1976 NIDA report and then adjusted for regional factor. Northeast factors are .94 from the 12–17 age group, and 1.13 for the 18+ age group.
[b]Massachusetts population statistics taken from the July 1976 *Survey of Buying Power Data Service* put out by Sales and Marketing Management Magazine.
[c]Column 1 × Column 2.

[2]"Current" being interpreted as having used marijuana in the past month.

Exhibit 4
MassNORML (A)

Attitude Questionnaire[3]

1. With which of the following statements would you most closely agree? (check one)
   53.5% A. Marijuana, in small amounts, is less dangerous than alcohol or tobacco.
   33.6% B. Marijuana, in small amounts, presents about the same dangers as alcohol and tobacco.
   12.9% C. Marijuana is more dangerous than alcohol or tobacco.
2. Individual use of marijuana (by persons over 18 years of age) in the privacy of the user's home
   76.0% A. Presents little or no danger to society.
   15.4% B. Presents a fair degree of danger to society (e.g., more dangerous than the similar use of alcohol).
   8.6% C. Is extremely dangerous.
3. With which statement ending do you most agree? (check one) Possession of small amounts of marijuana for personal use only (not for sale to others)
   73.3% A. Should not be punished by law.
   12.5% B. Should be punished with a fine, but without going to court (like a parking ticket).
   6.9% C. Should be punished with fine after going to court.
   1.3% D. Should be punished with a jail sentence.
   6.0% E. Should be punished with both a fine and a jail sentence.
4. People who are arrested for possession of small amounts of marijuana for personal use only (not for sale to others)
   87.6% A. *Should not* have a permanent record of the arrest on file with the police and courts.
   12.4% B. *Should* have a permanent record of the arrest on file with the police and court.
5. Marijuana is a plant that can be grown fairly easily by the user. Allowing cultivation would alleviate the need for a marijuana smoker to buy from outside sources.
   69.4% A. Cultivation of small numbers of marijuana plants for personal use (not for sale) *should* be allowed.
   30.6% B. Cultivation of small numbers of marijuana plants for personal use (not for sale) *should not* be allowed.
6. The casual not-for-profit sale of small amounts of marijuana to friends or acquaintances over 18 years of age (as opposed to large scale trafficking in marijuana)
   60.5% A. Should not be punished by law.
   14.2% B. Should be punished with a fine without going to court.
   13.3% C. Should be punished with a fine after going to court.
   2.6% D. Should be punished with a jail sentence.
   9.4% E. Should be punished with both a jail sentence and a fine.

[3]The numbers shown in each blank are the percentages of people providing that particular response.

Exhibit 4 (continued)
MassNORML (A)

Attitude Questionnaire[3]

7. People arrested for the casual, not-for-profit sale of small amounts of marijuana to friends or acquaintances over 18 years of age
   - 78.5% A. *Should not* have a permanent record of the arrest on file with the police and courts.
   - 21.5% B. *Should* have a permanent record.
8. Assume that your state representative voted in favor of the following bills:
   - A. Would the vote for each bill make you look *favorably* or *unfavorably* on the state representative at reelection time; or would it have *no effect* on the way you voted at reelection?
   - B. How strongly would you feel this?

8-1. A bill to *remove jail sentences for personal use* (not sale) of marijuana, but *maintain punishment by fine*.

56.1% favorably	___ I feel strongly
15.4% no effect	___ I feel mildly
28.5% unfavorably	___ I don't care much

8-2. A bill to *remove the need for court appearances for possession of small amounts for personal use* (not sale), but *retain punishment by fine* (similar to a traffic ticket system)

54.9% favorably	___ strongly
14.2% no effect	___ mildly
30.9% unfavorably	___ don't care

8-3. A bill to *remove all penalties* for possession of small amount for personal use (not sale)

64.9% favorably	___ strongly
9.5% no effect	___ mildly
25.6% unfavorably	___ don't care

8-4. A bill to *allow cultivation of small amounts of marijuana plants* for personal use (not sale)

58.3% favorably	___ strongly
11.3% no effect	___ mildly
30.4% unfavorably	___ don't care

9. To give your state representative a better idea of who is responding to this survey, please check the appropriate categories. (This is optional; do not fill this out if you do not care to.)

Sex: ___		Occupation: Student	25.0%
Age: 18–23	45.0%	Clerical	17.1%
24–29	35.0%	Sales	3.2%
30–35	8.6%	Craftsmen/foremen	12.5%
35–45	7.7%	Professional	32.4%
Above 45	3.6%	Managerial	5.6%

10. Is there any comment you desire passed on to your representative? Please use this space.

Other: 4.2%

Exhibit 5
MassNORML (A)

Comparison of Response Rates with Population and Prevalence of Use by Age-Group

(1) *Age Group*	*(2) Respondents* *Number*	*% of Total*	*(3)* *Subgroup Population (%)*	*(4)* *No. of Questionnaires Mailed to Subgroup*	*(5)* *Response Rate (%)*
18–23	99	45.0%	15.4[a]	246[b]	40.2[c]
24–29	77	35.0	14.3	229	33.6
30–35	19	8.6	8.5	136 ·	14.0
35+	25	11.4	61.8	989	2.5
Total	220[d]	100.0%	100.0%	1,600	15.0[e]

[a]Derived from Exhibit 5, Table III, "Prevalence of Use of Marijuana Among Subgroups of Massachusetts."
[b]Subgroup population (%) × 1,600 (total number of questionnaires mailed), assuring a random distribution of mailing.
[c]Number of respondents/number of questionnaires mailed.
[d]Total of 220 does not include the 20 respondents who did not give their age.
[e]Total response rate of 15% includes the 20 "no-age" respondents.

MassNORML (B)

As Cassidy and Dimitry were preparing to present the findings of an attitude survey commissioned by the Massachusetts branch of the National Organization for the Reform of Marijuana Laws (MassNORML) to the state legislative hearings, they were beginning to become apprehensive of the findings which had been derived from their voter survey conducted in South Boston. Their primary concern was that, although they had randomly selected the names for sampling from voter registration records, the response rate differed among various age groups. They were wondering what biases this might create in the results and how they could adjust their results to compensate for it.

Further complicating matters was the fact that the main local newspaper, *The Boston Globe*, ran a public forum questionnaire in the paper addressing the decriminalization issue (Exhibit 1). Results from the *Globe*'s survey would be made public approximately one week after MassNORML's results were presented to the Massachusetts state legislature. Cassidy and Dimitry feared that conflicting results would not only hamper their efforts but might leave the impression with legislators that much of the materials presented by MassNORML were biased.

MassNORML VOTER SURVEY

In the spring of 1977, MassNORML commissioned a voter survey in South Boston on voters' attitudes toward the decriminalization of marijuana. The original sample consisted of 1,600 randomly selected respondents from voter registration records. Of those sampled, there were 240 complete responses. Cassidy and Dimitry realized that, whenever there is a large percentage of nonrespondents, there is always the fear that the answers provided are not representative of the total sample or population.

Although the age distribution of the sample was unknown, since the voter registration records did not contain age information, the population's age distribution was known. This could be compared with the age distribution of the survey respondents, provided directly from the questionnaire. From Exhibit 2 it can be seen that, although the questionnaires may have been mailed out proportional to the number of individuals in each of the age categories, as would be expected from a random sample, they clearly were not returned equally across all age groups.

As such, Cassidy felt that it would be best to review the questionnaire results by age category. Two questions were felt to be most crucial and were selected for specific inspection. The detailed results for questions 2 and 3 are shown in Exhibit 3. Although there were some variances in responses for questions 2 and 3, the results for each age category were "pro-decriminalization." For every age category, there appeared to be a favorable attitude toward decriminalization.

In spite of these pro-decriminalization results, Cassidy felt that it was still necessary to adjust the results to account for the true age distribution. One way in which to deal with this disparity in response rates would be to weigh the answers with respect to their proportions in the population. Since the population's age distribution shown in Exhibit 2 were known, a weighted average could be calculated. For example, the percentage of people answering question 2, "Individual use of marijuana (by persons over 18 years of age) in the privacy of the users' home," with the response, "Presents little or no danger to society" could be calculated as $(.154 \times .845) + (.143 \times .727) + (.085 \times .588) + (.618 \times .704) = 71.9\%$.

CONCLUSION

Cassidy proceeded to adjust all survey results to account for the true age distribution in the population. He felt confident that he now had an accurate representation of the data to present to the Massachusetts state legislation.

Exhibit 1
MassNORML (B)

Boston Globe Decriminalization Survey, April 11, 1977

FORUM

Decriminalization of marijuana laws favored by readers

By Lise Bang-Jensen
Special to The Globe

By a margin of 1034-143 with 52 undecided, readers and students responding to the April 11 FORUM favored decriminalizing Massachusetts marijuana laws to make possession of one ounce or less punishable by a civil fine instead of a criminal fine and prison sentence.

Reader responses to this informal survey should not be interpreted as a scientifically drawn public opinion poll. Responses to mail surveys tend to come from persons who feel most intensely one way or the other about an issue.

Several bills are pending in the Massachusetts Legislature and in Congress to decriminalize possession of marijuana, which eight states including Maine have already done.

Those bills would not make it legal to possess marijuana. Nor would they make it legal to grow or sell it, which several readers called legally illogical.

Sale of marijuana is not legal in any state. Alaska is the only state permitting cultivation of marijuana.

Decriminalization means that a person caught with a specified amount of marijuana (usually one ounce of less) would be guilty of a civil offense not a crime.

In Massachusetts, the maximum penalty for possession of marijuana is a six-month jail sentence and a fine of $500. Most first offenders are given probationary sentences.

Several readers argued that those criminal penalties strain law-enforcement facilities, and do an offender more harm than the drug itself.

One Cambridge man, who described himself as a successful accountant, wrote: "I spent two years in prison for possession, which prevented me from becoming a doctor. Too many people are having their lives ruined by laws that are outdated and archaic."

Reader tally

Should possession of one ounce of marijuana or less be decriminalized and punished by a civil fine instead of a possible jail sentence?

	Yes	No	Undecided
Readers	731	84	3
Students	303	59	49
TOTAL	1034	143	52

Opponents of decriminalization argued that our drug-dependent society does not need another legal drug and that marijuana should not be decriminalized until there is conclusive evidence that it has no dangerous physical and pyschological side effects.

The Federal government, after reviewing hundreds of conflicting medical studies, concluded in a report released in March that marijuana cannot be given "a clean bill of health as some would hope. Nor does (evidence) support the fear and irrationality that still characterize some of the public debate."

Supporters justify decriminalization by saying that any pharmaceutical agent smoked or ingested has harmful side effects but that marijuana is less dangerous than alcohol, tobacco and other legal drugs.

For many supporters and opponents alike, decriminalization of marijuana possession is "one toe over the line," or a step toward legalizing the possession, sale and cultivation of marijuana.

Several readers proposed total legalization of marijuana and taxing it like alcohol or tobacco.

Among those responding to the FORUM were students from Amherst College, Greenlodge School (Dedham), Easton Junior High School, Minute Man Technical School (Lexington), Catholic Memorial High School (West Roxbury) and high schools in Norwood, Framingham and Marlboro.

Courtesy, *The Boston Globe*.

Exhibit 2
MassNORML (B)

Age Distribution of Population over 18 and of Sample

Age Group	*% of Population*	*% of Respondents*
18–23	15.4%	45.0%
24–29	14.3	35.0
30–35	8.5	8.6
36+	61.8	11.4

Exhibit 3
MassNORML (B)

Questionnaire Results by Age Category

Question 2: Individual use of marijuana (by persons over 18 years of age) in the privacy of the users' home

	Age of Respondents				
	18–23	*24–29*	*30–35*	*35–45*	*45+*
A. Presents little or no danger to society	84.5%	72.7%	58.8%	72.2%	66.7%
B. Presents a fair degree of danger to society (e.g., more dangerous than the similar use of alcohol)	8.3	19.5	17.7	16.7	33.3
C. Is extremely dangerous	7.2	7.8	23.5	11.1	0
Number of respondents	97	77	17	18	9

Question 3: Which statement ending do you most agree with? (check one) Possession of small amounts of marijuana for personal use only (not for sale to others)

	Age of Respondents				
	18–23	*24–29*	*30–35*	*35–45*	*45+*
A. Should not be punished by law	82.7%	69.7%	52.9%	72.2%	55.6%
B. Should be fined with a fine, but without going to court (like a parking ticket)	6.1	14.5	17.6	16.6	33.3
C. Should be punished with a fine after going to court	5.1	11.8	0	5.6	0
D. Should be punished with a jail sentence	2.0	1.3	0	0	0
E. Should be punished with both a fine and a jail sentence	4.1	2.7	29.5	5.6	11.1
Number of respondents	98	76	17	18	9

MassNORML (C)

Cassidy, MassNORML's state coordinator, felt confident that the survey results he was prepared to present to the Massachusetts state legislative Judiciary Committee were accurate and a fair portrayal of South Boston voters' attitudes toward decriminalization of marijuana. A questionnaire had been administered to a random sample of registered voters in the South Boston district, and the results had been adjusted to account for the varying response rates within different age categories.

Faced with the possibility of conflicting results from a similar survey being conducted by *The Boston Globe*, the largest circulated local newspaper, Cassidy felt he should take one final precautionary step. Cassidy presented his survey approach and results to his former college marketing professor for a final stamp of approval.

 This case was prepared by David J. Reibstein.

CONTACTING NONRESPONDENTS

Cassidy was advised that his weighting scheme was a good idea, but not necessarily a solution to the possible response bias. One possible problem not accounted for by his weighting approach was that the response bias may have existed across all age categories; that is, those that chose to respond were different from the nonrespondents regardless of age. For example, it was possible that the factor determining whether the individual would complete and return the questionnaire was "if they had ever tried marijuana before," not age. If this were true, the distribution of the responses across age categories would have been similar to that actually received (see Exhibit 1). Whether this was actually the case was unknown. It was suggested to Cassidy that the best way in which to address this question was to recontact the nonrespondents, in a further attempt to ascertain their attitudes toward the decriminalization issue.

This was a more difficult task than it

might seem on the surface. The first problem stemmed from the fact that the identity of the nonrespondents was unknown. No names were obtained in the original survey for fear of either creating some bias or further diminishing the response rate. It was felt that the likelihood of greatly decreasing the response rate by asking for respondent identification was particularly acute, given the illegality of the issue under question. Thus, if the sample were to be recontacted, it would be necessary to ask whether the person had responded to the earlier questionnaire.

The question of the method for resurveying the sample was also at hand. If another questionnaire were mailed to the original sample, there would be the possibility that only the same people would reply and the response bias problem would remain unsolved. A similar problem might result if a new sample were selected.

Hence, it was decided that a phone survey to the original sample would be a feasible approach. The limitations of a phone survey were felt to be shortening of the questionnaire and possible sample bias (those without phones or not at home at reasonable calling hours).

THE PHONE SURVEY

The objective of the phone survey was to test the reliability of the original mail survey and not to draw specific conclusions in and of themselves. It was decided to ask respondents whether they had returned the original questionnaire and, if so, to ask five key questions which had appeared on the original questionnaire.

Several difficulties were encountered in administering the phone survey. First, approximately 25% of the people listed on voter registration records had unlisted numbers. Second, in many cases repeated calls were necessary as there were many households where the respondent sought was not at home. It became necessary to restrict phone calls to between 5 P.M. and 8 P.M.

A total of 149 people was reached who had not completed the original mail survey. Of this set, only 90 (60.4%) were willing to answer the questions over the phone. As can be seen from Exhibit 2, the age distribution of the phone survey appeared to be much more representative of the age distribution of the population.

The responses from the phone survey and comparisons with the original survey are shown in Exhibit 3. As can be seen, the results appeared to be different on the first three questions, but on the question of primary significance to Cassidy and Dimitry, question 4, the attitudes appear to be more favorable to the decriminalization of marijuana. As a result, both Cassidy and Dimitry felt considerably more comfortable with their original results.

BOSTON GLOBE SURVEY

The Boston Globe had conducted a readership survey on the marijuana decriminalization issue. Readers, if they felt so inclined, could cut the ballot out of the newspaper, mark their opinion on marijuana decriminalization on the ballot, and send it, at their own expense, to the newspaper's office. The results of their survey were published in the paper one week after the Judiciary Committee's hearing. The results, shown in Exhibit 4, were even more pro-decriminalization than was the study commissioned by MassNORML, with 80% of the respondents favoring decriminalization.

Exhibit 1
MassNORML (C)

Marijuana Use and Percentage of the Responses by Age[1]

Age	% Having Tried Marijuana[2]	Age	% Responses
18–21	59%	18–23	45.0%
22–25	60	24–29	35.0
26–34	41	20–35	8.6
35+	7	36+	11.4

[1]Age categories differ because they were collected and reported by different organizations.
[2]Nationwide statistics taken from 1976 NIDA report and then adjusted for regional factor.

Exhibit 2
MassNORML (C)

Age Distribution of Respondents in Telephone Survey ($n = 90$)

Age	% of Respondents
18–23	15.6%
24–29	18.9
30–35	7.8
36+	52.2
NA	5.6

NA – not available.

Exhibit 3
MassNORML (C)

Phone Follow-Up Survey and Original Results

1. Which of the following statements would you most closely agree with? (check one)

Phone Survey	Original Survey	
42.7%	53.5%	A. Marijuana, in small amounts, is less dangerous than alcohol or tobacco.
33.7	33.6%	B. Marijuana, in small amounts, presents about the same dangers as alcohol and tobacco.
23.6	12.9%	C. Marijuana is more dangerous than alcohol or tobacco.

2. Individual use of marijuana (by persons over 18 years of age) in the privacy of the users' home

47.8	73.3%	A. Presents little or no danger to society.
36.7	15.4%	B. Presents a fair degree of danger to society (e.g., more dangerous than the similar use of alcohol).
15.6	8.6%	C. Is extremely dangerous.

3. Which statement ending do you most agree with? (check one) Possession of small amounts of marijuana for personal use only (not for sale to others)

38.1	73.3%	A. Should not be punished by law.
36.9	12.5%	B. Should be punished with a fine, but without going to court (like a parking ticket).
13.1	6.9%	C. Should be punished with fine after going to court.
0	1.3%	D. Should be punished with a jail sentence.
11.9	6.0%	E. Should be punished with both a fine and a jail sentence.

4. A bill to *remove the need for court appearances for possession of small amounts for personal use* (not sale), but *retain punishment by* fine (similar to a traffic ticket system)

72.2 54.9% favorably
14.4 14.2% no effect
13.3 30.9% unfavorably

5. To give your state representative a better idea of who is responding to this survey, please check the appropriate categories. (This is optional; do not fill this out if you do not care to.)

15.6	Age: 18–23 45%	Occupation: Student 25%
18.9	24–29 35%	Clerical 17.1%
7.8	30–35 8.6%	Sales 3.2%
11.1	35–45 7.7%	Craftsmen/foremen 12.5%
41.1	Above 45 3.6%	Professional 32.4%
5.6	No answer	Managerial 5.6%

Exhibit 4
MassNORML

Boston Globe Survey on Marijuana Decriminalization

Question: "Should possession of one ounce of marijuana or less be decriminalized and punished by civil fine instead of a possible jail sentence?"

	Yes	*No*	*Undecided*
Readers	731	84	3
Students	303	59	49
Total	1,034	143	52

Strategic Planning Institute (A)

Mark Chussil sat back in his chair in January 1979 and mused about how to proceed with his independent project in marketing. The Strategic Planning Institute (SPI), where Chussil had worked for two years before entering the MBA program at Harvard, recognized mutual interest in sponsoring a study that would attempt to diagnose the strengths and weaknesses of SPI's primary marketing tool. Management at SPI was especially interested in understanding why some companies decided to participate in the PIMS program, which SPI operated, and why other companies decided not to join. Concern about marketing was growing as the join rate dropped over time.

Chussil knew that the empirical orientation at SPI would influence how he went about his project. SPI would expect that there would be a firm basis for Chussil's conclusions and recommendations.

 This case was prepared by Mark Chussil under the supervision of David J. Reibstein.

THE STRATEGIC PLANNING INSTITUTE: PIMS

The primary activity of the Strategic Planning Institute was the PIMS (Profit of Market Strategy) program.

The PIMS Program

The PIMS program of the Strategic Planning Institute was a multicompany activity designed to provide an improved and innovative factual base for the business planning efforts of each participant.

Each member company contributed information about its experiences in several different business areas to a combined data base. The PIMS staff analyzed this experience to discover the general "laws" that determined what business strategy, in what kind of competitive environment, produced what profit results. The findings were made available to member companies in a form useful to their business planning.

The intent of the program was to provide business managers and planners with tools and data for answering such questions as

1. What profit rate was "*normal*" for a given business, considering its particular market, competitive position, technology, cost structure, and so on?
2. If the business continued on its *current track*, what would its future operating results be?
3. What *strategic changes* in the business have promise of improving these results?
4. Given a *specific* contemplated future strategy for the business, how would profitability or cash flow change, short-term and long-term?

In each case, the answers were derived from an analysis of the experiences of *other* businesses operating under *similar* conditions.

More specifically, the objectives of the program were the following:

1. To assemble a *data base* reflecting the business strategy experiences a group of participating companies.
2. To conduct a *research* program on that data base to discover the "laws of marketplace" that govern (a) profit levels, (b) other outcomes of strategic actions, and (c) outcomes of changes in the business environment.
3. To conduct an *applications program* to make the findings of the research available to participating companies in a form and manner they could effectively use.
4. To carry out such *ancillary activities* (publication, education, service to participants, study of planning methods, legislative recommendations, etc.) as would enhance the value of the entire program to its members and to the economy at large.

The confidential information entrusted to the institute by its member companies concerning their businesses was held under stringent conditions of data security and confidentiality, to minimize the possibility of leakage of such information among member companies or to outsiders.

History and Structure of PIMS

The PIMS program originated as an internal project of the General Electric Company, where it had been used for over a decade as a tool of corporate planning and division-level planning. The basic logic, methodological approach, and techniques of application were developed and tested there, by a team of people now heavily represented on the PIMS staff.

From 1972 to 1974, the PIMS program was established as a developmental project at the Harvard Business School and was located at the Marketing Science Institute (a research organization affiliated with the Harvard Business School). During this phase of its life, PIMS

1. Learned to operate on a multicompany basis.
2. Verified the basic GE research findings on a wider cross section of businesses and extended the parameters of strategy exploration.
3. Developed much of the current computer software package.
4. Stimulated interest in the comparative, quantitative analysis of the consequences of business strategy in a large number of companies and academic research centers.

In February 1975, to facilitate the evaluation of program beyond the academic stage to an operating system, PIMS was organized as an autonomous institute, focused explicitly on the analysis of strategic business plans. The Strategic Planning Institute was a nonprofit corporation, governed by its member companies, with a charter permitting not only academic research but also application activities of various kinds.

As of early 1979, well over 200 corporations were participants in PIMS. About 20% of the *Fortune* 500 companies were PIMS members. A considerable number of large European firms participated, and the proportion of members from other parts of the world, such as Australia and Brazil, was growing. The rest of the membership was composed of medium-sized American companies.

Each member company contributed to the PIMS data base, and in return received feedback in several forms.

The PIMS Data Base

The unit of observation in PIMS was a *business.* Each business was a division, product line, or other profit center within its parent company, selling a distinct set of products and/or services to an identifiable group of customers, in competition with a well-defined set of competitors and for which meaningful separation can be made of revenues, operating costs, investments, and strategic plans.

As of mid-1979, the data base consisted of information on the strategic experiences of over 2,000 businesses, covering periods of up to ten years. The information on each business consists of about 200 items, descriptive of the characteristics of the *market environment*, the state of *competition*, the *strategy* pursued by the business, and the *operating results* obtained. Exhibit 1 contains an illustrative list of the items of information in the data base.

The Research and Development Program

The research portion of the PIMS program consisted of a continuing analysis of the experiences reflected in the data base, to discover the empirical "laws" that determine what *strategy*, under what *conditions*, produced what *results.* The investigators used a variety of analytical tools, the most common being multiple regression analysis.

To date, PIMS had succeeded in identifying 30-odd factors that have a potent and predictable impact on profitability. Taken together, they accounted for about 80% of the observed variation in profitability across the businesses in the data base.

These factors were incorporated in a set of profit-predicting and cash-flow-predicting models that assigned to each factor its proper weight, judging from the experiences reflected in the data base. The models also indicated how the impact of each profit-determining factor was conditioned by other factors.

The models were designed to aid the assessment of strategic moves. An assumed *change* in one or several profit-influencing factors could be analyzed to determine the profit and cash consequences both *during* the time that the move was being executed and *after* it had been completed.

Feedback to Member Companies

Participating companies received three kinds of feedback from the institute:

1. Reports on the *general principles* of business strategy disclosed by the analysis of the data base.
2. *Specific reports* on *each* business the company had contributed to the data base.
3. Access to *computer models* in which the general strategic principles were incorporated, in a manner useful for strategy planning and simulation; plus instruction and counsel in the interpretation and use of these resources.

The specific reports on an individual business expressed the net impact of all research findings to date, in the form of (1) evaluative statements about that business and (2) strategy advice for that business. They were computer-generated reports, using the empirical models mentioned above.

The resources, research findings, and reports of the institute were available *only* to its member companies and not to other organizations or individuals. Subject to policies approved by the council of the institute, there were selected publications directed at the well-being of the economy at large, in areas in which the institute could make a useful contribution.

PIMS also offered other services, such as analysis of a portfolio of businesses. All the reports were based on models estimated on empirical evidence from the data base.

Companies found PIMS useful in a variety of ways. Profitability analysis showed companies whether current performance was up to par and what profitability strengths and weaknesses were present. This suggested what could be done to improve profitability; sometimes there were no feasible moves, and companies might consider harvesting or divesting more attractive than investing in some businesses. Portfolio analysis combined the results of several of the PIMS models to help companies find optimal strategies for balancing the actions of individual business units into corporate master plans that were greater than the sum of their parts. Even the process of filling out the data forms helped some companies to understand their businesses better than they did before.

THE BRIEFING SESSION

A day-long meeting (or briefing session) was designed to give a broad view of the PIMS program to potential clients. Staff members presented the concept of PIMS, selected research findings, brief explanations of PIMS models, and descriptions of major projects such as the start-up business project. Attendees received a loose-leaf binder containing more detailed expositions of the material presented during the day. Questions and answers were taken at any time. Staff members mingled with attendees during coffee breaks and lunch. Attendees were given badges with their names and their company names, which they wore during the day.

The briefing session was a primary PIMS marketing tool. It was usually the prospective member's first introduction to PIMS concepts and analyses, and the overwhelming majority of current members had attended one or more sessions before.

Companies might have been invited to briefing sessions in several ways. PIMS occasionally extended invitations by direct mail to top management of certain companies (e.g., the *Fortune* 250). Sometimes a manager in a company would read an article by or about PIMS in a business publication; upon calling PIMS for more information, he or she might be invited to a session. PIMS also sent speakers to various conferences (e.g., American Marketing Association), and those interested in learning more about PIMS were asked to attend a briefing session.

Briefing sessions were held in major cities in all parts of the country. Since late 1975, well over 100 sessions had been presented in 40 cities in the United States and Canada. The sessions were held in convention rooms in the better hotels in those cities. Attendance varied from 10 to 100 representatives of 5 to 30 companies, and each attendee was billed for the session at a standard rate, to recover expenses. Companies that already were PIMS members sometimes sent people to briefing sessions to introduce them to PIMS.

The Future for Briefing Sessions

The briefing session had been introduced in 1975 and quickly proved itself a useful tool to expose interested companies to PIMS. More recently, however, SPI noted a decline in the percentage of companies that joined PIMS after attending a briefing session. Management at SPI was understandably concerned about this trend and wanted to know how to change the briefing session to make it more effective. Although there was considerable experience at

SPI with briefing sessions, there had not been systematic investigation into what techniques were particularly effective in encouraging companies to join PIMS.

In general terms, SPI was interested in learning why some companies joined and others did not. Was the difference due to the type of person sent to a briefing session? Perhaps those in general management, or at top management levels, or with MBAs, or with technically oriented backgrounds were more (or less) likely to join than their opposites. Was the quality of briefing sessions deteriorating over time? Perhaps the standardization of the sessions or the growing attendance at recent sessions had a negative impact on joining. Had all the really interested companies already joined, so those that were attending more recent sessions were the tougher nuts to crack? If so, then there were presumably some differences between these two types of companies. Knowing the answers to these and other questions would have important implications for SPI's marketing strategy.

Identifying the Issues

As a first step in answering these questions, Chussil thought it was best to interview the SPI staff to get a grasp on the major issues he needed to address. Conversation with staff members suggested the following factors as being important to the attendee's perception of PIMS and the briefing session and hence to the company's decision to join or not to join:

- the attendee's rank in his or her company, whether it was line or staff, and in general management, planning, and so forth;
- previous attendance at a briefing session by representatives from the company;
- the position of the person who would make the join/not join decision;
- whether the company had a planning group, used computer models, used consultants, or the like;
- other company characteristics (e.g., diversification, profitability);
- the complexity, length, and emphasis (e.g., academic seminar versus sales pitch) of the material presented;
- the number of attendees at the session; and
- contact with PIMS staff members during the session.

However, relatively little was known concerning which of these (and other) factors were most important, or which were already addressed successfully at the briefing sessions.

Another problem was one of perceived differentiation from competitors. How was PIMS positioned in the marketplace? This could be broken into two separate components: (1) How did PIMS want to be positioned? and (2) How were customers presently viewing PIMS relative to alternative consulting firms? It was further recognized that this positioning most likely would differ by market segment. Because PIMS was a fairly new and rather complex planning tool, it was felt to be somewhat misunderstood. For example, some people perceived similarity between PIMS and the Boston Consulting Group (BCG), perhaps because the latter tries to address many of the same strategic problems and because both have noted the impact of market share as a determinant of profitability. However, their approach to answering these strategic questions was substantially different. BCG had high-caliber conventional consulting, whereas PIMS derived their suggestions empirically from cross-sectional data analysis. Management at SPI recognized that the market's (i.e., companies') perceptions of PIMS vis-à-vis strategy consulting firms was a key uncertainty.

Collecting the Data

Thinking of the question that his study would seek to answer, Chussil tried to decide whether to utilize personal interviews or a standardized questionnaire. There were several reasons why personal interviewing seemed unattractive. One was the sheer amount of time and expense involved in reaching former attendees scattered about the United States. This was aggravated further by the immense scheduling difficulties that were inevitable, even assuming that the attendees would be willing to devote their time. But a more serious objection was that personal interviewing seemed not to get at the right information effectively. Chussil felt that it was more important to get data from which broad patterns and trends would be observed and verified statistically. Personal interviewing seemed most effective for understanding nuances of expression and for allowing the interviewee to concentrate on what was important to him or her; however, the project appeared to require a large sample of responses to a well-established set of questions for which a broad-based questionnaire would be appropriate.

Such a questionnaire could be administered by mail or by phone. Mail seemed the obvious choice, since there would be no way to predict when would be a good time to find former attendees in their offices. Furthermore, because phoning people takes so much time, more responses could be obtained by a mass mailing.

A further question that needed to be resolved was who should be sampled. One choice was to sample member companies and determine their characteristics and perceptions of SPI. Alternatively, the focus could be on companies that had not joined SPI. This was where the future marketing effort would be directed. This could focus on either firms that had attended briefing sessions and elected not to join, firms that had never been to a briefing session, or both.

A disadvantage of contacting member companies was the fear of inundating the principal contacts with questions. Each member company was required to complete numerous questionnaires to be put into the data base; occasionally, special studies were conducted which again called for more questionnaire completion. Chussil certainly did not want to exhaust whatever "goodwill" existed by making it an onerous task to be an SPI member company.

On the other hand, it could prove worthwhile to have information on all who attended briefing sessions and compare those who elected to join to those who did not. The distinctions between these groups might provide a clue as to the type of attendee and company that SPI appealed to most. Because of this latter advantage, Chussil decided that it would be desirable to question both members and nonmembers who had attended a briefing session.

Upon the advice of the SPI staff, Chussil eliminated attendees of the first few briefing sessions held in 1975 both because the sessions had undergone extensive change since then and because perceptions dated 1975 were likely to be vague. In addition, those who attended sessions in the last year were excluded, since many had not yet decided whether or not to join. This left 690 companies who had sent representatives to briefing sessions in 1976 or 1977. Of the 690, 140 had joined PIMS and 550 had not. Chussil decided to send one questionnaire to the person in each company who had represented that company at the session. (If more than one person had come from a company, the questionnaire was sent to the person who had been invited originally). There was no sampling; the entire population was polled.

Designing the Questionnaire

Chussil's objective, upon completion of the study, was to be able to answer two specific questions: (1) Why did firms elect to join SPI?

and (2) How do companies view SPI as compared with other consulting agencies? He felt that by comparing those who elected to join versus those who did not he might be able to infer some of the rationale for joining, as well as identifying the types of firms, or individuals within a firm, that should be invited to briefing sessions. He believed that some individuals clearly perceived SPI differently from others. By determining if "joiners" positioned SPI differently from "nonjoiners," some clues to the difficulties which SPI might have to overcome might be brought to light.

The next task was how to design the questionnaire itself. The SPI staff had been very helpful in identifying important factors and questions about the briefing sessions to be answered. The questionnaire had to yield data that should be used to answer the many issues raised. On the other hand, the questionnaire had to be brief enough so that recipients would not be so distressed by its sheer bulk that they would destroy it instantly. Chussil also had to keep in mind that many of the nonjoiners who would receive the questionnaire were not "lost causes." If a company in the *Fortune* 100 did not join, SPI might contact them again at a later date. The questionnaire should not have an adverse effect upon the market.

Turning determinedly to his desk, Chussil started to draft a questionnaire.

Exhibit 1
Strategic Planning Institute (A)

Information on Each Business in the PIMS Data Base
(illustrative list)

Characteristics of the business environment
- Long-run growth rate of the market
- Short-run growth rate of the market
- Rate of inflation of selling price levels
- Number and size of customers
- Purchase frequency and magnitude

Competitive position of the business
- Share of the served market
- Share relative to largest competitors'
- Product quality relative to competitors'
- Prices relative to competitors'
- Pay scales relative to competitors'
- Marketing efforts relative to competitors'
- Patterns of market segmentation
- Rate of new product introductions

Structure of the production process
- Capital intensity (degree of automation, etc.)
- Degree of vertical integration
- Capacity utilization
- Productivity of capital equipment
- Productivity of people
- Inventory levels

Discretionary budget allocations
- R&D budgets
- Advertising and promotion budgets
- Sales force expenditures

Strategic moves
- Patterns of change in the controllable elements above

Operating results
- Profitability results
- Cash flow results
- Growth results

Strategic Planning Institute (B)

As responses to his questionnaire began arriving, Mark Chussil felt growing excitement at the prospect of understanding the strengths and weaknesses of the briefing session as SPI's main marketing tool.[1] SPI management was concerned about the general decline in the percentage of companies which attended briefing sessions and decided to join SPI. Had most of the potentially interested companies already joined? Could briefing sessions be made into a more effective marketing tool? Were they poorly focused or were they not addressing the concerns of the company representatives attending them? As the last days of March pushed toward the first days of April, the number of responses steadily rose, until there were certainly enough to ensure statistical reliability. Chussil turned eagerly to his first computer output and began to delve into the briefing session story.

EVOLUTION OF THE SURVEY

Mark Chussil decided to send a standard questionnaire by mail to the 690 companies that attended briefing sessions in 1976 and 1977. He spent the month of February designing the questionnaire. His first step was to talk extensively with members of the SPI staff who had considerable experience with briefing sessions, to get ideas as to what factors might be important. Their suggestions proved invaluable, and all expressed great interest in the results of the survey. In addition, Chussil attended a briefing session in New York to get a firsthand view.

Armed with all this information, Chussil put together a first draft. The draft had some 170 questions, typed on 30 pages, allowing generous space for comments. Chussil distributed a copy of the draft, along with a cover memo describing the purpose of the survey

 This case was prepared by Mark Chussil under the supervision of David J. Reibstein.

[1]For a complete description of the Strategic Planning Institute, the PIMS program, and the briefing session, see Strategic Planning Institute (A).

and the questionnaire, to each member of the SPI professional staff. Their comments were also very useful, covering not only which questions might be most helpful but also the phrasing of the questions. For example, one reaction focused on the phrase "PIMS and other consultants," which could position PIMS in the respondent's mind as being similar to some other firms. This might affect not only the respondent's perceptions and hence survey answers, but might even have an impact on the respondent's *future* perceptions of PIMS and hence reaction to later attempts at recruitment.

As expected, the most common suggestion was that the questionnaire length should be reduced. The opinions of the SPI staff were helpful to Chussil in pruning the questionnaire to 77 questions that fit neatly onto both sides of four pages (Exhibit 1). At the same time, some questions were reworded to request a categorical answer instead of a discrete number. For example, rather than asking for a company's precise marketing expenses to sales ratio, the questionnaire provided five boxes, each corresponding to a range of values (e.g., 0.0%–3.9%). The ranges were set up to match observed distributions in the PIMS data base.

Categorical questions were an important feature of the questionnaire. Open-ended questions would be difficult at best to categorize, which would make quantitative analysis almost useless. Equally important, a questionnaire requiring checkmarks only was quick and easy to fill out, presumably helping to boost the response rate. In this case, although this final questionnaire had 77 questions, it took only 10–15 minutes to fill out, based on pretesting of the questionnaire. This fact was stated clearly in the cover letter to each recipient, to prevent even the questionnaire's fairly modest length from deterring response.

After some thought, Chussil decided not to include "no opinion" as an alternative to any question. Although nothing would prevent a respondent from leaving a question blank, Chussil felt that offering "no opinion" as an option would make it too easy for the respondent to avoid the effort of making a choice.

SENDING THE SURVEY

Realizing that the people who were to receive the questionnaire were presumably busy executives, Chussil knew that, if he were to obtain a high response rate, he would have to do everything possible to make it easy for them to respond. Obviously, postage-paid, addressed envelopes would be provided. Another step was to assure the recipients in brief, individually addressed, cover letters, that only 10–15 minutes of their time would be required to complete the questionnaire. (The cover letter is reproduced as Exhibit 2.) In addition, the cover letter suggested that recipients *not* agonize over answers, saying that first impressions were pretty accurate. This was designed to encourage more fully completed questionnaires as well as a higher number of returned questionnaires in total.

It was suggested to Chussil that postcards be sent to questionnaire recipients several days before the survey was to be mailed, and several days after it was mailed. (Copies of the postcards are shown in Exhibit 3.) The premailing postcard would say that a questionnaire would be received in a few days and that taking a few minutes to complete it would be greatly appreciated. The postmailing postcard reminded the recipient to fill out the questionnaire and expressed gratitude if the recipient had already done so. He was told that controlled experiments showed that postcards such as these can have a major positive impact on a survey's response rate. The postcard scheme was adopted.

Exhibit 1

Strategic Planning Institute (B)

Questionnaire: Attitudes Toward a Scientific Approach to Strategic Planning

Please describe your position in your company:

1. Line staff

- ☐ (1) Line
- ☐ (2) Staff

2. Function

- ☐ (1) General management
- ☐ (2) Marketing
- ☐ (3) Production manufacturing
- ☐ (4) Finance
- ☐ (5) Accounting control
- ☐ (6) Planning
- ☐ (7) Operations research
- ☐ (8) Other

3. Level

- ☐ (1) Top management (CEO, VP, division head, etc.)
- ☐ (2) Assistant to top management
- ☐ (3) Middle management
- ☐ (4) Analyst/specialist
- ☐ (5) Other

4. Has your formal training been technically oriented (e.g., engineering)?

- ☐ (1) Nontechnical
- ☐ (2) Technical

5. Do you have an MBA degree?

- ☐ (1) No
- ☐ (2) Yes

6. In what functional area in your company did the person(s) work who had primary responsibility for making the decision to join (or not to join) PIMS?

- ☐ (1) General management
- ☐ (2) Marketing
- ☐ (3) Production manufacturing
- ☐ (4) Finance
- ☐ (5) Accounting control
- ☐ (6) Planning
- ☐ (7) Operations research
- ☐ (8) Other

7. Was the position of the primary decision maker(s) line or staff?

- ☐ (1) Line
- ☐ (2) Staff

8. Are you the first in your company to investigate PIMS?

- ☐ (1) No
- ☐ (2) Yes
- ☐ (3) Unsure

9. How did you <u>first</u> hear about PIMS?

- ☐ (1) Direct mail
- ☐ (2) Published article
- ☐ (3) Meeting
- ☐ (4) Someone in your company
- ☐ (5) Someone in another company
- ☐ (6) Educational program
- ☐ (7) Consultant

10. Please indicate the reason you attended the PIMS Briefing Session.

- ☐ (1) My own initiative
- ☐ (2) My manager <u>asked</u> me to attend
- ☐ (3) My manager <u>told</u> me to attend

11. About how many people from your company, including yourself, attended the Briefing Session?

☐ Attendees

12. Please indicate your opinion of the size of the Briefing Session, in terms of the total number of attendees.

- ☐ (1) Too few
- ☐ (2) About right
- ☐ (3) Too many

13. Please indicate your general level of interest in PIMS after attending the Briefing Session.

1	2	3	4	5	6	7
No interest		Moderate interest				Strong interest

14. Please indicate your opinion of the credibility of PIMS analyses.

1	2	3	4	5	6	7
Not at all credible		About the same as most consultants				Unusually credible

15. Please indicate your opinion of the value of PIMS analyses to your company

1	2	3	4	5	6	7
Not valuable at all		About the same as most consultants				Unusually valuable

16. Did you have a specific strategy problem in mind when you came to the Briefing Session?

- ☐ (1) No
- ☐ (2) Yes

On Questions 17-22, please indicate your perceptions of the Briefing Session on the following scales by circling one number on each.

17. Emphasis

1	2	3	4	5	6	7
Academic seminar						Sales pitch

18. Appropriateness of emphasis

1	2	3	4	5	6	7
Inappropriate						Appropriate

19. Length

1	2	3	4	5	6	7
Too short			About right			Too long

20. Complexity of material

1	2	3	4	5	6	7
Too simple			About right			Too complex

21. Professionalism of approach

1	2	3	4	5	6	7
Too little			About right			Overkill

22. Quality of speakers

1	2	3	4	5	6	7
Unusually low						Unusually high

23. Did you find contact with PIMS staff at the Briefing Session helpful in understanding and learning about PIMS?

1	2	3	4	5	6	7
Not at all helpful						Very helpful

24. What was the first action regarding PIMS taken by your company after the Briefing Session?

- ☐ (1) Arranged in-house PIMS presentation
- ☐ (2) Asked for additional PIMS information
- ☐ (3) Made a decision to join or not to join
- ☐ (4) Other

25. Were you satisfied with PIMS follow-up after the Briefing Session?

1 2 3 4 5 6 7
/ / / / / / /
Dissatisfied — Satisfied

On questions 26-35, please circle one number on each scale to indicate the degree of similarity you perceive between the services offered by each pair of organizations.

26. PIMS, Arthur D. Little

1 2 3 4 5 6 7
/ / / / / / /
Very dissimilar — Very similar

27. PIMS, Boston Consulting Group

1 2 3 4 5 6 7
/ / / / / / /
Very dissimilar — Very similar

39. Your in-house staff

1 2 3 4 5 6 7
/ / / / / / /
Little or no value — High value

To evaluate opportunities for corporate or divisional investment or divestiture (e.g., portfolio analysis):

40. PIMS

1 2 3 4 5 6 7
/ / / / / / /
Little or no value — High value

41. Arthur D. Little

1 2 3 4 5 6 7
/ / / / / / /
Little or no value — High value

42. Boston Consulting Group

1 2 3 4 5 6 7
/ / / / / / /
Little or no value — High value

43. Your in-house staff

1 2 3 4 5 6 7
/ / / / / / /
Little or no value — High value

To investigate competitive scenarios under alternative strategic moves or assumptions:

44. PIMS

1 2 3 4 5 6 7
/ / / / / / /
Little or no value — High value

45. Arthur D. Little

1 2 3 4 5 6 7
/ / / / / / /
Little or no value — High value

46. Boston Consulting Group

1 2 3 4 5 6 7
/ / / / / / /
Little or no value — High value

47. Your in-house staff

1 2 3 4 5 6 7
/ / / / / / /
Little or no value — High value

To produce specific strategic recommendations:

48. PIMS

1 2 3 4 5 6 7
/ / / / / / /
Little or no value — High value

49. Arthur D. Little

1 2 3 4 5 6 7
/ / / / / / /
Little or no value — High value

50. Boston Consulting Group

1 2 3 4 5 6 7
/ / / / / / /
Little or no value — High value

51. Your in-house staff

1 2 3 4 5 6 7
/ / / / / / /
Little or no value — High value

To help improve profitability or market share:

52. PIMS

1 2 3 4 5 6 7
/ / / / / / /
Little or no value — High value

53. Arthur D. Little

1 2 3 4 5 6 7
/ / / / / / /
Little or no value — High value

54. Boston Consulting Group

1 2 3 4 5 6 7
/ / / / / / /
Little or no value — High value

55. Your in-house staff

1 2 3 4 5 6 7
/ / / / / / /
Little or no value — High value

56. Please indicate your company's approximate yearly sales.

☐ (1) $10 million or less
☐ (2) $11-100 million
☐ (3) $101-500 million
☐ (4) $500 million or more

57. Please indicate your company's approximate degree of diversification.

☐ (1) Low (more than 75% of company sales in one product area
☐ (2) Moderate (50% to 75% of company sales in product area)
☐ (3) High (less than 50% of company sales in one product area)

58. Would you characterize strategic planning in your company as bottom-up (from divisions) or top-down (from top staff)?

☐ (1) Bottom-up
☐ (2) Top-down

59. Is strategic planning at your company done on a formalized, regular basis, or on an as-needed, episodic basis?

☐ (1) Formal
☐ (2) Episodic

60. Does your company have a functional group whose primary responsibility is strategic planning?

☐ (1) No
☐ (2) Yes

61. Does the planning group make use of computer models?

☐ (1) Never
☐ (2) Sometimes
☐ (3) Frequently
☐ (minus 1) No planning group

62. In your opinion, what is the primary strength or focus of your company?

☐ (1) Marketing
☐ (2) Production/manufacturing
☐ (3) Other

63. Has your company made use of outside strategy consultants in the past?

64. If your company has made use of consultants, how has the performance of those consultants been, in your opinion?

- ☐ (1) Poor
- ☐ (2) Acceptable
- ☐ (3) Excellent

For questions 65-77, please insert "your division" instead of "your company" if your interest in PIMS was for your division instead of for your company as a whole.

65. Please indicate your company's approximate pretax return on sales.

- ☐ (1) Less than 2.0%
- ☐ (2) 2.0-6.9%
- ☐ (3) 7.0-11.9%
- ☐ (4) 12.0-17.0%
- ☐ (5) More than 17.0%

66. Compared with your major competitors, was that return on sales

- ☐ (1) Considerably lower
- ☐ (2) About the same
- ☐ (3) Considerably higher

67. Please enter the average market share rank held by your company in its major product line.

- ☐ (1) Largest share
- ☐ (2) Second largest share
- ☐ (3) Third largest share
- ☐ (4) Fourth (or smaller) share

68. Please indicate your approximate share relative to your largest competitor in major product lines.

- ☐ (1) Your company more than 1.2 times the share of your largest competitor
- ☐ (2) Your company 0.8-1.2 times the share of your largest competitor
- ☐ (3) Your company less than 0.2 times the share of your largest competitor

69. Please indicate the approximate degree of your company's product quality, as perceived by your customers. Please include the quality of services, such as delivery time and repair support, in your evaluation.

Perceived product quality, relative to major competitors:

- ☐ (1) Much worse
- ☐ (2) Somewhat worse
- ☐ (3) About the same
- ☐ (4) Somewhat better
- ☐ (5) Much better

70. Please indicate your company's approximate degree of production automation.

- ☐ (1) Few or zero tasks automated
- ☐ (2) Many tasks automated
- ☐ (3) Most or all tasks automated

71. About what percentage of production employees in your company is unionized?

☐ % of employees unionized

72. Please indicate the approximate percentage of sales spent by your company on marketing. Please include as marketing media advertising, promotion expenses and sales force expenses. Please do not include physical distribution expenses.

Marketing/sales:

- ☐ (1) Less than 4.0%
- ☐ (2) 4.0-6.9%
- ☐ (3) 7.0-9.9%
- ☐ (4) 10.0-14.0%
- ☐ (5) More than 14.0%

Exhibit 2
Strategic Planning Institute (B)
Questionnaire Cover Letter

March 6, 1979

Within the last two years, you attended a PIMS Briefing Session conducted by the Strategic Planning Institute. At that time, you heard a unique concept: the application of science to strategic planning. I am very interested in your reactions to the PIMS approach, and I would be grateful if you would take a few minutes to complete the enclosed questionnaire. A stamped, addressed return envelope is included for your convenience.

Because your schedule is busy, the questionnaire has been designed to require only ten or fifteen minutes to complete. Answers require simply checking boxes or circling numbers. Please do not agonize over any of the questions; first impressions or recollections are quite accurate and are far more useful than no response at all.

Absolute anonymity is guaranteed. Although questionnaires have been marked to indicate which Briefing Session you attended, the questionnaire cannot be used to identify you or your company because many companies attended each Briefing Session.

This survey is being conducted as a student research project at the Harvard Business School with the cooperation of the Strategic Planning Institute.

Thank you for your cooperation.

Sincerely,

Mark J. Chussil

Mark J. Chussil

MJC/K
enclosures

Exhibit 3

Strategic Planning Institute (B)

Premailing and Postmailing Respondent Contract Messages

PREMAILING

In a few days you will receive a questionnaire for a survey on attitudes toward a scientific approach to planning. This survey is being conducted as a student research project at the Harvard Business School, with the cooperation of the Strategic Planning Institute. I would be grateful if you would take 10-15 minutes of your time to complete it. Thank you!

Mark J. Chussil

POSTMAILING

A few days ago, you received a questionnaire for a survey on attitudes toward a scientific approach to planning. The survey is being conducted as a student research project at the Harvard Business School, with the cooperation of the Strategic Planning Institute. If you have already completed the questionnaire, I would like to express my appreciation to you. If you have not, I would be very grateful if you would take a few minutes to fill it out. Thank you!

Mark J. Chussil

Exhibit 4

Strategic Planning Institute (B)

Typical Letter of Rejection

Office of

Assistant Secretary and
Associate General Counsel

Gentlemen:

Your request for information has been referred to me for reply.

In recent years, the volume of requests for information of various types from nongovernmental and governmental sources, including federal agencies, state agencies, and foreign governments, has increased to such an extent that we are unable to respond. Consequently, we have adopted the policy of not answering questionnaires except when required by law.

We are sorry that this circumstance exists and hope that you will understand. Thank you for considering ______ as a source of information.

Sincerely,

Exhibit 5
Strategic Planning Institute (B)

Analysis of Univariate Means

Variable Name	*Nonjoiner Mean (1)*	*Total Mean (2)*	*Joiners Means (3)*	*(1) – (3)*	*(1) – (2)*	*(2) – (3)*
1. Your line/staff	1.67	1.68	1.70			
2. Your function	3.45	3.58	3.85	NA	NA	NA
3. Your level	1.84	1.87	1.93			
4. Tech. degree?	1.51	1.53	1.55			
5. MBA degree?	1.52	1.50	1.49	NA	NA	NA
6. DMU function	2.22	2.34	2.59			
7. DMU line/staff	1.47	1.49	1.53			
8. First investigation	1.78	1.78	1.77			
9. First knowledge	3.02	3.03	3.06			
10. Why attended	1.36	1.34	1.29			
11. Number attendees	2.29	2.64	3.35	***		*
12. Size opinion	2.14	2.14	2.15			
13. Interest level	4.66	4.95	5.54	***	**	***
14. Credibility opinion	4.93	5.05	5.29	***		*
15. Value opinion	4.27	4.54	5.09	***	**	***
16. Specific problem?	1.20	1.23	1.30	*		
17. Emphasis perception	4.14	4.08	3.96			
18. Appropriate emphasis?	5.03	4.99	4.92			
19. Length perception	4.09	4.04	3.94			
20. Complex perception	3.84	3.90	4.01	*		
21. Professional perception	4.12	4.13	4.15			
22. Speaker quality perception	4.70	4.75	4.86			
23. Contact helpful?	4.81	4.82	4.83			
24. First action	2.78	2.57	2.14	***	**	***
25. Follow-up perception	4.96	5.02	5.16			
26. Similarity: PIMS–ADL	2.59	2.54	2.43			
27. Similarity: PIMS–BCG	3.92	3.90	3.87			
28. Similarity: PIMS–DRI	2.36	2.41	2.50			
29. Similarity: PIMS–you	2.83	2.85	2.89			
30. Similarity: ADL–BCG	3.65	3.58	3.42	*		
31. Similarity: ADL–DRI	3.12	3.12	3.12			
32. Similarity: ADL–you	3.29	3.25	3.17			
33. Similarity: BCG–DRI	2.81	2.77	2.69			
34. Similarity: BCG–you	3.75	3.77	3.81			
35. Similarity: DRI–you	3.16	3.14	3.08			
36. Profit: PIMS	4.67	4.89	5.36	***	*	***
37. Profit: ADL	3.86	3.86	3.86			
38. Profit: BCG	4.63	4.63	4.63			
39. Profit: You	4.92	4.84	4.70			
40. Portfolio: PIMS	4.47	4.59	4.85	**		
41. Portfolio: ADL	4.11	4.06	3.97	NA	NA	NA
42. Portfolio: BCG	4.72	4.74	4.79			
43. Portfolio: You	4.84	4.77	4.62			
44. Competition: PIMS	4.77	4.96	5.34	***		**
45. Competition: ADL	3.95	3.92	3.85			
46. Competition: BCG	4.48	4.43	4.31			
47. Competition: You	4.57	4.43	4.13	***		*
48. Recommendation: PIMS	4.30	4.45	4.75	**		*
49. Recommendation: ADL	4.02	4.02	4.01			
50. Recommendation: BCG	4.55	4.55	4.56			

Exhibit 5 (continued)

Variable Name	*Nonjoiner Mean (1)*	*Total Mean (2)*	*Joiners Means (3)*	*(1) – (3)*	*(1) – (2)*	*(2) – (3)*
51. Recommendation: You	4.93	4.86	4.73			
52. Improvement: PIMS	4.36	4.51	4.81	***		*
53. Improvement: ADL	3.92	3.92	3.92			
54. Improvement: BCG	4.48	4.45	4.39			
55. Improvement: You	4.77	4.68	4.49	**		
56. Annual sales	2.95	2.98	3.04			
57. Diversification	2.01	2.09	2.24	NA	NA	NA
58. Bottom-top plan	1.61	1.58	1.51	*		
59. Formal/episodic	1.40	1.37	1.31			
60. Planning group?	1.47	1.53	1.65	***		**
61. Use models?	1.48	1.59	1.84	***		*
62. Primary strength	1.69	1.69	1.68			
63. Use consultants?	1.92	1.93	1.97			
64. Consultant opinion	1.86	1.84	1.82			
65. Return on sales	2.94	2.93	2.91			
66. Relative return on sales	2.15	2.14	2.12			
67. Share rank	1.98	2.01	2.08			
68. Relative share	1.95	1.99	2.09	NA	NA	NA
69. Relative quality	3.93	3.90	3.83			
70. Automation	1.82	1.81	1.80			
71. Employees unionized	42.94	44.15	46.61			
72. Marketing/sales	2.67	2.68	2.72			
73. Relative marketing/sales	2.03	2.02	1.99	NA	NA	NA
74. R&D/sales	2.53	2.58	2.68			
75. Relative R&D/sales	1.95	1.95	1.95			
76. Real growth rate	3.51	3.44	3.28	**		
77. Growth/mature	1.75	1.78	1.84	*		

NA – Not available.

Key to significance levels:
* = At least .90.
** = At least .95.
*** = At least .99.

Olympia Brewing Company (A)

In May 1977 Fred Prentice and Andrew Lee, consultants with Data Economics, Inc (DEI), an economic forecasting and consulting company, were faced with a serious problem on a consulting assignment for the Olympia Brewing Company.

DEI had contracted with Olympia to provide an analysis of how future economic and demographic changes would impact the U.S. beer market. DEI had developed an econometric model, known as its age-income model (AIM), that could forecast the number of U.S. consumers grouped by both age and income characteristics. Since the consumption and/or purchase rates of most consumer products and services varied by the age and income of the consumer, DEI had found that forecasts of the number of consumers of different age-income characteristics could be used to forecast sales of particular products. However, for this approach to work, DEI needed to have data on consumption or purchase rates for different age-income groups. DEI had begun the project in January 1977, assuming that they had such data in the form of the Target Group Index (TGI) survey. The consumption rates provided by this survey had worked well in an earlier study for another client for wine and liquor products.

However, once DEI had analyzed the TGI data, they found that it had projected total 1975 U.S. beer consumption at about 70 million barrels. (The latest year of TGI data available was 1975. DEI made the projection of total 1975 U.S. beer consumption to check the validity of TGI data.) In contrast, statistics from the Bureau of Alcohol, Tobacco, and Firearms and from the Internal Revenue Service indicated a 1975 market size of about 150 million barrels. This latter figure was generally accepted in the beer industry.

Given this apparent severe underreporting of consumption by the TGI data, both Olympia and DEI executives were doubtful as to whether they had a sound basis for forecasting. Fred Prentice and Andrew Lee were par-

 This case was prepared by George S. Yip under the supervision of David J. Reibstein.

ticularly concerned since Prentice, a senior consultant in DEI's San Francisco office, was responsible for performing the consulting work, and Lee, a member of the consumer group at DEI's head office in Lexington, Massachusetts, had been the person primarily responsible for arranging the contract with Olympia. Prentice and Lee were, respectively, recent graduates of a well-known western business school and a well-known eastern business school.

INDUSTRY AND COMPANY BACKGROUND

In 1976 Olympia sold 7.1 million barrels of beer, out of an industry total of about 160 million barrels.[1] Beer was Olympia's only product. Olympia's sales revenues in 1976 were $354 million.

Industry Situation

Beer sales in the United States had undergone rapid growth since 1960, when sales were about 85 million barrels. This growth had coincided with the growth in number of the heaviest beer-drinking group, those aged 18–34 years. This group had grown from under 40 million to just over 60 million in 1976. Straightforward demographic projections showed that the numbers in this group would peak at about 68 million by 1985 and decline thereafter. Many in the industry were concerned about the implications of this demographic trend. The year 1976 had also seen an unexpected slowdown in the growth rate of beer consumption.

The major industry trend was its rapid consolidation. In ten years the number of independent brewing companies had shrunk from 118 to 49 by 1976. The five largest companies combined had 69% market share in 1976, and everyone in the industry expected this proportion to increase. Their collective share had been 53% in 1971. One estimate was that their share would reach 90% by 1980. The leading U.S. market shares by company in 1976 were[2]:

Anheuser-Busch	20%
Schlitz	17
Miller	12
Pabst	11
Coors	9
Olympia	4

Miller was the only major beer company owned by a firm outside the industry. It had been acquired in 1970 by Philip Morris, Inc., a major tobacco company. In 1976 Philip Morris' revenues, including Miller, were $4,293 million. Anheuser-Busch, the largest independent beer company, had 1976 revenues of $1,441 million. Miller's market share had been only 4% at the time of its acquisition. Philip Morris had injected sophisticated marketing techniques and huge amounts of cash into Miller. In 1975 Miller spent an estimated $3 a barrel on advertising, nearly three times the industry average. It was also estimated that by 1980 Miller would have spent $850 million on plant expansion since the acquisition. It was believed that much of this activity led to Miller's tripling of its market share.

Anheuser-Busch, Schlitz, and Miller were the only brewers with full national distribution. Many industry experts predicted that it would be very difficult for regional brewers to survive the industry's consolidation. Industry profitability had also been declining drastically.

[1]Manufacturer data reported to the Bureau of Alcohol, Tobacco, and Firearms.

[2]"Turmoil Among the Brewers: Miller's Fast Growth," *Business Week*, November 8, 1976.

Product Trends

In 1977 Olympia believed that the beer market was divided into the following segments:

	% Share	Average Retail Price ($ per six pack)
Imported	1.8%	$3.25
Super premium	5.7	1.89
Premium	51.8	1.69
Popular	24.5	1.49
Price	4.8	1.35
Low calorie	8.4	1.75
Malt	3.0	1.75

These segments were manufacturers', not necessarily consumers', designations. Leading imported beers were Carlsberg, Heineken, Lowenbrau, and Tuborg. "Premium" beers were generally considered to be Budweiser, Coors, Miller, Olympia, Pabst, Rolling Rock, and Schlitz. "Popular" beers were such brands as Falstaff, Hamm's, Lone Star, and Schaefer. "Price" beers included Ballantine, Iron City, and Red, White & Blue. Michelob was marketed by Anheuser as a brand a cut above premium beers.

In 1975 Miller had introduced the first widely successful low-calorie beer, Lite. The success encouraged the introduction of light beers by Anheuser-Busch and Schlitz. In January 1977 Olympia had introduced its own light beer, Olympia Gold. Olympia now considered that light beer was the major growth segment of the future.

Another possible growth segment was imported beers. Some industry sources thought that two factors favored this trend. First, increasing affluence might encourage the drinking of more expensive beers. Second, the continuing elimination of many regional brands, with their distinctive flavors, might open a slot for imports with their distinctive flavors. Miller had recently begun test marketing a domestically brewed Lowenbrau at a price 25% higher than Michelob's, under a licensing agreement with Lowenbrau Munich.

A third possible trend was the sale of 7-ounce bottles, aimed at women drinkers. The standard size was 12 ounces. Miller had had a successful introduction of the smaller size in 1972.

Olympia's Situation and Strategy

The Olympia Brewing Company owned three brands: Olympia, Hamm's, and Lone Star. In 1976 the Olympia and Hamm's brands accounted for 89% of company sales and Lone Star 11%. Olympia was brewed in Olympia, Washington (and had been since 1896), and distributed in 20 western states. California was its largest single market, and Olympia was one of the top brands there, with 9.4% market share.

Hamm's breweries and brand names had been acquired in 1975 for $22 million (in cash and assumed liabilities) from a group of independent Hamm's distributors. The latter had bought the Theodore Hamm Brewing Company from Heublein, Inc., in 1973. Heublein was a diversified distilling and fast-food (Kentucky Fried Chicken) company and had owned Hamm's since 1966. Heublein was estimated to have taken write-offs of $26.5 million on the sale. Hamm's was brewed in St. Paul, Minnesota, and distributed in 26 western and midwestern states.

In December 1976 Olympia had acquired the Lone Star brewery in San Antonio, Texas, for the equivalent of about $23 million in newly issued common stock. The acquisition increased the Olympia company's distribution coverage to 30 states and its industry rank to sixth.

In an interview in *Beverage World*, November 1977, Rick Schmidt, Olympia's president and chief executive officer, and great-grandson of the company's founder, commented,

> In an industry that's shrinking as fast as the brewing industry, we saw only one alter-

native for Olympia. We had to develop a national posture.

Today we're seeing rapid market segmentation in the brewing industry, where ten years ago the majority of the beer sold in the U.S. fell into two pricing categories: premium and popular, or regional. We're looking at major changes in brewing facilities—a trend toward a much more horizontal plant—a more efficient, faster kind of operation. We've seen a continuing shift from pure product orientation to a balance of product and marketing. And we'll continue to see further concentration in the industry, as well as greater segmentation of products as this industry moves closer and closer to a true packaged goods business.

In January 1976 Olympia had appointed a new vice president of marketing. This was Richard Harvey, a 28-year veteran of Coca-Cola Co. In the same *Beverage World* interview, Harvey commented,

[Olympia is] looking for a combination of people who have packaged goods marketing experience. We're blending them together with people who have brewing experience to try to introduce to our beer marketing all the promotion techniques and elements of the marketing mix that have worked for other impulse consumer goods products—candy, soft drinks, cigarettes.

We're competing with the top five breweries everyplace we sell now. We compete with regional breweries as we move farther and farther away from the Washington area and at the same time with regional breweries on the West Coast: with Heidelberg in Tacoma, which is part of the Carling chain; with Rainier in Seattle, which is part of the Heileman chain; and with Lucky in Vancouver, which is part of the Falstaff chain.

THE DEI CONSULTING PROPOSAL

In 1976 Tom Black, who had been director of brand planning at Olympia, was appointed director of corporate planning, a new position for the company, which reported to the president.

In analyzing his responsibilities for planning, Black had concluded that forecasts of beer market developments would be a useful tool. Data Economics had been doing economic forecasting and analysis for the Washington State government in the state capital, Olympia. Black had many contacts with the state government since the Olympia Brewing Company was one of the largest employers in the state. Through a state government intermediary, Black and some DEI representatives got together to discuss Olympia's planning and forecasting needs. After a number of meetings, DEI submitted a consulting proposal to Black in August 1976. The proposal discussed four marketing issues which DEI considered to be facing Olympia:

1. As a regional producer, decisions had to be made as to location and timing of geographic expansion.
2. As a competitor in a market situation which exhibited continuing product innovation, they needed to know what new products to launch, where, and when.
3. As a company with heavy investment in production and other facilities, an accurate forecast of demand of existing product lines was needed.
4. For consideration of merger and acquisition prospects, Olympia needed to know which geographic and product line mixes would best complement existing capabilities.

To help with these issues, Data Economics would provide Olympia with a forecasting and planning system. This system would consist of an econometric model of the outside economic and demographic environment with which Olympia interacted. The model would produce forecasts of industrywide demand for beer products, Olympia's market share of the beer market, and an analysis of the potential for new products. Specific applications would include:

1. product line forecasting, disaggregating by demographic and economic characteristics of consumers;

2. new product introduction evaluation, based on test marketing or survey results;
3. product mix decisions, for analyzing the cyclical and growth complementarity of individual existing or potential product lines to the total portfolio of Olympia's products; and
4. market potential evaluation, through examination of consumers and markets, for targeting market segments.

The resulting system would have simulation capabilities, including demographic and economic levers, would be theoretically supportable, and would rely not only on government and third-party (e.g., Target Group Index) data but also on survey and other data developed by Olympia's market research.

After a further meeting in November 1976, Black signed the contract in December to initiate the project in January 1977. In addition to Black, Ed Ojdana, manager of corporate planning, and Dennis Murphy, manager of marketing information systems, were involved in the project.

On the DEI side, Fred Prentice, a senior consultant in DEI's San Francisco regional office, was responsible for the project. As a consultant in a DEI regional office, Prentice had responsibility for several clients. These clients used the whole spectrum of DEI's services, not just consumer services, Andrew Lee, the marketing manager for DEI's consumer services, was responsible for developing contracts for consumer-related assignments. Since a DEI assignment involved inputs from the specialist head office groups, such as the consumer group, as well as from the regional consulting office, Lee also acted as a consultant to the regional consultant responsible for a project. Jay Levine, who was responsible for the age-income model, would provide guidance on how to link the age-income model to the custom models to be built for Olympia.

The project would begin by using DEI's age-income model to forecast how economic and demographic changes would affect beer consumption.

THE AGE-INCOME MODEL

The heart of DEI's consumer forecasting capability was the age-income model (AIM). This model was able to forecast the numbers of individuals and family units who would be in particular age and income categories for each year to 1990. AIM was linked to DEI's macroeconomic model. Thus, changes in national aggregate economic forecasts of, for example, GNP, unemployment, and inflation, could be disaggregated by the age-income model into the effects for particular age-income groups.[3]

As described earlier, the model forecast the *number* of consumers in different age-income categories, and these numbers were then linked to consumption and purchase data of particular product categories, to forecast sales of that category. DEI intended to use the Target Group Index as the source of consumption data for different age-income categories. The assumption behind this forecasting methodology was that product consumption patterns were primarily determined by the age and income of the consumer.

TARGET GROUP INDEX

The Target Group Index was an annual survey of approximately 30,000 adults. The primary purpose was to collect media and product usage information. Along with the W. R. Simmons survey,[4] the TGI survey was the primary source of data on exposure to printed media. (TGI also collected information on TV viewing habits, but being an annual survey it did not provide the detail of the more comprehensive and frequent A. C. Nielsen "ratings" of TV programs.) The main subscribers to the TGI survey were advertising agencies who used it

[3]This model had been developed by Dr. Jay Levine who, before joining DEI, had been an assistant professor of economics at Toronto University. Additional DEI services are described in Exhibit 4.

[4]In 1978 the Simmons and the Target Group Index surveys were merged and the total sample size slightly reduced.

primarily for media planning—the data on each respondent's product usage could be related to his or her media habits. A small number of advertisers also subscribed. Most, however, relied on their advertising agencies for analysis of the TGI data.

TGI provided their data in about 50 printed volumes. The data in the printed volumes were, of course, in pretabulated form and were, therefore, only a limited selection of the possible combinations—each of the 30,000 respondents (or "observations") had provided information on about 10,000 items (or "variables"). Access to the raw data (the 300 million or so pieces of information) was available from a small number of computer service bureaus to whom TGI had given computer tapes.

Soon after the development of the age-income model, DEI had recognized the usefulness of the TGI data and had arranged to become one of the computer service bureaus for the data. Axiom Market Research Bureau, the owners of TGI, stipulated that DEI could process their data only for advertisers who subscribed to the survey. Olympia Brewing Company had been a TGI subscriber for some time.

Data Collection

Data reported by TGI were collected in three steps. First, the interviewer made contact with the designated household and carried out a short personal interview which mainly collected demographic classification data. This initial personal interview was made with any responsible adult member of the household. Second, all members of the household aged 18 and over were asked to complete a booklet questionnaire which contained questions about products and services used or owned and about exposure to print and broadcast media. Third, the interviewer called again to collect the booklet questionnaires, checked them over, verified in particular the magazine reading claims recorded in them, and asked additional questions about the magazines read (for the reader quality report).

TGI had two different types of booklet questionnaires, one "for the person who does most of the shopping for groceries and household items" and one for other persons. The larger "shopper" booklet questionnaire used in the 1976 survey consisted of 76 pages of product usage questions, 17 pages of media exposure questions, and 4 pages of demographic and psychographic questions. Exhibit 1 reproduces the page containing the questions on "beer and ale."

Sample Design

The TGI sample represented the population aged 18 or over living in households in the 48 contiguous states. Separate samples were drawn in each of the largest 20 markets in the country (defined as ADIs), with each of these subsamples being large enough to be tabulated in special local market reports.

The sampling frame from which the sample was selected was a file of households with listed phones and/or registered automobiles maintained by the Reuben H. Donnelley Corporation. Except in certain rural areas, this was in street order. Interviewing clusters were selected by a systematic random procedure within each market, at a single stage of selection (i.e., the clusters themselves were not clustered, but were dispersed throughout the market). Clusters outside SMSAs were selected with half the probability of those inside, and the probabilities of selection also depended on economic index.

The interviewer was instructed to attempt interviews at all households listed in the selected clusters, together with other households that might be found in between these households: in this way, households which would not have appeared on the lists entered the sample.

Fieldwork

Up to seven attempts were made to get a personal interview at each designated household, and interviewers were instructed to make these attempts on different days and at different times of day.

Cooperating respondents were compensated by being offered a gift which they could choose from a selection. In addition, in households in which two or more people had been asked to complete the questionnaire, the household was offered a further special gift if both/all of them did so.

In 1975 TGI attempted to contact 35,151 occupied dwelling units and achieved 24,443 interviews (a 69.5% contact rate). Within these households there were 49,723 eligible adults and 30,497 (or 61.3%) completed booklets. Thus, the overall completion rate was 42.8%.

Weighting and Projection of the Sample

The sample was balanced to conform, within each area, to the estimated characteristics of the U.S. population for each of

- Race and census region (interlaced)
- County size
- Age
- Marital status
- Employment status/occupation
- Education
- Household income
- Head of household/nonhead

The 30,497 adults were weighted *on average* by 4,640 to project to a population total of 141.6 million. However, the range of weights was from less than 2,500 to more than 25,000.

DEI had found that there was a general problem in all surveys of getting adequate representation of young, single males. The TGI sample did not balance for age, area, and marital status simultaneously. However, the sample for 1975 had 2,323 men aged between 18 and 24 years and 2,092 single men, out of 30,497 adults in total. If the proportions of men 18 to 24 years and single men were distributed evenly, the expected number of single men aged 18 to 24 would have been 159 (2,323 × 2,092 ÷ 30,497 = 159).

TGI excluded from their sample of households sorority or fraternity houses, dormitories, military barracks, homes for the aged, hotels and motels that did not have permanent residents, and boarding houses with five or more lodgers.

The TGI survey showed that the incidence of beer drinking ("beer penetration rate" in DEI terminology) varied by both age and income. Exhibit 2 reproduces an exhibit from a DEI report to Olympia, presenting such data.

THE PROBLEM

As described earlier, DEI needed consumption data by age, income, and sex to link to the age-income model's demographic forecasts. The two sets of data would be used as follows:

No. of men[5] (e.g., 1980)	× % of beer drinkers[6] (1975)		
	×	Ave. no. of beers per drinker[6] (1975)	= total no. of beers[7] (1980)

The TGI survey did provide data by age-income-sex categories on the percentage drinking beer. However, it did not provide explicit data on the average number of beers consumed by each drinker. Instead the survey asked beer drinkers *how often* they drank beer (see Exhibit 1 for actual questionnaire):

[5]Was supplied by the age-income model forecasts for each of 36 age-income groups.

[6]To be supplied by market research data.

[7]A base case forecast based on demographic and economic changes only. Other factors, such as the average price of beer, would be incorporated in the final forecast; see (C) case.

- More than once a day
- Once a day
- 2 or 3 times a week
- Once a week
- 2 or 3 times a month
- Once a month
- Less than once a month

To convert these frequency estimates into volume estimates, Prentice and Lee, the DEI consultants, and Dennis Murphy, the Olympia marketing information systems manager, had together "guesstimated" the following pattern:

Claimed Frequency	*Average No. of 12-oz. Cans Per Week*
More than once a day	23
Once a day	9
2 or 3 times a week	6
Once a week	2
2 or 3 times a month	1
Once a month	0.5
Less than once a month	0.2

When this pattern was applied to the actual number of drinkers in each frequency category in 1975, the result was an estimate of an average of 4.9 cans per week per adult drinker (see Table 2 of Exhibit 3). Unfortunately industry sales statistics,[8] which Olympia accepted, indicated an average of 11.6 cans per week per adult drinker (see Table 1 of Exhibit 3). (The industry sales statistics were of course insufficient for the DEI project since the latter needed consumption statistics to feed into the age-income model.) Thus the TGI data on which DEI needed to base their forecasts showed a tremendous underreporting of beer consumption.

Both DEI and Olympia considered that the major source of the underreporting was that the TGI survey asked about *frequency* and not *volume* of drinking. Clearly the DEI/Olympia estimated weights linking frequency and volume were incorrect. These weights were actually the second set used. A first set, assuming fewer beers per frequency category, had produced an underestimate of two-thirds. DEI and Olympia felt they had no basis for trying a third set of weights.

In addition, DEI and Olympia wondered whether an annual survey was the most reliable way of collecting data on a daily activity like beer drinking. Also, they wondered whether the TGI sample included the heaviest beer drinkers, and how honest respondents would be about their drinking habits.

A meeting between DEI and Olympia had been arranged for June 30. At that time Olympia expected DEI to have a solution to the problem of the lack of realistic consumption rates. Without such consumption rates the age/income-based forecasts could not be made.

In preparation for this meeting Prentice wrote a memorandum to be sent to Olympia beforehand. (This is reproduced in full in Exhibit 3.)

After studying the memo, Lee realized that Prentice presented the problem well but that DEI had as yet no solution. He did not think that the meeting at Olympia on June 30 would go too well without a proposed solution in hand. Lee had had extensive experience of using market research data, having worked as a product manager and advertising account supervisor for Unilever in England. He had also taken a "Marketing Research Information Systems" course in his MBA program. Lee felt that his work experience and the course should provide the basis for developing a solution to the problem.

[8]Bureau of Alcohol, Tobacco, and Firearms data.

Exhibit 1
Olympia Brewing Company (A)
Beer and Ale Portion of TGI Questionnaire

BEER & ALE

1. Do you drink them? Yes 41 ☐ 1
   No ☐ 2

IF YOU DO

2. About how often do you drink them?

More than once a DAY	☐ 3
Once a DAY	☐ 4
2 or 3 times a WEEK	☐ 5
Once a WEEK	☐ 6
2 or 3 times a MONTH	☐ 7
Once a MONTH	☐ 8
Less than once a MONTH	☐ 9

3. What type do you drink?

	Most Often	Others
Regular beer	42 ☐	43 ☐ 1
Draft beer	☐	☐ 2
Ale	☐	☐ 3

4. What kind do you drink?

	Most Often	Others
Bottled	(42) ☐	(43) ☐ 4
Canned	☐	☐ 5
Keg	☐	☐ 6

5. Which brands do you drink?

	Most Often	Others
Ballantine	(42) ☐	(43) ☐ 7
Becks	☐	☐ 8
Blatz	☐	☐ 9
Budweiser	☐	☐ 0
Busch Bavarian	☐	☐ x
Carling Black Label	☐	☐ y
Carlsberg	44 ☐	45 ☐ 1
Coors	☐	☐ 2
Dixie	☐	☐ 3
Falstaff	☐	☐ 4
Genesee	☐	☐ 5
Grain Belt	☐	☐ 6
Hamms	☐	☐ 7
Heinekin	☐	☐ 8
Iron City	☐	☐ 9
Jax	☐	☐ 0
Kirin	☐	☐ x
Labatt's Blue	☐	☐ y
Labatt's 50	46 ☐	47 ☐ 1
Lone Star	☐	☐ 2
Lowenbrau	☐	☐ 3
Meister Brau	☐	☐ 4
Michelob	☐	☐ 5
Miller High Life	☐	☐ 6
Miller Lite	☐	☐ 7
Narragansett	☐	☐ 8
National	☐	☐ 9
Old Milwaukee	☐	☐ 0
Old Style	☐	☐ x
Olympia	☐	☐ y
Pabst	48 ☐	49 ☐ 1
Pearl	☐	☐ 2
Pfeiffer	☐	☐ 3
Piels	☐	☐ 4
Rainier	☐	☐ 5
Red Cap Ale	☐	☐ 6
Red, White & Blue	☐	☐ 7
Rheingold	☐	☐ 8
Rolling Rock	☐	☐ 9
Schaefer	☐	☐ 0
Schlitz	☐	☐ x
Schmidts	☐	☐ y
Sterling	50 ☐	51 ☐ 1
Strohs	☐	☐ 2
Tuborg	☐	☐ 3
Utica Club	☐	☐ 4
Wiedeman	☐	☐ 5

BRANDS NOT LISTED ABOVE
(Write in and mark):

________________	☐	☐
________________	(50)	(51)

Exhibit 2
Olympia Brewing Company (A)

Beer Penetration Rates
(proportion of population who drink beer)

Income	*18–24*	*25–34*	*35–44*	*45–54*	*55–64*	*65 and Over*	*All Ages*
Men							
Under $8,000	66.6%	63.3%	54.9%	44.4%	45.6%	37.1%	51.1%
$8,000–11,999	65.6	62.2	64.7	49.4	43.6	36.3	55.9
$12,000–14,999	69.2	73.0	60.3	67.8	55.4	56.7	66.0
$15,000–19,999	65.9	72.8	63.6	64.6	54.5	54.9	64.6
$20,000–24,999	75.1	77.9	73.5	65.3	66.8	42.9	71.3
$25,000 and over	66.7	71.3	75.9	75.7	56.3	52.2	69.6
All incomes	67.4	69.2	66.0	62.2	51.6	41.8	61.4
Women							
Under $8,000	44.1	41.2	32.2	34.1	23.1	11.7	27.6
$8,000–11,999	45.6	40.2	34.4	25.9	30.4	19.6	35.2
$12,000–14,999	52.2	38.5	32.3	29.1	26.7	19.8	35.6
$15,000–19,999	46.0	41.0	35.9	40.5	24.9	18.5	36.7
$20,000–24,999	48.3	46.7	37.7	40.0	33.9	26.5	41.6
$25,000 and over	53.1	46.7	42.2	38.2	34.9	28.0	42.2
All incomes	47.1	41.6	35.8	34.5	26.5	14.9	34.3
All adults							
Under $8,000	53.7	51.2	40.8	37.7	31.0	21.0	36.7
$8,000–11,999	54.6	50.6	49.1	36.6	36.8	28.7	45.1
$12,000–14,999	60.8	57.0	46.2	49.4	42.2	35.0	51.2
$15,000–19,999	56.3	57.0	50.1	52.6	40.5	34.9	50.7
$20,000–24,999	64.2	61.9	56.6	53.2	54.8	35.4	57.6
$25,000 and over	60.4	58.6	59.3	59.5	47.1	38.9	56.7
All incomes	56.9	55.1	50.5	47.9	38.4	26.0	45.1

Source: DEI report to the Olympia Brewing Company based on 1976 TGI Survey

Exhibit 3
Olympia Brewing Company (A)

Fred Prentice's Memorandum, May 1977
1975 Beer Consumption Estimates

Based upon the 1976 Target Group Index Survey

A Reconciliation

On March 2, 1977, I presented to Olympia Brewing Company a set of forecasts and historical estimates of total beer consumption. These estimates were based on beer consumption rates by age, income, and sex derived from the 1976 Target Group Index survey (measuring consumption behavior during calendar 1975). Applying the TGI consumption rates to the population—similarly distributed by age, income, and sex—resulted in an estimate of total 1975 U.S. beer consumption of 50.8 million barrels. This figure drastically underestimates industry data compiled from Treasury Department statistics (Bureau of Alcohol, Tobacco, and Firearms and the IRS), indicating actual beer consumption of about 148 million barrels.

For several months, this discrepancy has gone unexplained and has undermined the credibility of subsequent TGI-based analysis.

This memorandum attempts to summarize the procedure which produced the discrepancy and the factors which likely contributed to it. In the end, I hope to show that the discrepancy must reasonably be attributed to an arbitrary scheme of weights which were used to convert frequency-of-use data measured in the survey to volume-of-consumption data.

Step 1

The first step in the reconciliation is to figure out what answer TGI *should yield*, given that we know the approximate actual consumption of beer in 1975. Since TGI is used to measure behavioral rates for various classes of consumers, there is one single figure which must be reconciled against the "known" consumption: the overall consumption rate of the adult population. Table 1 shows how this key number is computed.

All the calculations in Table 1 represent historical facts, arithmetic conversions, or well-believed behavioral observations. Deducting the volume of malt beverages not incorporated in the TGI drinking rates, and converting into per capita drinking rates of adult drinkers, yields an average *intensity* rate of 11.6 cans per week per adult drinker. This number conflicts drastically with the average drinking intensity of 4.9 cans per week measured by TGI in 1975. What can explain these numbers?

Step 2

The fact is "known" that the average adult beer drinker drinks about 11.6 cans of beer per week. Using the weighting scheme in Table 2, TGI indicates a figure of 4.9 cans per week. Table 2 shows the details of this average drinking intensity.

The 1974 and 1975 TGI surveys are remarkably similar in terms of population weighted numbers of drinkers. Therefore, to avoid overreliance on a single survey, Table 2 utilizes the average 1974–1975 distribution of drinkers by frequency of use. Note that these two rows of figures are taken directly from the published TGI reports and have nothing to do with differing behavior by age, income, or sex. The bottom line of the table shows how the *average intensity* increases from .2 to 4.9 cans/week as the heavier and heavier drinkers are included in the average.

Figure 1 gives another interpretation of the data. If the entire U.S. adult drinking population were lined up by their true drinking intensity, it would be possible to draw a smooth curve rising from the bottom-left-hand to upper-right corners. The average height of the curve would be 11.6 (cans/week), but the exact shape of the curve cannot be determined from the TGI data. Instead, TGI forces us to break the curve into seven discrete pieces, corresponding to the seven allowed frequency-of-use responses. Thus, corresponding

Table 1

Computation of Overall Consumption Rate of Adult Population

1.	148 million barrels of malt beverages consumed in 1975
2.	− 8 million barrels of malt liquor and other beverages not included in the TGI drinking rates
3.	− 5 million barrels of beer drunk by people under 18
4.	= 135 million barrels of beer consumed by the adult population
5.	÷ 147 million adults in the United States in 1975
6.	= .918 barrels per year, per adult
7.	= 5.8 cans per week per adult: 1 can/week = .157 barrels/year; 1 can/day = 7 × 157 barrels = 1.099 barrels/year
8.	÷ 50% adult penetration rate
9.	= 11.6 cans/week per adult drinker

Table 2

Beer Drinkers by Frequency of Use
(Population Weighted, 000)

	>1/Mo.	*1/Mo.*	*2–3/Mo.*	*1/Wk.*	*2–3/Wk.*	*1/Day*	*>1/Day*	*Total*
(1) 1975 survey	11,454	5,782	12,969	9,239	16,712	6,608	4,955	67,719
(2) 1974 survey	9,354	5,139	11,991	9,819	17,576	7,176	6,194	67,249
(3) Average 1974–1975	10,404	5,460	12,480	9,529	17,144	6,892	5,575	67,484
(4) Percentage of total drinkers	15.4%	8.1%	18.5%	14.1%	25.4%	10.2%	8.3%	100%
(5) Cumulative drinkers	10,404	15,864	28,344	37,873	55,017	61,909	67,484	
(6) Volume weight[1] (cans/week)	.2	.5	1	2	6	9	23	
(7) Total volume[2]	2,081	2,730	12,480	19,058	102,864	62,028	128,225	
(8) Cumulative total volume	2,081	4,811	17,291	36,349	139,213	201,241	329,466	
(9) Cumulative average total[3] (cans/week)	0.2	0.3	0.6	1.0	2.5	3.2	4.9	

[1]This was the weighting scheme used to equate frequency with volume.
[2](7) = (5) × (6).
[3](9) = (8) ÷ (5).

Figure 1

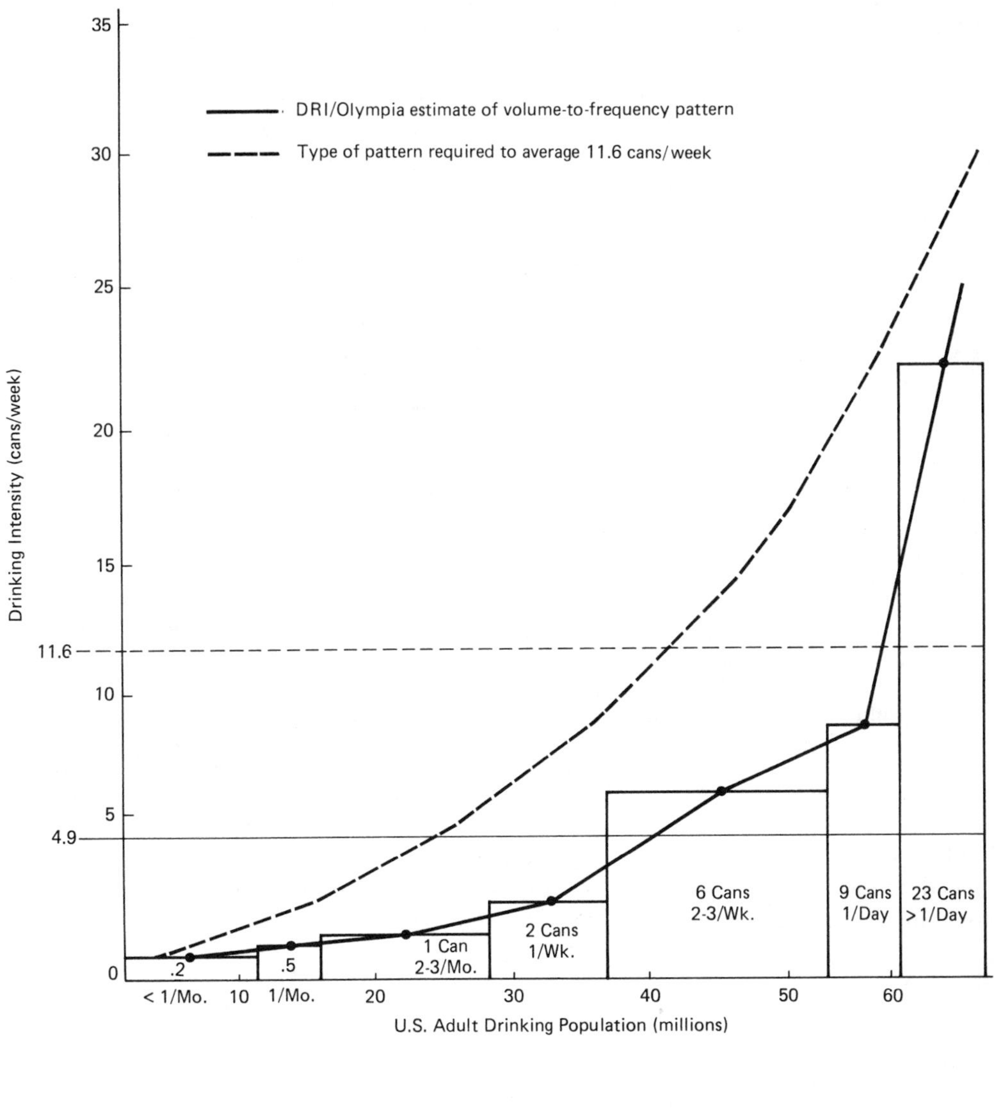

to any arbitrary scheme converting frequency to volume, we can draw a histogram which approximates a smooth curve. Figure 1 contains the histogram for the weighting scheme actually used. But this scheme produces an average intensity of 4.9 (based on the average 1974–1975 frequency distribution) and must therefore be an unrealistic scheme. In fact, any scheme that hopes to estimate actual 1975 beer consumption accurately must contain weights of more than double the magnitude of the current scheme!

The obvious question is: What is the true shape of the intensity profile in Figure 1? And how can it be measured? DEI proposes to answer these questions by drawing on the consumer expenditure survey which is now available on the DEI computer. This survey contains dollar expenditures on beer for the entire survey sample. It can therefore be used to construct a continuous profile of drinking intensity across the sample. Once this line is constructed, the proper discrete weighting scheme can be extracted from Figure 1.

Exhibit 4
Olympia Brewing Company (A)

Data Economics, Inc.

·DEI provided four basic services to its clients:

1. An economic data base of over 4 million time series.
2. Computerized models of the world economies and specific industries.
3. Time-shared software capabilities to link specific company data (e.g., sales) to outside economic variables.
4. Consulting support to facilitate a client's understanding of the economic environment and how the latter affected business decisions.

Since its founding in 1968, DEI had experienced rapid growth, with revenues increasing by about 50% each year. Its 1976 revenues were $17 million and 1977 revenues were expected to be about $24 million. At the beginning of 1977, DEI had about 500 clients including 60 of the top 100 U.S. industrial corporations. DEI was headquartered in Lexington, Massachusetts, with regional offices in New York; Chicago; Washington, D.C.; San Francisco; Pittsburgh; Houston; Toronto, and Brussels. DEI had over 400 employees of which 280 were full-time professional economists and consultants.

DEI's services were based on a number of large-scale econometric models. These models covered:

- U.S. economy
- Regional economics
- Consumer products
- Agriculture sector
- Fertilizer industry
- Steel industry
- Automobile industry
- Petrochemical industry
- Energy sector
- Transportation industry
- Forest products industry
- Paper and pulp industry
- Banking industry
- Insurance industry
- Materials and labor inflation rates
- Corporate financial analysis
- Canadian economy
- European economy
- Japanese economy
- Foreign currency

These models were all accessible on the DEI time-shared computer and were available in service packages similar to the consumer products service, packages of models, forecasts, data bases, software, and consulting support.

Olympia Brewing Company (B)

Data Economics, Inc. (DEI), an economic consulting company, had undertaken a market forecast study for the Olympia Brewing Company.[1] As part of that study, DEI needed market research data on current beer consumption for age-income-sex categories of consumers. The data which DEI had planned to use, the Target Group Index, had turned out to seriously underreport current beer consumption. Without accurate current data, DEI would not be able to forecast future consumption. The DEI team included Fred Prentice, a senior consultant in DEI's San Francisco office, and Andrew Lee, a member of the consumer group at DEI's headquarters in Lexington, Massachusetts. On June 30, DEI staff members were due to meet Olympia to present their recommendations for solving the consumption data problem.

On May 23, 1977, Lee reviewed the alternatives that he and other DEI executives had debated as a solution to the problem of the inadequate beer consumption data. Lee had personally concluded that DEI would have to obtain additional data. Both cost and time were major obstacles. DEI would have to absorb the cost, and 5 months of the 12-month contract with Olympia were already gone.

ALTERNATIVE A: NEW PHONE SURVEY

One obvious alternative was to conduct a fresh survey with questions about volume of consumption. However, DEI's age-income forecasting approach for consumer products made separate forecasts for each of 36 age-income groups in a 6 × 6 matrix [see Exhibit 2, (A) case]. Thus a very large total sample size would be required to provide adequate representation in each of the 36 cells—100 per cell was probably the minimum. Also, since men and women had markedly different beer consumption habits, the age-income forecast would

[1]See Olympia Brewing Company (A).

have to be done separately for each one. Thus, a minimum of 7,200 responses would be needed.

Lee thought that a telephone survey would be adequate to obtain the kind of information needed. However, because of the need to control for age, income, and sex, far more than 7,200 contacts would have to be made. At a total cost of the order of $25,000, this alternative seemed prohibitively expensive. Also Lee was concerned about whether or not people contacted at random would be willing to reveal their income over the phone.

ALTERNATIVE B: A DIARY PANEL

Lee was aware that a few market research companies collected detailed purchase and consumption data on some product categories on a regular basis. These were the "diary panel" services, where respondents maintained a detailed diary of expenditure and usage. The demographic characteristics of these respondents and their families were, of course, also recorded. The two main sources of such diaries were MRCA (Market Research Corporation of America) and NPD Research, Inc. (formerly National Purchase Diary Panel, Inc.). Unfortunately, neither included beer in their diaries.

MRCA conducted a regular National Household Menu Census, but this covered food items only. They also had a "textile panel" recording purchase and usage of clothing and other textile products.

NPD had a general diary service recording 50 categories of supermarket items. They also had three special panels recording purchases/usage of textiles, toys, and restaurants.

Advertisers would typically pay MRCA or NPD between $20,000 and $50,000 to subscribe to a product category. The president of NPD, Tod Johnson, had once explained to Lee that running a diary was a very expensive and difficult operation. Member "fatigue" was a major problem, and members had to be kept motivated. For example, NPD sent birthday cards to everyone in a panel member's family.

It did not seem practical for the DEI project to add a beer category to one of the diary services. First, the process would take several months. Second, the diary companies would require several companies to subscribe before they would add a category.

ALTERNATIVE C: SURVEY OF A PANEL

While MRCA and NPD maintained diary panels to collect specific data on a regular basis, some other market research companies maintained general-purpose panels for use in custom studies on an irregular basis. Market Facts, Inc., and National Family Opinion were the two leading companies that offered such a service.

The Market Facts Panel

Market Facts maintained a pool of about 60,000 "panelists." These were households that had agreed in advance to be available to act as survey respondents. Market Facts recorded and kept current the demographic characteristics of the panelists and their families. These characteristics included geographic location, population density of place of residence, type of dwelling unit, ownership of residence, household income, education level, occupation, employment status, household size, age, and marital status.

Since any one study used fewer than the total 60,000 panel households, the sample (e.g., 10,000 households) for that study could be drawn to achieve a particular distribution along one or more of the recorded demographic characteristics. Usually the sample would be drawn to achieve a distribution equivalent to the national one, for those characteristics (up to five) most critical for the study in question.

Advantages and Disadvantages of Panels

A criticism voiced by many market research users and suppliers was that the people who agreed to join panels were atypical of the general population. A specific problem was the well-known difficulty of recruiting young single persons.

Lee thought that this would be a major problem for a beer study were it not for the fact that they also had the TGI data. The TGI survey seemed to have reasonable representation of young singles of both sexes. The problem [see (A) case] was that it asked about frequency not volume. However, it seemed that if there was some way of relating a new panel-based survey to the TGI survey, DEI would be able to get the best of both worlds—accurate volume data and a representative sample.

THE DECISION TO USE MARKET FACTS

Lee had met Market Facts executives in exploring how DEI and a market research company might be able to collaborate. He thought that this was a perfect opportunity for a cooperative effort, and he arranged to visit Omar Bendikas, a vice president at Market Facts in charge of their panel operation.

On May 25, Lee met with Bendikas at Market Facts' Chicago head office. They were able to conclude that it would be possible to conduct the necessary survey at a very low cost, and they developed a research design. At the June 30 meeting at Olympia, Lee presented the proposed design. The Olympia executives Tom Black, Ed Ojdana, and Dennis Murphy agreed that DEI should proceed. On July 13, Ojdana visited DEI's offices in Lexington, Massachusetts, and was able to approve the questionnaire for mailout. The questionnaire had been designed between June 30 and July 13 by Lee in conjunction with Market Facts, Fred Prentice, Jay Levine, and John McNeil. McNeil had recently joined DEI as a senior consultant. He was formerly professor of marketing at the Cornell Graduate School of Business and Public Administration. McNeil held a Ph. D. degree in marketing from Purdue University.

THE MARKET FACTS SURVEY

The Research Design

It was realized that only a small amount of information was needed. This allowed the study to use Market Facts' "Data-Gage" technique. Each month Market Facts sent a single mailing to several thousand panel members. Each single mailing contained a small number of different short questionnaires. These questionnaires were each for different studies. However, the "Data-Gage" service grouped these questionnaires in the mailing to save mail and administration costs. The "Data-Gage" questionnaires were the size of computer keypunch cards. Both sides could be used. The "Data-Gage" approach cost much less per mailing than did an individual mailing of a questionnaire. An individually mailed questionnaire could be up to four 8″ × 11″ pages. However, it would have cost about three times as much per mailing.

The Questionnaire

The objective of the Market Facts survey was to provide volume information that would be related to the frequency information in the

TGI survey. Thus, the questionnaire asked two questions. The first question repeated the TGI frequency question of "About how often do you drink beer or ale?". The second question asked "How many beers did you drink yesterday?". The question also distinguished between beer bought from a store and that bought at bars and restaurants. In addition, there was a third set of questions on brands. Again the TGI question was repeated, here on the brands drunk "most often," and calibrated by a question on the brands drunk yesterday.

The questionnaire had instructions on one side of the card and questions on the other (reproduced in Exhibit 1).

The Sample

As described earlier, it was decided that the TGI survey was a correct representation of the distribution by demographic characteristics of the *incidence* and *frequency* of drinking. Since the objective of the survey was to calibrate *volume* with stated frequency, it was not necessary to select a sample representative of the national distribution of demographic characteristics. Instead, the sample was drawn to achieve

> the *national* distribution by census region and an *even* distribution by income category.

Also, the questionnaire card asked the panel member to give the card to the youngest household member of legal drinking age. Half the cards specified the youngest male, and half the youngest female.

Thus, the sample did not "represent" the U.S. market. Instead, it was designed to maximize the number of young respondents while controlling for region, income, and sex. This was because DEI and Olympia suspected that, within a frequency category, younger persons would drink a greater volume.

A sample size of 13,000 was chosen. Since two-thirds of men and one-third of women drank beer at all, and the Market Facts panel households averaged about two adults each with, on average, more women adults than men, it was estimated that about half the 13,000 households would have eligible beer drinkers. In fact, 5,621 usable replies were received, of whom 3,278 were from men and 2,343 from women.

The assumption that younger drinkers drank more, within a frequency category, seemed supported by the results (Exhibit 2).

The Mailing Procedure

Since it was known that the level of beer consumption varied by the day of the week, there were seven separate mailings of the questionnaire on six consecutive days. To handle the fact that there was no mail delivery on Sundays, one batch of the questionnaires was put in sealed envelopes with instructions to open and answer on Sunday. An alternative would have been to put every questionnaire in a sealed envelope, with instructions to open on a particular day. This was not done to save money.

The results confirmed that there was a strong day-of-week effect:

To correct for the day-of-week effect, it was necessary to develop a weight for each respondent to convert his or her actual consumption on a particular day of the week to one averaged over the entire week. Lee developed the following procedures for Market Facts to use in reweighting each respondent's consumption:

> Market Facts should first calculate an average beers per day, for each sex, for the week overall. This could not be done by grouping all male (or female) respondents and simply averaging over all seven days, because the sample sizes were different for each day. Instead the average had to be calculated for each day separately, as in

Table 1

Day	Index of Average Number of Beers		Number of Respondents		
	Males	*Females*	*Males*	*Females*	*Total*
Sunday	112	122	495	330	825
Monday	80	65	291	237	528
Tuesday	77	110	447	488	895
Wednesday	89	91	405	325	730
Thursday	79	96	453	302	755
Friday	119	84	577	291	868
Saturday	143	133	610	370	980

Table 1; then the week average should be obtained by averaging over the seven-day averages.

An index for the day of week would then be calculated by dividing a given day's average by the overall average. These are shown in Table 1.

Each day-of-week's index should then be converted to its reciprocal and divided by 100 (e.g., the males Saturday index of 143 became .70) to give the weight to apply to a particular respondent.

This weight should then be applied to a respondent's actual reported consumption (e.g., for a Saturday male respondent who reported 5 beers, his weighted consumption would be 5 × .70 = 3.50).

These reweightings would then allow the respondents to be analyzed in an age-income-sex framework, without having to worry about the day-of-week effect.

THE RESULTS

The results confirmed that the assumed volume weights originally assigned by DEI and Olympia to the TGI frequency responses were too low, as shown in Table 2. In addition, there

Table 2

Index of average beers per day[1]

TGI Frequency Category	*No. of Drinkers (millions)*	*Original Estimate All Adults*	*New Estimates*		
			All Adults	*Males*	*Females*
More than once a day	4.955	383	666	707	555
Once a day	6.608	150	362	384	321
2 or 3 times a week	16.712	100[a]	271	283	247
Once a week	9.239	34	140	145	127
2 or 3 times a month	12.969	16	85	87	78
Once a month	5.782	8	27	21	40
Less than once a month	11.454	3	12	12	12
Total	67.719				

[1]Table 2 indices are disguised.

[a]All indices calculated from this base of 100.

was not a single set of numbers to calibrate frequency to volume. Instead, the required calibration varied by both sex and age. For example, while the average volume index was 136 for males and 114 for females for the "once-a-day" frequency category, this figure ranged from 168 for "males 18–24 years" to 82 for "females 65 years and over" (see Exhibit 2).[2]

The overall average number for all drinkers was 11.4 beers per week. However, since the Market Facts survey was conducted in August, a high month for beer consumption, the 11.4 figure was rescaled to 10.3 on an annualized basis, from a seasonal index used by Olympia. This compared very favorably with the 11.6 target figure calculated from industry total sales volume. It was also a great improvement over the 4.9 beers per week calculated from the Target Group Index data. The Market Facts survey also showed that heavy drinkers were even more important than Olympia had suspected.

Ed Ojdana at Olympia was satisfied that they now had reasonable current consumption data on which to base forecasts. Thus, in October 1977, DEI were ready to provide the first set of forecasts of the U.S. beer market. The objectives of this first set were to forecast.

total U.S. beer consumption for each year to 1990 and

beer consumption in each of the 72 age-income-sex "cells" of the DEI age-income model.

[2]The indices in Exhibit 2 and Table 2 are not to the same base, in order to protect the confidentiality of this data.

The reason for this age-income-sex approach was twofold. DEI believed that a better total U.S. forecast could be obtained by forecasting consumption in each age-income-sex cell separately and then summing up the 72 cells. This was because consumption patterns were different in each age-income-sex cell. This differing pattern had been demonstrated by the Target Group Index data on the *incidence* and *frequency* of beer drinking [see Exhibit 2 of (A) case for incidence pattern by age-income-sex cell]. The Market Facts survey now confirmed that the *volume* of beer drinking also varied by age, income and sex (see Exhibit 2 of this case for average volume by age and sex).

The second reason for the age-income-sex approach was a strategic one. Not only did different age-income-sex groups have different consumption patterns, but they had different brand and product type preferences. For example, Olympia knew that their light beer appealed more to younger, affluent drinkers and more to women than to other types of beer. The Olympia brand overall did better with younger more affluent drinkers. If Olympia could forecast the future distribution of beer consumption volume by age-income-sex groups, they would be better able to allocate their brand promotion and product development efforts.

With these objectives in mind, DEI set out to prepare a forecast. John McNeil had taken over consulting responsibility for the Olympia project from Fred Prentice, who had left DEI to start his own consulting business.

Exhibit 1

Olympia Brewing Company (B)

The Market Facts Questionnaire

PLEASE READ OTHER SIDE FIRST

1. About how often do you drink beer or ale?

More than once a DAY	☐ 1	(18)
Once a DAY	☐ 2	
2 or 3 times a WEEK	☐ 3	
Once a WEEK	☐ 4	
2 or 3 times a MONTH	☐ 5	
Once a MONTH	☐ 6	
Less than once a MONTH	☐ 7	

2. How many beers did you drink yesterday (Count each 12 ounces as one beer)?

	Beers Bought From Store by You or Someone Else		Beers bought Elsewhere bar, restaurant, etc.	
None	☐ 0	(19)	☐ 0	(21)
1	☐ 1		☐ 1	
2	☐ 2		☐ 2	
3	☐ 3		☐ 3	
4	☐ 4		☐ 4	
5	☐ 5		☐ 5	
6	☐ 6		☐ 6	
7	☐ 7		☐ 7	
8	☐ 8		☐ 8	
9 or 10	☐ 9		☐ 9	
11 to 15	☐ 1	(20)	☐ 1	(22)
16 to 20	☐ 2		☐ 2	
More than 20 ...	☐ 3		☐ 3	

3. Below please write in the brand names of beer that you drink. Be sure to give the complete brand name such as "Miller Lite" or "Miller High Life" not just "Miller".

a. Brand you drink most often:

____

b. Other brands you drink:

____

____

c. Brand(s) you drunk YESTERDAY (next to each brand write the number of beers you drank)

	How Many
____________	______
____________	______

(J191)-I

Dear Panel Member,

Please give this card to the youngest female of LEGAL drinking age who drinks beer. If there is no female beer drinker, have the youngest male beer drinker answer my questions.

TO THE PERSON ANSWERING THIS CARD:

This survey is about beer drinking. (It does not include malt liquor.) To make it easier, I want you to answer the questions just for YESTERDAY. First, before answering the questions, write in your age and sex, and circle the day of the week TODAY.

AGE: ______ (14–15) Sex: Male 1 Female 2 (16)

Today is: Mon 1 Tues 2 Wed 3 Thurs 4 Fri 5 Sat 6 Sun 7 (17)

Exhibit 2
Olympia Brewing Company (B)

Frequency-to-Volume Calibration Table
(Indices only)[1]

			Males						Females					
Frequency	*All Males*	*All Females*	*18–24*	*25–34*	*35–44*	*45–54*	*55–64*	*≥65*	*18–24*	*25–34*	*35–44*	*45–54*	*55–64*	*≥65*
More than once a day	250 (405) 98.4%	196 (46) 97.6%	277 (63)	278 (141)	256 (69)	219 (52)	180 (37)	184 (33)	226 (5)	228 (12)	198 (8)	181 (11)	245 (5)	106 (6)
Once a day	136 (358) 91.9%	114 (95) 90.0%	168 (75)	143 (101)	107 (67)	151 (49)	100 (35)	103 (21)	135 (11)	109 (21)	110 (19)	153 (12)	96 (16)	82 (12)
2 or 3 times a week	100[a] (965) 68.2%	87 (379) 64.8%	108 (277)	108 (314)	95 (170)	106 (83)	70 (67)	49 (41)	87 (117)	87 (107)	95 (56)	73 (56)	82[b] (27)	67 (12)
Once a week	51 (395) 40.5%	45 (260) 35.1%	52 (90)	58 (139)	34 (66)	66 (42)	38 (33)	38 (14)	72 (100)	62[a] (77)	42 (39)	58[b] (13)	25[b] (19)	19 (9)
2 or 3 times a month	31 (492) 26.3%	28 (509) 23.5%	33 (107)	40 (150)	15 (99)	25 (56)	31 (45)	38 (25)	30 (171)	27 (177)	12 (64)	33[b] (43)	24 (27)	37 (20)
Once a month	7 (167) 11.3%	14 (221) 12.9%	7 (44)	7 (54)	2 (30)	8 (18)	14 (15)	12 (4)	12 (64)	10 (74)	4 (33)	3 (19)	12[b] (16)	29 (11)
Less than once a month	4 (507) 6.2%	4 (842) 4.4%	7 (98)	3 (152)	3 (91)	5 (54)	4 (58)	3 (41)	2 (194)	5 (281)	2 (105)	9 (84)	1 (84)	7 (71)

[1]Key:
250 = Average number of beers yesterday.
(405) = number of respondents.
98.4% = Percentage drinking yesterday.
[a]All indices from this base of 100.
[b]Consumption numbers in these cells have been "smoothed" to reflect relationships with surrounding numbers.

Ocean Spray Cranberries, Inc. (A)

In December 1971, the research team from Appel, Haley, and Fouriezos, Inc., under the direction of Russell Haley, presented the results of a survey among 200 cranberry sauce users to Jerry Melvin, brand manager of Ocean Spray's cranberry sauce products, and Ken Witham, manager of marketing research at Ocean Spray. Brand management had requested the study to find ways of repositioning its cranberry sauce, which had experienced no sales growth in the late 1960s and had actually registered a 6% sales decline in fiscal 1970. The research team had completed a pilot study which was to be the basis for an expanded survey of consumers' product attitudes, personality patterns, and life-style characteristics relevant to canned cranberry sauce and cranberry jelly. The management group had requested the presentation as an interim review of the project, which had resulted in expenditures of about one-third of its alloted budget.

THE COMPANY AND THE CRANBERRY INDUSTRY

Practically all processing and marketing of cranberries[1] have in recent years been made by various cooperatives. The sales of fresh cranberries were lower than in the 1950s and early 1960s, whereas the processed products had almost doubled their sales. However, the yield per acre increased faster than the amount which could be marketed profitably, so the industry became confronted with a significant surplus problem. The surplus was by 1968 serious enough to cause growers to resort to the Agriculture Marketing Agreement Act of 1937.[2] The Cranberry Marketing Act of 1968 stipulated that no new acreage was to be developed over the next six years. Some 87% of

[1]Cranberry is, according to *Webster's New World Dictionary*, "a firm, sour, edible red berry, the fruit of any of several trailing evergreen shrubs of the heath family."

[2]Under this act growers can regulate and control the size of an agricultural crop if the federal government and more than two-thirds of the growers by number and tonnage agree to a plan for restriction.

all growers voted in favor of the order, making it binding on all cranberry growers.

In the early 1970s, 99% of the industry's sales of cranberries had been made by various cooperatives. In 1970 production was slightly above 2 million barrels. Around 370,000 barrels went to fresh sales and 1,400,000 barrels to processing. The difference between production and utilization represents economic abandonment. The "set-aside" amounted in 1970 to more than 40 million pounds. Between 1965 and 1970, U.S. production and utilization (i.e., fresh sales and processed) of cranberries developed as follows:

	1965	*1966*	*1967*	*1968*	*1969*	*1970*
Production (000 bbl.)[1]	1,437	1,599	1,404	1,468	1,823	2,037
Utilized (000 bbl.)	1,423	1,578	1,313	1,413	1,760	1,845
Average price received by growers ($/bbl.)[2]	$15.60	$15.60	$15.50	$16.50	$16.30	$12.90

[1] 1 barrel = 100 pounds.
[2] Price per barrel is based on utilized cranberries.
Source: Annual reports of Crop Reporting Board, Statistical Reporting Service, USDA.

The cooperatively owned Ocean Spray Cranberries, Inc., of South Hanson, Massachusetts (OSC) dominated cranberry growing, processing, and distribution in the United States. Its sales volume had developed as follows:

	Fiscal Years Ending in August					
	1965	*1966*	*1967*	*1968*	*1969*	*1970*
OSC sales (000 bbl.)	967	1,036	1,054	1,145	1,265	1,197
OSC sales (millions)	$44.4	$50.9	$55.4	$62.5	$70.8	$71.4

Source: Company annual reports.

As a growers' cooperative, OSC was tax exempted as long as 95% or more of its business was cranberry based. Year-end operating profits were determined by deducting from sales all manufacturing, marketing, administrative and other expenses; advances on berries delivered by the growers; and any retained earnings. Total net proceeds (equivalent to operating profits before taxes) were then divided by the number of barrels of cranberries received by OSC, and the resulting average pool price was used to pay each member-grower on the basis of cranberries delivered to OSC. Operating figures from 1963 through 1970 are listed in Exhibit 1.

OSC was the largest cooperative and had operations in all the principal growing areas of North America: Massachusetts, New Jersey, Wisconsin, Washington, Oregon, British Columbia, and Nova Scotia. Over 800 growers were members of the OSC cooperative in 1971, and there was very little year-to-year change in that number.

The Ocean Spray brand name had been in use since the 1920s for canned cranberry products. Product development activities over the years expanded the retail line of Ocean Spray cranberry products to include the following as of late 1970:

Fresh cranberries
Jellied cranberry sauce
Whole-berry cranberry sauce

Deluxe cranberry-raspberry sauce	Grape-berry juice drink
Cranberry juice cocktail	Low-calorie cranberry products
Cranberry-orange relish	Institutional cranberry products
Cranapple drink	Industrial cranberry products
Cranprune juice drink	

Operations were divided among four divisions: Food Service, Government and Industrial, International, and Retail. The retail operations accounted for the major part of OSC's total sales. Brand managers were responsible for retail marketing. Exhibit 2 shows the marketing organization.

Many of the OSC products enjoyed good retail distribution. The company used 85 food brokers to contact the retailers. These brokers were assigned all OSC retail products in their areas, which could be quite large. There was, for example, only one broker for New England. Twelve OSC field salesmen functioned mainly as regional managers, supervising the activities of the brokers.

OSC spent substantial monies in the advertising and sales promotion of its products. The promotional budget included "early shipping allowances" well in advance of Thanksgiving, in-store display allowances, couponing and special price-margin features for all products, and local food store advertising programs. OSC's own advertising for all brands exceeded $5 million annually between 1968 and 1970. Well above 75% of this advertising supported cranberry juice cocktail and cranapple juice drink. Most consumer advertising was directed through network television.

OSC products sold at significantly higher prices than did those of competitive brands at both retail and wholesale level. A price differential of 10 to 15% was quite common. Competition was mainly from private labels. The OSC president had the view that the "competitive pressure at the retail level being generated by private store-label merchandise is steadily increasing and represents a serious challenge in all of our current marketing strategies."

New product opportunities in old or new product categories were pursued actively by OSC. During fiscal 1970 two new sauce products (cranberry-raspberry sauce and a deluxe cranberry sauce) were being tested as well as a jellied form of applesauce. The number of tested but rejected product ideas from earlier decades was considerable.

OSC had a strong position in the Canadian market and its products were also sold in the United Kingdom and West Germany. Plans were being made to penetrate the Swedish and Dutch export markets.

MARKETING RESEARCH AT OSC

The marketing research department consisted of one manager, Ken Witham, and one secretarial assistant. Witham spent considerable time supervising or monitoring field tests of new marketing programs. These tests mostly dealt with new products, but sometimes special research projects were undertaken to measure the effectiveness of new advertising or promotional vehicles and messages for mature products. Usually, new product tests required most of Witham's attention. The department was also involved in preparing sales analyses and quarterly forecasts for financial planning and budgeting.

Witham could suggest new marketing research projects, but normally the brand managers took such initiatives. They had also to seek approval for the research budget. In the definition and planning stages of a project, Witham's role was mainly an advisory one. He would make comments on how the new project related to previous research and the costs and benefits of different research approaches and techniques. He would also be in charge of establishing and maintaining contacts with outside suppliers of marketing research. Outside firms were used in the data collection and analytical phases of special projects, and Witham participated in the interpretation phases of each study with the brand managers and representatives of the research supplier.

In a typical year there were 5 to 10 projects with a total budget of around $150,000. This sum did not include salaries, which amounted to around $30,000. The advertising agencies responsible for various product groups would occasionally undertake marketing research in connection with their handling of OSC accounts.

Apart from these research efforts OSC also bought syndicated marketing information. OSC management received Nielsen Index reports bimonthly on all retailed cranberry products. These reports contained information gathered by retail store audits about price, shelf position, in-store promotion, and estimated sales volume of OSC and competing brands. Monthly SAMI reports on warehouse withdrawals were purchased for the sauce products during the main selling season. For beverage products only, a third syndicated data base was purchased from the operators of the MRCA National Consumer Panel, a diary-based service reporting within household purchasing activities over continuous time periods for a variety of consumer products. Occasionally, OSC would buy other syndicated information, for example, the MRCA National Household Menu Census. In a typical year, OSC spent approximately $200,000 for syndicated marketing information.

Marketing of OSC Cranberry Sauce

Industry sales of cranberry sauce totaled about 6 million cases (1 case = 24 pounds) annually. It had been learned from previous research that more than 90% of all U.S. households consumed some cranberry sauce during a year. A large consumer segment with very high usage consisted of relatively old people. For most consumers cranberry sauce was purchased and used a couple of times a year. The four months from October to January accounted for 60% of retail sales.

OSC's sauce was sold in two forms—whole berry and jellied. A cranberry-raspberry sauce and a deluxe sauce were in test markets during the fall of 1970. Retail sales and marketing expenditures for the OSC jelly and whole-berry sauce were as follows (year ending August 31):

Jelly and Whole Berry	*1965*	*1966*	*1967*	*1968*	*1969*	*1970*
Retail unit sales (million cases)[1]	4.25	4.53	4.54	4.64	4.55	4.25
Advertising (000)[2]	$240	$226	$214	—	—	$ 72
Promotion (000)	446	473	312	$182	$344	605
Total	$686	$699	$526	$182	$344	$677

[1]A. C. Nielsen
[2]Company records.

The overall marketing strategy for sauce during the latter half of the 1960s was characterized as a milking strategy. Marketing support was curtailed sharply in 1964 for two reasons. First, the brand had not responded to previous advertising, and, second, cutbacks were necessary to fund introduction of the juice product and still maintain grower returns. The only noticeable advertising efforts for sauce during this period were an outdoor campaign in 1965–1967 and newspaper supplement ads at Easter in 1970.

OSC retailed 8-ounce and 1-pound packages at a higher price than competitors. A retail price of around 27¢ was common for the 1-pound can. Other brands, if any, were usually sold at 3 to 7¢ less per can. It was difficult to estimate the retail markup on sauce, because retailers set price drastically different dependent on whether or not the sauce was in season or out of season. During off season, a common retail markup was 18%. However, many retailers used sauce as a "loss leader" during the peak season. One New York retailer had sold the OSC sauce for 21¢ to those customers who purchased more than $5 worth of other goods.

The brand manager for sauce worked with the sales division in planning in-store promotion activities. Broker commissions varied between 3 and 5% based on OSC factory prices, depending on volume generated in the broker's market. Management was satisfied with the results obtained by the brokers during the major season, but less so regarding off-season activities.

Limited couponing was used before or after the main fall season, but brand management could not find economic justification for using coupons in connection with peak selling seasons. However, some food retailers included coupons for OSC sauce in their newspaper ads during the major selling season.

Despite some losses to private labels, OSC still had a dominant position in cranberry sauce. Its brand name was truly a household name. No other manufacturer of sauce had a national market. The competitors relied almost entirely on selling their cranberry sauce under private labels. Many fruit or vegetable cooperatives as well as other manufacturers having a canning operation were active during the main season. On an annual basis, private labels accounted for around 26% of the sauce volume in 1970–1971, and this share had been increasing very slowly.

OSC did participate in cranberry private-label business to a very limited extent in the 1960s. No concerted effort was made to gain such business. In fiscal 1970, OSC sold around 100,000 cases of sauce under private labels, which represented an addition to regular sauce sales of around 2%. OSC usually received 2–4¢ less for the 1-pound can of sauce when sold as private label. This was offset by savings in distribution and production costs (another sauce formula was used). The private-label business was not the responsibility of the OSC sauce brand manager although he was kept informed aboout it.

OSC sold three times more jelly than whole-berry sauce. This ratio had been very stable during the 1960s. However, the ratio was about 4 to 1 in New England and 2 to 1 in California. The brand manager had so far not found any good explanation for the regional differences. He knew, however, that the whole-berry sauce was used relatively more often as an ingredient in preparing a meal. The two products were always advertised and promoted jointly. It was felt that management did not have a clear indication as to how the marketing of the two variants could be differentiated beneficially.

Previous Market Research for Sauce

While handling the OSC sauce and drink accounts, the McCann-Erickson advertising agency undertook in 1962 an "Exploratory Motivation Survey of Consumer Attitudes Toward Cranberries." This study followed a general format which McCann-Erickson called "MARPLAN '62." The study had a great impact on OSC management, and it was often referred to or reviewed in the following years.

The MARPLAN study found that cranberry sauce was tradition bound, almost synonymous with Thanksgiving and turkey. It indicated that this aspect of the image was not likely to change. The rejection of cranberry sauce by nonusers who have tried it seemed to be a fairly permanent factor. Close analysis of the verbatims and ratings suggested that rejection was based primarily on taste.

It seemed unlikely that nonusers could be taught to like cranberries by advertising. The study concluded that, if advertising were to be used, the effort would have to be substantial. Advertising should be aimed at overcoming the force of habits and traditional views among year-round users and in-season-only users rather than persuading rejecters to become triers again. However, OSC management opted for the implicit alternative of minimal advertising and promotional expenditures.

In 1967 OSC had purchased information from the MRCA National Household Menu Census. The survey gave demographic data on sauce users and nonusers. When the results of the 1967 study were compared with those of MARPLAN '62, a shift in the age distribution of the sauce franchise to a reduction in the annual usage in younger age groups was apparent.

Incidence of cranberry sauce usage in preceding 12-month period

Age of Female Head of Household	*1962 MARPLAN*[1] *(n = 2,027)*	*1967 MRCA*[2] *(n = 4,000)*
Under 25	68%	59%
25–34	85	75
35–44	91	99
45–54	88	95
55+	83	81
Average	85	85

[1]Based on claimed usage.
[2]Special survey conducted among members of the MRCA National Consumer Panel.

MARPLAN '62 and the Menu Census also revealed that, even though many households used sauce with chicken servings, sauce was used only in connection with 6% of all chicken servings. In the brand manager's eyes this was an opportunity for growth. Another possibility for growth read from these reports was the fact that, if the "seasonal" users could be stimulated to buy one additional can, this would represent around 25% increase in total volume.

Apart from reports from the sales organization, the brand manager received Nielsen retail audit reports and SAMI warehouse shipment figures during the peak sales season. These standardized reports were helpful for short-term marketing planning and control. However, it was equally clear that they were not particularly designed to be used in analyzing and developing long-term strategy for OSC's cranberry sauce.

Developments During 1969–1971

Before joining OSC as a brand manager in 1969, Jack Walsh had worked with the General Foods Company. There he had been witness to many attempts to increase sales and/or market share of commodity-like food products. These attempts centered primarily on advertising, positioning, and occasionally product quality, since changing other marketing variables such as price or distribution was deemed unprofitable. According to Walsh, the management and marketing process dealt with trying to identify large consumer groups which seemed to be similar to medium- or heavy-user groups. If one group of consumers only differed markedly as to the amount consumed of a certain product when compared with another group, then it ought to be possible to "convert" this group of lighter users to a group of heavier users.

A central question in these studies was choosing which specific consumer characteristics to measure. In addition to traditional measures of product usage—demographic and socioeconomic characteristics—some market segmentation studies had begun experimentation with newer measures of consumers' lifestyles, their attitudes toward a product class, and their beliefs about the kinds of benefits a product should provide. Although studies of consumers' attitudes and product usage patterns were not new, it became fashionable to refer to the more recent research efforts as psychographic studies. Whereas demographics referred to the characteristics of an individual or a population in terms of its age, sex, and location, psychographics included any of a range of more or less systematic measures of a consumer's (or a group's) personality as it related to the scenarios of purchase and consumption of a given product category.

Jack Walsh's first task was brand management of the cranberry cocktail and sauce businesses. He saw three ways in which to increase sauce sales and profits: (1) gain in market share by selling part of production under private label, (2) by more aggressive pricing and merchandising of the OSC sauce, or (3) expansion of sauce demand by stimulating heavier usage among various consumer segments. Various opinions were held by the members of the OSC management as to which was the best way to go and, above all, whether or not any offensive marketing action was likely to help OSC's position in the market for cranberry sauce. Walsh himself argued that there were opportunities to expand the sauce market. "We have a premium brand of an inexpensive food product which two out of every three U.S. households buy once or twice a year. The marketing challenge is to raise this to twice or three times a year."

Possible reasons for infrequent usage of sauce came easily to mind, and the following explanations were popular among OSC managers: "Many consumers consider cranberry sauce as a tradition strictly connected with the Thanksgiving and Christmas holidays and the turkey meal;" "many find it inconvenient to serve;" and "many housewives don't buy it more often because some family members don't like the taste."

Management's thinking about the role of consumer advertising was affected by the experiences from the substantial effort made in the early 1960s. The objective at that time had been to promote sauce consumption year round. Cranberry sauce as an accompaniment to a variety of meals was featured in the advertising copy. The advertising program was stopped because little consumer reaction was observed. Measurements of advertising results showed the early 1960s program had failed to make consumers more aware of sauce advertising in out-of-season periods.

Walsh thought that the sauce market was ripe for an application of psychographic research along the lines he had experienced while at General Foods. The sauce business was very important for OSC, because it accounted for around 40% of growers' returns. Top management, on the other hand, was not convinced that advertising would be a sound investment for these reasons:

1. The "milking" strategy seemed to be successful.
2. Past advertising efforts had not succeeded in generating sufficient sales growth to "pay out."
3. Marketing funds would have to be diverted from OSC drinks which were growing rapidly.
4. Lack of any OSC exclusivity in previous creative submissions made it likely that growth resulting from successful advertising would be disproportionately shared with price brands, whose cranberries were supplied by growers who were not members of the Ocean Spray cooperative.

For these reasons it had been reluctant to spend money on the advertising of OSC sauce or, for that matter, invest substantial sums in sauce marketing research.

When the sales of OSC sauce products decreased by nearly 7% in fiscal 1970, management became more willing to take action. The decline was due to a combination of a 3% drop in total sauce sales and the inroads of low-priced, private-label products in selected major markets.

Management abandoned the milking strategy of 1965–1969 and implemented a merchandising and promotion program in 1970 that was credited with stabilizing a declining situation. While advertising spending in fiscal 1970 was limited to a $72,000 Easter campaign, $605,000 was spent on promotion and merchandising activities. Brand management's plan for the 1971 fiscal year, approved late in the summer of 1970, called for an increase of over $500,000 in spending for sauce to be divided approximately equally between advertising and promotion, and some of those funds could be diverted for research studies if justified properly with top management.

In this situation, just after the selling season of fall 1970, Walsh outlined a marketing research project which could give management information about how the apparent market expansion opportunity should best be seized. His memorandum to key personnel at OSC and the advertising agency, Young & Rubicam (who had obtained the sauce account late in the 1960s), stated that the project would

> (a) observe the psychodemographic characteristics of heavy sauce users; (b) generate hypotheses for their high service frequency; and (c) develop selling propositions which, delivered against similarly profiled light/nonusers, will position regular sauce service as complementary to their life style.

The ultimate objective was to "turn on" some segment of light and/or nonusers of sauce.

As Walsh saw it, the direction for development of communication approaches would come from observation and analysis of heavy-user subgroups. He gave the following simplified example of how this would be done:

> One segment of heavy users may be characterized by a "Family Centered" orientation, where meals are a medium for expressing affection for family and where it can be concluded that the role of sauce is to communicate affection at common, easily-prepared, or otherwise "unspecial" meals.
>
> Next, this segment would be viewed against normative data to determine potential (that is, incidence in the total consumer universe) and reachability (in terms of media habits).
>
> Were the above completed and were "Family Centered" concluded to be the optimal target, the Agency would go to work. Advertising would be produced which communicated the life style of the target audience and positioned cranberry sauce service as complementary to or supportive of that style. The desired end result would be target prospects "self-selecting" ("Hey, that's me"), perceiving sauce service out-of-season as desirable and commencing to buy the product. For the heavy users necessarily reached, the advertising would reinforce and, hopefully, stimulate their already profitable behavior pattern.

Walsh foresaw the need to work with "an agency trained in psychodemographics who would provide the formal game plan;" in the meantime, he indicated that the following research activities would take place:

1. Screen for a statistically reliable sample of heavy users.
2. Segment sample through psychological testing and analysis by a research firm (include demographic and media habit data by segment).
3. Generate hypotheses for the sauce usage of each segment in context of their now available psychographic profiles or life-styles.
4. Select the most promising segment.
5. Develop and test the selling platform for that segment.

Late in December 1970, Walsh's superiors agreed to a marketing research project for sauce, mainly to help management better evaluate and plan the increased marketing spending on sauce.

Having set out research objectives, guidelines for the methods to be used, and organization of the project, Walsh initiated and participated in a series of meetings with agency and OSC marketing managers and research specialists. Late in the spring of 1971, OSC invited the agency and two other marketing research firms to submit proposals and bid for the project. These two firms were Daniel Yankelovich, Incorporated, and Appel, Haley, Fouriezos, Incorporated. The latter came out as the winner. An important factor was that Russell Haley of AHF had successfully completed similar consulting assignments for General Foods. Walsh was familiar with this work.

In the spring of 1971, Walsh was promoted to group product manager and Jerry Melvin became brand product manager for sauce. Melvin was earlier an assistant to Walsh.

THE FRUIT POSITIONING STUDY

By the end of the summer 1971, the research project was a major concern of Walsh, Melvin, and Witham. Haley's proposal had called for "a benchmark study of the market for cranberry sauce." The overall proposed study was to be the development of an understanding of cranberry sauce users—their behavior, attitudes, opinions, and beliefs. Walsh decided that the study would focus only on the sauce product category and would not investigate other OSC products in any depth.

The research objectives were formulated as follows:

1. To identify and describe the kinds of women who use cranberry sauce.
2. To provide an understanding of what consumers are seeking in choosing between complementary products for use—in salads and with main food courses.
3. To look into the consumption of various food types as sources and potential sources of cranberry sauce usage.
4. To describe consumer usage patterns with regard to cranberry sauce.
5. To identify broad media types for OSC sauce in getting across its message to consumers.
6. To investigate new product or line extension possibilities.

It was argued that guidance for formulation of three basic components of the marketing strategy would result from a fulfillment of the above research objectives. The three components were in the words of the AHF proposal as follows:

1. *Positioning:* Where are additional sales most likely to originate? Should the product or its image be modified to maximize its long-term sales appeal and, if so, how?
2. *Market target:* Who are the best prospects for cranberry sauce?
3. *Buying incentives:* What should be said about OSC's cranberry sauce to make it most attractive to its market target?

At the meeting of the brand group, OSC research, and Haley, it was agreed that the project should have three phases with a final report in early spring 1972. The cost of the three phases would be about \$45,000, with a ±10% contingency for unforeseen costs or savings. The three phases were to cover (1) exploration of areas to be covered, (2) development of measurement tools, and (3) measurement of the market on a national basis.

Phase 1: Exploration of Areas To Be Covered

The immediate purpose of the first phase was to define the competitive environment and to compile lists of product attributes, consumer beliefs, and personality and life-style characteristics of special relevance for cranberry sauce consumption. Past research on the cranberry sauce market consisted mainly, as has been mentioned, of the MRCA study from 1967 and the so-called MARPLAN study from 1962. These studies were reviewed in search of areas to be measured. Witham put down a one-page list of hypotheses concerning the activities, opinions, life-styles, and demographics of heavy users of cranberry sauce. According to Witham heavy sauce users

1. Use cranberry sauce with a variety of meats and numerous preparations (i.e., fried, broiled, cold meats, as well as baked).
2. Perceive sauce as a part of the meal rather than a garnish or a symbol of tradition.
3. Have sauce in their kitchen as a staple year round.
4. Often make their own sauce or relish when fresh cranberries are available.
5. Feel that the sauce has a food value as well as an attractive appearance and good taste.
6. Often use sauce as an ingredient in cooking.
7. Consider sauce a convenient, inexpensive food item.
8. Have (demographics) larger families, several children living at home, better education, a 30- to 45-year-old female head-of-house, a higher family income, and up-scale socioeconomic characteristics.
9. Have a life-style which includes a wife/mother who enjoys cooking, active participation in community affairs, being concerned with nutrition of the family and quality of environment, preference for natural foods versus synthetics, a planned food budget and shopping from a shopping list, and strong family ties.

Melvin, the sauce brand manager, gave the AHF team a list of 41 cranberry sauce usage hypotheses, for example, "since sauce is perceived as appropriate for formal meals, the difference between heavy and light users has to do with the number of formal meals served" and "new products like Shake 'n Bake are cutting into the sauce business."

To supplement management's judgment, two focused group sessions were conducted among women who used cranberry sauce. The first group session was conducted in Boston among ten heavy users. The light-user group was gathered in Kansas City. A light user had to have used only one can of cranberry sauce within the past year and had not served any within the past month.

One finding was that several of the women were concerned about serving a colorful meal. A difference between the two groups was the food items chosen to make a meal more colorful. The heavy users primarily chose cranberries whereas the light users specified a combination of green and yellow vegetables, salads, and beets. Cranberry sauce was not mentioned by this group particularly because they considered it to be strictly a traditional food.

Twenty women were also the subjects for a perceptual mapping exercise. Each respondent was asked to make judgments about which two out of a set of three food items were most alike in terms of use. Twenty-four food accompaniments, including cranberries, were considered in this way. Figure 1 was developed using the perceived similarities data and suggests how the 20 respondents positioned cranberries relative to other foods. In discussing this map with OSC managers, Haley suggested that the two dimensions could be interpreted as "spicy-nonspicy" and "condiment-side dish." Cranberries were perceived as average on the first scale and more of a side dish or fruit than a condiment on the second scale.

Phase 2: Development of Measurement Tools

The qualitative results from phase 1 were used to design a questionnaire. Marketing management made several extensions and modifications of the questions which the research team first suggested, and the list of questions became quite lengthy. Management and the AHF staff came up with 75 questions dealing with attributes of ideal canned fruit products, 103 questions on overall opinions and feelings about cranberry sauce, and 55 questions on personality and life-style. The 75 questions on attributes were to be replicated for jellied and for whole-berry cranberry sauce, respectively. Traditional questions on product usage and on various demographical variables were also to be included.

A pilot test was conducted in fall 1971 to try to determine which of the many items best reflected strong, underlying consumer dimensions in the cranberry sauce market. That such dimensions of attitudinal or other character existed was believed by both OSC marketing management and the AHF research team.

Two hundred females living in ten different market areas were interviewed personally in their homes. The procedure to select the sample was thought to approximate acceptably a national probability sample. Potential respondents were screened personally to determine if they had purchased canned cranberry sauce in the past year. Around 220 females had to be contacted to yield a sample of 200 qualified respondents.

The personal interview lasted around 30 minutes. It covered purchasing and usage of cranberry sauce, brands, frequency of serving various foods, and demographic and socioeconomic variables. A self-administered questionnaire containing questions about the subjective areas mentioned previously (overall opinions and feelings about cranberry sauce) was given to the respondent at the end of the personal interview. The interviewer picked up the completed questionnaire later the same day. A promised gift was delivered in return for the completed questionnaire.

Figure 1

Perceptual map of various food accompaniments

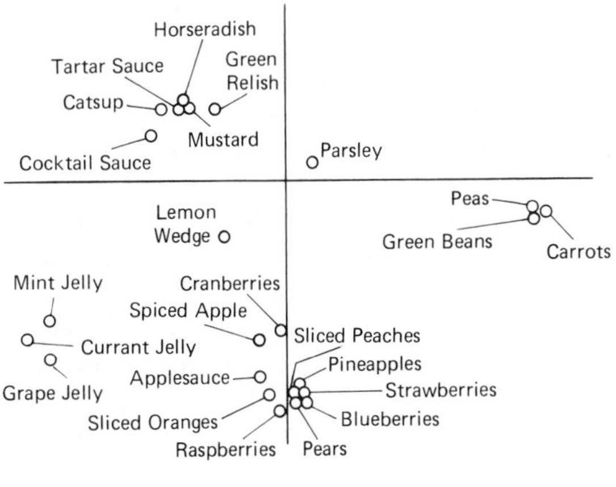

Analysis of Pilot Test Data

A major objective of the pilot test was to investigate the extent to which consumers in fact exhibited the characteristics that management had hypothesized. The self-administered portion of the pilot survey questionnaire contained 383 separate items covering five separate areas of inquiry:

Set	*Type of Data*	*No. of Items*
1	Attributes of an ideal canned fruit	75
2	Perceived attributes of jellied cranberry sauce	75
3	Perceived attributes of whole-berry cranberry sauce	75
4	Overall attitudes and feelings about cranberry sauce	103
5	Self-description of personality and life-style	55
	Total number of self-administered items	383

The pilot questionnaire had been constructed to cover as many different characteristics of consumers and the product category as could conceivably be relevant to the purchase and use decision process of important market segments. The research strategy involved letting the data and subsequent analysis determine which subsets of all the original items were of more or less analytical and managerial interest, rather than strictly relying on "expert judgment" as a basis for building a more succinct list of final items. Whatever redundancy might be present in the original items would thus be identified and could be eliminated, and furthermore, if certain items seemed to be tapping a fundamental consumer or product characteristic not explicitly measured, that characteristic could be inductively identified. The pilot questionnaire, then, was thought of as a preliminary and exploratory vehicle that would shape the form and content of a smaller, final set of questions to be employed in phase 3 of the project.

The five data sets were analyzed one at a time—however, always in combination with a sixth group of variables. This sixth group consisted of

1. cranberry sauce usage—heavy or light
2. age—young or old
3. meat consumption—heavy or light
4. fruit (and vegetable) consumption—heavy or light
5. education—high school or further

Respondents were given the values 1 or 0 in the coding of these variables. It was hoped that, by including these basic marketing variables, the analyses would give results which were easier to understand.

The computerized data analysis was done in five steps and repeated for each of the five sets of data. Exhibit 3 illustrates the analytical procedure as it applied to the fifth data set—"Description of Personalities and Life-styles." The steps were as follows:

Step	*Analysis*
1.	Calculation of means and standard deviations of the responses to each item (Exhibit 3).
2.	Preparation of a matrix of the pariwise correlations between these items (A portion of the 56 × 56 correlation matrix is shown in Exhibit 4).
3.	The use of a computerized data analysis technique called principal components analysis to identify which sets of variables tended to be scored by respondents according to a consistent pattern. The output of the principal components analysis was a series of factors.
4.	Each factor consisted of a set of weights (called loadings) which showed the degree of association between each variable and an underlying theoretical pattern of responses. Loadings could range between −1.0 and 1.0, and loadings that were near zero indicated there was no association between a variable and a particular factor. Exhibit 5 lists the loadings of the 56 personality and life-style variables on the first of the 13 factors.
5.	The theoretical response pattern represented by a given factor was then identified using the following procedure: a list of highly loaded variables was compiled for each of the 13 factors. Exhibit 6 is such a list as prepared by the factor analysis program for factor 1. The list was then inspected and the research team made a judgment regarding what underlying phenomena seemed to best explain the factor. Factor 1 was judged to be a measure of cooking enthusiasm and was so labeled. This process was repeated for the remaining 12 personality and life-style factors, resulting in the labels listed in Exhibit 7.
6.	Exhibit 8 lists the labels given to factors extracted from five types of data: the attributes of ideal canned fruit products, the attributes of jellied cranberry sauce, the attributes of whole-berry cranberry sauce, the respondents' overall attitudes and feelings about cranberry sauce, and the respondents' self-descriptions of personality and life-style.

The use of the principal components analysis had suggested the possible underlying dimensions of consumers' attitudes toward the product category and had identified a relatively small subset of important variables in each of the five types of measurements. The research team then began construction of a revised questionnaire—with no redundant or irrelevant items—to be used in a full-scale survey.

The revision of the pilot questionnaire resulted in changes so that instead of the 75 original questions on attributes of ideal canned fruit products, jellied and whole-berry cranberry sauce, the research team now wanted to use 33 questions; 43 of the original 75 had been dropped and 1 added. Furthermore, of the 103 questions on overall attitudes and feelings about cranberry sauce, only 2 were retained. An additional set of 20 question items would be included. Finally, of the 51 statements regarding personality and life-style, 17 were dropped. This part would consist of the remaining 34 plus 1 additional item.

Preparations for a Full-Scale Survey

A meeting was held between the research team and the marketing research and brand managers from OSC to report on the results of the pilot test. In discussing the planned full-scale consumer survey, the research team reiterated the earlier objectives for phase 3 of the project. A larger sample would result in more reliable estimates of the attitudes and behaviors of cranberry sauce users. Furthermore, the pilot test had enabled the research team to develop a better version of the questionnaire.

Haley's brief to the OSC managers contained the following question areas suggested for phase 3:

1. The personal interview
   a. Usage of main dishes with which cranberry sauce may be eaten.
   b. Usage of and overall attitudes toward competitive complementary products.
   c. Occasions of use.
   d. Brand awareness and trial.
   e. Brand loyalty.
   f. Demographic characteristics.
2. The self-administered questionnaire
   a. Attitude ratings of whole-berry and jellied cranberry sauce.
   b. Desirability of product attributes and benefits.
   c. Images of branded and private-label cranberry sauce.
   d. Perceived compatibility with various main dishes.
   e. Beliefs.
   f. Personality and life-style characteristics.
   g. Exposure patterns to different types of media.

It was suggested that personal interviews should be conducted regarding consumer usage of cranberry sauce and the demographic profile of the respondent. Live questions would ask about the frequency of serving various meats and complementary products (e.g., cranberry sauce) with these meats, cranberry sauce purchases, and so on.

The other items discussed above would be measured by a self-administered questionnaire. The questionnaire would include some questions on TV, radio, and newspaper exposure patterns as well as questions regarding readership of 24 general- or female-audience magazines. This magazine list was, according to the account manager at Young & Rubicam, "totally representative of the books which would be considered for a magazine effort for sauce." In the communication to the AHF team he had, however, added that it was "highly improbable that all of the magazines would ever be used."

To obtain around 1,000 qualified respondents (purchased one or more cans in the last year), it seemed likely that around 1,200 women would have to be contacted in their homes. If standard estimates for the costs of this kind of fieldwork were used, the OSC managers figured that the additional expenditure for phase 3 would amount to around $30,000. About $12,000 had been spent through the completion of phase 2. Phase 3 costs would include the data collection, analysis, and reporting to OSC management. The research team promised delivery of a report in March 1972. The field interviews would be made in late January and early February. Melvin was concerned about the timing because he had to prepare the marketing plan well before the new fiscal year started in September 1972.

Preliminary reports for the 1971 fall selling season indicated that OSC cranberry sauce sales were up by around 5% compared with those of the previous year. Melvin attributed the increase to the fact he had mustered an almost 80% higher marketing expenditure budget in fiscal 1971 than in fiscal 1970. He certainly hoped that the AHF study would give indications about how the marketing effort should be directed to give even better results in 1972. Since phases 1 and 2 largely confirmed the brand manager's assumptions about cranberry consumers, it was not clear to him whether the final phase would produce the desired direction for future marketing.

Exhibit 1

Ocean Spray Cranberries, Inc. (A)

Financial Review, Fiscal Year Ended August 31, 1963–1970

	1963	*1964*	*1965*	*1966*	*1967*	*1968*	*1969*	*1970*
Net sales ($000)	32,294	37,430	44,401	50,909	55,429	62,513	70,815	71,365
Barrels sold (000)	938	978	967	1,036	1,054	1,145	1,265	1,197
Per 1,000 barrels ($)	34.4	38.3	45.9	49.1	52.6	54.6	56.0	59.6
Selling, marketing, and administrative expenses ($000)	6,314	7,441	9,264	10,590	11,774	11,512	12,983	12,896
Per 1,000 barrels ($)	6.73	7.61	9.58	10.2	11.2	10.1	10.3	10.8
Net proceeds ($000)	11,369	13,607	15,788	17,584	17,534	18,652	20,298	20,536
Net proceeds as a % of net sales (%)	35.2	36.4	35.6	34.5	31.6	29.8	28.7	28.8
Total capital employed ($000)	7,190	7,198	6,597	6,858	7,201	9,781	11,628	13,699

Source: Company annual reports.

Exhibit 2
Ocean Spray Cranberries, Inc. (A)

Partial Organization Chart, Fall 1971

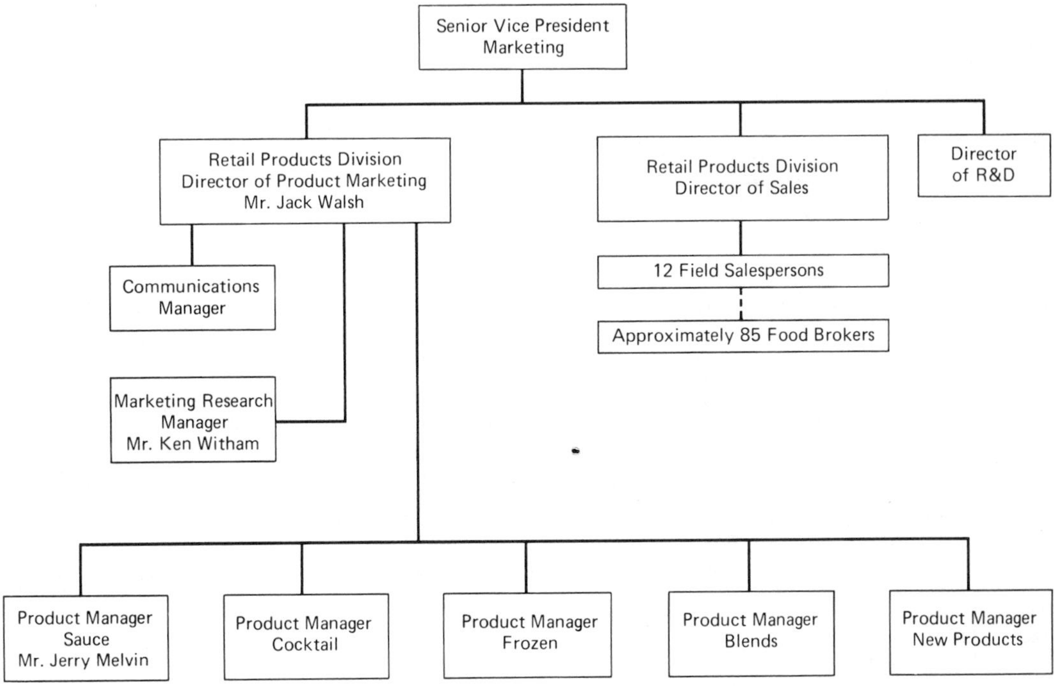

Exhibit 3
Ocean Spray Cranberries, Inc. (A)

Analysis of "Decription of Personalities and Life-Styles" Data: Means and Standard Deviations of "Descriptions of Personalities and Life-Styles"

Variable No.	*Label*	*Mean*	*Standard Deviation*
1.	I like to have friends over for dinner	2.04	1.02
2.	I prefer fresh vegetables to canned or frozen products	2.23	1.15
3.	I watch my calories carefully	3.17	1.31
4.	I like to rough it and live simply	3.22	1.17
5.	I'm not a good cook	3.60	1.29
6.	I believe in things my parents believed in	2.68	0.91
7.	I'm a nervous sort of person	3.09	1.28
8.	I usually get together with the family for holiday meals	1.73	1.04
9.	When I see something I like, I buy it	2.65	1.02
10.	I prefer natural foods to ones with artificial ingredients	1.95	1.06

Variable No.	Label	Mean	Standard Deviation
11.	I really enjoy eating	1.63	0.88
12.	I don't feel well, but don't know what is wrong	4.30	1.03
13.	I enjoy having lots of people around	2.43	1.07
14.	I tend to be good to myself	2.44	0.97
15.	I like to cook new dishes	2.08	1.05
16.	I usually serve several relishes and other extras at holiday meals	1.70	0.87
17.	I try to serve my children the things they like to eat	2.01	1.00
18.	I like to have my meals planned and organized in advance	2.16	1.10
19.	I often buy store brands instead of national brands	2.91	1.17
20.	I like to look for sales in the grocery store	1.92	1.10
21.	I am frequently on a diet	3.25	1.35
22.	I think Sunday is a traditional day	2.38	1.24
23.	I have few pains	3.20	1.40
24.	I enjoy cookouts	2.19	1.16
25.	My family appreciates the work I put into a meal	2.05	0.97
26.	I like to prepare fancy dishes even if they take a long time	2.70	1.30
27.	I am in better health than most of my friends	2.67	1.15
28.	The foods I serve reflect my moods	2.86	1.14
29.	I like to keep busy in leisure time	2.03	1.06
30.	I usually get to cook things for my husband	1.88	1.19
31.	I plan my life carefully	2.79	1.10
32.	I enjoy cooking more for guests than for the family	3.47	1.25
33.	I like to balance my meals carefully to make sure they're nutritious	1.84	0.87
34.	I like to prepare colorful salads	2.15	1.04
35.	In running my home, I think of how mother would do things	3.50	1.19
36.	I enjoy entertaining at home	2.10	1.04
37.	I wish I were not so shy	3.57	1.33
38.	I try to get color and taste contrast in my main meals	2.00	0.97
39.	I rarely serve leftover foods	3.32	1.25
40.	Food advertising interests me	2.56	1.22
41.	I enjoy taking time to prepare meals	2.28	1.03
42.	I serve quite a few casseroles	2.90	1.05
43.	I always keep some fruit around for the family	1.51	0.75
44.	We prefer plain and simple foods	2.19	0.90
45.	I believe we are on earth to enjoy ourselves	2.23	0.95
46.	I like to cook	1.84	1.01
47.	I think the meat is the most important part of the meal	1.78	0.85
48.	I enjoy being active	1.63	0.73
49.	I enjoy serving spicy dishes	2.89	1.11
50.	Meals are a way to express affection for the family	2.11	1.05
51.	I feel guilty about wasting food	1.84	1.12
52.	Sauce: Heavy/light user	0.52	0.50
53.	Age: Younger/older	0.39	0.49
54.	Meat: Heavy/light user	0.43	0.50
55.	Fruit: Heavy/light user	0.51	0.50
56.	Education: High school/+	0.65	0.48

Key to variable numbers:

51. Respondents answered along a five-point scale ranging from "describes me completely" (1) to "describes me not at all" (5).
52. Respondents who stated that they had purchased ≥ 7 cans of cranberry sauce in the past year were considered to be heavy users. Heavy users were given the value 1 and light users 0 on this variable.
53. Respondents in the age ≤ 34 years were given the value 1.
54. Heavy users were those who reported a total score ≥ 31 on questions regarding the frequency of eating meats during an average month. Nine different meats were mentioned and a seven-point scale was used. Heavy users were given the value 1.
55. Heavy users (1) were those who reported a total score on 16 fruits and vegetables.
56. Respondents with high school as highest grade were given the value 1.

Exhibit 4
Ocean Spray Cranberries, Inc. (A)

Sample from Matrix of Pairwise Correlations of "Descriptions of Personalities and Life-Styles"

		1 I like to have friends over for dinner	2 I prefer fresh vegetables to canned or frozen products	3 I watch my calories carefully	4 I like to rough it and live simply	5 I'm not a good cook	6 I believe in things my parents believed in	7 I'm a nervous sort of person	8 I usually get together with the family for holiday meals	9 When I see something I like, I buy it	10 I prefer natural foods to ones with artificial ingredients
Food advertising interests me	40	.197	−.002	.172	.166	.108	.230	.144	.122	.081	.106
I enjoy taking time to prepare meals	41	.362	.145	.179	.193	−.234	.205	.005	.030	.090	.216
I serve quite a few casseroles	42	−.033	.172	.105	−.023	.027	.056	−.054	−.067	−.053	.102
I always keep some fruit around for the family	43	.184	.123	.132	.077	−.076	.056	.143	.111	.127	.162
We prefer plain and simple foods	44	−.046	.070	.060	.086	.126	.130	.078	.027	−.009	.136
I believe we are on earth to enjoy ourselves	65	.223	.166	.166	.171	.070	.091	.073	−.010	.134	.354
I like to cook	46	.323	.084	.132	.137	−.248	.149	.011	.013	.068	.147
I think the meat is the most important part of the meal	47	.191	.052	.037	−.039	−.056	.163	.004	.111	.131	−.004
I enjoy being active	48	.225	.153	.108	.041	−.021	.179	−.111	.016	.030	.172
I enjoy serving spicy dishes	49	.161	.082	.120	.072	−.106	−.063	−.043	−.024	.142	.104
Meals are a way to express affection for the family	50	.207	.161	.085	.166	−.095	.213	.081	.031	.008	.248
I feel guilty about wasting food	51	−.026	.072	.074	.139	.031	.229	.145	−.076	−.259	.266
Sauce: Heavy/light user	52	−.065	−.005	.024	.086	.102	−.047	.160	−.203	−.031	.054
Age: Younger/older	53	−.038	.045	.143	−.025	.019	.048	−.013	−.042	−.066	.162
Meat: Heavy/light user	54	−.020	−.101	−.054	−.001	.109	−.011	.031	.033	.005	−.157
Fruit: Heavy/light user	55	−.015	−.091	−.052	−.033	.114	.023	−.005	.023	−.123	−.109
Education: High school/+	56	.129	.002	.037	−.198	−.132	−.076	−.091	−.130	.004	−.052

Exhibit 5

Ocean Spray Cranberries, Inc. (A)

Detailed Listing of Factor No. 1[1]

Variable No.	*Loading*	*Variable No.*	*Loading*
1	.3181	29	.0059
2	−.0005	30	.1188
3	.0222	31	.0052
4	.1522	32	−.0747
5	−.4790	33	.0713
6	.0026	34	.1572
7	−.0962	35	.0830
8	−.0224	36	.2865
9	.0163	37	−.0482
10	−.0274	38	.1051
11	.3798	39	.0970
12	.0591	40	−.0651
13	.0576	41	.6165
14	−.0359	42	.0987
15	.5778	43	.0274
16	.2069	44	−.3540
17	.0666	45	−.0569
18	.1351	46	.7470
19	−.0125	47	.1416
20	−.0444	48	.0265
21	.0629	49	.4987
22	−.0020	50	.4555
23	.0866	51	.1326
24	.2609	52	−.1613
25	.3921	53	−.0679
26	.5584	54	−.0393
27	.0945	55	−.0539
28	.1781	56	.0460

[1]Loadings determined by equimax rotation of the 13-factor pinci-pal components solution.

Exhibit 6

Ocean Spray Cranberries, Inc. (A)

Factor Analysis of "Descriptions of Personalities and Life-Styles":
Managerial Summary, Factor 1
(5.9% Variance Explained)

Assigned Variable No.[1]	*Loading*	*Label*
46	.7470	I like to cook[2]
41	.6165	I enjoy taking time to prepare meals
15	.5778	I like to cook new dishes
26	.5584	I like to prepare fancy dishes even if they take a long time
49	.4987	I enjoy serving spicy dishes
5	−.4790	I'm not a good cook
50*	.4555	Meals are a way to express affection for the family
25*	.3921	My family appreciates the work I put into a meal
11*	.3798	I really enjoy eating
44*	−.3540	We prefer plain and simple foods
24*	.2609	I enjoy cookouts
16*	.2069	I usually serve several relishes and other extras at holiday meals

[1]A variable was assigned to factor 1 if the absolute value of the largest loading of that variable on any of the 13 factors was equal to or greater than .30 and the absolute value of the loading of the variable on factor 1 was within .15 of the absolute value of the maximum loading. An * indicated that the variable had been assigned to more than one factor.
[2]Interpretive label: "cooking enthusiast."

Exhibit 7

Ocean Spray Cranberries, Inc. (A)

Summary of Interpreted Factors For the "Descriptions of Personalities and Life-Styles"

Factor No.	*Interpretative Label*	*% of Total Variance*	*Cumulative Percentage*
1	Cooking enthusiast	5.9%	5.9%
2	Sociable	5.8	11.7
3	Conscious meal planner	4.9	16.6
4	Traditional values	4.4	21.0
5	Active	4.2	25.2
6	Husband/family oriented	4.1	29.3
7	Dreamer	3.9	33.2
8	Weight watcher	3.9	37.1
9	Self-indulgent	3.7	40.8
10	Economically minded	3.7	44.5
11	Youth orientation	3.7	48.2
12	Light users	3.4	51.6
13	Healthy	3.1	54.7

Exhibit 8

Ocean Spray Cranberries, Inc. (A)

Labels Given to Factors Extracted from Five Types of Data

First Ten Factors in Order of Extraction	*Attributes of Ideal Canned Fruit Products*	*Attributes of Jellied Cranberry Sauce*	*Attributes of Whole-berry Cranberry Sauce*	*Overall Attitudes and Feelings about Cranberry Sauce*	*Self-description of Personality and Life-style*
1	Convenience orientation	Appropriate for all meats	Appropriate for traditional/formal meals	Rejection of frequent use	Cooking enthusiast
2	Attractive appearance	Attractive color	Easy accessibility	Family usage and interest	Sociable
3	Used with a variety of meats	Nourishing	Brings out variety of meat flavors	Perfect for special occasion meals	Conscious meal planner
4	Nutritive value	Traditional yet formal	Consistency	Appropriate for all meats	Traditional values
5	Fancy/special meals	Easy accessibility	Appetizer/snack	Elegant/fancy food	Active
6	Unique taste	Snack food	Wholesome	Tastes good/good for you	Husband/family oriented
7	Less frequent uses	Sharp taste	Sharp taste	Jellied form preferred	Dreamer
8	Adaptable	Every day food	Heavy users of meat/fruit	Unique taste	Weight watcher
9	Relish association	Sweet/unusual taste		Negative taste aspects	Self-indulgent
10	Heavy users of meat/fruit	Smooth		Because of mom	Economically minded

III

ANALYSIS FOR MARKETING DECISIONS

3

Quantifying and Forecasting Demand

"Daisy" (B)

RESEARCHING THE WOMEN'S SHAVING MARKET

Shortly after SRD's top executives decided that SRD should further pursue the women's shaving market, the newly created task force of SRD's Marketing Research Department and the J. Walter Thompson Company's Research and Planning Department convened. Following the recommendation of SRD's market researchers, it was decided that they would gather objective data regarding blade and razor usage and consumer demographics, while the J. Walter Thompson group would focus more on the subjective aspects of why women shaved and how they felt about it.

 This case was prepared by Nancy J. Davis under the supervision of Steven H. Star.

THE SRD MARKETING RESEARCH DEPARTMENT'S SURVEY

For their survey, SRD's market researchers selected a sample of 2,500 women, 13 years of age or older, which was representative of the total female shaving population in the continental United States. Of these women, about 75% had removed hair from their legs and/or underarms during the past month. The interviews were conducted in person at the respondents' homes during the last week of January 1974. In the interview, the woman was shown illustrations of razors and blades and was asked what brand and type of razor and blade she was then using. (See Exhibit 1 for illustrations.) After giving her response, she was offered 25¢ for the actual blade, and two-thirds of the women who shaved with wet razors complied. The purpose of this was to measure the comparison between the blades women thought they were using and the blades they actually were using. About one-third of those who provided their blades said either that they didn't know what blade they were using or that they were using a blade other than those they were actually using. Therefore, the statistics were not as precise as SRD researchers would have liked.

From the data gathered, the researchers determined that slightly over 75% of the women interviewed, or 65 million women on a national basis, removed hair from their underarms and/or legs either by shaving or by using depilatories and waxes. In 1967, the comparable percentage had been about 70%. The respondents who showed the least incidence of hair removal were women over 55 years of age, nonwhites, and women in lower socioeconomic groups. On average, the respondents shaved their underarms about 85 times per year and their legs about 90 times per year. During the summer months, the frequency with which the women shaved increased by about 50%.

Of the women in the study who shaved their legs and/or underarms, about four-fifths said that they used a wet razor for their last shave and one-fourth said that they used an electric razor for their last shave. The total exceeded 100% because some used different razors for their underarms and their legs. Of the wet shavers, about half used a double-edge razor, less than one-fifth used a Trac II, a Schick Super II, or a Wilkinson Bonded, and about one-fifth used an injector razor. Continuous-band razors, disposable razors, and single-edge razors were used by almost 20%. Double-edge razors were especially strong among older, lower socioeconomic, nonmetropolitan, nonwhite, and southern women. Trac II and the bonded systems were stronger among younger, up-scale, metropolitan, white, and Eastern demographic groups. Injector usage was highest among whites and in the South, while band usage was higher among up-scale, white, and younger (18–34) groups. Disposable razors were weakest among older women, and depilatory usage was predominant among nonwhite and lower-income women.

Of the 1,344 women who shaved with a wet razor, more than half or, on a national basis, about 30 million women had used Gillette blades for their last shave. Gillette double-edge blades were used by about a third of these women and by about 70% of all double-edge blade users. About 10% of all wet shavers used Trac II blades.

When SRD's researchers questioned the women about the quality of the shave they received from the various systems, new systems such as Trac II, Lady Sure Touch, and Flicker all received higher ratings than did older double- or single-edge systems. Among these women, Trac II had by far the highest "conversion level": about two-thirds of those who tried it had converted to it from their previous system. Flicker and Wilkinson Bonded both had a conversion level somewhat lower, and Lady Sure Touch had the lowest conversion level of about one-third.

About half of the women who shaved with wet razors shaved with a new blade which they did not share with someone else. Of the remaining, about one-fourth said that they shaved with a used blade which someone else had cast off. Lady Sure Touch and Flicker were most often purchased by the women who intended to use them, and they were used almost exclusively by those women. Trac II and Schick Super II were shared the most. More than a third of the women who used these systems were using a blade that had first been used by someone else. The women who did not share a blade thought that, on the average, they used about ten blades a year. (See Exhibit 2 for a sample page from the SRD questionnaire and the categories of information gathered and Exhibit 3 for selected data derived from the survey.)

THE J. WALTER THOMPSON COMPANY'S SURVEY

In February 1974, Alison Yancy of the J. Walter Thompson Company began gathering information about how women felt about shaving and what their shaving habits were. Her major source of information was a series of six "creative development" sessions, each of which was attended by nine or ten women who had agreed to participate in the research. In all, 57 women attended. The criteria for selection were (1) that the women normally shaved at least twice a month and (2) that she usually used a regular wet razor, not an electric one. Yancy accepted all brands of razors except the Gillette Trac II. Trac II users were disqualified because Yancy thought that she might use these women to test the new product if SRD did in fact develop one, and she was sure that such a product would contain the Trac II system. She recruited the following groups:

Under Age 25	*Ages 25–34*
1 group of working women	1 group of working women
1 group of housewives	1 group of housewives
1 group of college students	
1 group of high school students	

The women did not know the study was being done for Gillette.

Each creative development session consisted of three phases of interviewing: a self-administered questionnaire, a personal interview with Yancy, and a focus group session. Yancy stated that it was essential to have the self-administered questionnaire and the personal interview precede the group session so that the women being interviewed would have their own ideas and opinions regarding shaving firmly planted in their minds. Otherwise, once in a group session, one or more particularly strong, vocal respondents often swayed others to their position, and the dissenting voices were not heard. The self-administered questionnaire which Yancy used is shown in Exhibit 4. In the personal interview, Yancy questioned the women in depth on their responses to this questionnaire.

From the 57 women interviewed, Yancy learned that, while the women tended to perceive shaving products and the act of shaving as masculine, they considered the end results to be feminine. Most said that shaving made them feel cleaner and more feminine, but they did not view it as a glamorous or pleasant task. Most considered it a necessary evil, comparable to eyebrow plucking. They felt that the dictates of modern American society were such that, for a woman to be considered well groomed, feminine, and appealing to men, her skin should be smooth and almost totally void of hairy stubble. Thus, they said, young girls were conditioned at an early age via romantic stories, mass consumer advertising campaigns, and peer groups to believe that removing hair, particularly from the legs, was necessary for social acceptance. Many said that they began shaving their underarms partly for social grooming and partly for personal hygiene but that they began shaving their legs almost solely for personal grooming. They said that, once they started shaving, they had to keep it up because hair growing out caused their legs to itch. The women surveyed felt that shaving did not add to their appearance in a positive sense but that it prevented potential "detraction" from their appearance by removing unsightly hair.

Fifty-four of the women said they preferred a blade razor to an electric razor even though, with a blade razor, shaving was time consuming, tedious, and messy and involved a number of steps. They said further that cutting and nicking were constant problems, especially on the back of the ankles, knees, and thighs and under the arms. Cutting apparently produced negative feelings, not so much because of the pain, but because of the time and bother required to stop the bleeding and because of the unsightly appearance of scabs and/or Band-Aids. Skin irritations were also a problem, especially when deodorant was applied immediately after shaving the underarms. In spite of these complaints, however, when asked what they would do if it were socially acceptable not to shave, 29 said that they would continue to shave as usual and only 13 said that they would not shave at all.

Most of the women said that they shaved in the evening during the latter part of the week and that for special occasions they would shave more frequently, more carefully, and more thoroughly. Moreover, they were more likely to use toiletry products such as shaving cream for special occasions. Fifty-one said they shaved before, during, or after a bath.

Yancy learned that, on average, the women interviewed spent about ten minutes shaving their legs and about five minutes shaving their underarms. Concerning preshaving preparations, 65% used soap and water, 10% shaved dry, and 25% used shaving cream. Most women held the razor in the same hand throughout the shaving process. They shaved their legs in an upward direction, beginning with the front and then proceeding to the backs and the thighs. The latter procedure required considerable bending, twisting, and stretching, they said.

The final item on the personal questionnaire consisted of a list of characteristics associated with shaving. The women were first asked to rate each characteristic on a ten-point scale, where one point meant "extremely unimportant" and ten points meant "extremely important." Then they were asked to rate their own razors' performance on each characteristic. The results for the 57 respondents were as follows:

	Characteristics/ Benefits Rating	
Characteristics	*Importance (avg.)*	*Own Razor (avg.)*
No nicks or cuts	9.54	6.51
Close shave	9.28	7.95
Easy to control	7.86	6.68
Adjustable to underarms/legs	7.58	3.81
Convenient to use	7.42	7.54
Economical	7.14	6.82
Safe to dispose of blades	6.88	7.53
Fast shave	6.40	6.54
Feminine razor	3.56	4.54
Attractive razor	2.96	4.84

See Exhibit 5 for selected data produced by this study.

Exhibit 1

"Daisy" (B)

Razor and Blade Illustrations

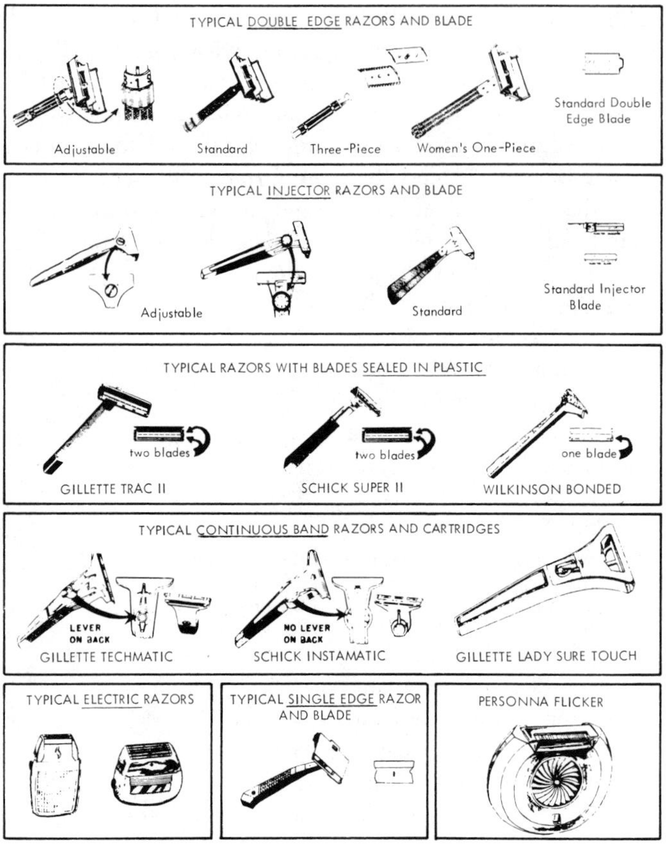

Exhibit 2
"Daisy" (B)

Sample Page from the SRD Questionnaire

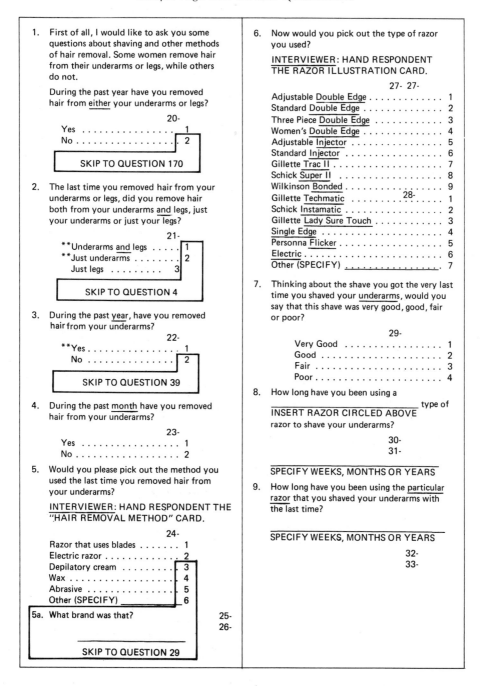

1. First of all, I would like to ask you some questions about shaving and other methods of hair removal. Some women remove hair from their underarms or legs, while others do not.

   During the past year have you removed hair from either your underarms or legs?

   20-
   - Yes 1
   - No . . . . 2 — SKIP TO QUESTION 170

2. The last time you removed hair from your underarms or legs, did you remove hair both from your underarms and legs, just your underarms or just your legs?

   21-
   - **Underarms and legs 1
   - **Just underarms 2
   - Just legs 3

   SKIP TO QUESTION 4

3. During the past year, have you removed hair from your underarms?

   22-
   - **Yes 1
   - No . . . . 2 — SKIP TO QUESTION 39

4. During the past month have you removed hair from your underarms?

   23-
   - Yes 1
   - No 2

5. Would you please pick out the method you used the last time you removed hair from your underarms?

   INTERVIEWER: HAND RESPONDENT THE "HAIR REMOVAL METHOD" CARD.

   24-
   - Razor that uses blades 1
   - Electric razor 2
   - Depilatory cream 3
   - Wax 4
   - Abrasive 5
   - Other (SPECIFY) __________ 6

   5a. What brand was that? 25- 26-

   ____

   SKIP TO QUESTION 29

6. Now would you pick out the type of razor you used?

   INTERVIEWER: HAND RESPONDENT THE RAZOR ILLUSTRATION CARD.

   27- 27-
   - Adjustable Double Edge 1
   - Standard Double Edge 2
   - Three Piece Double Edge 3
   - Women's Double Edge 4
   - Adjustable Injector 5
   - Standard Injector 6
   - Gillette Trac II 7
   - Schick Super II 8
   - Wilkinson Bonded 9

   28-
   - Gillette Techmatic 1
   - Schick Instamatic 2
   - Gillette Lady Sure Touch 3
   - Single Edge 4
   - Personna Flicker 5
   - Electric 6
   - Other (SPECIFY) _________________. 7

7. Thinking about the shave you got the very last time you shaved your underarms, would you say that this shave was very good, good, fair or poor?

   29-
   - Very Good 1
   - Good 2
   - Fair 3
   - Poor 4

8. How long have you been using a ____________________ type of razor to shave your underarms?
   (INSERT RAZOR CIRCLED ABOVE)

   30-
   31-

   ____
   SPECIFY WEEKS, MONTHS OR YEARS

9. How long have you been using the particular razor that you shaved your underarms with the last time?

   ____
   SPECIFY WEEKS, MONTHS OR YEARS

   32-
   33-

Exhibit 2, continued

Type of Information Gathered by the SRD Survey

Data Category	*Specifics*
1. Incidence of hair removal	Past-year hair removal Underarms Legs Past-month hair removal Underarms Legs
2. Last hair removal method	Wet/dry/other Type/brand of razor used last (if any) Brand of blade used (if any) Length of time using last used razor
3. Facts about razor ownership	Self-ownership/borrow New or used Method of acquisition (self purchase, gift, etc.) Sharing of razor
4. Last used blade	Brand and type Number of shaves per blade Was last used blade new or used before? Sharing of blade Who purchased blades?
5. Shave preparation and time of shave	Method of preparation Shave cream type (if any) Brand of shave cream Sharing of shave cream Who purchased shave cream Who decided on brand After-shave lotion or cream (if any) Type Brand Proximity time of hair removal to bath or shower
6. Frequency of hair removal for both underarms and legs	Past 24 hours Past month Summer Winter
7. History of respondents' hair removal	Age when first removed hair Previous blade Purchase intention All razors ever tried
8. Razor and blade I.D.	Interviewer records type brand and color Purchase of blade in razor Interviewer records brand of package seen
9. Trial and satisfaction with new systems (Lady Sure Touch, Flicker, TRAC II)	Method of acquisition Sharing Who shared Shaving frequency Repurchase Satisfaction overall and on specific shaving attributes
10. Difficulties in shaving certain areas (knees, ankles, etc.)	Incidence of problem Area of problem Problem always present when shaving? Any razor ease problem? Any razor make problem more difficult?

11. Corporate image	Rating of Gillette Co. Schick Co. Personna (ASR) Co. Wilkinson Co.
12. Attitudes toward shaving	Rating on scale of pleasant users Importance of various shaving attributes Closeness Nicks and cuts Shaves per blade Comfort
13. Demographics	Skin condition (dry, oily, average) Age Marital status Occupation Telephone Education Family income Socioeconomic status Race

Exhibit 3

"Daisy" (B)

Responses to the SRD Questionnaire[1]

Table 1

Incidence of hair removal among women in past month[1]
(razors and/or depilatories)

Removed Hair from	*% of Women Interviewed*[2]
Both underarms and legs	59%
Underarms only	17
Legs only	8
Underarms and/or legs	84%
Total underarms	76
Total legs	67
Did not remove hair	16

[1]To be read "59% of the women surveyed removed hair from h both their underarms and legs in the past month."
[2]Total sample = 2,500 women.

Table 2

Frequency of hair removal among women who shaved in the past month[1]

Frequency Rates	*Underarms*	*Legs*
Winter	73	77
Summer	109	115
Winter/summer average	85	90

[1]To be read "The women who shaved in the past month shave their underarms at an annual rate of 73 times during the winter (September–April) and 77 times during the summer (May–August)."

[1]All data in Exhibit 3 have been disguised and are not useful for research purposes.

Exhibit 3, continued

Table 3

Index of incidence of hair removal among women during the past month[1]
(razors and/or depilatories)

	Both Underarms and Legs	*Underarms Only*	*Legs Only*	*Underarms and/or Legs*	*Total Underarms*	*Total Legs*	*Did Not Remove Hair*
Sales region							
East	93	109	125	97	96	96	109
South	99	82	100	96	96	99	114
Central	106	100	75	104	105	104	86
West	97	100	125	99	97	99	105
Age							
13–17	105	73	200	105	100	110	82
18–24	132	55	50	117	120	127	40
25–34	137	55	75	122	124	133	23
35–44	119	73	100	112	112	118	59
45–54	100	155	150	110	108	103	64
55+	33	164	125	56	53	39	318
Residential location							
Major metro	97	109	100	99	99	97	105
Minor metro	105	91	125	104	103	106	86
Other urban	93	127	100	99	99	94	105
Nonmetro	99	82	100	97	96	99	114
Urban	95	100	100	97	96	96	114
Suburban	111	91	150	110	108	113	64
Rural	93	100	100	95	95	94	118

Marital status							
Married	110	100	100	108	108	109	73
Single	81	100	125	86	84	84	150
Race							
White	108	82	100	104	104	107	86
Nonwhite	30	227	50	59	59	31	309
Education							
College	117	100	75	113	115	115	55
Noncollege	92	100	125	95	93	94	118
Occupation							
Housewife, employed	111	109	50	108	111	107	73
Housewife, not employed	95	100	100	95	95	96	118
Other, employed	105	145	100	110	111	104	64
Other, not employed	79	100	25	79	82	76	173
Student	111	64	150	106	104	113	77
Household income							
Under $7,000	57	118	125	69	66	61	218
$7,000–9,999	108	100	75	105	107	106	82
$10,000–14,999	117	91	150	115	114	119	45
$15,000 and over	125	82	50	115	119	121	45

[1]The formula to be used to interpret the data in Tables 3 through 8 is $(Y - X)/X =$ ________ %, where X and Y are values in the same column and row Y is being compared with row X. Comparisons cannot be made *across* columns. For example, Table 3 is to be read "On the average, women in the East remove hair from both their underarms and legs 6.1% less frequently than do women in the South." The calculation is as follows $(93 - 99)/99 = -6.1\%$.

Exhibit 3, continued

Table 4

Index of incidence of hair removal among women[1]
(women removing hair in past month—razors and/or depilatories)

Type of Razor Last Used	*Removed Hair from Both Underarms and Legs*	*Underarms Only*	*Legs Only*	*Total Underarms*	*Total Legs*
Adjustable double edge	100	100	100	100	100
Standard double edge	94	150	60	102	92
Three-piece women's double edge	98	136	40	103	94
Total double edge	96	136	60	102	94
Adjustable injector	111	71	—	105	105
Standard injector	105	93	40	103	101
Total injector	107	86	20	104	102
TRAC II	109	71	40	103	105
Super II	116	21	60	102	113
Wilkinson Bonded	110	64	40	103	94
Total plastic sealed	110	64	40	103	106
Techmatic	117	29	20	104	112
Instamatic	117	36	—	105	110
Total band	117	29	20	104	112
Lady Sure Touch	110	79	—	105	103
Flicker	117	36	—	105	110
Total disposable	115	50	—	105	108
Single edge	77	271	—	105	72
Electric	107	57	100	100	107
Depilatories/waxes	81	179	180	96	87

[1]To be read "Of the women who removed hair in the past month, users of a standard double-edge razor were 6% less likely to remove hair from both underarms and legs than were users of the adjustable double edge. Similarly, they were 50% more likely to remove hair from underarms only than were users of the adjustable double edge." Comparisons cannot be made *across* columns.

Table 5

Index of incidence of hair removal among women[1]
(women removing hair in past month—razors and/or depilatories)

Type of Blade Last Used	*Removed Hair from Both Underarms and Legs*	*Underarms Only*	*Legs Only*	*Total Underarms*	*Total Legs*
Gillette Platinum-Plus double edge	100	114	60	102	98
Gillette Stainless double edge	100	117	80	101	99
Gillette Super Silver double edge	100	114	60	102	98
Gillette Carbon double edge	85	193	80	101	85
Gillette Blue double edge	95	136	80	101	94
Techmatic	117	29	20	104	112
TRAC II	107	79	40	103	103
Gillette Injector	101	129	—	105	95
Lady Sure Touch	110	79	—	105	103
Total Gillette	101	117	60	102	99
Schick double edge	106	86	40	103	102
Personna double edge	102	121	—	105	97
Wilkinson double edge	188	193	40	103	85
Competitive injector	107	79	40	103	103
Wilkinson Bonded	110	64	40	103	106
Schick Super II	116	21	60	102	113
Other blade	110	114	60	102	98

[1]To be read "Of the women who removed hair in the past month, users of the Techmatic were 17% more likely to remove hair from both underarms and legs than were users of Gillette Platinum-Plus double edge and were 75% less likely to use the Techmatic for removing hair from underarms only than were users of Gillette Platinum-Plus double-edge blades." Comparisons cannot be made *across* columns.

Exhibit 3, continued

Table 6

Index of frequency of shaving per year expressed as an annual rate—demographics[1]
(respondents were women who shaved during the past month)

	Winter		*Summer*		*Annual Average*	
	Underarms	*Legs*	*Underarms*	*Legs*	*Underarms*	*Legs*
Sales region						
East	88	86	92	95	91	90
South	122	114	104	101	117	106
Central	102	100	100	101	101	100
West	108	109	101	103	104	105
Age						
13–17	107	94	112	105	111	101
18–24	132	125	128	122	129	122
25–34	128	125	119	118	123	120
35–44	93	89	92	88	93	89
45–54	70	66	64	63	67	64
55+	55	62	47	52	49	55
Residential location						
Major metro	105	102	99	99	101	100
Minor metro	107	103	101	99	104	101
Other urban	92	94	103	109	99	103
Nonmetro	102	100	98	99	100	99
Urban	107	105	97	100	101	101
Suburban	105	100	104	101	105	101
Rural	97	92	97	95	97	94
Marital status						
Married	103	100	97	96	99	98
Single	107	105	106	107	107	106
Race						
White	107	102	101	100	103	101
Nonwhite	72	80	67	75	69	76
Education						
College	117	112	111	112	113	111
Noncollege	98	95	94	94	96	95
Occupation						
Housewife, employed	102	97	93	92	97	94
Housewife, not employed	100	97	93	93	96	95
Other, employed	110	117	102	111	105	112
Other, not employed	100	108	96	109	97	109
Student	115	102	118	112	117	108
Household income						
Under $7,000	88	92	81	87	84	90
$7,000–9,999	97	94	91	92	93	93
$10,000–14,999	110	103	104	101	107	103
$15,000 and over	117	112	114	112	115	112

[1]To be read "Of the women who shaved during the past month, those who lived in the South shaved their underarms 39% more frequently in the winter than did those living in the East." Comparisons cannot be made *across* columns.

Table 7

Index of frequency of shaving per year expressed as annual rate—blade used for last shave[1]
(all past-month shavers)

	Winter		*Summer*		*Average*	
	Underarms	*Legs*	*Underarms*	*Legs*	*Underarms*	*Legs*
Gillette Platinum-Plus double edge	108	103	96	93	101	94
Gillette Stainless double edge	103	103	102	97	103	96
Gillette Premium double edge	105	103	100	96	101	96
Gillette Super Blue double edge	103	120	91	106	96	112
Gillette Blue double edge	72	83	79	107	76	98
Gillette Thin double edge	93	108	90	104	92	106
Gillette Carbon double edge	93	108	89	105	91	108
Total Gillette double edge	102	100	96	99	97	100
Regular Techmatic	122	126	117	116	119	120
Adjustable Techmatic	130	122	138	139	135	131
Total Techmatic	125	125	126	125	125	125
TRAC II	110	114	114	112	112	112
Gillette Injector	147	166	129	154	136	159
Lady Sure Touch	125	117	116	113	120	114
Total Gillette	110	108	107	108	108	110
Gillette Import double edge	103	175	87	76	93	75
Schick Platinum/Stainless double edge	102	102	110	102	107	102
Schick Chrome double edge	197	194	101	105	100	100
Total Schick double edge	98	197	104	104	101	101
Personna Stainless/chrome double edge	60	91	42	55	49	70
Personna Tungsten double edge	78	91	79	96	79	94
Personna Face Guard double edge	113	74	117	88	115	82
Total Personna double edge	80	86	78	81	79	84
Wilkinson double edge	95	100	94	102	95	101
Total competitive major brand double edge	100	98	97	98	97	98
Competitive injector	122	108	116	99	117	102
Wilkinson Bonded	133	117	128	126	131	124
Schick Super II	110	106	109	107	109	108
Schick Instamatic	135	129	108	112	119	119
Personna Flicker	128	126	123	132	125	130
Single edge	68	71	59	59	63	64
Other blade	88	114	76	103	81	109

[1]To be read "Of the women who shaved during the past month, those who used a Gillette Platinum-Plus double-edge blade shaved their underarms during the winter 4.9% more frequently than did those who used a Gillette Stainless double-edge blade." Comparisons cannot be made *across* columns.

Exhibit 3, continued

Table 8

Index of frequency of shaving per year expressed as annual rate—last razor used[1]
(all past-month shavers)

	Winter		*Summer*		*Average*	
	Underarms	*Legs*	*Underarms*	*Legs*	*Underarms*	*Legs*
Adjustable double edge	100	97	93	99	96	99
Standard double edge	100	98	94	95	97	96
Three-piece double edge	92	75	50	85	67	81
Women's double edge	103	111	110	111	108	111
Total double edge	98	98	94	98	96	99
Adjustable injector	123	122	113	119	117	120
Standard injector	123	114	109	102	115	108
Total injector	123	117	110	108	116	111
TRAC II	110	114	114	111	112	113
Super II	115	111	111	108	112	109
Wilkinson Bonded	133	118	128	126	129	123
Total sealed in plastic	115	114	117	114	116	114
Techmatic	127	125	128	126	127	125
Instamatic	130	129	95	105	109	115
Total band	127	125	112	123	124	124
Sure Touch	125	117	116	113	127	114
Flicker	128	126	112	132	125	130
Total disposable	127	123	121	126	124	125
Single edge	58	69	52	58	55	63
Total blade razors	110	108	104	105	107	106
Electric	82	78	79	79	80	79

[1]To be read "Of the women who shaved during the past month, those who used a three-piece double-edge razor used it 8% more frequently to shave their underarms during the winter than did those who used either an adjustable double-edge or a standard double-edge razor." Comparisons cannot be made *across* columns.

Table 9

Type of razor last used among women[1]
(underarms and/or legs past month)

Multiple Mention	*% All Past Month Shavers*	*% Past Month Blade Shavers*
Total double edge	42%	54%
Total injector	8	11
TRAC II	11	14
Super II	2	3
Wilkinson Bonded	4	5
Total plastic sealed	15	22
Total band	6	7
Lady Sure Touch	1	1
Flicker	3	4
Total disposable	4	5
Single edge	1	1
Total blade razors	77	100
Electric	23	
Sample size	1,794	1,344

[1]To be read "42% of all past month shavers used a double-edge razor for their last shave."

Exhibit 3, continued

Table 10

Index of type of razor or other method used for last shave in past month according to age[1] (past-month hair removers—underarms and/or legs)

	13–17	*18–24*	*25–34*	*35–44*	*45–54*	*55+*
Total double edge	100	84	100	103	113	121
Total injector	54	115	131	77	108	77
TRAC II	143	143	114	114	57	71
Super II	200	300	200	100	100	*
Wilkinson Bonded	133	133	100	*	*	67
Total plastic sealed	155	164	118	91	55	64
Total band	89	133	122	67	78	33
Sure Touch	100	200	100	200	—	*
Flicker	100	100	67	100	*	33
Total disposable	100	125	75	125	*	25
Single edge	*	100	100	100	100	400
Total blade razors	97	106	108	92	94	92
Electric	113	79	79	113	125	167
Total razor users	102	101	102	100	100	100
Depilatories, waxes, etc.	75	75	75	100	150	100

[1]The formula to be used to interpret the data in Table 10 through 15 is $(S - R)/R =$ ________%, where R and S are values in the same row, and column S is being compared with column R. Comparisons cannot be made *down* columns. For example, Table 10 is to be read as follows: "Of the women who removed hair in the past month, those between ages 18 and 24 were 16% less likely to use a double-edge razor than were women between ages 13 and 17." The calculation is made as follows: $(84 - 100)/100 = -16\%$.

*Minimal.

Table 11

Index of type of razor or other method used for last shave in past month according to income and education[1]
(past-month hair removers—underarms and/or legs)

	Household Income				*Education*	
	Under $7,000	*$7,000–9,999*	*$10,000–14,999*	*$15,000+*	*Noncollege*	*College*
Total double edge	118	103	103	89	105	95
Total injector	108	100	85	100	92	100
TRAC II	71	100	100	143	100	129
Super II	200	200	200	200	200	100
Wilkinson Bonded	100	67	67	133	100	67
Total plastic sealed	91	100	100	145	109	109
Total band	78	100	78	122	89	122
Sure Touch	100	100	100	100	100	100
Flicker	33	100	67	100	67	67
Total disposable	50	100	75	100	75	75
Single edge	100	100	100	100	100	200
Total blade razors	123	100	94	123	99	100
Electric	75	100	129	96	100	104
Total razor users	99	101	102	102	101	102
Depilatories, waxes, etc.	150	100	100	50	100	75

[1]To be read "Of the women who removed hair in the past month, those whose household income was under $7,000 were 14.6% more likely to use a double-edge razor than were women whose household income was between $7,000 and $9,999." Comparisons cannot be made *down* columns.

Exhibit 3, continued

Table 12

Index of type of razor or other method used for last shave in past month according to residential location[1]
(past-month hair removers—underarms and/or legs)

	Major Metro	*Minor Metro*	*Other Urban*	*Nonmetro*	*Urban*	*Suburban*	*Rural*
Total double edge	89	100	97	81	103	92	113
Total injector	92	100	115	92	108	85	92
TRAC II	143	100	29	86	114	129	71
Super II	200	200	200	200	200	200	300
Wilkinson Bonded	67	100	67	100	67	100	67
Total plastic sealed	127	109	55	100	109	127	91
Total band	100	100	100	78	100	100	78
Sure Touch	100	100	—	100	100	100	100
Flicker	67	67	133	100	100	67	67
Total disposable	75	75	100	100	100	75	75
Single edge	100	200	400	100	100	100	200
Total blade razors	95	100	97	6	103	94	100
Electric	108	104	92	88	88	125	104
Total razor users	100	101	100	102	104	101	101
Depilatories, waxes, etc.	125	100	100	50	100	75	125

[1]To be read "Of the women who removed hair in the past month, those who lived in minor metro areas were 12.4% more likely to use a double-edge razor than were those who lived in major metro areas." Comparisons cannot be made *down* columns.

Table 13

Index of type of razor or other method used for last shave in past month according to marital status and race[1]
(past-month hair removers—underarms and/or legs)

	Marital Status		*Race*	
	Married	*Single*	*White*	*Nonwhite*
Total double edge	103	100	100	116
Total injector	108	69	100	43
TRAC II	114	114	114	100
Super II	200	200	200	100
Wilkinson Bonded	67	133	100	33
Total plastic sealed	109	127	118	82
Total band	100	90	100	44
Sure Touch	100	100	100	100
Flicker	67	100	67	67
Total disposable	75	100	75	75
Single edge	100	100	100	100
Total blade razors	101	96	100	87
Electric	100	104	104	75
Total razor users	101	100	102	90
Depilatories, waxes, etc.	100	120	60	375

[1]To be read "Of the women who removed hair in the past month, married women were 3% more likely to use a double-edge blade than were single women." Comparisons cannot be made *down* columns.

Exhibit 3, continued

Table 14

Index of type of razor or other method used for last shave in past month according to region[1]
(past-month hair removers—underarms and/or legs)

	East	*South*	*Central*	*West*
Total double edged	95	113	103	95
Total injector	85	131	85	85
TRAC II	129	100	100	114
Super II	200	200	200	200
Wilkinson Bonded	100	100	67	67
Total plastic sealed	127	109	100	109
Total band	89	78	100	111
Sure Touch	100	100	100	200
Flicker	67	100	100	67
Total disposable	75	100	100	100
Single edge	*	100	200	200
Total blade razors	95	109	99	97
Electric	108	75	113	104
Total razor users	100	102	102	100
Depilatories, waxes, etc.	125	75	75	150

[1]To be read "Of the women who removed hair in the past month, women in the South were 18.9% more likely to use a double-edge razor than were women in the East." Comparisons cannot be made *down* columns.
*Minimal.

Table 15

Index of type of razor or other method used for last shave in past month according to occupation[1]
(past-month hair removers—underarms and/or legs)

	Housewife Employed	*Housewife Not Employed*	*Other Employed*	*Other Not Employed*	*Student*
Total double edged	105	100	105	108	89
Total injector	85	115	100	69	69
TRAC II	86	114	100	29	143
Super II	200	100	100	—	300
Wilkinson Bonded	100	67	100	167	133
Total plastic sealed	100	100	100	64	164
Total band	78	89	89	168	111
Sure Touch	100	100	100	—	200
Flicker	100	67	67	—	67
Total disposable	100	75	75	—	100
Single edge	200	200	100	—	100
Total blade razors	97	100	99	94	99
Electric	121	96	92	108	112
Total razor users	102	101	99	97	102
Depilatories, waxes, etc.	125	100	150	175	75

[1]To be read "Of the women who removed hair within the past month, the housewives who were employed were 5% more likely to use a double-edge razor than were housewives who were not employed." Comparisons cannot be made *down* columns.

Exhibit 3, continued

Table 16

Blade used for last shave in past month[1]
(underarms and/or legs)

Multiple Mention	*% Past-Month Blade Shavers*
Gillette Premium double edge	22%
Gillette Carbon double edge	15
Total Gillette double edge	37%
Techmatic	6
TRAC II	14
Gillette Injector	4
Lady Sure Touch	1
Total Gillette	62%
Gillette Import double edge	1
Schick double edge	7
Personna double edge	4
Wilkinson double edge	6
Total competitive major brand double edge	17%
Competitive injector	7
Wilkinson Bonded	5
Schick Super II	3
Schick Instamatic	1
Personna Flicker	4
Single edge	1
Open blade	2
Sample size	1,344

[1]To be read "22% of the women who shaved with a blade during the past month used a Gillette Premium double-edge blade for their last shave."

Table 17

Who decided on brand of blades purchased[1]
(past-month wet shavers—underarms and/or legs)

	Respondent (%)	Husband (%)	Other (%)
Gillette Platinum-Plus double edge	70%	18%	12%
Gillette Stainless double edge	66	18	16
Gillette Carbon double edge	77	5	18
Techmatic	77	9	14
TRAC II	57	24	19
Gillette Injector	49	40	11
Lady Sure Touch	90	5	5
Import double edge	71	12	17
Schick double edge	75	15	11
Personna double edge	71	18	11
Wilkinson double edge	55	20	15
Competitive injector	73	16	11
Wilkinson Bonded	57	14	29
Schick Super II	74	11	15
Schick Instamatic	74	10	16
Personna Flicker	91	4	6
Other blade	69		19
Total	70	15	15

[1]To be read "Of the women who used Gillette Platinum-Plus blades and who had shaved within the last month, 70% decided which brand of blades they would purchase."

Exhibit 3, continued

Table 18

Who bought last shave blade package[1]
(past-month wet shavers—underarms and/or legs)

	Respondent Bought (%)	*Husband Bought (%)*	*Someone Else Bought (%)*
Gillette Platinum-Plus double edge	76%	16%	8%
Gillette Stainless double edge	75	12	13
Gillette Carbon double edge	83	6	11
Techmatic	78	9	13
TRAC II	67	16	17
Gillette Injector	64	28	9
Lady Sure Touch	82	12	6
Import double edge	77	12	11
Schick double edge	71	23	6
Personna double edge	82	12	6
Wilkinson double edge	69	21	10
Competitive injector	75	17	8
Wilkinson Bonded	65	11	24
Schick Super II	71	7	22
Schick Instamatic	74	15	11
Personna Flicker	90	—	10
Other blade	73	15	11
Total	75	13	12

[1]To be read "Of the women who used Gillette Platinum-Plus blades and who had shaved within the last month, 76% actually purchased the blades themselves."

Table 19

Ownership of last shave razor[1]
(past-month shavers)

	Self-owned, Not shared (%)
Adjustable double edge	48%
Standard double edge	55
Three-piece double edge	67
Women's double edge	80
Adjustable injector	48
Standard injector	58
TRAC II	41
Super II	49
Wilkinson Bonded	59
Techmatic	54
Instamatic	60
Sure Touch	98
Flicker	95
Electric	70
Total double edge	56
Total injector	54
Total bonded	46
Total band	55
Total disposable	96

[1]To be read "Of the women who had shaved in the past month with adjustable double-edge razor, 48% owned the razor themselves and did not share it with anyone else."

Table 20

Age began shaving[1]
(among all women who shaved)

Age	*Underarms (%)*	*Legs (%)*
10–13	33%	36%
14–15	35	34
16–17	13	12
18–19	10	9
20+	9	9
Total	100%	100%

[1]To be read "33% of the women who shaved said they began shaving between the ages of 10 and 13."

Table 21

Shaving preparation last used[1]
(among wet shavers)

Shaving Preparation	*Underarms (%)*	*Legs (%)*
Shaving cream	31%	34%
Shave dry	8	5
Water only	10	8
Soap and water	50	52
Preshave	1	1
Sample size	1,323	1,127

[1]To be read "31% of the wet shavers said they used shaving cream when they shaved their underarms."

Exhibit 3, continued

Table 22

Time of hair removal[1]

	Underarms				*Legs*			
	Before Bath (%)	*During Bath (%)*	*After Bath (%)*	*Other Time (%)*	*Before Bath (%)*	*During Bath (%)*	*After Bath (%)*	*Other Time (%)*
Total	27%	36%	31%	6%	24%	39%	30%	7%
Region								
East	32	27	35	6	31	28	33	8
South	23	44	26	7	20	47	26	7
Central	28	34	31	7	24	39	30	7
West	21	44	29	6	17	46	19	9
Education								
College	24	42	28	6	21	43	28	8
Noncollege	27	34	32	7	25	38	30	7
Occupation								
Housewife, employed	24	37	33	6	25	38	30	7
Housewife, not employed	29	34	30	7	27	37	29	7
Other, employed	31	34	29	6	27	37	29	7
Other, not employed	29	41	26	4	15	47	35	3
Student	17	45	33	5	13	47	30	10
Race								
White	26	37	31	6	23	40	29	8
Nonwhite	35	26	33	6	33	36	31	—
Age								
13–24	17	46	31	6	16	47	30	7
25–34	21	51	24	4	18	53	24	5
35–54	35	26	32	7	24	28	30	8
Over 55	42	10	37	11	27	16	28	10
Household income								
Under $7,000	27	30	35	8	24	34	35	7
$7,000–9,999	25	39	30	6	23	43	28	6
$10,000–14,999	28	34	31	7	25	35	31	9
$15,000+	25	43	28	4	21	45	27	7
Frequency of removal								
Less than once a month	61	—	39	—	56	17	27	—
1–3 times/month	34	20	37	9	31	25	34	10
4–11 times/month	23	47	26	4	20	48	27	5
12–29 times/month	7	69	23	1	8	66	23	3
Every day	10	70	25	—	13	64	14	9
Method of removal								
Blade razor	18	47	30	5	15	51	28	6
Electric razor	51	0	40	9	45	0	41	14
Waxes, etc.	45	11	33	11	40	15	23	12

[1]To be read "Of all the women in the East who removed hair, 32% did so before bathing."

Exhibit 4
"Daisy" (B)

The J. Walter Thompson Company
Questionnaire

Name: ____________________ Address ______________________________

Telephone No.: ____________________ Age: ________ School/Year in School: ______________________
(if applicable)

1. At approximately what age did you first begin to shave?

 ____

2. Why did you first start shaving? What were the reasons?

 ____

 ____

3. When you first began to shave, what type of razor did you use (electric, double edge, single edge, injector, etc.)?

 ____

4. Which of the following statements best describes your current shaving habits. (check one)

 ___A I use a blade razor all the time.

 ___B I use a blade razor most of the time, and occasionally use an electric shaver.

 ___C I use an electric shaver most of the time, and occasionally use a blade razor.

 ___D I use an electric shaver all the time.

5. Is your current razor a men's razor or one that is specifically made for women? (check one)

 ___A men's razor ___A women's razor ___Don't know

6. Which of the following types of blade razors do you use most often. (check one)

 ___Double-edge razor (blades on both sides of razor)

 ___Single-edge or injector (one blade only)

 ___Continuous-band (Techmatic, Instamatic, etc.)

 ___Twin-bladed razor (two blades on one side)

 ___Disposable razor (Flicker, Lady Sure Touch)

7. What brand of blade razor are you currently using?

 ____

Exhibit 4, continued

8. How did you obtain your current razor? (check one)

____Purchased it

____Was given to me as a gift

____Someone else's castoff; other family member gave it to me

____Borrowed, share it with someone else

9. How long have you used this current razor? (check one)

____Less than 1 month ____1-2 years

____Less than 6 months ____2-5 years

____6 months-1 year ____More than 5 years

10. What do you particularly like about the blade razor you are currently using? Please list everything that you like about it.

____

____

____

11. What, if anything, do you dislike about the blade razor you are currently using?

____

____

____

12. Do you use a blade razor that requires the blade to be changed? In other words, to change blades, do you have to remove one and replace it with another?

____No ____Yes

12a. If you answered Yes to Question 12, do you load and unload the razor yourself, or do you have someone else do it for you? (check one below)

____Load and unload it myself

____Have someone else do it for me

If someone else changes your blades, please explain why you don't do this yourself. Give all reasons.

____

____

____

13. Which of the following types of razor blades do you use?

____Double-edge (edges on both sides of large blade)

____Single-edge/injector (one edge on small blade)

____Continuous-band (many edges on one band)

____Twin-bladed (two edges on one side of blade)

____Use disposable razor, don't buy blades

____Other ______________________________
(please describe)

14. Which of the following brands of razor blades do you buy or use most often?

____Gillette ____Schick

____Personna ____Wilkinson

____Other (please specify brand)___________________

15. Which of the following statements best describes how you obtain the blades you use. (check one)

____I buy them myself

____Other family member buys/roommate buys

____Whole family uses same brand, so anyone buys

16. How often do you usually shave? (check one)

____Every day ____At least once a week

____Every 2-3 days ____Less than once a week

17. Approximately how many shaves do you get from each razor blade (consider shaving both legs and underarms as one shave)

____

18. What qualities or characteristics are important to you in shaving. In other words, what do you expect or want a shaver to do for you. List everything that you consider important and number them in the order of their importance to you.

____

____

____

____

____

____

Exhibit 4, continued

19. If you were going to go out and buy a new blade razor today, what would you look for? What would this razor look like and what would you expect it to do? List everything that would enter in to your final decision.

____

____

____

____

20. Think about your feelings and attitudes toward shaving. Then look at the grooming functions listed below. Consider your feelings toward each of these and compare them with your feelings about shaving. Which one is most similar to your feelings about shaving? Check one of these and then explain why your feelings toward shaving and this other grooming function are similar.

____Applying make-up　　____Eyebrow plucking

____Bathing　　____Brushing teeth

____Pedicures　　____Hair care

____Manicures

They are similar because_________________________

____

____

21. Which is the most difficult area of the body for you to shave, your underarms or your legs?

____Underarms　　Why__________________________

____Legs　　____________________________

____

____

22. Other than possibly nicking or cutting yourself, what other problems do you have with the actual act of shaving? What problems or difficulties of any kind do you have while shaving?

____

____

____

23. Do you feel that a woman's shaving needs differ from those of a man? In other words, does the shaving of underarms and legs require something of a razor that a man's razor simply can't do very well?

____Yes What?________________________________

____No ________________________________

____

24. What do you feel could be improved on current razors that would be more helpful to a woman's shaving needs?

____

____

25. Following is a list of incomplete sentences. Please read each one and complete the sentence to reflect your feelings on each idea.

A. I think that body hair on a woman is ____________

____

B. The primary motive for a woman shaving is ________

____

C. When I need a shave, I feel ________________

____

D. After shaving, I feel ____________________

____

E. The best things about shaving are ____________

____

F. The worst things about shaving are __________

____

G. After I have used my razor, I usually put it ___

____

H. The specific place where I am most likely to shave my legs is ________________________ (tub, shower, sink, etc.)

Exhibit 4, continued

26. Following is a list of multiple-choice statements. For each of these statements, read all choices and check the one which most closely describes your own feelings. For several of these statements, it is possible that you may want to check more than one of the choices.

A. When I shave, I cut or nick myself

____Almost every time
____Occasionally
____Hardly ever

B. When I shave, I get a rash or skin irritation

____Almost every time
____Ocassionally
____Hardly ever

C. During the summer months, I usually shave my legs

____More frequently than during winter months
____Less frequently
____About the same

D. When I shave my legs, I usually use

____Shaving cream
____Soap
____Just water
____Something else
____Nothing

E. After I shave my legs, I usually use

____A cream or lotion
____Something else
____Nothing

F. Once you start shaving hair it

____Hastens hair growth
____Makes hair coarser
____Makes hair darker
____Doesn't effect hair

G. If it were socially acceptable <u>not</u> to shave, I would

____Continue to shave my underarms and legs
____Shave only my underarms
____Shave only my legs
____Not shave at all

STOP. DO NOT TURN PAGE

1. Earlier in this questionnaire, you were asked to compare shaving with one of a number of other grooming functions. Think about all these functions again, including shaving (read list below). Now, rate all of these functions in the order of their importance to you.

___Applying make-up	___Hair care
___Bathing	___Manicures
___Brushing teeth	___Pedicures
___Eyebrow plucking	___Shaving

2a. (Hand Respondent Attribute List A) Here is a list of attributes or characteristics which you may or may not consider to be important to you in your normal shaving routine. Above this list is a scale which rates these attributes on their importance - from extremely important to extremely unimportant. Using this scale, tell me how important each of these benefits or characteristics is to you. (Record below)

2b. (Hand Respondent List B) Now think about your current razor and how it performs or relates to each of these descriptions. Using the scale at the top of the page, rate your own razor. For instance, on "no nicks or cuts," if you never have any trouble with your razor cutting you, you might choose "10" - "excellent description." If you cut yourself almost every time you shave, you might consider this a "poor description."

	2a	2b
No nicks or cuts	___	___
Fast shave	___	___
Convenient to use	___	___
Easy to control	___	___
Safe to dispose of blades	___	___
Close shave	___	___
Attractive razor	___	___
Feminine	___	___
Adjustable to legs/underarms	___	___

Exhibit 5
"Daisy" (B)

Responses to the J. Walter Thompson Company Questionnaire[1]

Table 1

Age First Began to Shave	*No. of Respondents*
12	18
13	19
14	11
15	6
16	1
17	2
Total	57

Table 2

Brand of Razor Currently Using	*No. of Respondents*
Gillette	24
Schick	17
Personna Flicker	7
Wilkinson	5
Don't know	4
Total	57

Table 3

Current Razor Being Used	*No. of Respondents*
Men's	30
Women's	22
Don't know	5
Total	57

Table 4

How Current Razor Was Obtained	*No. of Respondents*
Purchased it for self-use	33
Received as gift	6
Someone's castoff	10
Share with someone else	8
Total	57

[1]These data have been disguised and are not useful for research purposes.

Table 5

Type of Razor Used Most Often	*No. of Respondents*
Double edge	24
Injector	16
Band	6
Twin-bladed	3
Disposable	8
Total	57

Table 6

Length of Time Current Razor Has Been Used	*No. of Respondents*
Less than 1 month	2
1–6 months	6
6 months–1 year	10
1–2 years	17
2–5 years	14
More than 5 years	8
Total	57

Table 7

Frequency of Shaving	*No. of Respondents*
Every day	2
Every 2–3 days	14
At least once a week	30
Less than once a week	11
Total	57
More in summer	49
Less in summer	0
About the same	8
Total	57

Table 8

Blades Bought and/or Used Most Often	*No. of Respondents*
Gillette	25
Schick	18
Wilkinson	9
Personna	4
Other	1
Total	57

Table 9

How Blades Are Obtained	*No. of Respondents*
Purchased by respondent	35
Purchased by other family member/roommate	14
Whole family uses same brand, so anyone buys	8
Total	57

Table 10

Number of Shavings per Blade	*No. of Respondents*
1	3
2	3
3	5
4	3
5	12
6	5
7	6
10	8
15	2
18	1
20	1
40	1
Don't know	7
Total	57

Olympia Brewing Company (C)

In 1977, Data Economics, Inc. (DEI), an economic forecasting and consulting company had undertaken a market forecast study of the U.S. beer market for the Olympia Brewing Company.[1] The first step was to forecast the beer consumption that would be accounted for by different age and income groups, in a 6 × 6 age-income matrix, for men and for women. DEI had a model, the age-income model, which forecast the number of men and women in the 6 × 6 matrix, but required market research data on the average beer consumption rate in each age-income-sex category. The Target Group Index (TGI), an annual syndicated survey, provided incidence and frequency data by age-income-sex category. It did not have volume data. DEI commissioned a special study using the Market Facts survey panel. This study obtained frequency and volume data. These data were used to convert the TGI frequency estimates into volume estimates. The conversion was made so that the larger TGI sample (30,000 respondents) could be used as the base of the DEI forecast. The Market Facts sample was less than 6,000.

John McNeil, the DEI consultant responsible for the project, developed the forecast in two stages. First, he developed what DEI called a "momentum" forecast. This was a forecast of what total beer consumption would be if consumption rates in each age-income-sex cell remained constant and only the number of persons in each cell changed. Second, McNeil combined the momentum forecast with other variables to develop an econometric model to forecast total beer consumption.

THE MOMENTUM FORECAST

The basic procedure was to forecast "cell" consumption in each of the 72 (6 × 6 × 2) age-income-sex cells and then sum across all 72 cells to obtain "total" consumption. The forecast

[1]See Olympia Brewing Company (A) and (B).

period was each year from 1976 to 1990, with 1976 as the base.

For a given forecast year (e.g., 1980), the cell consumption was obtained thusly:

$$C_{1980} = N_{1980} \times P_{1976} \times R_{1976}$$

where

C_{1980} = cell consumption of beer (number of beers) in 1980.

N_{1980} = the number of persons forecast to be in that age-income-sex cell in 1980, for example, males 18–24 years, $12,000–14,999 income.

P_{1976} = the proportion in that cell who drank beer at all in 1976, for example, 69.2% for males 18–24 years, $12,000–14,999 income [see Exhibit 2 of (A) case]. The source for this was the Target Group Index surveys.

R_{1976} = the consumption rate, or daily number of beers, per drinker, in that cell. The source for this was the Market Facts survey.[2]

Thus, by developing a momentum forecast, it was possible to isolate the impact of changing age, income, and sex distribution on total beer consumption. McNeil developed such age-income-sex forecasts for each year from 1976[3] to 1990. Exhibit 1 illustrates the forecasts for the beginning year, for "All Adults" (adding men and women).

After developing the momentum forecasts for each year, McNeil summarized the results by taking the overall total number for each year (i.e., the lower-right-hand corner numbers in Exhibit 1, for example, 127,842,000 beers per day for 1976) and computing the overall annual growth rate:

[2]The Market Facts survey was conducted in 1977 but it was assumed that the consumption rates per drinker would have been very similar in 1976.

[3]The year 1976 was treated as a "forecast" year, even though the forecast was made in 1977, since no actual 1976 data existed.

Table 1

Momentum forecast growth rates: total beer, 1977–1990

Year	*Growth Rate*	*Year*	*Growth Rate*
1977	2.1%	1984	1.1%
1978	1.9	1985	1.1
1979	1.7	1986	0.9
1980	1.9	1987	0.5
1981	1.9	1988	1.0
1982	1.4	1989	1.2
1983	1.0	1990	0.9

After analyzing the results, McNeil thought that the following comments could be made. The momentum forecast of total beer consumption called for a growth rate of about 1.9% through 1981 and the slowing to a rate of about 1.0%. The slowdown seemed caused by two reasons:

1. The post–World War II "baby boom" which brought about a rapid increase in the number of consumers aged 18–35 would pass through this age bracket and cause rapid growth in the 35–44 age group in the 1980s. Since beer consumption was not as high in the 35–44 group as in the 18–35 group, the growth in beer consumption would be lower.
2. The age-income model was based upon DEI's long-term macroeconomic forecast. Since this forecast called for slower growth in the 1980s than in the 1970s, there would be fewer people moving into the upper-income brackets. Since beer consumption was positively related to income, the growth rate would decline.

The momentum forecast in terms of the complete age-income tables contained a lot of information. The large volume of the information made it somewhat difficult to obtain a clear view of the strategic implications of the changing age-income distribution. One approach was to calculate the percentage of total beer consumption which was consumed by each age-income cell. This calculation could be made for 1976 and each future year. (Exhibit 2 contains such tables for 1976 for women, men, and all adults.) Several points could be made about the changing consumption patterns.

1. The beer consumer was aging. In 1976, 25.1% of beer had been consumed by consumers between 18–24; this figure would drop to 21.3% in 1986. Growth was coming in the 25–34 age bracket (26.8 to 29.3%) and in the 35–54 age bracket (32.3 to 34.2%). The same patterns would hold for men and women.
2. The beer consumer would have more income. In 1976, 41.6% of total beer had been consumed by people with incomes less than $12,000, whereas only 28.6% had been consumed by people with incomes greater than $20,000. By 1986, these percentages would be reversed.
3. By 1986, the two dominant beer-drinking groups would be consumers who made $20,000 and over and who were either in the 25–34 or the 35–54 age bracket. For example, the 25–34 years, over $20,000, all adults cell would increase their share of beer consumption from 7.4% in 1976 to 13.9% in 1986.

THE ECONOMETRIC MODEL

After developing and analyzing the momentum forecast, McNeil moved to the next stage, the econometric model.

First, he used the procedure in the momentum forecast to produce a momentum "backcast" for 1960 to 1975, that is, to simulate what past beer consumption would have been if the 1976 beer-drinking incidence and consumption rates by age-income-sex cell had remained constant, while only the numbers in those cells changed. McNeil then compared this momentum backcast with the actual total beer consumption from 1960 to 1975.[4] Exhibit 3 shows a plot of the ratio of actual to backcast.

As shown in Exhibit 3 the ratio was about .85 in 1960 and gradually increased to about 1.08 in 1975. Thus, the age-income-sex momentum approach underforecasted by 8% in 1975 and overforecasted by 18% (1.00 ÷ .85) in 1960. Another way of looking at this ratio was that actual consumption increased at a faster rate from 1960 to 1975 than would have been accounted for by age-income-sex factors alone.

McNeil thought that two other factors that might have accounted for this faster than predicted growth rate were price and advertising. During the 1960–1975 period the price of beer had fallen steadily in real terms. Exhibit 4 illustrates that the ratio of the consumer price index (CPI) for beer relative to the overall consumer price index had fallen from 1.057 in 1960 to a low of .858 in 1974. This meant that the price of beer relative to other consumer items was about 20% lower in 1974 than in 1960. Another possible factor was beer advertising, which had risen steadily over the period.

To check whether these two additional factors, falling relative price and increasing advertising, might have accounted for the faster than expected growth rate of consumption, McNeil ran a multiple regression. He formulated the regression equation as

$$\log Y = b_0 + b_1 \log X_1 + b_2 \log X_2$$

where

Y = ratio of actual backcast consumption.
X_1 = ratio of CPI for beer to overall CPI.
X_2 = total beer advertising.

He used logarithms to deal with possible nonlinearities. He had 16 observations, one for each of the years 1960 to 1975. The results were as follows:

[4]As mentioned in the (A) case, the industry total was available from government statistics.

	Estimate	*Standard Error*	*Probabilities of Sign*
b_0	5.770	.756	1.00
b_1	−1.223	.127	1.00
b_2	.088	.065	.81

R squared (adjusted for degrees of freedom) = 0.9399.

Thus it seemed that the price and advertising variables were very effective in explaining the change in the ratio of the actual to backcast consumption. The coefficient b_1 for the price variable was highly significant, at over the 99% level. However, the coefficient b_2 for the advertising variable was not significant at even the 90% level. If he had correctly specified the model, without including some unmeasured factor that had caused consumption to rise, the value of −1.223 for the price coefficient could be interpreted that for each 1% decline in the relative price of beer there was a 1.22% increase in actual consumption relative to the backcast (where the backcast was what consumption would have been based just on age-income-sex factors).

Next, McNeil ran a second regression with actual consumption and (1) the age-income backcast, (2) the relative CPI for beer, and (3) advertising, as the independent variables. He found that the three variables together now explained 98.6% of the variation in actual consumption, and the contribution of each factor was as follows:

Explanatory Variable	*Contribution to Explained Variance*
Age-income backcast	60%
Relative price	35
Advertising	5

The fit for this model is shown in Exhibit 5.

SUMMARY

McNeil now had two sets of forecasts. First, he had the forecasts by age-income-sex cells from the momentum forecast. Second, if the econometric model were correct, he had a way of adjusting the momentum forecast to account for how future price and advertising changes might affect the propensity to consume beer. Since he expected the relative price of beer to continue to decline, and the level of advertising to continue to rise, the total market forecast would be higher than that produced by the age-income model.

It was now early October. On November 8, DEI was due to meet with Olympia to present the results of this first stage of the consulting project. At that time Olympia would expect both a justification of the forecasts and an interpretation of its implications for Olympia's marketing strategy.

Exhibit 1
Olympia Brewing Company (C)

Momentum Forecast: All Adults Total Beers Per Day Per Age-Income Cell in Constant 1976 Dollars
(000)

	Age Group						
Income	*18–24*	*25–34*	*35–44*	*45–54*	*55–64*	*65 and Over*	*All*
Under $8,000	13,147	7,151	2,733	2,812	2,882	3,730	32,455
$8,000–11,999	7,464	5,302	2,521	2,024	1,901	1,544	20,757
$12,000–14,999	4,551	4,960	2,204	2,137	1,390	707	15,949
$15,000–19,999	4,380	7,484	3,445	4,098	2,038	720	22,166
$20,000–24,999	1,820	5,707	3,478	3,227	1,823	312	16,367
$25,000 and over	755	3,695	5,464	7,174	2,438	621	20,149
All incomes	32,118	34,298	19,847	21,473	12,472	7,635	127,842

Exhibit 2
Olympia Brewing Company (C)

Cell Percentages of Total Beer Consumption in Constant 1976 Dollars

	Age Group				
Income	*<25*	*25–34*	*35–54*	*55 and Over*	*All Ages*
Men					
Under $12,000	15.4%	9.9%	7.6%	7.6%	40.6%
$12,000–19,999	6.8	9.9	9.5	4.3	30.6
$20,000 and over	1.9	7.2	15.6	4.1	28.9
All incomes	24.2%	27.0%	32.8%	16.0%	100.0%
Women					
Under $12,000	17.7	9.4	8.6	8.4	44.1
$12,000–19,999	7.3	9.3	8.7	2.7	28.1
$20,000 and over	2.2	7.7	14.0	3.9	27.8
All incomes	27.2%	26.4%	31.3%	15.1%	100.0%
All adults					
Under $12,000	16.1	9.7	7.9	7.9	41.6
$12,000–19,999	7.0	9.7	9.3	3.8	29.8
$20,000 and over	2.0	7.4	15.1	4.1	28.6
All incomes	25.1%	26.8%	32.3%	15.7%	100.0%

Exhibit 3
Olympia Brewing Company (C)

Ratio of Actual to Backcast Consumption, 1960–1975

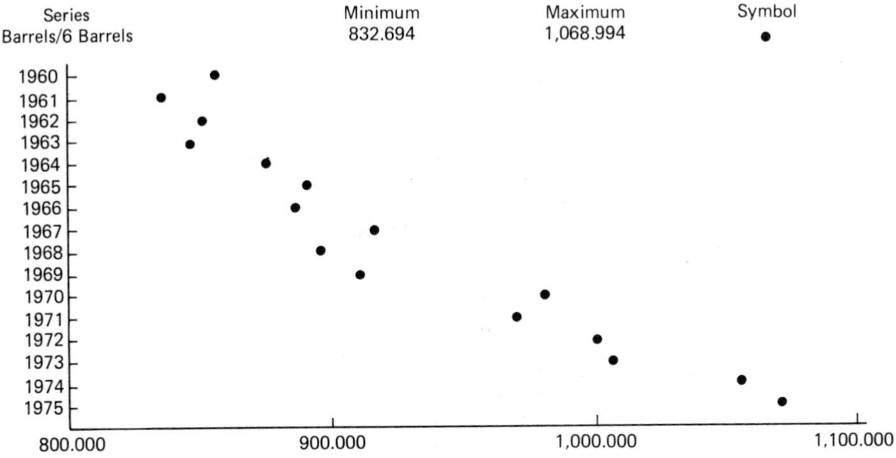

Exhibit 4
Olympia Brewing Company (C)

Ratio of CPI of Beer to CPI, 1960–1975

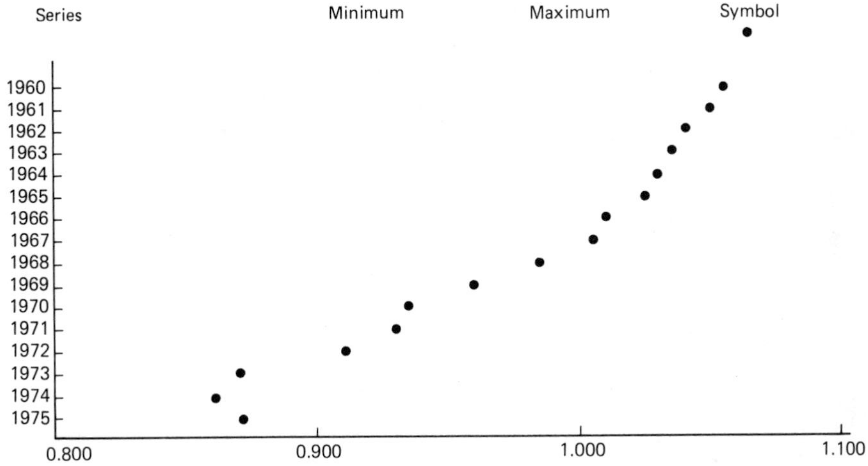

Exhibit 5
Olympia Brewing Company (C)

Model Fit: Total Beer Consumption, 1960–1975

Date	*Actual*	*Fitted*	*% Error*
1960	88,928,883.000	87,159,913.373	−1.989%
1961	87,925,801.000	89,552,953.525	1.851
1962	90,693,253.000	91,137,359.803	0.490
1963	91,493,577.000	93,239,414.706	1.908
1964	96,247,413.000	95,326,615.535	−0.957
1965	100,306,727.000	98,875,573.030	−1.427
1966	101,510,307.000	102,155,697.359	0.636
1967	107,310,356.000	105,799,887.713	−1.408
1968	107,470,430.000	108,573,949.381	1.027
1969	111,866,595.000	113,512,371.171	1.471
1970	122,550,191.000	120,975,354.711	−1.285
1971	123,850,399.000	124,730,773.990	0.711
1972	130,740,585.000	130,174,156.595	−0.433
1973	133,960,457.000	139,539,967.002	4.165
1974	142,311,977.000	141,617,674.322	−0.488
1975	146,853,088.000	141,891,139.004	−3.379

Units = barrels/year (one can per week per adult drinker is approximately equivalent to 1.1 barrels per year in sales).

Franklin Corporation (A)

Darkened hallways and the removal of every second lamp from the lighting fixtures in his office were just two more reminders in a swelling stream of information that had become very disturbing to the marketing director of the Commercial and Industrial Group (CIG) of Franklin Corporation's Lamp Products Division. Although the division's annual planning cycle had concluded in late September 1973, nobody had anticipated the sudden and severe changes in the U.S. energy situation resulting from announced reductions in oil imports.

Now, in December 1973, the director was heavily involved in preparing forecasts that reflected both the immediate national atmosphere of energy conservation and the almost certain long-term increases in the price of electrical energy. The senior vice president of the Lamp Products Division had given each of the division's marketing groups the opportunity to submit revised 1974 forecasts, and the director had decided to concentrate on the forecast for the CIG's sales of fluorescent lamps. Fluorescent lamps accounted for about half the group's dollar sales and were expected to be the hardest hit of the CIG products.

THE INDUSTRY

Franklin was one of four major manufacturers of electric lamps in the United States. Two of the other manufacturers maintained physical distribution facilities and sales forces that were roughly equivalent to Franklin's, while the third manufacturer employed significantly fewer salespersons and had only about one-half the number of physical distribution outlets as the three other major manufacturers. In addition to the four major manufacturers, the industry was populated by approximately half a dozen manufacturers whose market shares were very small.

The four major manufacturers competed on the basis of product quality, availability, technical features, design assistance for the lighting plans for new construction projects, working capital, and price. Each company's product line included more than 5,000 separate lamp products, and firms would occasionally seek advantageous marketing positions by stockpiling part of the product line and then announcing special price promotions on the accumulated products. The advantages of lower unit costs gained using this tactic had to be weighed against the risks of poor market response to the promotion, competitor's matching of the special prices, and the costs of carrying excessive inventories. Nonetheless, each firm frequently used its working capital investment as a competitive tool.

The mix of types of lamps manufactured by the industry was shifting in 1973 from the traditional incandescent lamps (which turned electrical energy into light by passing it through a wire filament) and fluorescent lamps (which turned electrical energy into light by passing it through a gas which caused specially coated glass surfaces to glow) to HID lamps. HID lamps used metallic vapors, usually sodium or mercury based, to generate light that was more focused, had less glare, and was produced at higher efficiencies than were possible with fluorescent lamps, which were in turn more efficient than incandescent lamps.

All the manufacturers were scrupulously careful to avoid the appearance, occasion, and practice of price collusion, and a strong sense of competitive zeal pervaded the industry. With respect to fluorescent lamps, price differentials between competitors were small and were not uniformly in one company's favor.

FRANKLIN'S COMMERCIAL AND INDUSTRIAL GROUP

Franklin Corporation's Lamp Products Division was functionally organized, with vice presidents of marketing, manufacturing, engineering, and financial control reporting to the division senior vice president. The vice president of marketing headed three separate market management groups, a product management group, a marketing services group, and a marketing development group. The Commercial and Industrial Group was headed by a marketing director who oversaw the activities of 8 regional sales managers, 30 district sales managers, and about 250 sales representatives. The CIG served over 5,000 active accounts segmented as follows:

1. Industrial—interior and outdoor lighting products purchased by manufacturing plants and companies.
2. Commercial—similar products purchased by builders and operators of retail chains, shopping malls, and commercial developers.
3. Electrical contractors.
4. Utilities.
5. Political—states and municipalities who purchase lighting products for public use, principally for highway and street lighting purposes.
6. Communications—studio and theater lighting and special lamps for TV studios.
7. Main street—lamp and lighting products purchased by individual stores and small business that lacked a centralized network purchasing function.

Franklin's two other market management groups focused on lamp products used by consumers and by original equipment manufacturers.

CIG sales representatives divided their time between calls on nearly 1,300 distributors and missionary sales contacts with electrical contractors, architects, consulting illuminating engineers, and maintenance departments. New business was sought in the form of both new customers and new product applications. Although the amount of fluorescent lamps that went into new sockets accounted for less than 20% of the fluorescent lamp market, suppliers of the first lamps had an advantage when the lamps needed to be replaced. The CIG sales force could rely on Franklin's District Engineering staff and the Lamp Product Division's Lighting Engineering Group for technical assistance in preparing quotes and designs.

In the lamp industry, manufacturer-distributor loyalties were important with respect to servicing large numbers of smaller accounts, but for larger orders the inventory and selling functions shifted toward the manufacturers. In fact, when bidding for a larger order, manufacturers would often choose to negotiate with more than one distributor to arrive at a desired price to quote to the ultimate customer. In those cases, delivery would be effected via the "most cooperative" distributor, or the manufacturer might elect to sell direct if that would be most advantageous to the seller and buyer.

About 10% of CIG's dollar sales in 1973 were accounted for by HID lamps, and the remainder was divided evenly between incandescent and fluorescent products.

FORECASTING AT THE CIG

The CIG submitted its planned sales volume and budget in July for the next calendar year. After discussing these plans within the Lamp Products Division and perhaps with Franklin's corporate management, budgets were approved in September. The annual forecasts were the results of intensive analysis of market trends and efforts to estimate the effects of suggested marketing programs. In the final analysis, the CIG forecast was a compromise between what the director wanted to commit the organization to deliver and what higher-placed managers demanded. Their demands could be based on independent forecasting, the use of optimistic plans to achieve top results, the demands from their superiors, or a combination of these factors.

The setting of sales quotas for each district manager and salesperson was an important tool for planning and control in the CIG. Salespersons or district managers with average performance received about 15 to 20% of their salary in the form of bonus payment. The bonus formula was geared to stimulate the field sales force to achieve results which were above the historic growth trend of the U.S. lamp business, of about 6½% per year, expressed in constant prices. The bonus formula for 1973 centered on a planned 10% increase in sales. The sales quota thus became 110% of 1972 sales. If a salesperson or a district manager achieved such an increase, he or she would receive about $1,000 in bonus. The bonus increased rapidly with sales results above the 10% growth figure, although nobody could receive more in bonus payments than was received in base salary. Salespersons had to reach 90% of the sales quota to receive any bonus at all.

In preparing forecasts, the CIG marketing director relied on assistance from the manager of sales forecasting and the manager of marketing management science, both of whom reported to the marketing development director. These organizational relationships are sketched in Exhibit 1. The sales forecasting manager used two types of procedures in forecasting CIG fluorescent lamp unit sales: district managers' forecasts and exponential smoothing forecasts.

For the first method, the district managers were required to send forecasts for the next three months on the twenty-fifth day of each month to Franklin. District managers were given information about the seasonality pattern of the sales in their districts, new marketing programs, and general economic trends for selected sectors of the U.S. economy. Some district managers asked their sales personnel to prepare comparable forecasts for their accounts, but there was little uniformity among the district managers' forecasting procedures.

The sales forecasting manager felt that these field sales forecasts had acceptable reliability. Most of the forecasts for the first month were within an error margin of 5%. He felt that the three-month forecasts were even more accurate, because sudden jumps and declines in sales tended to even out. To prepare the monthly total CIG district managers' forecast, he summed each of the districts' forecasts without trying to adjust for individuals' suspected forecasting errors.

It often happened that the forecast for a particular month produced by the district managers changed substantially as the month came closer in time. The sales forecasting manager compiled the data shown in Exhibit 2 to indicate some of the dynamics of the short-term sales forecasting system. The district managers were also asked once a year to submit an annual forecast. These forecasts were, however, usually far off the mark.

A second forecasting method input actual sales data into a computer program that used exponential smoothing procedures to extrapolate sales trends. Sales trends were projected monthly for a one-year time horizon. The sales of many CIG products were forecasted using this procedure, which adjusted for seasonal and long-run trend effects.

The sales forecasting manager saw these forecasts as an efficient way in which to sum up the historical trends, and they were produced in much greater product detail than the district managers' forecasts. He thought that exponential smoothing did not produce reliable annual forecasts, but its results for the next three months were considered to be a valuable part of the analytical support for forecasting.

THE ECONOMETRIC FORECASTING MODEL

Complementing the judgmentally derived district managers' forecasts and the somewhat mechanical exponential smoothing forecasts were forecasts determined by a model which had been built for the CIG by the manager of marketing management science, Eric Nielsen. He had joined the group in 1968 after receiving a master's degree in management science from a well-known school of engineering, science, and agriculture and had gradually won Franklin's acceptance of his forecasts prepared from measures of national and industry economic activity.

Nielsen's approach to forecasting required the following types of data and analytical tools:

1. Historical sales data for the industry and, for Franklin, by product type. All lamp manufacturers regularly submitted production and shipments figures to the U.S. Department of Commerce, which published industry aggregate statistics on shipments and made them available to any interested party.
2. Historical figures for a wide variety of economic indicators related to financial markets, the construction industry, and other major sectors of the U.S. economy.
3. Predicted future values of the data described in the preceding requirement.
4. A flexible computer system for integrating data with families of regression programs and simulation models.

Nielsen relied on Applied Models, Inc. (AMI), to provide these capabilities. AMI had gained national recognition for its work in forecasting a wide range of economic parameters and offered its clients access to data, forecasting models, a time-sharing computer system, an extensive software library, and personal consulting services in the use of these capabilities. The annual fees paid AMI for the services used by Franklin amounted to about $16,000 plus an additional charge of $1,000 for a rented computer terminal placed next to Nielsen's desk. Nielsen was the principal user of the AMI system at Franklin. Since he was knowledgeable in the use of econometric methods, he did not make use of the AMI consulting staff.

Nielsen's model was a system of six interrelated equations arranged in a hierarchy so that the output of each equation became one of the inputs to the next equation in the sequence. Although each equation was different, most equations used combinations of environmental data, industry data, and the outputs from preceding equations as inputs or independent variables.

Nielsen described the building of each level of the model as an exercise in practical econometrics, where statistical theory was merged with his knowledge of the industry's competitive structure, environmental trends, and internal marketing decisions to produce systems of regression equations consistent with a variety of practical and theoretical criteria. Nielsen's first decisions were to choose the six dependent variables forecasted by the six equations of the model: three industry sales variables and three Franklin sales variables. He then designed the right-hand side of each equation.

He started off by considering more than 30 economic variables for possible inclusion in the six equations. Those candidate variables had been selected using his and others' judgments as to which variables might be related to sales of ballasts or fluorescent lamps. Nielsen then chose subsets of the 30 candidate variables by applying the following decision rules, which were commonly used in regression analysis.

1. The regression coefficient for the variable had to have the expected sign.
2. The variable had to have a significantly strong statistical relationship with the dependent variable. Operationally, Nielsen insisted that the t-statistic for a regression coefficient of an independent variable should be well above 1.
3. Third, the number of variables included in the final regression equations was influenced by the desire to explain a high proportion of the variation in their respective dependent variables. The R-squared statistic was a suitable measure of the goodness of fit of the regression equation to the observed data.
4. Finally, the equations had to demonstrate that they were not likely to violate the assumption of least squares regression models that the residual terms were uncorrelated. In time-series analysis such as Nielsen performed in building his models, a common problem was that residuals were apparently correlated over time—thus increasing or decreasing systematically over the time periods for which the regression model was estimated. This problem was called serial correlation or autocorrelation and was indicated by the Durbin–Watson statistic, computed and printed out by the AMI software. Nielsen felt that Durbin–Watson values that exceeded about 1.0 indicated that serial correlation was not a problem in any given regression equation.

After using these decision rules to build preliminary regression models, Nielsen used other procedures to refine the models into the equations he used to prepare the final forecasts. He discussed his research strategy with the casewriter:

> If a regression equation is unacceptable on the basis of the regression statistics, several options are open for improving the equation. We can return to our theory and there seek hints about possible adjustments and then repeat the regression analysis with a new set of variables. Or we can take a look at the plot of the regression and adjust for factors which might have been ignored in the equation.
>
> For instance, if the plot of fluorescent lamp sales seems to lag the shifts in the economic variables, we can adjust the equation for the length of this lag.
>
> If the fit is still unacceptable and we don't want to abandon our theory, we can examine more closely past sales developments for clues to the source of the misfit. For example, were the sales figures "distorted" by strikes among employees, suppliers or distributors in the industry? Were the sales

figures affected by price changes in the industry? If we find that these, or any other factors, have severely distorted the sales figures over the period covered by the regression analysis, we have again two choices. We can attempt to estimate the effect of these sudden alterations upon the sales figures and introduce a "dummy variable" to isolate the distortions. Or we can shorten the time frame of the regression analysis so that the sales figures cover only the period during which no severe distortions are apparent.

Using the AMI data base and computer software, Franklin and industry sales figures, and his procedures for fitting models to data, Nielsen's model's equations had as many as eight independent variables which in turn were often weighted and lagged or dummied to be consistent with the ways in which Nielsen and the marketing managers at Franklin perceived general economic trends and the competitive interrelationships among the major manufacturers. For example, the first equation, which forecast quarterly domestic shipments of fluorescent ballasts,[1] took the following form:

Industry domestic ballast unit shipments (000) $= a_0 + a_1x_1 + a_2x_2 + a_3x_3 + a_4x_4 + a_5x_5$

where

a_0 = an intercept term fitted by the regression analysis.

a_1–a_5 = regression coefficients estimated by ordinary least squares procedures, applied to the five respective independent variables.

x_1 = the investment in private, nonresidential structures expressed in billions of 1958 dollars, lagged weighted average for six preceding quarters.

x_2 = the index of unit labor costs in the private nonfarm sector, 100 in 1967, lagged weighted average for two quarters.

x_3 = the index of output per worker-hour in the private nonfarm sector, 100 in 1967, lagged weighted average for three quarters.

x_4 = the difference between the average yield on new issues of high-grade corporate bonds and the average market yield on U.S. government three-month Treasury vills, expressed in percentage points, lagged weighted average for four quarters.

x_5 = the current production index for nondurable manufacturing, 100 in 1967.

When the equation was fitted to quarterly, seasonally adjusted data from the interval 1956:3 to 1973:2, all the regression coefficients met Nielsen's criteria for effectiveness. The standard error for the forecast was slightly over 1.3 million units, which was about 3.5% of the 1972 level for industry ballast shipments. The R^2 value was .968, which suggested the equation did a very good job of describing variation in industry domestic fluorescent lamp shipments over the time interval.

To get a visual impression of this regression equation, Nielsen used the AMI software to obtain a plot of the actual ballast shipments and those estimated (of fitted) by the regression equation. The plot is shown in Exhibit 3.

[1] A ballast was an iron bar wrapped with wire used in all electrical discharge devices to prevent current surges from melting a fuse or destroying a fluorescent tube. Franklin did not manufacture ballasts, but Nielsen forecast the demand for ballasts since it was strongly related to the new demand for fluorescent lamps themselves. New lamp demand accounted for between 15 and 20% of fluorescent unit sales in 1973 and had always been more difficult to forecast than replacement demand for fluorescent lamps. On average, a new ballast served 1.8 lamps over its life. Ballast shipments data were available from the Department of Commerce.

Commenting on this particular regression, Nielsen pointed out the following:

> As we can see from this plot, the equation performs quite well in picking up the major economic cycles in the economy. Each of the recessions of 1957–58, 1960–61, 1969–70 and the mini-recession of 1967, and the subsequent economic recoveries had a definite effect on the fluorescent ballast shipments. The explanatory variables used in the equation appear to do quite well in explaining the variation of ballast shipments due to these economic fluctuations.
>
> Regarding the different explanatory variables, the Federal Reserve Board's production index represents the physical volume of production for all nondurable manufacturers and provides a measure of short- and long-run variations in economic activity. Fixed investment in nonresidential structures measures the construction of (and additions or alterations to) nonresidential buildings, farm structures, and utilities. This variable, though a lagged version, estimates the impact of construction on shipments of lamp ballasts. The positive coefficient indicates that, as construction activity increases, ballast shipments increase, and vice versa. This lag structure indicates that this occurs with some delay, which is expected since new ballasts are installed later in the construction cycle. Obviously, I tried a lot of different lagged versions of x_1 before I decided that I had found the one I wanted to use for forecasting.
>
> Credit availability, as measured by the credit crunch variable, has a negative effect on ballast shipments. Apparently, as credit availability tightens, modernization programs for improved lighting are postponed, which would, therefore, postpone the demand for the ballasts.

Several of the remaining five equations in the model used the industry ballast shipments forecast as an independent variable. Many of those equations also used dummy variables to adjust for "buy-ins" or temporary surges in industry or corporate sales due to announced price increases. Other dummy variables adjusted the data to account for threatened strikes, special "one free with a dozen" promotions on certain items, and factors related to competitors' own strikes and promotions.

The level 2 equation of the model used the industry ballast forecast and several other variables to estimate the industry domestic shipments of fluorescent lamp units. The level 3 equation estimated total shipments of fluorescent lamps, including domestic and foreign shipments, using the forecast of domestic shipments from Level Two.

The level 4 equation of the model used the industry domestic shipments forecasts, modified by terms for Franklin's promotional campaigns, and the ballast shipments forecast, to predict Franklin's factory shipments of all types of fluorescent lamp products. Termed the "field shipments forecast," it included all units shipped by the CIG, Consumer and OEM marketing groups.

The domestic shipments forecast of level 5 included both lamps shipped under the Franklin brand name and Franklin-manufactured lamps sold under private labeling programs. The sixth equation estimated total Franklin shipments, domestic and foreign, based on earlier estimates of industry shipments of lamps and ballasts. The structure and the interrelationships among the six forecasting equations making up the model are described in Exhibit 4.

Several times each year, additional figures would become available for the various equations. Nielsen used the new data to update the old regression equations. Usually only very small changes were observed since the regression coefficients had been found to be relatively stable when estimated over different time periods. Nielsen made a special effort to update the equations in the fall of each year, when market plans and accounting budgets were prepared for the following year.

The same approach taken for building and using the quarterly forecasting model was used to develop sales forecasting models to support five-year marketing plans. Instead of using quarterly data, Nielsen employed annual aggregates of the same variables. AMI made available the comparable annual data on business conditions as well as the predicted values of these conditions during the coming five-year period.

When Nielsen started working on econometric approaches to forecasting, only a few managers understood the procedure he employed, and many were quite doubtful about its value to Franklin. However, the econometric forecasts had been able to build up a fairly good track record in the past, and Nielsen's work seemed to be accepted by a wider circle of managers. A comparison of the econometrics-based forecasts with the actual sales results is shown in Exhibit 5. Additional technical detail on the econometric model's equations is presented in Exhibit 6.

THE CHANGING ENVIRONMENT IN FALL 1973

In September 1973, the AMI economists expected the economy to slow down. The gross national product (GNP), expressed in real terms, was predicted to grow at annual rates of only around 1.5 to 2.0% during the first half of 1974 before the business climate was expected to improve again.

Nielsen's quarterly forecasting model indicated that the slowdown of the economy was expected to reduce gradually the rate of growth in lamp shipments. The prediction for Franklin domestic shipments of fluorescent lamps pointed to figures for the later half of 1974 which were less than 4% higher than those expected during the same period in 1973.

As the fall progressed, the managers of the CIG received, through many channels, information about the nation's energy problems and consequences for CIG customers and sales. The national and regional mass media gave broad coverage to pending and implemented energy-related decisions by both public and private authorities. Conspicuous use of lighting was the focus for many news stories, with the explicit or implicit theme that lighting could and should be reduced significantly. Lighting as a target for energy conservation had seemed remote, if at all conceivable, in the summer of 1973. Most public attention at that time had been given to the plights of the independent oil and gasoline distributors.

Oil prices continued to increase much faster than in previous years, and these higher prices started to cause substantial price hikes by electric utilities. In mid-October, the CIG managers received a few pieces of information of the kind that would later in the year flood the office. A salesman in Seattle had heard through a distributor that the Boeing Company had disconnected 192 of the 238 lights in the parking lot of one of its plants. A district engineer in southern California reported that Safeway, a supermarket chain, planned to switch off every other lighting fixture in its stores.

In early November, the federal government was actively preparing emergency legislation to deal with energy conservation. The pace of the political process was hurried in anticipation of the Arab oil embargo on deliveries to the United States, which was to take effect by mid-November. It was generally expected that there would be a shortfall of around 17% of petroleum for the winter 1973–1974.

At first the CIG marketing director took a wait-and-see attitude. He did not want to act without having a better understanding of the short- and long-term impact of the changes which apparently were underway. There were, however, good reasons to be concerned about CIG future sales. The industry shipments of fluorescent lamps were down by around 3% in the third quarter of 1973 compared with those in the previous year. Franklin's domestic shipments were down even more. Despite price increases in the preceding periods, the sales value of the shipments had also declined. Elsewhere, requests were being received by the field sales force that were directed toward getting or purchasing empty Franklin lamp packages. These packages would be used for safe storage of removed lamps.

Exhibit 1
Franklin Corporation (A)

Lamp Products Division Organization Chart, fall 1973

- Division Senior Vice President and General Manager
  - Vice President, Controller
  - Vice President, Manufacturing
  - Vice President, Engineering
  - Vice President, Marketing
    - Marketing Director, Original Equipment Manufacturers
    - Marketing Director, Consumer Products
    - Marketing Director, Commercial and Industrial Products
      - Marketing Manager
      - National Sales Manager
        - Regional Sales Managers (8)
          - District Sales Managers (30)
            - Sales Representatives (250)
    - Director, Marketing Development
      - Manager, Sales Forecasting and Planning
      - Manager, Marketing Management Science, (Eric Nielsen)
      - Manager, Marketing Research
      - Manager, Manpower Development
    - Director, Marketing Services
    - Director, Product Management

Exhibit 2
Franklin Corporation (A)

District Managers' Combined Forecasts of Monthly Shipments (units), September–November 1973

Field Forecast Submitted	*Forecast Month* September	October	November
August 25	1,533	1,467	1.433
September 25	—	1,683	1,667
October 25	—	—	1,600
Actual	1,409	1,705	1,756[a]

[a]An industrywide price increase to take effect in December 1973 was announced early in November 1973.

Exhibit 3

Franklin Corporation (A)

Plots of Actual and Fitted Values of Industry Ballast Shipments, 1956–1973

DATE	ACTUAL	FITTED	PLOT +=ACTUAL +=FITTED
56 3	6867.	6664.	++
56 4	6494.	6541.	+
57 1	6529.	6462.	+
57 2	6241.	5997.	++
57 3	5922.	6208.	++
58 1	5330.	4924.	++
58 2	5353.	5459.	++
58 3	5773.	5757.	+
58 4	6155.	6000.	++
59 1	6325.	6135.	+
59 2	7040.	6936.	+
59 3	7027.	6950.	+
59 4	7049.	7249.	++
60 1	7612.	8227.	++
60 3	6556.	7210.	+ +
60 3	6509.	6729.	+
60 4	6780.	6873.	++
61 1	7085.	6524.	++
61 2	8001.	7488.	+ +
61 3	7536.	7567.	+
61 4	7604.	7681.	+
62 1	8303.	7735.	++
62 2	8322.	8203.	+
62 3	8594.	8792.	++
62 4	8512.	8950.	++
63 1	8571.	8123.	++
63 2	8415.	8854.	++
63 3	9600.	9365.	++
63 4	9501.	9742.	+
64 1	9860.	.1019E+05	+
64 2	.1010E+05	.1041E+05	++
64 3	.1016E+05	.1049E+05	++
64 4	.1067E+05	.1081E+05	+ +
65 1	.1158E+05	.1135E+05	++
65 2	.1207E+05	.1181E+05	+
65 3	.1203E+05	.1203E+05	+
65 4	.1247E+05	.1257E+05	++
66 1	.1219E+05	.1282E+05	++
66 2	.1354E+05	.1227E+05	+ +
66 3	.1262E+05	.1224E+05	++
66 4	.1332E+05	.1228E+05	+ +
67 1	.1192E+05	.1195E+05	+
67 2	.1027E+05	.1165E+05	+ +
67 3	.1155E+05	.1189E+05	++
67 4	.1092E+05	.1124E+05	+ +
68 1	.1320E+05	.1291E+05	+
68 2	.1254E+05	.1297E+05	++
68 3	.1239E+05	.1284E+05	++
68 4	.1302E+05	.1306E+05	+
69 1	.1336E+05	.1309E+05	++
69 2	.1359E+05	.1322E+05	++
69 3	.1374E+05	.1367E+05	++
69 4	.1287E+05	.1313E+05	++
70 1	.1165E+05	.1244E+05	+ +
70 2	.1395E+05	.1266E+05	+ +
70 3	.1337E+05	.1275E+05	+ +
70 4	.1189E+05	.1157E+05	++
71 1	.1112E+05	.1204E+05	+ +
71 2	.1097E+05	.1196E+05	+ +
71 3	.1109E+05	.1205E+05	+ +
71 4	.1200E+05	.1217E+05	+
72 1	.1224E+05	.1274E+05	++
72 2	.1372E+05	.1374E+05	++
72 3	.1349E+05	.1361E+05	+
72 4	.1448E+05	.1404E+05	++
73 1	.1511E+05	.1408E+05	+ +
73 2	.1434E+05	.1502E+05	+ +

Exhibit 4
Franklin Corporation (A)

Structure of Econometric
Forecasting Model of Fluorescent Lamps

		Y_5	Y_4	Y_3	Y_2	Y_1	X_1 Investment in private nonresidential structures ($B 1958)	X_2 Index of unit labor costs private nonfarm sector (1967=100)	X_3 Index of output per man hour private nonfarm sector (1967=100)	X_4 Degree of credit crunch as explained in text	X_5 Production index nondurable manufacturing (1967=100)	X_6 Capital stock of private nonresidential structures ($B 1958)	X_7 Dummy variable for quarters of a "buy-in"	X_8 Dummy variable for quarters following a "buy-in"	X_9 Dummy variable for quarter of lamp industry strike threat	X_{10} Dummy variable for quarters of Franklin special promotions	X_{11} Pretax income for electrical machinery industry ($B)
Industry total shipments of fluorescent ballasts	Y_1						●	●	●	●	●						
Industry total shipments of fluorescent lamps	Y_2					● ●[1]	●				●	●	●	●	●		
Industry domestic shipments of fluorescent lamps	Y_3				●												
Franklin field shipments of fluorescent lamps	Y_4				●	●										●	
Franklin domestic shipments of fluorescent lamps	Y_5		●			●											●
Franklin total shipments of fluorescent lamps	Y_6	●		(●)	●	●											

● Column head variable used as independent variable in a regression equation to estimate the row head variable.

(●) Indicates that the sign of the independent variable is reversed before regression parameters are estimated.

1 Y_1 used per Level One estimate and also in weighted, lagged form.

Exhibit 5
Franklin Corporation (A)

Nielsen's Econometric Model: Forecasts Versus Actual Fluorescent Lamp Sales, 1972–1973
(millions)

	1972			1973		
	Forecast Prepared August 1971	*Actual*	*% Error in Forecast*	*Forecast Prepared September 1972*	*Actual Estimated December 1973*	*% Error in Forecast*
Industry domestic	274.0	280.0	−2.1	300.0	291.0	3.1
Franklin domestic						
Field sales	23.3	24.0	−2.9	25.8	24.7	4.5
Private label	1.7	1.7	−1.8	1.7	1.6	4.3
Total	25.0	25.7	−2.7	27.5	26.3	4.6
Franklin export	1.0	1.2	−19.2	1.3	1.8	−27.4
Franklin total	26.0	26.9	−3.3	28.8	28.1	2.5

Exhibit 6

Franklin Corporation (A)

Technical Description of Certain Regression Equations

Level 1 Equation: Industry Total Unit Shipments of Fluorescent Lamp Ballasts, Quarterly (000)

R^2	.968
Standard error of the regression	520
Durbin–Watson statistic	1.64
Intercept term	−46,110
Intercept term *t*-statistic	−4.0

	Raw Variable	*Transformation*	*Coefficient*	t-*Statistic*
X_1	Investment in private nonresidential structures ($B 1958)	$A = (.4)(X_{1,t-1})$ $B = (.3)(X_{1,t-2})$ $C = (.2)(X_{1,t-3})$ $D = (.1)(X_{1,t-4})$ Temp = $A + B + C + D$ $X_1 = X_1/\text{temp}$ $A = (.9)(X_{1,t})$ $B = (.1)(X_{1,t-1})$ $X_1 = A + B$	7,704	4.1
X_2	Index of unit labor costs private nonfarm sector (1967 = 100)	$A = (.4)(X_{2,t})$ $B = (.6)(X_{2,t-1})$ $X_2 = A + B$	−5,457	−2.6
X_3	Index of output per worker-hour private nonfarm sector (1967 = 100)	$A = X_{3,t-1}$ $X_3 = X_3/A$	39,950	3.6
X_4	Credit crunch: average yield on new issues of high-grade corporate bonds minus average market yield on three-month U.S. Treasury bills (%)	$A = X_4$ $B = X_{4,t-1}$ $C = X_{4,t-2}$ $D = X_{4,t-3}$ $X_4 = A + B + C + D$	−158.4	−3.7
X_5	Production index for nondurable manufacturing (1967 = 100)	None	16,510	15

Exhibit 6, continued

Level 2 Equation: Industry Domestic Unit Shipments of Fluorescent Lamps, Quarterly (000)

R^2	.993
Standard error of the regression	1,316
Durbin-Watson statistic	1.56
Intercept term	−52,250
Intercept term *t*-statistic	−19

	Raw Variable	*Transformation*	*Coefficient*	*t-statistic*
Y_1	Forecast of industry total shipments of fluorescent lamp ballasts, from level 1	None	.7114	2.7
Y_1	Forecast of industry total shipments of fluorescent lamp ballasts, from level 1	$A = (.4)(Y_{1,t-1})$ $B = (.3)(Y_{1,t-2})$ $C = (.2)(Y_{1,t-3})$ $D = (.1)(Y_{1,t-4})$ $Y_1 = A + B + C + D$	1.696	6.6
X_1	Investment in private nonresidential structures ($B 1958)	$A = (.4)(X_{1,t-3})$ $B = (.3)(X_{1,t-4})$ $X_1 = X_1 - A - B$	188.8	1.1
X_5	Production index for nondurable manufacturing (1967 = 100)	None	22,760	1.7
X_6	Capital stock of private nonresidential structures ($B 1958)	$A = (.1)(X_{6,t-1})$ $B = (.2)(X_{6,t-2})$ $C = (.3)(X_{6,t-3})$ $D = (.4)(X_{6,t-4})$ $X_6 = A + B + C + D$	199.6	17
X_7	Dummy variable for quarters of a "buy in" due to advance announcements of industry price increases	1957:1, $X_7 =$ .5 1959:2, $X_7 =$ .5 1968:1, $X_7 =$ 1.0 1971:1, $X_7 =$ .5 1973:2, $X_7 =$ .7 All other quarters, $X_7 =$ 0.0	8,468	9.2
X_8	Dummy variable for quarters following a "buy in"	1957:2, $X_8 = -0.5$ 1959:3, $X_8 = -0.5$ 1968:2, $X_8 = -1.0$ 1971:2, $X_8 = -0.5$ All other quarters, $X_8 =$ 0.0	5,252	5.1
X_9	Dummy variable for quarter of lamp industry strike threat	1966:3, $X_9 =$ 1.0 All other quarters, $X_9 =$ 0.0	3,902	2.8

Level 4 Equation: Franklin Corporation Field Unit Shipments of Fluorescent Lamps, Quarterly (000)

R^2	.986
Standard error of the regression	513
Durbin–Watson statistic	2.3
Intercept term	−648
Intercept term *t*-statistic	−7.8

	Raw Variable	*Transformation*	*Coefficient*	*t-statistic*
Y_3	Industry domestic shipments of fluorescent lamps, units, from level 2	None	.0844	18
Y_1	Forecast of industry total shipments of fluorescent lamp ballasts, from level 1	$A = (.4)(Y_{1,t-2})$ $B = (.3)(Y_{1,t-3})$ $C = (.2)(Y_{1,t-4})$ $D = (.1)(Y_{1,t-5})$ $Y_1 = A + B + C + D$	.0600	2.3
X_{10}	Dummy variable for quarters of Franklin special promotions	1962:2, $X_{10} = 1.0$ 1 free with 10 1962:3, $X_{10} = -.5$ Internal record-keeping problems 1965:4, $X_{10} = 1.0$ Federal excise tax eliminated on lamps 1969:1, $X_{10} = -1.0$ Distributors hold off, anticipating Q2 "buy-in" 1970:3, $X_{10} = -1.0$ Competitors regain positions lost during recent strikes	381	4.6

Exhibit 6, continued

Level 5 Equation: Franklin Corporation, Domestic Unit Shipments of Fluorescent Lamps, Quarterly (000)

R^2	.992
Standard error of the regression	421
Durbin–Watson statistic	1.5
Intercept term	38
Intercept term *t*-statistic	0.5

	Raw Variable	Transformation	Coefficient	t-statistic
Y_4	Forecast of Franklin's field shipments of fluorescent lamps, from level 4	None	.344	25
Y_1	Forecast of industry total shipments of fluorescent lamp ballasts, from level 1	$A = (.8)(Y_{1,t})$ $B = (.2)(Y_{1,t-1})$ $Y_1 = A + B$	.0985	4.6
X_{11}	Pretax income for electrical machinery manufacturers (SIC 36, $B)	$A = (.4)(X_{11,t})$ $B = (.6)(X_{11,t-1})$ $X_{11} = A + B$	−209.9	−4.8

Level 6 Equation: Franklin Corporation Total Unit Shipments of Fluorescent Lamps, Quarterly (000)

R^2	.996
Standard error of the regression	290
Durbin–Watson statistic	1.11
Intercept term	111.4
Intercept term *t*-statistic	2.3

	Raw Variable	Transformation	Coefficient	t-statistic
Y_5	Forecast of Franklin's domestic shipments of fluorescent lamps, from level 5	None	.3175	40
Y_3	Forecast of industry total shipments of fluorescent lamps, from level 3			
Y_2	Forecast of industry domestic shipments of fluorescent lamps, from level 2			
Temp	Industry export shipments of fluorescent lamps, computed by subtracting Y_2 from Y_3	Temp $= Y_3 - Y_2$	.1012	5.1

Franklin Corporation (B)

Among the marketing managers at the Commercial and Industrial Group (CIG) of Franklin Corporation's Lamp Products Division, the expectation that 1974 would be a "pretty good year" was widely abandoned by November 1973. An embargo on Mideast oil had caused energy prices to rise rapidly, and many energy conservation programs were being hurried into place in households and corporations everywhere. Conspicuous among these was an apparent nationwide effort to reduce the use of lighting for all but the most important applications. Many existing lamps were being removed from service, and it appeared that both new and replacement lamp demand would be severely reduced.[1]

The CIG marketing director concluded that the 1974 budgeted sales levels, approved in September 1973, would now be impossible to meet, and he asked for and received permission to submit a revised marketing budget for the CIG. The manager of sales forecasting and planning was asked to arrange a new round of sales forecasts. At the end of October, the CIG district sales managers received requests to make estimates of the effects of the energy problems on 1974 and 1975 sales of all product categories. Depending on product category, a compilation of these estimates showed 10 to 20% lower sales volumes than the ones used to prepare the 1974 budget.

The district managers' field sales forecasts were considered very important, because the other available forecasts relied on data and analyses of the pre–"energy crisis" era. Trade magazine editors were approached in an effort to gather more information about the situation and the thinking of others. Through public statements and other sources, it was learned that one competitor had lowered its 1974 lamp forecast about 20%, most of which was due to weaknesses in the prospects for fluorescent lamps in industrial and commercial markets.

[1]See Franklin Corporation (A) for useful background information.

ADAPTING THE ECONOMETRIC MODEL

At the end of October, AMI issued new 1974 forecasts for the variables used in Nielsen's fluorescent lamp sales forecasting model. Most AMI estimates had been revised downward. Despite this, Nielsen obtained a higher industry forecast when he used the new AMI variables. The 1974 shipments came out 0.3% higher than in the previous forecast. The basic reason for the higher lamp prediction seemed to stem from very small changes in the regression coefficients, which resulted when data from the second quarter of 1973 were used in re-estimating the model's regression equations. An announced price increase had caused strong shipment and sales activities in that quarter.

Nielsen had to think about ways of making the model more appropriate for a market in which quite a few customers already had or were about to take products out of usage. His model did not capture this market behavior. In discussing his forecasts with the marketing managers, the extent of empty fluorescent lamp sockets had come up as a key issue. CIG had field observations on lamp usage, and many managers saw a gradually changing lamp usage factor for the remaining years of the 1970s. Nielsen decided to make direct use of this lamp usage factor in his model. He had a couple of weeks to review and revise the model.

Starting with the ballast equation, Nielsen reasoned that the ballast shipments to new installations would continue to be influenced in a way that was consistent with his old equation. There might be some gradual changes affecting the replacement ballast market, but since this portion was less than 20% of all ballast sales, he decided to just update the old equation by adding data from the third quarter of 1973 and discarding those from the periods before 1964.

Regarding the equation for industry shipments of fluorescent lamps, Nielsen pruned out the production index variable which was only making a very marginal contribution to the explanation of the changes in the forecast variable.

Further revisions in regression strategy seemed to promise no marked improvement in the existing model. Nielsen decided that analysis of historic data would not be enough to produce a useful quarterly lamp forecast for 1974–1975. Somehow the fact of emptied lamp sockets had to be brought to bear on the forecast. He concluded that a lamp usage factor should be introduced noneconometrically in the otherwise classical regression-based system of models. He reasoned that the estimated relationships between variables would remain largely intact, although the whole market might be reduced in size due to widespread reductions in lamp fixture utilization.

Nielsen had always viewed the terms in his forecasting equations as either bearing on replacement demand or new demand. Replacement demand would be adversely affected by the degree to which energy conservation programs caused existing lamp sockets to be taken out of service. The percentage of existing sockets in service at any point in time was not known, but this could be built into the equations through the use of a new variable, U, termed a "utilization factor." Replacement demand terms in the model would thus be multiplied by U to estimate declines in shipments to that part of the market.

New demand had always been associated with the shipments of fluorescent ballasts and by the mix of ballasts going into new and replacement service. That mix was likely to change from its present 80% new installations to something higher than that. Nielsen chose the term A to represent the proportion of ballast shipments going into new installations. New demand terms in the model would be modified to show decreases in shipments due to U, by multiplying the ballast terms in each equation by the expression

$$1 + A(1 - U)$$

There was no clear consensus on the value of U for 1974 or 1975. It was assumed that U was 100% in the third quarter of 1973, and after polling the CIG managers Nielsen selected values of U between 84.1 and 87.9% for 1974 and between 83.3 and 90.5% for 1975. The A value had traditionally been 80%, and Nielsen chose to try 82% in his restructured equations.

The ways in which the adjustment factors were introduced into the equation forecasting industry domestic shipments of fluorescent lamp units is demonstrated in Exhibit 1. A further revision of the model was considered which used management's estimates about the degree of usage of lamps that were left in sockets, but the expected weighted average usage was within 1% of normal usage for an average filled socket and was dropped from further consideration.

With these assumptions, the forecast for 1974 industry domestic shipments of fluorescent lamps was 18% lower than the one Nielsen has submitted in late September. The forecast for total shipments, including exports, was similarly lowered. Since the forecasting equations for Franklin shipments were tied directly to the industry shipments equation, Nielsen obtained forecasts for Franklin shipments that were 18% lower than the forecasts produced in September. This was a revision in the same direction which CIG managers thought the sales forecast would have to be changed. The marketing director asked Mr. Nielsen to plug in a utilization factor which was 8% farther below those established as most probably by the CIG managers. At that level, the Franklin 1974 forecast came down an additional 8%, calculated on the November forecast level. The results of the new round of forecasting methods are listed in Exhibit 2.

The marketing director noted that the September commitment forecast for the CIG had been based on a 6% increase of the then-expected sales result for 1973. Even though the last quarter of 1973 had many signs of market weaknesses, the announcement of a price increase for December had helped to keep up shipments through November.

The forecast for which the director eventually obtained approval for the CIG would become a group commitment. CIG management would be held responsible and rewarded in line with this commitment, and the bonus compensation up to the CIG sales force would depend on this level of commitment. The director was doubtful whether such forecasts, however he might arrive at them, should in the future be the basis for the bonus payment formula.

Exhibit 1
Franklin Corporation (B)

Comparison of Unadjusted and Adjusted Level 3 Equation

Dependent Variable: Industry Domestic Unit Shipments of Fluorescent Lamps, Quarterly (000)

Intercept Term −51,490

	Independent Variables	*Regression Coefficient (unadjusted)*	*Adjustment Multiplier*
Y_1	Forecast of industry total shipments of fluorescent lamp ballasts[1]	1.0	$1 + A(1 - U)$
X_1	Investment in private, nonresidential structures ($B 1958)[1]	647.3	None
X_6	Capital stock or private, nonresidential structures ($B 1958)[1]	221.0	U
X_7	Dummy variable for quarters of a "buy in" due to advance announcements of industry price increases[1]	7,387	None
X_8	Dummy variables for quarters following "buy-ins"[1]	6,172	None
X_9	Dummy variable for quarter of lamp industry strike threat[1]	4,467	None

[1]Weighted, summed, lagged, or dummied as described in Exhibit 6 of Franklin Corporation (A) case.

Exhibit 2
Franklin Corporation (B)

Summary of Fluorescent Lamp Unit Forecasts,
December 1973
(000)

Source of Forecast	*1974 CIG Shipments*
September 1973 CIG budget	22,000
September 1973 forecasts provided by econometric model	22,300
December 1973 forecasts provided by econometric model	
Utilization factor = 1.00	20,800
Utilization factor = .86	18,000
Utilization factor = .78	16,300
November 1973 district managers' forecast	18,700

4

Product Positioning

"Daisy" (C)

POSITIONING

By March 1974, the task force researchers had developed considerable information on the women's shaving market, and the task force product development group had designed Daisy, a disposable shaver created specifically for women. At this point, Bryan Dwyer, now product manager for Daisy, and the task force had to determine exactly how Daisy should be positioned. After considering Daisy's various attributes, the J. Walter Thompson Creative Department had developed audiovisual material for seven basic advertising concepts, each of which emphasized one specific attribute of Daisy. The J. Walter Thompson Research Department then tested these concepts with a group of women. From the women's responses, Dwyer and his task force would determine which features of Daisy should be emphasized and which would be played down.

 This case was prepared by Nancy J. Davis under the supervision of Steven H. Star.

THE DEVELOPMENT OF DAISY

Over the last decade the members of SRD's product development group had conducted periodic studies to determine the characteristics that women preferred in shaving products. In recent years, they had made films of women shaving to see how women grasped razors, the angle at which they approached the skin, and so forth. As talk of a major effort in the women's market increased, they began to do both in-plant and out-of-plant tests of handles of various lengths, plus tests of a stubby shaving unit without a handle which was somewhat comparable to Flicker. The women preferred a unit with a handle slightly longer than that of Lady Sure Touch, about the same length as that of Lady Trac II.

The product development group also tested shaving units of different weights. The heaviest was a double edge unit weighing about 64 grams while the lightest weighed about 5 grams. Generally speaking, the lighter units were more often preferred, although units weighing 10 grams or less were usually considered too light. It was almost certain that the Trac II system would be used in the new product, but the group still tested several configurations—a unit with a Trac II system on both sides, a unit with single blades on each side, different angles of the Trac II system, and a "guarded edge" blade that had been dulled slightly with a metallurgical coating.

After carefully reviewing the results of the product development group's studies and the consumer research done by Dwyer's task force and the J. Walter Thompson Research Department, SRD managers identified five features which they considered necessary for a successful product for women. The first requirement, they thought, was that the Trac II system be used. They estimated that the twin-bladed shaving system would account for 25% to 30% of the total 1974 blade market in the United States, and they expected continued rapid expansion in 1975. Women would increasingly be interested in twin-bladed shaving, they thought, as male shaving attitudes and word of mouth concerning the system's superiority increased. They felt that Lady Trac II represented the ultimate in a close, safe shave, but since it was merely a colored-handle version of the men's Trac II, it was not obviously designed especially for women.

A second requirement for success, management thought, was that a woman would purchase and use the product herself, without sharing it with anyone. Consumer research had indicated that this would most likely happen if the product was disposable. Although Lady Sure Touch had never enjoyed much success, Flicker had been quite successful. SRD management had interpreted this as meaning that indeed there was a potential market for a disposable shaver. Management also pointed out that disposability would strengthen the product's position with the trade because, if the product used replaceable cartridges, retailers would have to carry separate cartridges for it, and SRD's salespeople would have to obtain pegboard space for them. These cartridges would probably not differ from regular brown Trac II cartridges except that they would be colored, and SRD already had trouble getting retailers to carry enough of the brown cartridges. In fact, even though SRD had nearly a 60% share of blade sales, it had been able to maintain only slightly more than 40% of available pegboard space. The final key factor in favor of a disposable product was that it would generate more contribution per user than did SRD's other systems.

SRD's third requirement for a successful product, according to SRD management, was that the product must provide the highest retail turnover of any female shaving product to maximize trade interest. The fourth requirement was that the product be featured in a uniquely feminine package to maximize consumer interest. And the fifth requirement was that SRD's design staff create a completely unique display system, the aim of which would be to generate consumer trial.

The product which SRD's development group had now designed especially for women was "Daisy," a lightweight (13 grams) disposable shaver with a permanently locked-on, nonreplaceable Trac II cartridge. The handle was curved near the head of the shaver to provide better visibility and easier access to hard to reach areas such as behind knees. Daisy was molded out of high-impact polystyrene. Around the handle were indented Daisy designs which acted as grips and provided aesthetic appeal. The name "Gillette" was also molded into the handle. Each shaver had its own clear safety cap which protected the shaver's cutting edges during shipment and which was especially convenient when the consumer packed the shaver for traveling. (See Exhibit 1 for a picture of Daisy.)

CONSUMER RESPONSES TO PRODUCT POSITIONING CONCEPTS

To determine the relative emphasis which should be given to Daisy's different features, the J. Walter Thompson Company's Creative Department produced seven possible positioning concepts, each of which emphasized a particular feature or benefit of the shaver. These were as follows:

Positioning Concept	*Major Feature/Benefit*
Blind spots	Curved handle for closeness and safety
Daisy loves me	Product name, safer than older razor
Twin-bladed shave	Hysteresis[1] demonstration showing closeness
Bows to a woman's needs	Shaver designed specifically for a woman's needs, a new design
A girl shouldn't have to	Disposability, convenience of not changing blades
Wouldn't hurt a thigh	Safety, no nicks or cuts
Under 50¢/a dollar	Low price

[1]A hysteresis demonstration illustrated how the Trac II system worked. It showed the first blade lifting the hair, cutting off part of it, and holding it up while the second blade cut the rest of the hair very close to the skin surface. This type of illustration was used heavily in the early advertisement for the men's Trac II.

The research team's task now was to obtain reactions of women currently using a wet shaving system to these various approaches to Daisy's introduction. In all, six sessions were conducted, and the same 57 women who had participated in the survey Alison Yancy conducted in February also participated in this study. All respondents shaved at least twice a month, usually with a wet razor. The specific groups were as follows:

Under Age 25	*Age 25–34*
1 group of working women	1 group of working women
1 group of housewives	1 group of housewives
1 group of high school students	
1 group of college students	

Each group of nine or ten women again arrived at the J. Walter Thompson Company at an appointed time. About a week before the sessions, the women had been sent a sample Daisy shaver and had been asked to use it before coming to the sessions. Before the women screened the position concepts, Yancy spent about 30 minutes chatting with them about their experiences shaving with Daisy.

The creative material for each of the seven position concepts consisted of an idea board (a graphic representation of what one might see in a commercial) and an audio track which included the general message about the product which would appear in a commercial. The respondents were shown the idea boards and listened to the audio tracks of each concept. The order in which the concepts were presented varied from one group to the next. Immediately after each presentation, the women were asked for their reactions. The concepts, audio tracks, and responses were as follows.

Concept 1: Blind Spots

Audio Track:

> Announcing the end of blind spots. Introducing the Daisy disposable shaver.
>
> The Daisy's curved head makes it easier to see what you're shaving . . . especially underarms, calves, and ankles.
>
> And the Daisy's twin blades give you the closest, safest shave possible. The blades are recessed and permanently locked in. You never have to change them. So, after weeks of shaving, throw the whole thing away.
>
> Gillette's new disposable Daisy . . . designed to shed some light on the blind spots.

Consumer responses to the "Blind Spots" concept:

> I think the blind spot is a good point because you can't see under your arms unless

if you're in the shower or in the tub and you go crosswise.

I like this idea because I think that in order to get at the blind spots and everything . . . you'd get a good shave that way because there are a lot of places that are hard to reach.

I have a real hard time getting behind my knees and I shave up over my knees because of the short skirts. It does seem to get in there. I like the shape because of that.

I really like the shape of it . . . you've got a secure feeling in your hand with this. It's a nice shape. It fits right in the palm of your hand and I like the curve on it better than a straight-edge razor.

The thing is, I noticed with this razor—and it hasn't been said—but with my razor, my Lady Sure Touch, I never know the angle to hold it at, 'cause if I hold it too far this way, I don't get any hair, and if I hold it too far this way all I get is skin. And on this one, it's the end is like it's flat, so there's only one angle you can hold it at and so you kind of just have to get the right angle and that would be important to me.

I interpreted it as being like there are certain spots around your leg that it's difficult to see, and I thought that they were saying that this razor was going to make you be able to *see* those spots you can't see.

It did say that you *get to* the blind areas that you do have difficulty shaving if you shave . . .

Well, the idea of the blind spots is appealing to me because I have trouble *getting to* the blind spots.

I think with the straight handle you're right there on your leg and you want to see what you're doing and either you take it away or you lift it up. At least this way, with the curve there, there's some type of space that you can *see* what you're doing, without having to take it off and putting it back down.

In other words, you could take this either way, if your blind spots are where the regular razor misses or where you can't happen to see, this will cover both.

When you can see what you're doing, you won't miss patches of hair and have to go back over it again.

It gets into it on the basis of you can see better rather than on the basis of you won't knick yourself. It's more credible in a way.

Well, it says that you could see what you're doing so you won't get cut . . . it was a lot better . . . it brought out the point a little more.

My immediate reaction to that one, without having held it up to my leg and out to see that it did do that—let you see around—was, well, that's silly, the curved handle. It doesn't make any bit of difference. This one, unless it like actually showed on TV like better than just those pictures that it really did curve out, there would be no way for me to tell that it really did.

It says so many good things at the beginning of the commercial and then at the end they just say about throwing it away. I don't feel so guilty.

Concept 2: Daisy Loves Me

Audio Track:

My new Daisy loves me. My old razor loves me not.

Daisy shaves me smooth, cuts me not . . . because its twin blades shave me closely and they're recessed for safety.

Daisy shaves me easy, worries me not . . . because its new curved head makes it easier for me to see what I'm doing.

And Daisy lasts for weeks . . . bothers me not because I never change a blade. I just throw the whole thing away.

Gillette's new disposable shaver. Daisy loves me.

Consumer responses to the "Daisy Loves Me" concept:

It hits the eye. It teases the imagination. What's it going to do, you want to try it.

To get people's attention. I think by hearing some type thing a lot of people pay more attention to something like that than getting facts. You know, a lot of times you hear things, if it has a rhyme to it, your ear pays more attention to it than a regular talking type thing.

It's an original, stupid commercial. It will stick in your mind.

When I first heard the ad, I thought it was cute and liked it and then I was trying to think of where I heard it . . . the other Gillette Soft and Dri commercial has the same idea to it.

Of course, you could get confused with, you know, Daisy in your tank.

It sounds like the toilet bowl thing.

It must remind me too much of the Soft 'N Dri commercial. I don't like the way they just keep saying, loves me, they just kept repeating that too much.

It's a good commercial, but I don't think it says enough about the razor. I think more force is put on the name rather than what the blade does. I'd rather have a commercial that just told me what something does, without that loves me, loves me not. I just prefer straight facts.

It said a lot, but it was really all hidden in the loves me, loves me not.

I said I didn't like it . . . if the daisies would be in the commercial that's not what we're advertising. You're not advertising flowers, you're advertising a shaver. And I don't think flowers have anything to do with it except the name.

I like what they do on the premise of the Daisy, Daisy loves me, loves me not. I thought it was very cute advertising. If I was looking through a magazine, that was being advertised, I would look at it twice.

I think if it were in a magazine it would be a good advertisement, because you could stop and you could look at it . . . but for on TV it would probably be another one where you'd get up and get yourself a cup of coffee.

I also do not like a commercial where it degrades the intelligence of a person and I think this Daisy business is very juvenile.

I get to the point where this loves me, loves me not, is like adding sugar on top of frosting.

It's too cute, I mean, to the point of yuck!

I think the cliché is sort of childish. I mean, I don't disapprove of clichés, but that one is just that's already bordering on the hackneyed. The approach is a little bit too childish and too flippant.

It's so degrading, it talks down to you so much.

Concept 3: Twin-Bladed Shave

Audio Track:

Introducing the disposable Daisy. The first twin-bladed shaver you use for weeks and then throw away without ever changing blades.

Watch how the twin blades work. The first blade shaves close and then before that stubborn hair snaps back, the second blade shaves it clean away.

And because Daisy's twin blades are recessed and locked in place, there's no safer shave.

The new disposable razor from Gillette . . . don't let a close shave pass you by.

Consumer responses to the "Twin-Bladed Shave" concept:

The only part I like is the hair part, where it misses the one and then it catches the second one which tells me it's better than a regular shaver.

This one shows exactly what it will do, to the point. I think the idea of getting the second hair, you know, 'cause a lot of times when I shave, as I'm shaving, I watch closely and I have to keep going back.

I sort of liked that one . . . it's a real graphic description, I think, and I can relate to that a whole lot better . . . it presents it in a more like factual manner instead of a real frivolous.

Two blades should be a closer shave.

This is good . . . a lot of times I'll start shaving and feel like I've gone right over and it didn't take that much hair off. And I've had to go over again.

This one says to me that you're getting a smooth, close shave with a double-edge razor that will pick up what's left from the first cut and will pick up the stubble after the first blade cuts the hair.

Where does the hair go, when you're cutting your hair now, where does it go. It's going into the blade of the razor, in here. Now how can you use it over and over again without removing the razor to clean it . . . it's like accumulating and accumulating. That's the way to dull a razor.

It's going to get clogged up.

A lot of times I have to open up my razor to take the blade out, and there is hair clogging.

They have other women's razors out that are twin blades, but this isn't emphasizing the shape of it . . . or that it doesn't cut you and they've had other twin-blade razors out for women that say the same thing . . . I think the shape is the most appealing thing to me.

I don't really think that that's the most important thing. There's other razors out that have them too, so I don't think that's most important.

I don't believe that it actually pulls up the hair and goes over it again. I just can't see how it's physically possible that a razor could actually pull up a hair.

I would just wonder if that second blade is gonna take the skin with it . . . it's funny 'cause when I saw it [demo] for the men's razors, I guess I just don't worry about my husband chopping his face up, you know. But I do worry about me chopping my legs up.

I don't find it offensive, but I don't find it believable either.

I wondered about that. I've never really looked at one follicle of hair. It should shave it the first time.

I don't care if the razor has one or two blades, as long as it's clean, close, comfortable, and I'm not gonna get nicked or cut. These are the important things to me.

To me you're not getting across what you really want to get across about the new shape. It's a safer shave, cleaner shave, for hard to reach areas, and the fact that that's really a totally new shape in a razor.

The reason I don't like it is because they all stress that they'll give you a close shave. Of course, they indicate because it's got a twin blade, it will get the one behind it, but I think they should stress more the fact that it's curved in such a position that it can get to the parts that we usually chop. To me that would hit home quicker.

Well, it doesn't show the difficult areas that you think about shaving, like underarms or by your ankles or under the legs.

I wouldn't sit through it 'cause I know this whole spiel already about pulls the hair and this and that.

I don't like, if it's a repeat of that same commercial . . . sometimes I'll be marking papers and watching television and if something is interesting, I'll put my head up and if I turn my head up and see hairs being cut off twice, I'll put my head back down. The shape would be more important, just one shot of the shape.

It reminds me of a man's commercial.

They're copying and we've already been through all this with the previous commercials showing the diagram of the hair being done, so that's just repetitive.

It's just like the men's razor—the Trac II.

Concept 4: Bows to a Woman's Needs

Audio Track:

Introducing the Daisy . . . the first shaving instrument that bows to a woman's needs.

Gillette curved the handle so you can see around your own curves.

And locked in two blades so you never have to change them . . . and made the Daisy disposable so after weeks of clean, safe shaving, you toss the whole thing away.

The Daisy from Gillette . . . the company smart enough to see the difference between men and women's shaving needs.

Consumer responses to the "Bows to a Woman's Needs" concept:

I'm becoming sensitive to different advertisements that have to discriminate.

I don't like the way she says for a woman's needs. I mean, I feel like they're advertising a feminine hygiene deodorant.

On the other hand, the more liberated you want to be distinct from a man, you don't have to use the same thing a man uses in the beginning.

I resented the emphasis put on women. The razor made for a woman, because it seems to be that that's what they're doing in the advertising business, is they're using the whole idea of women's liberation to push their products when a lot of them are not at all liberated . . . as soon as I hear any kind of commercial like that, I automatically turn it off.

It just says, they shape the handle. It's made so you can see around your curves. I mean, it doesn't say anything to me. It doesn't say anything about the safety of it, the closeness of it.

It does say a lot, but it doesn't emphasize the things I think are important like safety. I mean, it mentions it, but not really, and closeness, alright it kind of mentions it but . . .

We have different problems than a man does. We have problems getting around the ankle and the back of the leg.

It told me that you can move it around your curves which is what a woman needs. I mean, our leg doesn't look like a man's face, you know. My leg is curved and I need it to curve around that bump.

It sounded good, real good, cause it expressed a lot about a shaver itself. It says that they know the difference that a man's razor should be something different than a woman's razor and that they're not putting them both on the same level, but that it is geared to a woman's needs and not a man's needs.

. . . you do need a different kind of razor cause you're not shaving your face. What could be more appropriate for a woman than a woman's razor? Like even Women's Lib would have to say yeah.

I think it's telling you what you want to know exactly about the curved razor and that's what we want to know, that the razor is curved and it will be easy for us to get the back of our legs and the shins, and that's exactly what this tells you.

I like that commercial because it's more direct than the others. It tells you right out and it's not so much of the art work involved. It shows the blade and that's the thing, and it explains the razor in full detail and that's it, explaining why it's built the way it is and what its purposes are, which is what we want to know.

I like the curvature of the handle, the head on it. It looks like it would be easy to hold, it's light and I think women would be prone to get it 'cause of the shape.

What my particular problem is with shaving is reaching the back of my thighs and reaching the back of my ankles. That one hits it to a tee, that's what it told me.

I think the idea of the curve is terrific. It's easier to see, especially when you're shaving your underarms.

. . . because I know myself when I shave under my arms especially it's rather difficult for us to see what you're doing and you have to get around areas where . . .

The first thing I thought when I saw that was that it was flexible, it moved . . . I thought, gee, maybe it's like those dolls that have wire in them that bends in different ways.

I also felt it looked like it was movable.

The particular picture makes it look as if it's bendable.

Concept 5: A Girl Shouldn't Have To

Audio Track:

There are some things a girl just shouldn't have to do . . . and changing blades is one of them.

So, Gillette created Daisy, the new disposable shaver.

The Daisy, with Gillette's famous twin blades permanently locked in for week after week of close, safe shaves.

But Daisy's priced so low you won't mind throwing it away. New disposable Daisy, two for about a dollar.

Great new throw-away idea.

Consumer responses to the "A Girl Shouldn't Have To" concept:

. . . what do they mean by weeks, three or ten?

Why shouldn't a girl have to throw away a razor blade? It's as though we're real delicate, can't touch a blade at all.

I mean, 16-year-old boys do it all the time, why can't 16-year-old girls change blades . . . it's like underrating them, because you know, like for heaven's sake, you touched the razor, you'll kill yourself.

It seems silly to me that they say there are some things a girl shouldn't have to do. I mean, I can think of a few things a girl shouldn't have to do, but changing my blades isn't one of them.

I don't like it either, it just annoys me this business about a woman, a girl shouldn't have to change a razor blade . . . why shouldn't a woman have to change a razor blade, she changes a tire.

It doesn't say anything about the product other than it's disposable and my biggest complaint on this I think it's a waste of natural resources.

Now we're in the energy crisis and this and that, and about plastic, you know, and then you figure they make them and then it's gonna be thrown away, and it's just a waste of money to me.

I hate razor blades laying around with little kids.

Well, I think it's not as important stressing that you don't have to change the blade. I think it's more important to stress that it's safer and it's closer.

There were a lot of good ideas expressed in this one that weren't expressed in the first one, but they put the emphasis on the wrong thing, changing the blade.

I think it was a nice idea of not having to change the blade, but it . . . doesn't say much about the product. It just says you know, you don't have to change the blades.

. . . it doesn't stress . . . they didn't really say why it will give you a close shave, because of the contour of it, the recessed blades, because of double blades, all it says it's something a woman shouldn't have to do. It's patronizing.

There's so much to this razor that it's really a good idea that makes me want to buy it. But this commercial told me that it's disposable, that it's cheap and it said once that it was a safe shave . . . but it didn't tell me enough. I'd never, I wouldn't buy it.

I mean, I know this product is gonna come out anyway. It's just a matter of which commercial. But my opinion is that it shouldn't emphasize disposability for people who can't stand disposable stuff.

The only thing that bothers me about this is this one in particular is emphasizing the one thing that I really don't like about it and that's its disposability.

I think it's a waste of natural resources. I do. I mean, here we are trying to conserve whatever resources we have and you are given two products, you know, that you use one and you throw it away and you have this perfectly good case that you can never use again. It just goes into the wastebasket. I think there should be a way of maybe changing the top where you don't have to dispose of the whole thing at once.

I think that's very important. I think that's good. I like just using things and throwing them away, buying new things.

Concept 6: Wouldn't Hurt a Thigh

Audio Track:

Introducing the Daisy from Gillette. The first women's shaver that wouldn't hurt a thigh . . . or ankle or knee or skin or underarm.

The Daisy's twin blades are recessed and permanently locked in at a safe angle, so there's no way to hurt yourself.

Then, after weeks of close, safe shaving, throw the whole thing away and pick the other Daisy.

The Daisy . . . it wouldn't hurt a thigh.

Consumer responses to the "Wouldn't Hurt a Thigh" concept:

I like it because it was cute and it's catchy when you see it.

I agree, I think this is the best one. It's got a tingle to it.

I think it's cute. It's real attention getting. It won't hurt a thigh. I like that.

It says a big thing about it not cutting you and trying to make it a little bit funny. I think they're trying to make it a little amusing to you . . . I think they're making fun of it themselves a little bit too, the company is making fun of it, but they're trying to get across to you that it will work.

There's no way to hurt yourself. I like it better and it won't hurt a thigh. Well, you know, a lot of catchy ads like the Alka Seltzer always has an ad that you remember or something. I won't hurt a thigh. I don't know, but no way you can hurt yourself, I would remember that.

The fact that it doesn't cut you is the most impressive thing to me. So it's the most important thing to stress.

It's recessed, it's not gonna dig into you.

Well, it states what you want to know about the razor itself. That it's curved and so you can't hurt yourself . . . and it's a recessed blade so that right there means that it's gonna be difficult to cut or nick yourself.

I like the idea of not having to change the blade, but then I don't like the idea of after a couple uses having to throw it away. It doesn't say how long you're going to be able to use it before you're going to be able to throw it away. It says a couple of weeks, but it depends on how long you're going to shave, how many times a week you shave, and how dull that blade is going to be.

Concept 7: Under 50¢/a Dollar

Audio Track:

Gillette introduces the new disposable shaver for under 50¢ (under a dollar). The Daisy . . .

Two blades . . . one to shave you close, the other to shave you closer. Permanently locked in at a safe angle so you never change blades. The Daisy . . . weeks of close, safe shaving before you throw the whole thing away.

Two Daisy shavers for 99¢ and that's less than 50¢ apiece.

The new Daisy disposable shaver. Don't let a good shave or a good deal pass you by.

Consumer responses to the "Under 50¢/a Dollar" concept:

When I think of it for under 50¢, I think of some cheap little thing.

. . . if they say it's under 50¢, it sounds like you're getting a good deal . . . but the first thing that will come into my mind is gee, that's too cheap.

I just want to say that the Daisy, first disposable shaver under a dollar, leads me to believe there's only one for under a dollar.

The one thing that really bothers me about this is that it's misleading as far as I'm concerned about the price.

Very misleading, because originally it's telling you 50¢ and then it's coming back and saying you have to get two for 99¢. You can't get it for 50¢, you have to buy it for 99¢.

I think the emphasis should be on what it does. I mean you do want the cost, but . . .

Price is important, but I don't think it's the major thing. Most of us are more concerned with the safety factor, the ease of use, than the price. The price enters into it, but I think the other considerations are more important. Is it going to do the job?

I don't think that money should be the main thing because a lot of people will say, yeah, under a dollar, but how long is it gonna last.

All they do is tell you that it's cheap and disposable.

The only thing I don't like, you keep saying after weeks. It depends how much you're going to shave and how thick your hair is, how coarse your hair is, and everyone is going to get more or less shaves.

I just don't believe all this business of weeks and weeks. That this one blade is going to last for weeks and weeks.

THE DECISION

As the SRD task force and the J. Walter Thompson researchers reviewed these comments about Daisy, they were well aware that the women surveyed had expressed both positive and negative feelings about virtually every one of Daisy's attributes. Whether the feature being emphasized was Daisy's curved handle, its name, the Trac II shaving system, the convenience of not having to change blades, the closeness of the shave, or the product's price, some women thought it was great while others were at best skeptical. The SRD and J. Walter Thompson groups now had to weigh the relative importance of these responses and generalize as best they could about how well they probably reflected the opinions of most women in the 15- to 34-year-old age group. Specifically, they had to assign some priorities to the various features so that the Creative Department would know exactly what the thrust of their advertisements should be. (See Exhibit 2 for sample of Flicker's advertising.)

Exhibit 1
"Daisy" (C)

Picture of Daisy

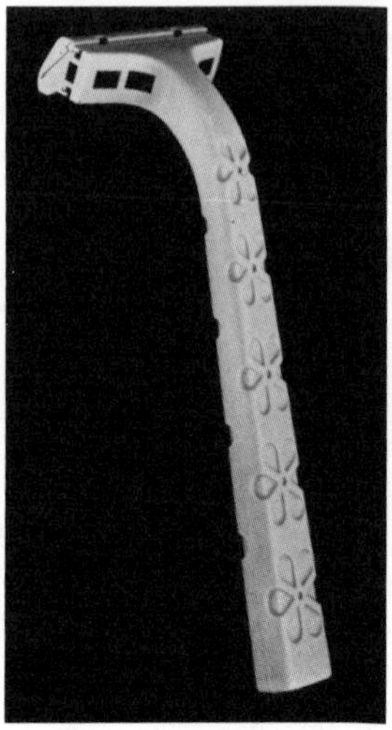

Exhibit 2
"Daisy" (C)

Sample Flicker Advertisements: TV Storyboard

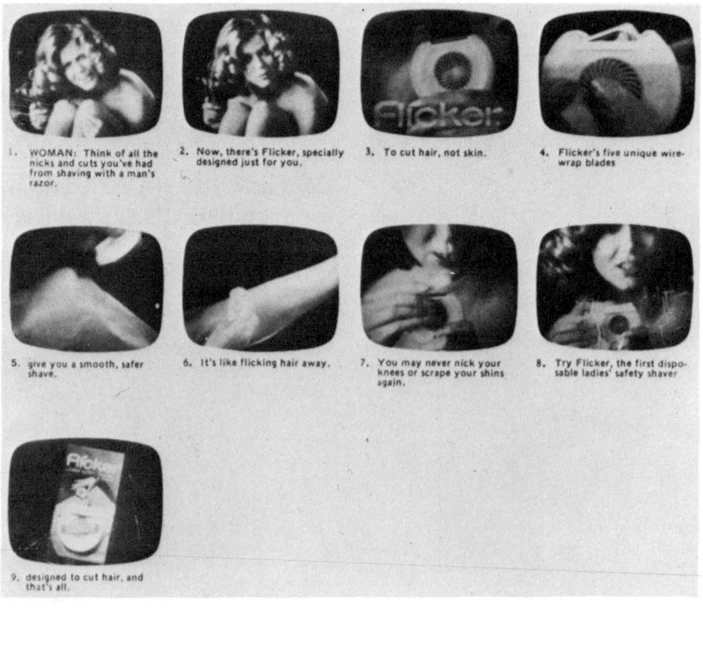
1. WOMAN: Think of all the nicks and cuts you've had from shaving with a man's razor.
2. Now, there's Flicker, specially designed just for you.
3. To cut hair, not skin.
4. Flicker's five unique wire-wrap blades
5. give you a smooth, safer shave.
6. It's like flicking hair away.
7. You may never nick your knees or scrape your shins again.
8. Try Flicker, the first disposable ladies' safety shaver
9. designed to cut hair, and that's all.

Strategic Planning Institute (C)

Mark Chussil had originally started on a project for the Strategic Planning Institute (SPI) in January 1979. It took until late April 1979 before data had been collected and analyzed. Now it was necessary to convert the analysis into a sensible strategy for SPI.

Chussil began by reviewing the results he had obtained. He knew he had to first assess who joined the PIMS (Profit Impact of Market Strategy) program how they differed from nonjoiners and what type of briefing sessions were most successful and how the market viewed PIMS versus strategy consulting firms. Based on this, he would have to recommend a strategy for SPI.[1]

[1]For a complete description of SPI, the PIMS program, the briefing session, and the survey, see Strategic Planning Institute (A) and (B).

RESULTS FROM THE SPI SURVEY

In March 1979, Mark Chussil sent standardized questionnaires to the 690 companies that had attended an SPI briefing session in either 1976 or 1977. Two hundred ninety-two (42%) were returned, with approximately one-third coming from companies that had decided to join the PIMS program.

In assessing the briefing sessions, an initial step was to determine who, within the organizations, attended. Two-thirds of those attending briefing sessions listed their position as "staff," with 34% in general management, 16% in marketing, and 35% in planning. There seemed to be a connection with function and company size. The general managers predominantly came from smaller companies, marketers from above-average-sized companies, and planners generally from larger companies. This was not surprising to Chussil, since larger companies were more likely to have a separate planning group.

The distribution of the job function of "the person who makes the decision about whether to join PIMS," however, was markedly different. Over two-thirds of the decision makers were in general management, 21% more were in planning. Overall, half were line managers. This meant that in roughly half the companies that attended briefing sessions, PIMS had to be sold to two audiences, namely, the attendees and the decision maker from another functional area.

Not only did they have to sell an audience in a different function, but they also had to sell an audience of higher status. Fifty-three percent of the briefing session attendees designated themselves as "assistants."

How attendees first heard of PIMS also yielded some interesting results. Twenty-three percent first heard of PIMS in a published article. Another 21% first came into contact via a PIMS mailing. The largest category, representing 36% of the attendees, first heard of PIMS from someone in their company. This number was more than enough to account for all the attendees who indicated they were specifically asked to attend by their managers. This implied to Chussil that mailings which did not produce large turnouts of those specifically invited were definitely not wasted. In addition, familiarizing managers with PIMS, even if they cannot attend a session, can help spread the word.

Who Joins PIMS

One of the most striking results of this study was that there were no systematic differences between the performance and market characteristics of companies that joined and companies that did not. Data were collected on annual sales, return on sales (ROS), ROS relative to competitors, share rank and relative share, product quality, degree of automation, unionization, marketing/sales and relative marketing/sales, and R&D/sales and relative R&D/sales; there were no differences between joiners and nonjoiners on these factors.

There were some important differences in environmental and structural terms. Companies who described the majority of their sales as coming from mature products were significantly more likely to join (36% versus 23%) than were "growth" companies. Similarly, companies in declining or slow-growing markets were more likely to join than were those in extremely fast-growing markets (43% versus 16%), though there was no difference between slow-growth and moderate-growth businesses. Chussil's interpretation of this was that planning takes on added importance in the minds of managers later on in the business life cycle. It was noteworthy that rapid-growth businesses indicated significantly lower levels of *interest* in PIMS, but they found PIMS as *credible* as did lower-growth businesses.

Certain structural differences were apparent between joiners and nonjoiners. Not surprisingly, highly diversified firms had a higher join rate (38%) than did highly focused firms (26%). To a diversified company, PIMS offered an objective way in which to evaluate a number of business units.

The planning process also seemed to be different between joiners and nonjoiners. Interestingly, the join rate was higher among firms that characterize their planning process as bottom-up rather than top-down (40% versus 29%). This might have been due to the fact that bottom-up companies tended to be larger in terms of sales, and larger companies tended to support two other activities that had positive impacts on joining: planning groups and the use of models. It came as no surprise to Chussil that companies with planning groups had much higher join rates (40% versus 25%) and that companies that used computer models (far more likely in companies with planning groups) showed join rates considerably above those that never or seldom used models (42%

versus 18% and 26%). Curiously, companies with formal planning systems did not join significantly more frequently than did those that did ad hoc planning (36% versus 29%).

As for the personal characteristics of briefing session attendees, those who were MBAs were no more likely to join than were non-MBAs, and holders of technical degrees were no more likely to join than were those without a technical background. Whether the attendee was line or staff, and whether the decision maker was line or staff, also made no difference. However, their *job functions* made a big difference, as shown.

Join rate (mean, 33%)

Function	*Attendee*	*% of obss*[1] *(n = 285)*	*Decision Maker*	*% of obss (n = 285)*
General management	28%	34%	32%	68%
Marketing	28	16	29	6
Planning	42	35	44	21
Production, finance, accounting	37	9	18	4
All others	13	6	25	1

[1]The term *% of obss* means percentage of the observations.

As Chussil expected, planners were by far the most frequent joiners. To some extent this was also linked to company size, because the larger companies are more likely to have a planning group, to use computer models, and to send a planner to the sessions.

Chussil felt that the marketing attendees were the most interesting of the attendees. The planners and the general managers were basically in agreement in the interest and attribute scales on the questionnaire,[2] but the marketing attendees consistently (though not always significantly) rated PIMS higher. Two representative examples are shown.

1. Question 15: Please indicate your opinion of the value of PIMS analysis to your company (1 = not valuable at all, 7 = unusually valuable).

Function	*Value Opinion*
General management	4.57
Marketing	4.84
Planning	4.51
Overall mean = 4.56	

2.

Function	*Average Value of PIMS Services/Expertise on Five Measures (survey nos. 36, 40, 44, 48, 52)*
General management	4.64
Marketing	5.03
Planning	4.61
Overall mean = 4.70	

Why did marketing attendees feel so good about PIMS? Their responses showed that they were especially enthusiastic about PIMS' capabilities for competitive analysis and profitability/share improvement, which were traditional marketing concerns. Why then didn't they have a join rate higher than that

[2]Level of interest in PIMS, belief in the value and credibility of PIMS analyses, and evaluation of PIMS services/expertise regarding profitability, portfolio analysis, competitive analysis, strategic recommendations, and performance improvement were measured. These evaluations were requested in an absolute sense and were compared with similar evaluations of other firms to get relative evaluations.

shown earlier? Was it that they had the problem of selling to a different audience? Marketers represented 16% of the attendees yet only 5% of the decision makers. This meant that at least 65% of the marketers must convince someone *in another functional area* to join PIMS. By contrast, only 40% of the planners faced this problem. In addition, planners took a more general view of the business, whereas marketers were likely to want PIMS as a marketing tool, as evidenced by the particular capabilities that excited them, thus aggravating the internal selling problem. Those attendees in general management were likely not to have this internal selling problem.

One more important distinguishing characteristic between people who joined and people who do not was whether they had a specific strategy problem in mind when they attended the briefing session. Only 23% of the attendees indicated that they had such a problem in mind, but these people had a join rate substantially higher than those without: 42% versus 30%. Chussil felt that there were two useful messages here. One was that thinking about strategy problems seemed to be effective in making PIMS "relevant" to the potential joiner. The second was that only a few people were in this most receptive state of mind when they attended a session. Clearly, this would have important action implications.

The Briefing Session Itself

As can be seen in Exhibit 1, the join rate had declined over time. The trend among recent sessions seemed rather flat. However, this masked two other trends shown in Exhibit 2.

Although PIMS' national and regional sessions had about the same average join rate, the regional sessions had not lost their effectiveness. One reason might be that the average attendance at regional sessions was less than half that of others, which slowed penetration.

The other two types of sessions that PIMS had held that were represented in the survey data were the *Fortune* sessions and topic-oriented sessions (e.g., troubled businesses). Average attendance at the *Fortune* sessions was 68, by far the largest of the sessions, and average joining was 20%, considerably below the averages of the other session types. Topic-oriented sessions, although rather sparsely represented in the survey data, had a mean join rate of 44% with attendance averaging 36, slightly above that for PIMS sessions.

The story of attendance was also interesting. Perhaps the oddest part of the story is that respondents overwhelmingly (82%) thought that the attendance at sessions was "about right" with essentially total disregard for the number of people actually present at the session! Apparently belying their statements, there appeared to be a significant negative relationship between joining and attendance, as shown in Exhibit 3. However, this relationship was due largely to the correlation between session size and session type. Small sessions tended to be the regional ones, PIMS and topic-oriented sessions were of moderate size, and *Fortune* sessions were large. The average attendance at PIMS sessions had not changed over time, and the regional sessions showed only a small shift (from 12 to 15 attendees). There was a lower number of each of the other types, so their shifts (*Fortune* up, topics down) had rather little impact. Because session sizes had remained fairly stable, it seemed that a large part of what was attributed to size may really have been due to other factors such as penetration (PIMS sessions) or unfocused sessions (perhaps *Fortune*).

However, because of the correlation of numerous different factors, it was difficult to directly isolate a single factor which was linked with the join rate. The fact that session alone had no impact on attendees' interest in PIMS, perceptions of PIMS credibility and value, and opinion of speaker quality implied that the size alone should not be designated as the driving force determining join rate.

One other characteristic pertained to the perceived emphasis at the briefing session. Respondents were asked to evaluate the sessions they attended on a scale ranging from "academic seminar" (1) to "sales pitch" (7). Chussil saw three messages in the data. One was that the mean was slightly over 4; this, plus a look at the distribution of responses, indicated that sessions appeared as sales pitches about as often as academic seminars. Second, there was a strong correlation showing that the seminar was thought more appropriate than the sales pitch. Third, the join rate among general managers and marketers was unaffected by where on this spectrum the session they attended happened to fall, but the join rate for planners—PIMS' best customers—plummeted when the session appeared to have been a sales pitch.

PIMS' Position

The last question Chussil wanted to address was how PIMS was viewed relative to strategy consulting firms. Among the data gathered were "similarity" ratings on which respondents were asked to indicate the similarity they perceived between various consulting firms and PIMS. The scale went from 1 (very dissimilar) to 7 (very similar). The questions purposely did not ask about similarity along specific dimensions; rather, using a technique called multidimensional scaling, a computer program can take these perceived similarities and display where the firms are "located" in space, relative to each other, in the respondent's mind. The graphed distance between two firms was proportional to the degree of dissimilarity between them. The analyst would then have to study the plots to see where firms were located and to try to understand on what dimensions they were perceived to differ.

The similarity data collected for this survey showed some interesting results even prior to analysis with multidimensional scaling. Chussil felt the most important one, which came as no surprise to him, was that PIMS was perceived as being considerably more like BCG (similarity of 3.9) than like ADL, DRI, or "your" (the respondent's) planning group (2.6, 2.5, and 2.9, respectively). What *did* come as something of a surprise to Chussil was that none of these perceptions varied significantly between joiners and nonjoiners. Joiners saw PIMS as being as similar to BCG as did nonjoiners.

Planners saw PIMS as being less similar to ADL and DRI than did general managers, but even they perceived PIMS as being most similar to BCG. This meant that the problem of differentiation from BCG was persistent even among planning professionals.

What distinguished the joiners from the nonjoiners when PIMS and BCG are believed to be so similar? The evaluative ratings of BCG were essentially constant among joiners and nonjoiners, but the ratings of PIMS were not (obviously, PIMS ratings were higher among joiners). Nonjoiners found PIMS about as good as BCG on the evaluative scales, but joiners found PIMS significantly better. Given the similarity ratings, this meant that in a certain sense PIMS was merely considered better at what BCG did, rather than PIMS being perceived as something different.

The multidimensional scaling was used to provide a graphic representation of similarities between firms in a multivariate context.[3] Exhibits 4–9 show these "perceptual maps" for the following groups:[4]

[3]In a way, a single similarity index is to multidimensional scaling as a single correlation is to multiple regression.

[4]The scales on the charts are completely arbitrary. Location relative to other points is all that matters; a chart contains exactly the same information if read upside down, in a mirror, etc. (A good fit was achieved in all cases.)

Exhibit 4 = all observations
Exhibit 5 = all nonjoiners
Exhibit 6 = all joiners
Exhibit 7 = general management joiners
Exhibit 8 = marketing joiners
Exhibit 9 = planning joiners

It was the job of the analyst to interpret what the axes represented; the program merely positioned the firms in such a way as to agree most closely with the interfirm distances supplied by the similarities.

Although Chussil was not entirely confident of his interpretation, he felt the axes represented a macro versus micro orientation (*X* axis) and a tool versus advice service (*Y* axis). On Exhibits 4–6, the left appeared to be macro and on 7–9 the right seemed to be macro; on all except 7, up seemed to indicate tool.

One of the most striking characteristics of these maps was the interaction between PIMS and BCG, especially the relationship among PIMS, BCG, and the respondent's company in Exhibits 5 and 6. Nonjoiners perceived BCG as lying almost directly on a straight line drawn from themselves to PIMS. Chussil's interpretation was that nonjoiners saw PIMS as a "poor man's BCG," because they did not understand the use of PIMS as a tool and because (as discussed earlier) they did not believe that PIMS offered service or expertise superior to BCG's. In addition, BCG was more like themselves, talking a language more familiar to them, and so on. Joiners, on the other hand, had a much clearer perception of PIMS as a tool and of BCG as advice. PIMS was perceived by them as being unique, because no other firm was even remotely in the direction of PIMS. PIMS also was located much closer to the joiner's company.

Exhibit 9 indicated to Chussil that planners tended to be the more knowledgeable buyers of strategic services. Planners differentiated so well between the four firms that each was far in its own quadrant, signifying a unique bundle of services. In contrast to Exhibit 5, the nonjoiners had identified each firm effectively on only one dimension each.

General managers (Exhibit 7) saw themselves as advice-oriented, which is what general management does, and as a combination of macro and micro concerns. They appeared to join PIMS because they perceived PIMS as having a strong micro orientation shared by no one else. The fact that PIMS was also perceived as a tool was nice, but (1) others were tools, too, and (2) it was nothing special to general management to offer a tool, because to general management *everything* was a tool.

From Chussil's perspective, the appeal of PIMS to the marketer (Exhibit 8) probably was due to the strong micro image, which to the marketer signified an important closeness to the market and to performance therein.

Chussil concluded from these maps that there were substantial misperceptions on the part of the market and that PIMS meant different things to different people.

PIMS' Recommended Strategy

The hard task which confronted Chussil was to evolve all his analysis into a new strategy for PIMS. He felt that the longer he spent poring over the data, the more he could learn. In spite of the unlimited richness, he knew that he had to stop analysis, at least temporarily, and begin to make recommendations to SPI management.

Based on the data, he felt that he could make three strong suggestions.

1. The most important recommendation was one that PIMS was already starting to implement: *differentiate*. The survey provided ample evidence that there was considerable confusion and misunderstanding on the part of the potential member. Traditional presentations seemed to fall short. Briefing sessions could include a section to show *explicitly* how PIMS was different from other strategy ser-

vices. This could be a matter-of-fact, low-key section, essentially listing the ways that PIMS was unusual, or it could at the opposite extreme be an aggressive exposition of why PIMS was superior to other approaches. Based on the findings that showed that a sales pitch emphasis was unappreciated, a calm, reasoned explanation of where PIMS was positioned in the marketplace seemed more appropriate. Such a campaign could be extended to the media, because published articles were shown to be an important part of the process of bringing a company into PIMS.

2. A second major action would be to *focus* the briefing sessions. PIMS sold to at least three markets with different interest, objectives, and orientations: general managers, marketers, and planners. That these are different markets was clear from their different join rates, perceptual maps, and evaluations of particular services, arising from their different functional needs and organizational ranks. A large part of the session would be common to all three, and because attendees must often convince decision makers in other functional areas to join, there must also be reasonable discussion of the broad variety of PIMS tools and services. However, the orientation of the session, the war stories discussed, and the particular tools emphasized offered room to focus on specific buyer groups. Although interest in attending focused sessions may be higher than for traditional ones, this may mean somewhat smaller sessions; nonetheless, smaller sessions had enjoyed better join rates than had larger ones because of the freedom of the attendee to ask questions and interact with PIMS staff—in short, to learn more. In fact, this was probably the best way to make the sessions small.

3. Finally, it appeared that sessions should have a greater *problem orientation.* The join rate was higher for those who arrived with specific problems in mind, but there were few of these people. Nonetheless, PIMS should actively promote thinking in terms of problems to be solved. One way would be for materials sent to prospective attendees (or to registered attendees whose session has not yet occurred) to emphasize problems: a few one-paragraph case descriptions of common situations, saying that PIMS can help solve these problems. Thinking in these terms may not only intrigue the person enough to come to a session; more important, it could remind the person of similar situations that he or she had encountered, helping to see how PIMS could address their own real-life problems. Another way that was employed occasionally was to begin the session with descriptions of a few problems and then *show* how PIMS could help to solve them. Although the two approaches were not mutually exclusive, the second was more likely to boost the join rate, while the first may help attract people to the sessions. It was important that the examples chosen to illustrate PIMS analysis could offer an ideal opportunity to focus the sessions as suggested above.

Chussil was confident that his recommendations were supportable by the data and that PIMS management would soon begin implementing his suggestions.

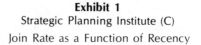

Exhibit 1
Strategic Planning Institute (C)
Join Rate as a Function of Recency

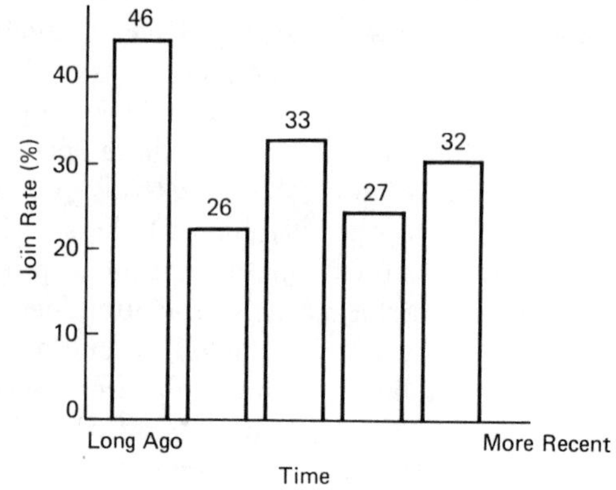

Cutpoints chosen so that roughly equal numbers of observations fall in each column

Exhibit 2
Strategic Planning Institute (C)

Join Rate as a Function of Recency and Type of Session

Join Rate (%)

Time	National Sessions	Regional Sessions
Old	53 (n = 38)	34 (n = 33)
	30 (n = 23)	32 (n = 28)
Recent	19 (n = 42)	37 (n = 57)

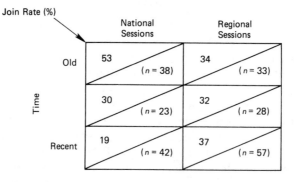

[1]National sessions does not include the *Fortune* sessions or "topic" sessions, such as troubled businesses.

Exhibit 3

Strategic Planning Institute (C)

Join Rate as a Function of Size of Audience at Briefing Session

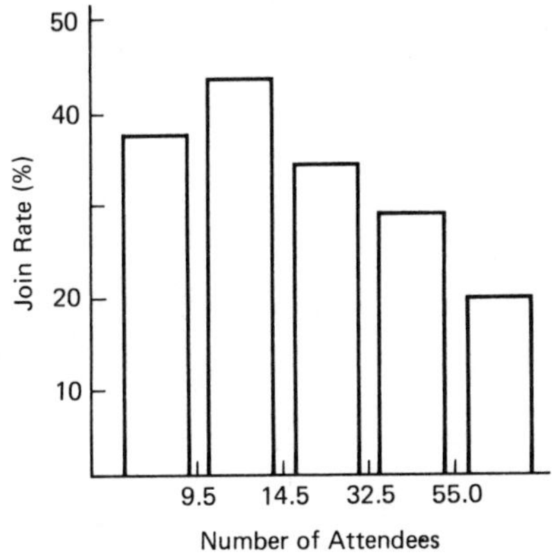

Exhibit 4

The Strategic Planning Institute (C)

Perceptual Map—Joiners and Nonjoiners Combined

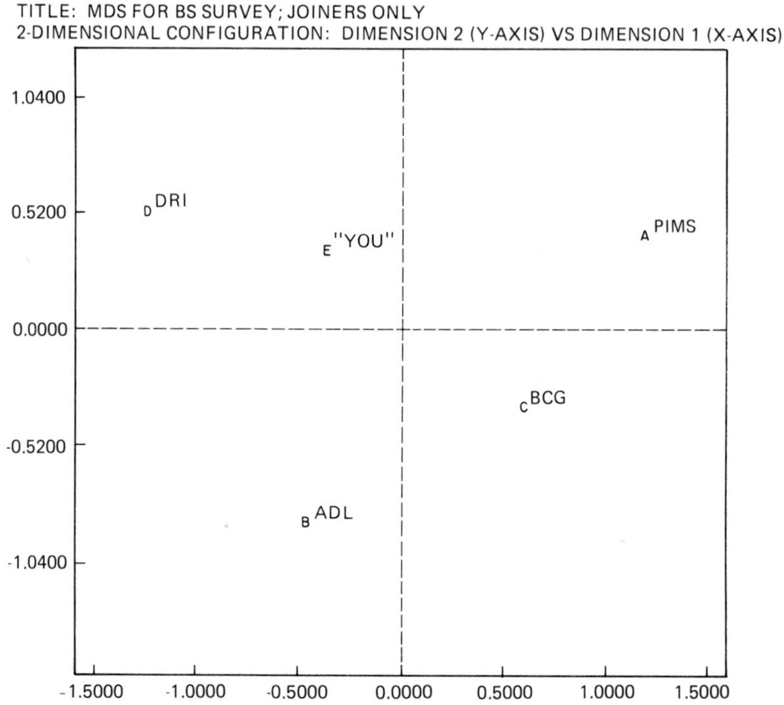

Exhibit 5
The Strategic Planning Institute (C)

Perceptual Map—Nonjoiners Only

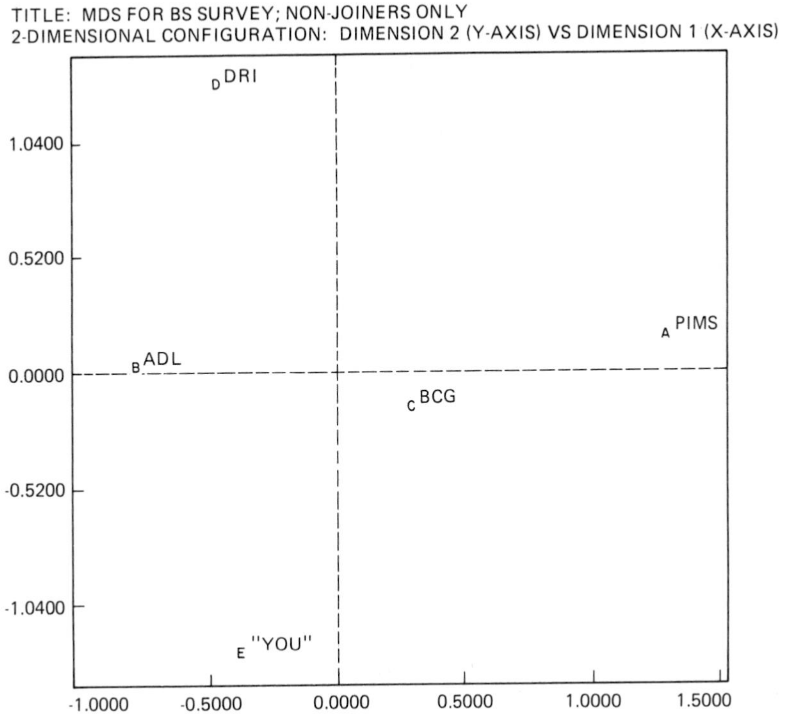

Exhibit 6
The Strategic Planning Institute (C)

Perceptual Map—Joiners Only

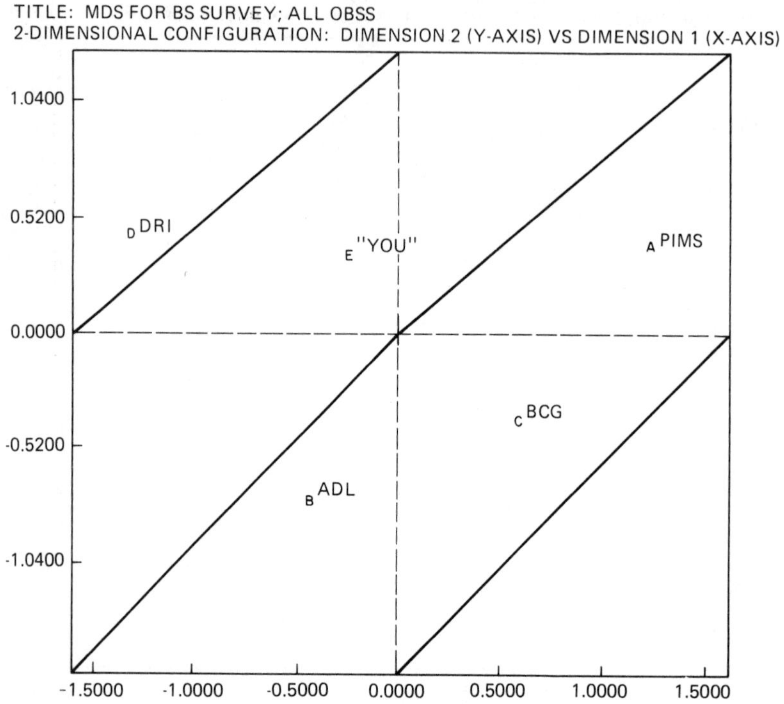

Exhibit 7
The Strategic Planning Institute (C)

Perceptual Map—General Management
Joiners Only

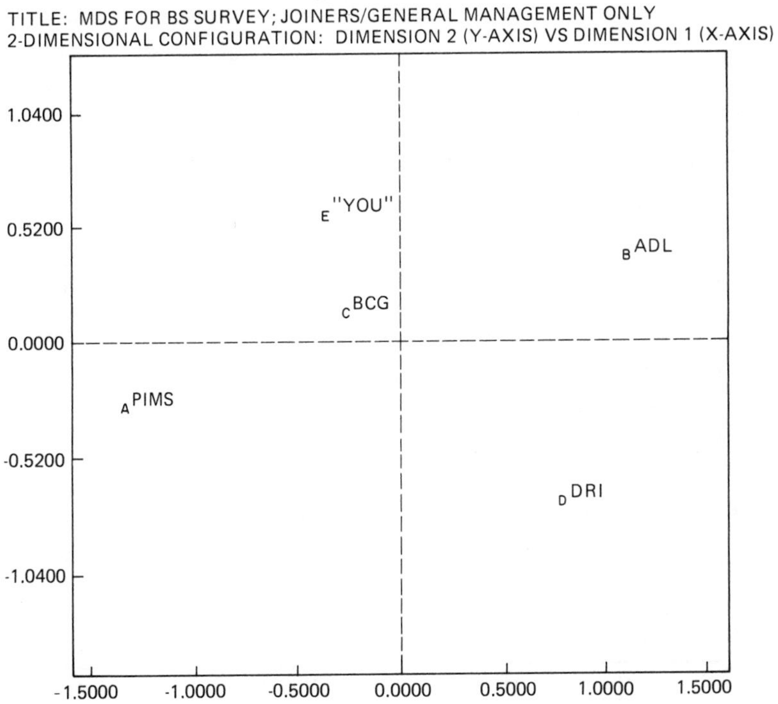

Exhibit 8
The Strategic Planning Institute (C)

Perceptual Map—Marketing Joiners Only

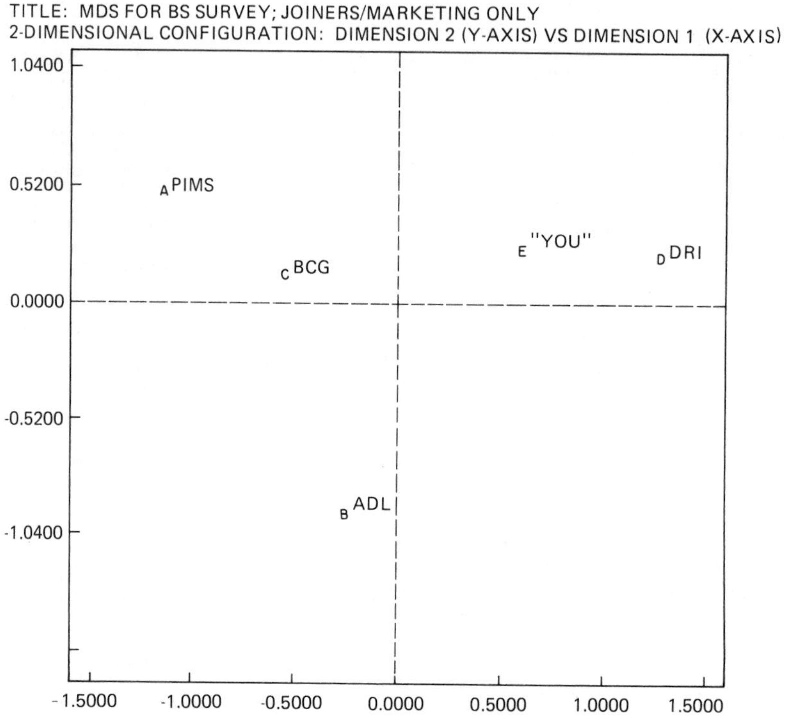

Exhibit 9

The Strategic Planning Institute (C)

Perceptual Maps—Planning Joiners Only

TITLE: MDS FOR BS SURVEY; JOINERS/PLANNERS ONLY
2-DIMENSIONAL CONFIGURATION: DIMENSION 2 (Y-AXIS) VS DIMENSION 1 (X-AXIS)

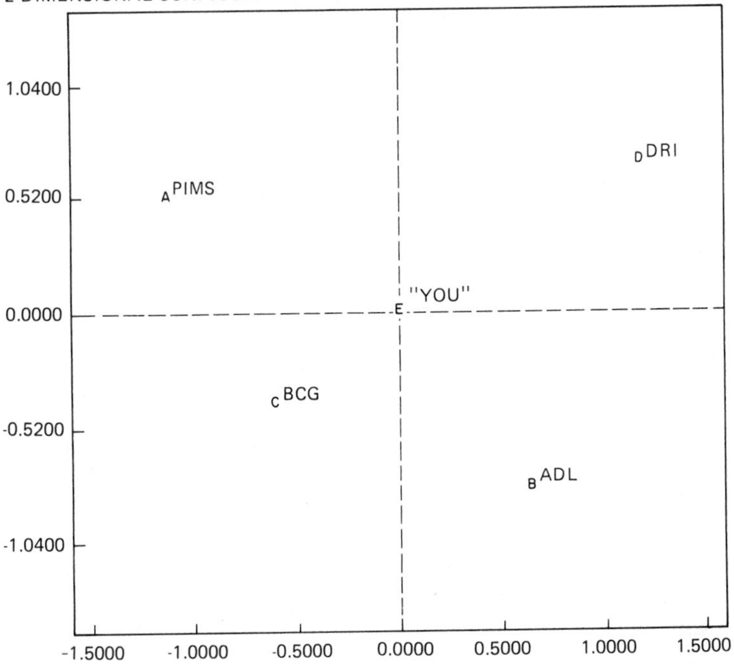

Ocean Spray Cranberries, Inc. (B)

FINDINGS OF THE FRUIT POSITIONING STUDY

Russell Haley of Appel, Haley, Fouriezos, Inc. (AHF), presented in March 1972 the conclusions of the fruit positioning study to the managers of marketing and marketing research at Ocean Spray Cranberries, Inc. (OSC), and the advertising agency personnel involved with OSC sauce products.[1] A 305-page report and additional computer printouts were also handed over by Haley. The study was generally given a favorable reception by the OSC managers. They noted that some findings confirmed those of a study undertaken in 1961–1962 by McCann-Erickson.

According to Haley, the central marketing problems for cranberry sauce were (1) relatively low per capita use and (2) an aging franchise. He suggested the following as five promising ways of increasing consumption:

1. Promoting cranberry sauce as a versatile poultry and meat accompaniment.
2. Changing people's perceptions of cranberry sauce.
3. Reminding people to use it.
4. Focusing communications efforts more sharply on potentially productive market segments.
5. Introducing new products.

The AHF research team stated in its 305-page report that "four clearcut attitudinal segments were found in the cranberry sauce market." These were labeled as follows:

Segment 1: Convenience oriented
Segment 2: Enthusiastic cooks
Segment 3: Disinterested
Segment 4: Decorators

Each consumer segment was described in a variety of ways. For instance, when compared with all consumers, the convenience-oriented segment was said to have "a higher

[1]For details of the exploration and pilot test phases of this research and for additional industry and company background, see Ocean Spray Cranberries, Inc. (A).

preference for jellied form of cranberry sauce relative to whole berry," and "a higher share of people 45 years or older."

Background

At the invitation of OSC management, the marketing research firm Appel, Haley, Fouriezos, Inc., had conducted the final phase of a three-phase consumer research study about cranberry sauce. The overall purpose of the study was to develop a better understanding of cranberry sauce users—their behaviors, attitudes, opinions, and beliefs. This would be accomplished by achieving the following research objectives:

1. Identifying and describing the kinds of persons who use cranberry sauce.
2. Providing an understanding of what consumers are seeking in choosing between complementary products for use such as in salads or with the main course.
3. Looking into the consumption of various food types as sources and potential sources of cranberry sauce usage.
4. Describing consumer usage patterns with regard to cranberry sauce.
5. Identifying broad media types for OSC sauce for getting across its message to consumers.
6. Investigating new product or line extension possibilities.

The cost of the whole project would be \$44,500 ± 10% contingency for unforeseen costs or savings. The project was proposed in three phases which covered (1) exploration of areas to be covered, (2) development of measurement tools, and (3) measurement of the market on a national basis.

The purpose of the first phase was to define the competitive environment and to compile lists of product attributes, consumer beliefs, and personality and life-style characteristics of special relevance for cranberry sauce consumption. To this end, two focused group sessions were conducted among 20 women who were either heavy or light users of sauce in the past year. The results from phase 1 were used in designing a questionnaire. The tentative list of questions was quite lengthy. The purpose of phase 2 was to determine which of the many questions best reflected underlying consumer dimensions in the cranberry sauce market. Data for phase 2 were collected by a pilot survey undertaken in the fall of 1971, in which a sample of 200 females living in ten market areas was interviewed personally.

Analysis of the pilot test data resulted in substantial revisions of the questionnaire. Between 30 and 98% of the items were dropped or exchanged within parts of the questionnaire. The structure of the questionnaire was, however, basically retained for later use in a national survey. Thus, most of the questions dealt with the following five areas:

1. Opinions about attributes of ideal canned fruit products.
2. Opinions about attributes of jellied cranberry sauce.
3. Opinions about attributes of whole-berry cranberry sauce.
4. Overall attitudes and feelings about cranberry sauce.
5. Descriptions of personalities and life-styles.

The new questionnaire also included some questions on exposure patterns to broadcast and newspaper media as well as questions regarding readership of 24 national magazines for general or female audiences. At a meeting with Haley late in 1971, OSC management agreed to proceed with phase 3.

Phase 3

The purpose of the third phase—a national survey—was to provide a better understanding of the attitudes and behavior of cranberry sauce users and to suggest potentially innovative ways of segmenting the existing demand for sauce. The respondents were sampled from 47 areas, 37 of which were Standard Metropolitan Statistical Areas, and the remaining 10 were nonmetropolitan counties. Quotas of persons to be interviewed were then established for each area, for example, 12 for Larimer County (Ft. Collins), Colorado, and 100 for New York. Blocks or roads were selected randomly from maps of the sampling areas. A list with names of blocks or roads was given to each interviewer, who was directed to contact and screen personally a given number of females according to a specific procedure for choosing households within a block or road. The interviewers made daily reports through their supervisors to AHF of the number of completed interviews with eligible respondents. As in the pilot survey, potential respondents were screened personally to determine if they had purchased canned cranberry sauce in the past year. Around 1,300 women were contacted and 1,004 of them qualified as respondents and participated in the interviews.

Analysis of the Sample in the Aggregate

Before seeking the identity of potentially interesting homogeneous subgroups within the sample, the AHF research team examined the characteristics of the entire sample of 1,004 respondents. Frequency counts of the total sample on various demographic and socioeconomic characteristics compared with available national distributions were as follows:

Characteristics	*AHF Sample (n = 1004)*	*1970 U.S. Population Census*
Age		
18–39	42%	44%
40–64	47	40
65+	11	16
	100%	100%
Education		
High school or less	66	79
Some college or more	34	21
	100%	100%
Employment		
Full- or part-time employed	22%	42%
Children		
Have children 18 years or under living at home	63%	55%

The most commonly accepted opinions or beliefs about cranberry sauce reflected its traditional nature, food value, and integration as part of a meal rather than a garnish. The percentage of all respondents strongly agreeing or disageeing with different belief statements is shown in Exhibit 1.

When consumers were asked about their inventory of cranberry sauce, 48% of them said that they had at least one can at home. Of the 48%, 85% reported they had OSC cans. Since more than half of the respondents agreed strongly with the statement that "I probably would serve more cranberry sauce if I thought of it, but I don't," Haley suggested that promotions be directed toward building increased in-home inventories and stimulation of product usage.

It was found that "nutritious" and "has vitamins" were said to be "extremely important" characteristics of an ideal canned food product by 46% and 37%, respectively, of all interviewed cranberry sauce users. However, only 22% and 19%, respectively, "agreed completely" that jellied cranberry sauce had these characteristics. The research team concluded that a fortified product would help to provide reassurance in these areas.

The researchers thought that a second new cranberry sauce product might be one with "a consistency more similar to that of applesauce." They argued that "one principal reason for the popularity of cranberry sauce is its convenience in use. If it were made even more convenient (so that it could be easily spooned out of the can or stored in refrigerator dishes) it might provide a worthwhile stimulus to sales."

The research team found grounds for the statement that cranberry sauce is sold "in a somewhat ambiguous competitive environment, being perceived as something of a cross between a fruit and a garnish." A perceptual map developed as part of the phase 1 research was put forward in support of this statement. Of the various food accompaniments, cranberry sauce products were perceived to be "closer" to applesauce than to catsup. This map was based on data collected from 20 women who had participated in the phase 1 focused group interviews.

When the research team examined the ways in which cranberry sauce and jelly were served, they discovered the following reported usage patterns:

Application	*% of Cranberry Serving Occasions*
Accompaniment to meats	84%
As a vegetable substitute	3
In plain or molded salads	9
In cooking (glaze or topping)	1
In baking	1
In desserts or dessert toppings	1
Total	100%

By combining information on consumers' frequency of use of the sauce with various meats and the frequency of eating these meats, it was found that chicken, roast beef, and pork were worth special consideration for future advertising copy and package label. The method and data which led the research team to this conclusion were the following:

> Each respondent was given a score based on her frequency of use of cranberry sauce with an individual meat—5 for "always," 4 for "frequently," 3 for "sometimes," 2 for "seldom," and 1 for "never." The average score for light users was subtracted from the average score for heavy users. (25% of all users were classified as heavy users and 28% as light users.) The results were multiplied by the frequency of eating as individual meat and this figure in turn was multiplied by 100. In other words, the numbers in the following table are indicative of the relative amounts of volume which would result if light users were to behave like heavy users.

Jellied	*Index*
Fried chicken	187
Baked or roast chicken	180
Leftover chicken	130
Roast beef	125
Broiled chicken	120
Pork/pork chops/pork roast	105
Hamburger	86
Ham	80
Leftover beef	76
Leftover turkey	60

Whole Berry	*Index*
Baked or roast chicken	180
Fried chicken	119
Pork/pork chops/pork roast	105
Leftover chicken	104
Baked or roast turkey	102
Broiled chicken	96
Hamburger	86
Roast beef	75
Leftover turkey	72
Steak	68

Management observed that the aggregated sample analyses were not inconsistent with the findings of the MARPLAN '62 study which they had received in 1962. One of the major differences between the 1962 study and the AHF study, however, was AHF's determination to identify subsets of the entire sauce market in psychographic terms and to suggest variations in OSC's strategy based on the resulting market segments.

Determining Psychographic Market Segments

The method used by AHF to determine a segmentation strategy and structure for the cranberry sauce and jelly market was described to the casewriter by Tibor Weiss, senior vice president of AHF. The data collection phase of phase 3 had produced three separate categories of information dealing, respectively, with life-styles, personality, and product attribute judgments.

These data were eventually input to a cluster analysis program, but first the original data sets were reduced to a smaller number of important variables. Instead of using individual items of the questionnaire as possible bases for clustering, a small number of summed scales were constructed. For example, four scales of various belief items were constructed as follows. Using judgment supported by factor analysis, a few items were selected and their responses were added together to form a new scale, thus creating a new variable or item.[2] The four resulting belief scales and the tentative labels attached by the AHF research team were

Scale 1 = "Traditional"	6 − ("I usually keep a can of cranberry sauce in the cupboard year round") + "I don't like to serve cranberry sauce too often because it loses its significance." [Note that $(6 - x)$ reverses the polarity of item x; thus $S_1 = (6 - x_4) + x_{15}$.]
Scale 2 = "Cook and Bake"	"I often use jellied cranberry sauce as an ingredient in cooking and baking" + "I use whole cranberry sauce as a cooking or baking ingredient" ($S_2 = x_{13} + x_{11}$).
Scale 3 = "Serving Interest"	"Cranberry sauce is served with pork because it cuts the grease" + "Cranberry sauce should be served only on Thanksgiving and Christmas" + "I serve cranberry sauce to cool hot food" + "A firmer jellied sauce is a higher-quality cranberry sauce" ($S_3 = x_8 + x_{21} + x_{20} + x_7$).
Scale 4 = "Food Value"	"Cranberry sauce is part of the meal rather than a garnish" + "Cranberry sauce has food value as well as an attractive appearance and good taste" ($S_4 = x_3 + x_2$).

[2]This new scale is sometimes called a cumulative or Guttman scale.

Similarly, six summed scales of personality items and six summed scales of benefit items were also constructed. The full list of belief variables is included in Exhibit 1.

The belief scales, personality scales and benefit scales then were compared for their potential as bases for defining market segments. Each set of scales was used in the cluster analysis program separately producing three possible interpretations of market structure.

The cluster analysis program assigned individual members of the sample into groups so that all members of a given group were relatively similar in terms of the belief, personality, or benefit characteristics input to the program and that each successive group would be relatively dissimilar when compared with all other groups. A more explicit description of the cluster analysis in included as Exhibit 3. The research team at AHF decided that the beliefs data provided the best of the three bases or clustering and that there were four clusters that were of managerial consequence. Those clusters were named "convenience oriented," "enthusiastic cook," "disinterested," and "decorator."

When the four segments were compared on some standard marketing variables, the results were as follows:

To enrich the understanding of the four clusters, a variety of psychographic and traditional marketing variables were cross-tabulated against cluster membership patterns. The resulting tabulations were presented by Haley as a means of making the clusters more lifelike, more humanistic, and more realistic potential targets for the OSC marketing strategy. In turn, the clusters were described according to their central tendencies as indicated by the following types of measurements:

1. Key benefits of ideal fruit products.
2. Key beliefs about cranberry sauce products.
3. Key food related life-style characteristics.
4. Key attitudes toward cranberry sauce products.

Segment Size (%)	*Convenience Oriented (n = 299)*	*Enthusiastic Cook (n = 257)*	*Disinterested (n = 270)*	*Decorator (n = 178)*	*Total (n = 1004)*
All respondents	30%	25%	27%	18%	100%
Total volume purchased	34	32	16	18	100
Jellied	35	29	17	19	100
Whole berry	30	40	14	16	100
Heavy users (19 or more cans per year)	27	38	13	25	25
Medium users (7 to 18 cans per year)	48	45	40	54	46
Light users (6 or less cans per year)	25	18	47	21	28
Total	100%	100%	100%	100%	100%
Noticed price difference between OSC and other brands	34%	37%	30%	36%	34%
Purchased 10 OSC cans of last 10	75%	74%	76%	74%	75%
Age distribution					
18–39	36%	35%	58%	37%	42%
40–64	53	56	35	44	47
65+	11	9	6	17	10
	100%	100%	100%	100%	100%

5. Product usage behavioral tendencies.
6. Demographics.
7. Media exposure patterns.

Exhibit 2 lists the between-cluster comparisons for each of the characteristics and also compares the individual clusters with the population means on many individual items.

Presentation to Management

In his presentation to OSC management, Haley said the four clusters were "four clearcut attitudinal segments." He went on to say that "three of the four segments just described are attractive targets and, based on the information now available to us, tailormade campaigns can be designed for each segment." He described these campaigns in terms of buying incentives, copy visuals, copy tonality, promotions, and media, as follows:

Comparisons of the clusters which differed in volume consumed and in types of cranberry products used led the research team to talk about "a cycle running through the market." The lightest sauce users seemed to strongly favor the jellied form. At the next heavier usage level, people became somewhat more frequent users of the jellied form. At a still higher level were heavier users who used both whole-berry and jellied sauce, favoring whole berry because of its usefulness in cooking and baking. Finally, there was the real cranberry enthusiast who employed fresh berries in making her own sauce.

The researchers did not think that efforts to attract nonusers held large promise. This had also been the conclusion of a similar though nonsegmented study undertaken in 1962 by McCann-Erickson. Moreover, only 23% of the households originally contacted were nonusing households. Some researchers thought that light users might be difficult to motivate because of their relatively low inter-

	Target Clusters		
	Convenience Oriented	*Enthusiastic Cook*	*Decorator*
Buying incentives	Position as a convenient, versatile meat accompaniment rather than as a special-purpose product. A natural food.	Both jellied and whole berry can be promoted for this segment. Color, versatility, and usefulness as a cooking/baking ingredient are desirable claims.	A good way of dressing up your meats and leftovers. A way of interjecting a festive note at mealtimes.
Copy visuals	Informal settings, family meals; baked/roast chicken particularly good.	Larger family scenes or scenes with guests. Big eaters.	Mature models, slight accent permissible, leftovers particularly good.
Copy tonality	Brisk, matter of fact. These women are not involved in cooking.	Friendly, sociable; reflecting interest in people and in cooking.	Reassuring, reinforcing. Emphasis on color. These people already love cranberry sauce.
Promotions	Tie-ins with chickens, and meats.	Recipes, cookbooks, salads; not price conscious.	Price promotions are apt to be especially effective.
Media	Small-space reminders in newspapers, *Ladies' Home Journal, Reader's Digest, TV Guide, Good Housekeeping.*	*Family Circle, Woman's Day, Better Homes & Gardens, Good Housekeeping, McCall's, Ladies' Home Journal.*	*True Story, True Romance, Reader's Digest.*

est in cooking. Their general advice was that the best point of emphasis seemed to be somewhere in the middle of the usage cycle. "People at this point have shown their acceptance of cranberries. However, by the standard of heavy cranberry users or average applesauce users, their volume of consumption is still low. Thus we believe that a huge potential lies in this intermediate group. Moreover, we believe that a marketing strategy aimed at increasing the consumption of this group will, at the same time, draw new users into the market."

Haley also offered suggestions regarding pricing of jellied and whole-berry sauce. "Since the jellied form has the greatest expansion potential, its price should be kept as low as is economically feasible. However, people who consume whole berry are less price conscious. Therefore, it should be possible to allow the price to float a little upward without damage to unit sales volume. Thus it appears that whole berry can safely be established as a higher profit margin item."

Shortly after OSC management had received the study, Melvin, brand manager for sauce, requested his advertising agency to develop advertising campaign proposals in light of the findings regarding market segmentation. Melvin's first reactions were that the study certainly was a needed updated version of the old 1962 study and, furthermore, that it would give him information to propose a more efficient advertising and promotion program. The right segmentation of the franchise should produce a much higher efficiency. There were, however, different opinions as to which of the four segments ought to be the prime target. Melvin felt the "convenience-oriented" group would be best, but Walsh, director of product marketing, argued for the "enthusiastic (or creative) cooks." The discussion about selecting a segment dealt also with the practical problems of identifying and reaching a particular consumer segment.

Melvin thought also that the broad approaches to advertising used in the previous two seasons had not worked too well and should be re-evaluated in light of some of the new findings. He noticed that the respondents generally overstated their volume of sauce consumption. It seemed that OSC had a huge potential in just bringing actual volume up to claimed volume of consumption.

Exhibit 1

Ocean Spray Cranberries, Inc. (B)

Consumer Opinions or Beliefs (Overall Attitudes and Feelings) Regarding Cranberry Sauce
(Sample Size = 1,004)

Variable Number	*Belief Statement*	*Agree Completely/ Strongly*	*Disagree Completely/ Strongly*	*Difference*
1	Cranberry sauce is a traditional food.	92%	3%	89%
2	Cranberry sauce has food value as well as an attractive appearance and good taste.	87	4	83
3	Cranberry sauce is part of the meal rather than a garnish.	72	17	55
4	I usually keep a can of cranberry sauce in the cupboard year round.	65	26	39
5	I probably would serve more cranberry sauce if I thought of it, but I don't.	57	31	26
6	I serve cranberry sauce with turkey to add moistness.	43	39	4
7	A firmer jellied sauce is a higher-quality cranberry sauce.	29	34	−5
8	Cranberry sauce is served with pork because it cuts the grease.	26	37	−11
9	Cranberry sauce is too tart to serve with spicy foreign foods.	16	56	−40
10	I often make my own cranberry sauce when fresh cranberries are available.	26	68	−42
11	I use whole cranberry sauce as a cooking or baking ingredient.	20	69	−49
12	Cranberry sauce is appropriate for roasted whole chicken but not for broiled or fried chicken.	16	67	−51
13	I often use jellied cranberry sauce as an ingredient in cooking and baking.	16	74	−58
14	I feel almost patriotic when I serve cranberry sauce.	10	71	−61
15	I don't like to serve cranberry sauce too often because it loses its significance.	9	77	−68
16	I'll eat cranberry sauce in a restaurant, but I don't serve it very often at home.	12	80	−68
17	Cranberry sauce dries up in the can before it is used up.	8	79	−71
18	All brands of cranberry sauce are made by Ocean Spray.	5	80	−75
19	Eating cranberries can cause health problems.	3	78	−75
20	I serve cranberry sauce to cool hot food.	6	81	−75
21	Cranberry sauce should be served only on Thanksgiving and Christmas.	5	87	−82

Exhibit 2
Ocean Spray Cranberries, Inc. (B)

Characterization of Four Consumer Segments[1]

Type of Measurement	*Segment 1: Convenience Oriented* ($n_1 = 299$)		*Segment 2: Enthusiastic Cook* ($n_2 = 257$)		*Segment 3: Disinterested* ($n_3 = 270$)		*Segment 4: Decorator* ($n_4 = 178$)	
Key benefits of ideal food products rated "very important"	Quick	4%	Appropriate for holidays	4%	Different taste	−1%	Easy availability	12%
	Goes well with turkey	4	Goes well in salads	3	Festive	−1	Appropriate for formal meals	11
	Easy to serve	3	Colorful	3			Acceptable to everyone	10
	Smooth consistency	3					Appropriate for holidays	9
							Variety of uses	9
							Available year round	9
							Festive	8
							Quick	8
							Has vitamins	8
							Sweet taste	8
Key beliefs rated "agree very much"	Part of meal rather than garnish	20	Use whole cranberry sauce as a cooking/baking ingredient	21	Would serve more cranberry sauce if I thought of it, but I don't	1	Firmer jellied sauce is higher quality	23
	Has food value as well as attractive appearance	15	Usually keep can year round	14			Cranberry sauce is served with pork because it cuts the grease	17
	Usually keep can year round	13	Often makes own cranberry sauce when fresh berries are available	10			Usually keep can year round	17
	Traditional food	5	Often use jellied cranberry sauce as a cooking/baking ingredient	9			I serve cranberry sauce with turkey to add moistness	15
			Cranberry sauce is one of favorite foods	7			Cranberry sauce is one of favorite foods	3
							Should be served only on Thanksgiving and Christmas	5

Key life-styles rated "describes me completely"	Prefer natural foods to ones with artificial ingredients	1	Enjoy being active	9	Prefer fresh vegetables to canned or frozen products	0	I believe we are on earth to enjoy ourselves	16
			Like to cook	8			Nutrition conscious	11
			Like to cook new dishes	7			Believe in things parents believed in	10
			Enjoy taking time to prepare meals	7			Interested in food advertising	10
			Like to prepare fancy dishes	6			Gets together with family for holidays	8
			Like to prepare colorful salads	6			Prefer natural foods to ones with artificial ingredients	8
			Sociable	6			Serve children the things they like to eat	7
			Like beef on the rare side	6			Like to look for sales in the grocery store	7
							Enjoy taking time to prepare meals	7
Attitudes	See cranberry sauce as a convenient staple.							
Main attitude	High on preference of jellied form relative to whole berry		High on seeing cranberry sauce as a cooking/baking ingredient		See cranberry sauce as a change of pace		See cranberry sauce as a means of sprucing up meals	
Supporting attitudes rated "agree very much"	High on rejection of whole berry	6%	Low on rejection of whole berry	−16%	High on rejection of whole berry by adults and children	9%	Low on rejection of whole berry	−3%
	High on brand awareness	4	Low on rejection of jellied	−4	High on rejection of jellied by adults and children	7	Low on rejection of jellied	−1
	High on regular brand OSC	2	Low on preference of jellied over whole berry		High on preference of jellied relative to whole berry		High on preference of jellied form relative to whole berry	
	High on future OSC purchase intention	2	High in seeing OSC as costing more	−3	Low on brand awareness	−3	Low on future OSC purchase intentions	−3
	High on seeing OSC as costing more	2			Low on regular brand OSC	−2		

Exhibit 2 (continued)

Type of Measurement	Segment 1: Convenience Oriented ($n_1 = 299$)		Segment 2: Enthusiastic Cook ($n_2 = 257$)		Segment 3: Disinterested ($n_3 = 270$)		Segment 4: Decorator ($n_4 = 178$)	
Behavior rated "tend to do frequently"	High on eating baked/roast chicken	9	High on use of whole berry with turkey	13	High on consumption of pork, and fried chicken	5	Favors jellied and applesauce as accompaniments	
	High on eating left-over chicken	3	High on consumption of all meat, poultry, and fish	6	Low on accompaniments, including cranberries		Low on jellied with chicken	−7
	High on eating applesauce as accompaniment	4	High on use of 16-oz. cans	8	Low on use of 16-oz. cans	−7	High on consumption of leftover beef, leftover chicken, and broiled chicken	7
	High on use of cranberry sauce as meat accompaniment	2	High on serving cranberry sauce on all occasions	10	High on use of cranberry sauce as a meat accompaniment only		Low on use of 16-oz. cans	−3
	High on serving cranberry sauce on all occasions, especially informal meals	3–6			Low on serving cranberry sauce on all occasions	−11	Low on using cranberry sauce on all occasions	−4
					Serve cranberry sauce at Thanksgiving and Christmas			

Key demographics	45 and older	5	40 to 64	6	18 to 39	10	65 and older	7
	Low on college	−3	High on college or more	2	High on some college	3	High on some high school or less	8
	High on United States as parents' country	2	High on United Kingdom as parents' country of origin	7	High on children living at home	11	Low on children living at home	−8
			High on upscale occupation of household head	3	High on United States as parents' country of origin	5	High on Germany/Austria, Italy, and Russia as parents' country of origin	3
					High on middle occupation of household head	4		
Media	Buy newspapers	2	Buy newspapers	3	Buy newspapers	−5	Buy newspapers	−1
	Above-average readership of		Above-average readership of		Low on magazines		Above-average readership of	
	Ladies' Home Journal	3	*Family Circle*	8			*True Story*	4
	Reader's Digest	2	*Woman's Day*	8			*True Romance*	2
	TV Guide	2	*Better Homes & Gardens*	6			*Reader's Digest*	2
	Good Housekeeping	2	*Good Housekeeping*	5				
			McCall's	5				
			Ladies' Home Journal	5				

[1]The percentages to the right of each item show the difference between the frequency count (%) for the segment and the frequency count for the total sample on the item.

Exhibit 3
Ocean Spray Cranberries, Inc. (B)

Construction and Interpretation of Belief Clusters

The Appel, Haley, and Fourezios, Inc., research team used two complementary data analysis techniques to form the four belief clusters presented to the Ocean Spray Company brand management team. The two techniques require the use of large digital computers and have many specific forms depending upon how they are programmed, but generically they are known as cluster analysis and multiple discriminant analysis. While both methods have been applied to impersonal objects and to variables observed over classes of objects, it is most illustrative to think of the two methods as they are applied routinely to samples of individual consumers. Cluster analysis is a procedure for forming an arbitrary number of relatively homogeneous subgroups of individuals within a larger, heterogeneous sample of respondents. Multiple discriminant analysis is a procedure for interpreting the differences between a number of existing groups of respondents.

CLUSTER ANALYSIS

Cluster analysis can be performed in a variety of ways, and many statistical algorithms have been written that have essentially the same objective: to form homogeneous groups of respondents drawn from a heterogeneous population. Procedures are either aggregative (proceeding by combining individuals into groups and smaller groups with individuals or other smaller groups to form larger groups) or disaggregative (proceeding by taking the entire sample—the largest possible group—and breaking it into successively smaller groups of increasing homogeneity). Both aggregative and disaggregative procedures have been written that allow for an individual respondent to be reassigned from an existing subgroup to a newer subgroup that better matches the characteristics of that respondent.

Users of cluster analysis are not required to know in advance how many, or what kind of clusters they eventually will choose. The purpose of the analysis is to suggest several alternative clustering arrangements from which analysts must select one that best meets their particular information needs. The analyst, perhaps in consultation with management, must decide how many clusters will make up the "solution" to the grouping problem being addressed. The analyst has the additional burden of interpreting the solution, first in terms of descriptions of the central tendencies of the resulting clusters and eventually in terms of what the clusters imply for purposes of marketing decision making.

MULTIPLE DISCRIMINANT ANALYSIS

Cluster analysis is used to form groups, and multiple discriminant analysis is used to interpret the statistical differences between a given number of existing groups. Given a set of existing groups, multiple discriminant analysis can also be used to predict into which existing group a new individual, not presently a member of any of the existing groups, is more likely to be classified. Thus multiple discriminant analysis, working with an existing set of groups, is used to perform tasks of interpretation and classification. Because it works with grouped data, it is a good counterpart technique to cluster analysis. Together, the two methods give the analyst a series of procedures that can be used to form groups from survey observations, interpret some of the underlying differences between those groups, and develop a classification scheme for predicting the group membership of individuals not represented in the original sample.

THE AHF SEGMENT BUILDING PROCESS—CLUSTER ANALYSIS

The sample was split in two halves of 502 respondents each and separate cluster analysis solutions were determined for each sample. This split-half technique was used to give the researchers an opportunity to judge the stability of the cluster solutions. The two subsamples consisted of individuals with even and odd identification numbers; thus there would be reason to expect strong similarities between the two cluster solutions except in the event that the relationships between the beliefs variables and homogeneous population subsets were spurious. A series of cluster analyses were performed using a top-down, hierarchical, disaggregative algorithm. Briefly, this computer program worked in the following way:

1. All respondents were first assigned to a single group.
2. The respondent farthest from the cluster mean or centroid was then selected as the centroid for a second cluster.
3. All respondents were sequentially tested to determine if a reassignment to the second cluster would reduce the within group sum-squared error, a statistical measure of within group homogeneity.
4. When it was no longer possible to reduce the within group sum-squared error by reassigning any single respondent to the second cluster, then that individual farthest from either of the two centroids became the centroid for a third cluster and the reassignment process was repeated.
5. The number of clusters was allowed to increase to some maximum number of clusters, set by the researcher. This number was set at six.
6. When this limit was reached, the program automatically terminated.

After constructing four product belief scales, six personality scales, and six product use benefit scales, each set of scales was used as the basis for two cluster analyses—one for the 502 respondents with even numbers and the second for the 502 with odd numbers. The clustering solution derived from the four belief scales lead to the highest ratio of between group variation to within group average variation as calculated for all solutions. The computer printouts contained the following values for this ratio:

Number of Clusters:	2		3		4		5		6	
Sample Halves:	*Even*	*Odd*	*Even*	*Odd*	*Even*	*Odd*	*Even*	*Odd*	*Even*	*Odd*
Beliefs	238	231	175	194	159	153	123	124	79	85
Personalities	143	146	82	81	66	71	50	46	44	44
Benefits	112	119	101	101	59	66	57	51	36	51

The belief clusters were therefore selected as the basis for deriving the market segments eventually presented to OSC management. Haley considered the belief items to have the most direct implications for marketing.

Looking at the cluster solutions for the belief items, it seemed clear that the samples should be divided in no less than four clusters. With only two or three clusters, the third belief scale, serving interest, appeared not to be a basis for between-cluster differentiation as indicated in the table of F-ratios shown below. On the other hand, it seemed that little was gained by using more than four clusters.

Number of Clusters:	2		3		4		5		6	
Sample Halves:	*Even*	*Odd*	*Even*	*Odd*	*Even*	*Odd*	*Even*	*Odd*	*Even*	*Odd*
Univariate *F*-ratios										
Scale 1, "Traditional"	1,214	1,117	337	413	340	377	392	347	358	289
Scale 2, "Cook and bake"	101	53	452	600	275	307	380	283	330	294
Scale 3, "Serving interest"	5	4	19	20	198	186	169	194	193	247
Scale 4, "Food value"	228	318	407	320	273	255	248	345	268	295
Average within group sums of squares (*W*)	2.02	2.05	1.51	1.48	1.14	1.13	.92	.91	.78	.79
Between group sums of squares (*B*)	484	474	263	287	182	174	114	112	66	62
B/W ratio	238	231	175	194	159	153	124	123	85	79

Means (and standard deviations)

Group	Size	Traditional X_1	Cook and Bake X_2	Serving Interest X_3	Food Value X_4
Cluster 1	134	3.15 (1.30)	2.51 (0.80)	7.60 (1.83)	9.40 (0.81)
Cluster 2	123	3.24 (1.38)	6.55 (1.82)	7.64 (2.04)	8.27 (1.45)
Cluster 3	148	6.51 (1.56)	2.90 (1.36)	8.33 (2.20)	6.99 (1.80)
Cluster 4	97	3.32 (1.48)	3.18 (1.71)	11.61 (2.44)	7.97 (1.65)
Total, "odd half"	502	4.19	3.74	8.60	8.13

The similarities between the "even" and "odd" halves of the sample were judged quite acceptable and gave the research team confidence that there were systematic relationships between the belief measurements and stable consumer subgroups. One of the two four-cluster solutions was chosen as the basis for a complete classification of the 1,004 respondents. The "odd" solution was chosen because of apparently cleaner delineations, as measured by generally larger F ratios, of the four clusters on the four scales.

CLASSIFYING THE REMAINING RESPONDENTS: MULTIPLE DISCRIMINANT ANALYSIS

Having accepted a cluster solution, the AHF team used the structure of the "odd" groups to define a strategy for classifying the entire sample. The classification strategy employed multiple discriminant analysis (MDA). The means and standard deviations of the scale values for each of the four clusters were as shown in this table.

The computer program used was a stepwise discriminant analysis program called BMD07M selected from the Biomedical Computer Programs library written at the Health Science Computing Facility of the University of California, Los Angeles. The program calculated a discriminant function for each cluster with coefficients similar to those in regression analysis. The classification rule based on this set of discriminant functions was that a respondent should be assigned to cluster 1 if the value of L_1 was higher than the values of L_2, L_3, and L_4, which were obtained by plugging the respondent's values on each of the four X's into the functions. The following four functions were obtained:

Discriminant functions

		Constant	Traditional	Cook and Bake	Serving Interest	Food Value
L_1	=	-24.66	$+0.2505X_1$	$-0.0915X_2$	$+1.128X_3$	$+3.984X_4$
L_2	=	-24.87	$+0.3488X_1$	$+2.123X_2$	$+0.8438X_3$	$+3.082X_4$
L_3	=	-21.73	$+2.187X_1$	$+0.2419X_2$	$+0.9776X_3$	$+2.521X_4$
L_4	=	-26.29	$-0.0481X_1$	$+0.0572X_2$	$+2.182X_3$	$+3.067X_4$

As shown, this classification of the "odd" sample using that rule led to a near perfect (92% correct) classification of the 502 respondents.

The respondent was allocated to the cluster to which he or she was most likely to belong. The AHF analysts had by these procedures obtained the following four clusters:

Classified by Cluster Analysis	*Number of Respondents Classified by MDA*				
	Cluster 1	*Cluster 2*	*Cluster 3*	*Cluster 4*	*Total*
Cluster 1	127	0	1	6	134
Cluster 2	11	111	1	0	123
Cluster 3	2	4	141	1	148
Cluster 4	8	4	1	84	97
Total	148	119	144	91	502

The same set of discriminant functions were then used to classify the remaining 502 respondents from the "even" sample into one of the four clusters. A probabilistic estimate that the respondent belonged to a certain cluster was computed. The discriminant function coefficients were used to compute the four *L*-values for each respondent. The resulting *L*-values were then considered to be normally distributed around the *L*-values of the four cluster means and using the assumptions of the normal distribution, probabilities of group membership were computed. Respondent 256, for example, was found to have a .94 probability of being a member of cluster 2. The group membership probabilities for a few members of the odd sample are shown now:

Cluster	*No. of Respondents*
1	299
2	257
3	270
4	178
Total	1,004

The discriminant functions were also useful in interpreting the obtained clusters, for example, since cluster 2 was strongly associated with high scores on scales 2 and 4, the interpretive label "enthusiastic cook" seemed appropriate. Additional interpretations of the clusters were made using cross-tabulations such as those presented in Exhibit 2.

Respondent No.	*Probabilities of Group Membership*				*Group Assignment*
	Group 1	*Group 2*	*Group 3*	*Group*	
255	.52440	.31081	.00028	.16449	1
256	.04790	.93954	.00127	.01127	2
257	.00280	.99135	.00100	.00484	2
258	.00021	.78391	.21548	.00037	2
259	.49128	.13987	.32159	.04724	1
260	.24562	.00029	.00109	.75299	4

5

Communications Strategies

AdTel Ltd.

In 1974, the Barrett Foods Company[1] held a 30% national market share of peanut butter sales and enjoyed a position of market leadership. Its closest and toughest competition came from the Mullen Foods Company, which had a 28% national market share. The balance of the peanut butter market was fragmented among half a dozen "price" brands and private-label brands.

Although Barrett's peanut butter sales volume had grown steadily in the past three years, for several reasons it had not grown as fast as the category itself. For one thing, Mullen Foods had been outspending Barrett in terms of trade deals. This gave Mullen a gross margin advantage to the retailer. Mullen had also increased its TV advertising expenditures to roughly $2 million, the same level as Barrett's TV budget. Another factor contributing to Barrett's failure to keep pace with the category growth rate was the 40% increase in the cost of peanut butter during the previous two years. Predictably, consumers has become more price conscious, and Barrett management believed that the increasing shelf price differences between their product and the price and private-label brands had become significant in the consumer's selection decision. Finally, Barrett management was concerned about the effectiveness of their advertising copy in this new competitive environment. For ten years, their advertising had had a contributing theme. However, this theme had never been carried on the peanut butter itself.

In the face of declining market share, Barrett management had asked the AdTel Company to conduct a "heavy-up" test to determine the payout on a $6 million TV advertising expenditure versus their current TV spending level. Management had decided that a minimum 15% sales increase (on an equivalent units base) read at a minimum 90% confidence level would be required before implementing the heavy spending nationally.

[1]Although the product and the data in the case have been disguised to protect the strict confidentiality of a client's test, the basic findings and resulting decision alternatives are derived from an actual AdTel spending level test.

ADTEL BACKGROUND

AdTel was founded in 1968 as an outgrowth of a consulting project initiated by the Advertising Research Foundation. Since 1972, it had been a subsidiary of Booz-Allen & Hamilton. The company's expertise was in testing and measuring the sales effectiveness of alternative TV advertising, consumer promotions, and introductory campaigns for new products within a single market.

To do this testing and measuring AdTel had developed a total minimarket system comprised of 2,000-family-per-market, ongoing, consumer purchase diary panels. To control all variables except the one being tested, in each of its unique test markets AdTel utilized a dual-cable CATV system and two balanced consumer diary panels of 1,000 households each. By this approach, AdTel overcame some of the drawbacks of other widely used testing techniques and facilities.

The "dual-cable" concept employed the following unique combination of resources to determine consumer acceptance of new packaged goods and to measure the sales effects of TV advertising alternatives on new or established brands.

Dual-Cable TV Systems

In each of AdTel's three test markets, the TV sets owned by half the cable subscriber households were wired to the "A" cable; the sets owned by the other half were wired to the "B" cable. Highly sophisticated electronic equipment allowed AdTel to control the signal carried over the cables. A push of a button blocked the "on-air" commercial broadcast by the network or local stations and simultaneously cut in the desired test commercial on one side of the cable, while the other side carried the regular commercial. The ability to test TV advertising alternatives within a single market represented a major cost and control breakthrough in TV advertising research.

Large Consumer Diary Panels

In each test market AdTel maintained on an ongoing basis a 2,000-family panel (1,000 "A" and 1,000 "B" cable households). The panels were carefully balanced according to demographic characteristics and store shopping preferences. The panel families recorded their purchases in weekly diaries. AdTel used these consumer sales data and highly sophisticated models to forecast product viability, national market shares, and sales volumes. One of the major benefits of panel data was the ability to determine a very precise demographic profile of a test brand's franchise. This allowed the client to "target" subsequent media and promotion efforts with a high degree of precision.

Limited Retail Distribution

The "minimarket" name was derived from the fact that the test brand was stocked in relatively few retail outlets (typically 50 or less) located only within the cable household shopping area. Although the number of stores carrying the test brand was small, they represented approximately 90% of the all-commodity volume generated within the cable.

Due to overlapping distribution channels, it was usually impossible for AdTel's packaged-goods clients to confine distribution of a test brand to AdTel's cable area. Therefore, AdTel employed the services of another Booz-Allen subsidiary, Market Audits, to warehouse the new product. Market Audits paid "co-operation" monies to the major retail factors to force distribution of the new product into the cable area. Distribution and pricing of the new product were controlled by Market Audits throughout the test. The cost benefits derived from this limited distribution were significant. For example,

1. pilot plant or bench-top production could be used since a relatively few retail outlets carried the product, and
2. media costs were comparatively small since minimarket tests were conducted in small markets.

AdTel had carefully avoided publishing the specific locations of these minimarkets, even though their names were open secrets in the marketing community. It was essential to the validity of the test results that the people in these markets operated under a real-life situation and were not aware of the relationship between their purchase diaries and cable TV. (See Exhibit 14 for additional background on AdTel.)

ADTEL TESTING AND MEASUREMENT ADVANTAGES

AdTel was retained by Barrett to measure the sales effects of the spending level test because management believed that there were cost and control advantages inherent in the AdTel dual-cable system.

One cost advantage to Barrett resulted from reduced incremental media costs. An estimated $50,000 in expenditures could be eliminated because the AdTel system allowed one client to cut in test brand advertising over time owned corporately for other brands not in the test category.

Also, AdTel's ability to test TV advertising alternatives within a single market was considered a control advantage. In traditional approaches, the sales effects of variables (competitive trade and consumer promotions, retail shelf environment, spot TV expenditures, weather, etc.) made it difficult to read tests conducted between supposedly matched markets. However, in the AdTel approach these variables were held in balance for both the test and control cells.

Design of Barrett's Spending Level Test

The basic design of the test was to triple advertising spending on panel A from a $2 million rate per year nationally to a $6 million rate per year nationally.

Media weight on the two AdTel panels was controlled as follows:

Period	*Quarters*	*Panel A "Heavy-up"*	*Banel B "Control"*
Pretest	1st ASO 2nd NDJ	National Strategy 60 GRPs/wk[1]	
Test	1st FMA	180 GRPs/wk	60 GRPs/wk
	2nd MJJ		
	3rd ASO	180 GRPs/wk	60 GRPs/wk
	4th NDJ	180 GRPs/wk	60 GRPs/wk

[1]A gross rating point (GRP) equals the number of commercial impression opportunities expressed as a percentage of the population in a market.

Thus, the extra advertising plan was run on panel A with the national plan on panel B as a control.

To avoid distortions of the data cuased by families joining and dropping out of the panel during the test, a "static" sample was created to include only those families returning at least 80% of their diaries during the 12-month period. This procedure ensured an accurate reflection of trend and repeat data, as opposed to "apparent" trial or repeat due to families joining or dropping from the panel. As a result, there was a sample of 829 families on panel A and 922 on panel B.

All volume measures in the test were expressed in equivalent units, where one equivalent unit equaled 12.0 ounces.

Volume Trend Test Results

As can be seen in Exhibit 1, the panel A "heavy-up" strategy resulted in significantly greater equivalent unit volume for Barrett peanut butter than did the panel B "control" strategy. On a volume-per-family basis,[2] purchases of Barrett peanut butter increased by 18.5% under the "control" strategy from the pretest to the test periods. During the same time periods, purchases of Barrett peanut butter increased by 34.5% under the "heavy-up" strategy. The net result was about 16% more Barrett peanut butter brand volume in favor of the "heavy-up" strategy during the test year.

For most of the measures in the test, AdTel used a statistical test designed to measure whether differences between the panels were real or possibly random. As is indicated on Exhibit 1, the difference between the panels for Barrett peanut butter volume trends is significant at a 96% level of confidence. This means that there was a difference between the panels, but it does not necessarily mean that the difference was 16% at a 96% level of confidence. Additional statistical testing would have been required to determine this.

Trendwise, the two panels were very well matched in terms of Barrett peanut butter's unit volume per panel family during the pretest periods. This created even more confidence in the test results. The better performance on panel A came primarily during the last half of the test. One's first reaction might be that the "heavy-up" advertising had no effect, since differences between the panels did not start until later. However, in most "heavy-up" AdTel tests, a three- to six-month lag between the initial advertising start-up and the test effects is commonly observed. This demonstrates the cumulative effect of the advertising.

[2]Expressing volume measures on a "per-panel-family" basis provided a common denominator for comparing the two panels.

Moreover, it is interesting to observe that the difference between the panels were at first quite small and then began to escalate, reaching the greatest divergence during period 35 (see bottom part of Exhibit 1). In period 36, panel A (heavy-up) declined to the panel B level. Although this was a significant decline, it was probably a random fluctuation.

As had already been noted, panel A (heavy-up) did 16% better than did panel B (control), relative to the pretest period, for the one-year test period. However, this difference occurred primarily in the second half of the year. If the volume increase for only the second half of the year (periods 30–35) were considered, the difference would have been 40% (62.1%–22.2%):

Monthly mean equivalent units per family

Panel	*Pretest 19–24*	*Test 30–35*	*Difference*	*% Change*
A	.29	.47	.18	+62.1%
B	.27	.33	.06	+22.2

Whether to view this test as having caused a 16%, 40%, or some other percentage improvement in sales is a policy decision based on how a company measures advertising payout. For this reason, AdTel felt that it could not go beyond this point in making an economic evaluation.

For additional brand volume and market share results, see Exhibits 2 through 7.

Diagnostics

An important question to explore was *why* higher Barrett sales resulted from the "heavy-up" strategy. Diagnostically, there were a number of possible reasons for the better Barrett peanut butter sales performance on the "heavy-up" panel:

1. an increase in the number of families buying Barrett peanut butter
   a. achieved by attracting users of other brands and/or
   b. achieved by attracting previous infrequent or nonusers of Barrett peanut butter
2. an increase in Barrett peanut butter volume per buying household
   a. achieved by increasing the usage of the brand and/or the product class and/or
   b. achieved by increasing Barrett peanut butter share among Barrett peanut butter buyers

Exhibit 8 displays the percentage of reporting panel families purchasing Barrett peanut butter per period (penetration); Exhibit 9 charts Barrett peanut butter volume per Barrett peanut butter brand buyer (brand buying rates). Referring to Exhibit 8, Barrett peanut butter's mean four-week penetration increased by 22.0% under the "heavy-up" strategy and by only 17.9% on the "control" panel from the pretest to the test period. This better improvement in Barrett peanut butter's penetration on the "heavy-up" panel was significant at a 96% level of confidence. Additionally, Exhibit 9 indicates that the "heavy-up" strategy led to a greater increase in Barrett peanut butter volume per buyer on panel A relative to panel B (+9.5% versus +3.9%). Thus, the positive effects of the "heavy-up" strategy on Barrett peanut butter volume could be traced to both more Barrett peanut butter brand buyers per period (hypothesis 1) and to a heavier Barrett peanut butter buying rate per period (hypothesis 2).

Exhibit 10 also indicates that the percentage of reporting panel families purchasing peanut butter showed a more substantial increase on panel A (+18.9%) than on panel B (+16.2%) during the test period. This means that Barrett peanut butter's improved penetration per period under the "heavy-up" strategy was attributable primarily to an attraction of previous infrequent or nonusers of peanut butter to the product class.

Referring to Exhibit 11, while total peanut butter volume per buyer increased by 9.6% in the "control" panel, a 19.8% increase in product class buying rates was observed for the "heavy-up" panel.

Changes in Dealing Activity

In an attempt to determine whether any other factors (other than advertising) may have caused the improvements in Barrett peanut butter's product class volume levels on panel A, AdTel analyzed changes in Barrett peanut butter and total peanut butter dealing activity from the pretest to the test periods. Exhibit 12 displays the percentage of Barrett peanut butter volume purchased on a consumer recognized deal,[3] and Exhibit 13 presents the same measure for total peanut butter. Referring to Exhibits 12 and 13 the more favorable volume performance on panel A for Barrett peanut butter and the product class is not attributable to significantly different levels of dealing between the panels. Dealing was at almost identical levels on both panels during both the pretest and the test periods.

SUMMARY OF TEST RESULTS

For the one-year test period, Barrett peanut butter volume was 16% greater under the "heavy-up" advertising strategy. This just barely met the breakeven point for the advertising payout of 15%. However, it took almost half a year before any differences started to occur. During the last six months, Barrett peanut butter's sales were 40% greater on the "heavy-up" panel.

[3]These are referred to as "consumer recognized" deals since the housewife was asked to indicate whether the purchase was made on deal and therefore depended upon her perceptions of the purchase transaction.

REACTION OF BARRETT FOODS' MANAGEMENT

After reviewing the results of this test, Barrett's president asked his marketing management group to submit their written recommendations regarding the implementation of the $6 million advertising plan and to use the test data to support their decision. In addition, he asked for recommendations for additional testing, if any, which appeared to be warranted by the results of the business building test.

Exhibit 1
AdTel Ltd.

Barrett's Volume Per Reporting Panel Family
(equivalent units basis)[1]

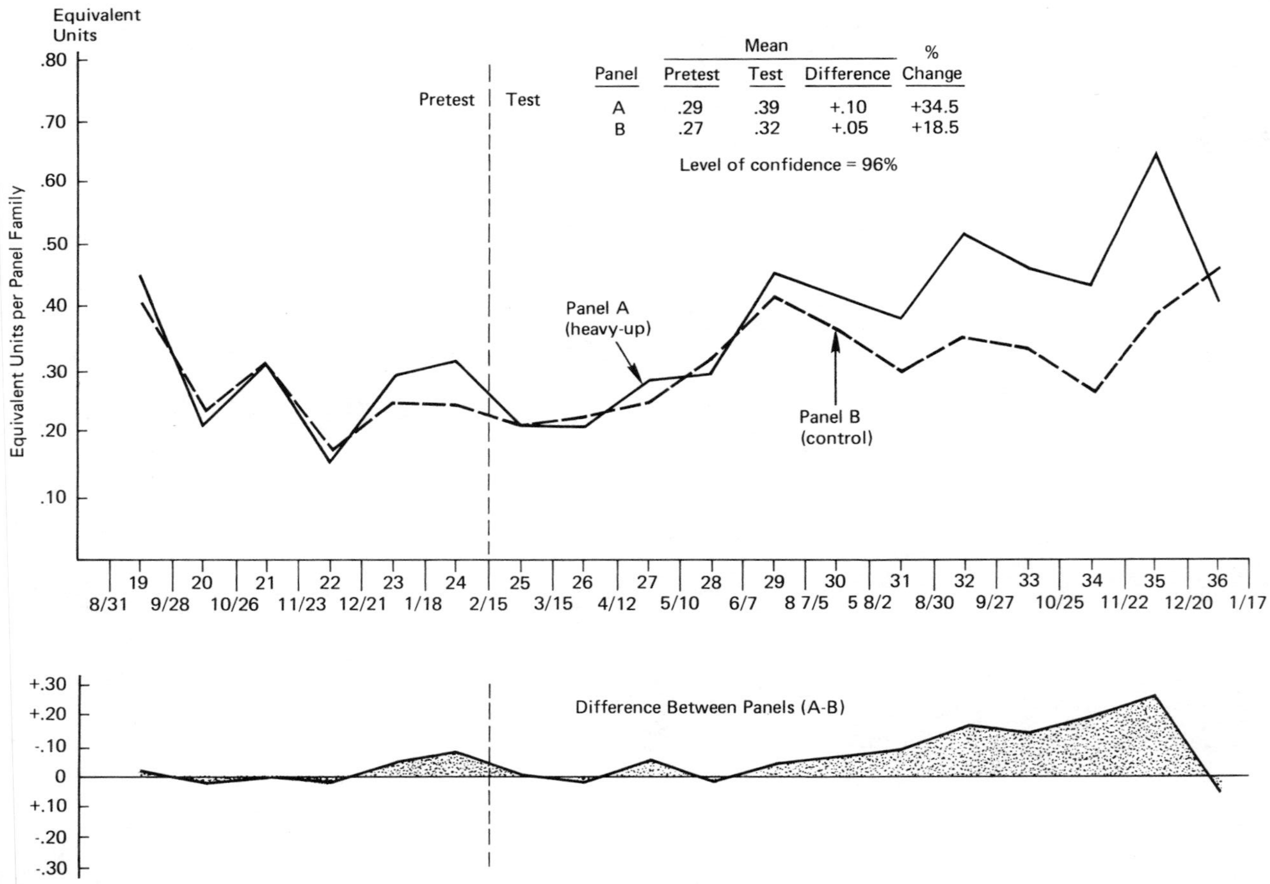

Panel	Mean: Pretest	Mean: Test	Mean: Difference	% Change
A	.29	.39	+.10	+34.5
B	.27	.32	+.05	+18.5

Level of confidence = 96%

[1]One equivalent unit equals 12.0 ounces.

Exhibit 2
AdTel Ltd.

Barrett's Share of the Category
(equivalent units basis)[1]

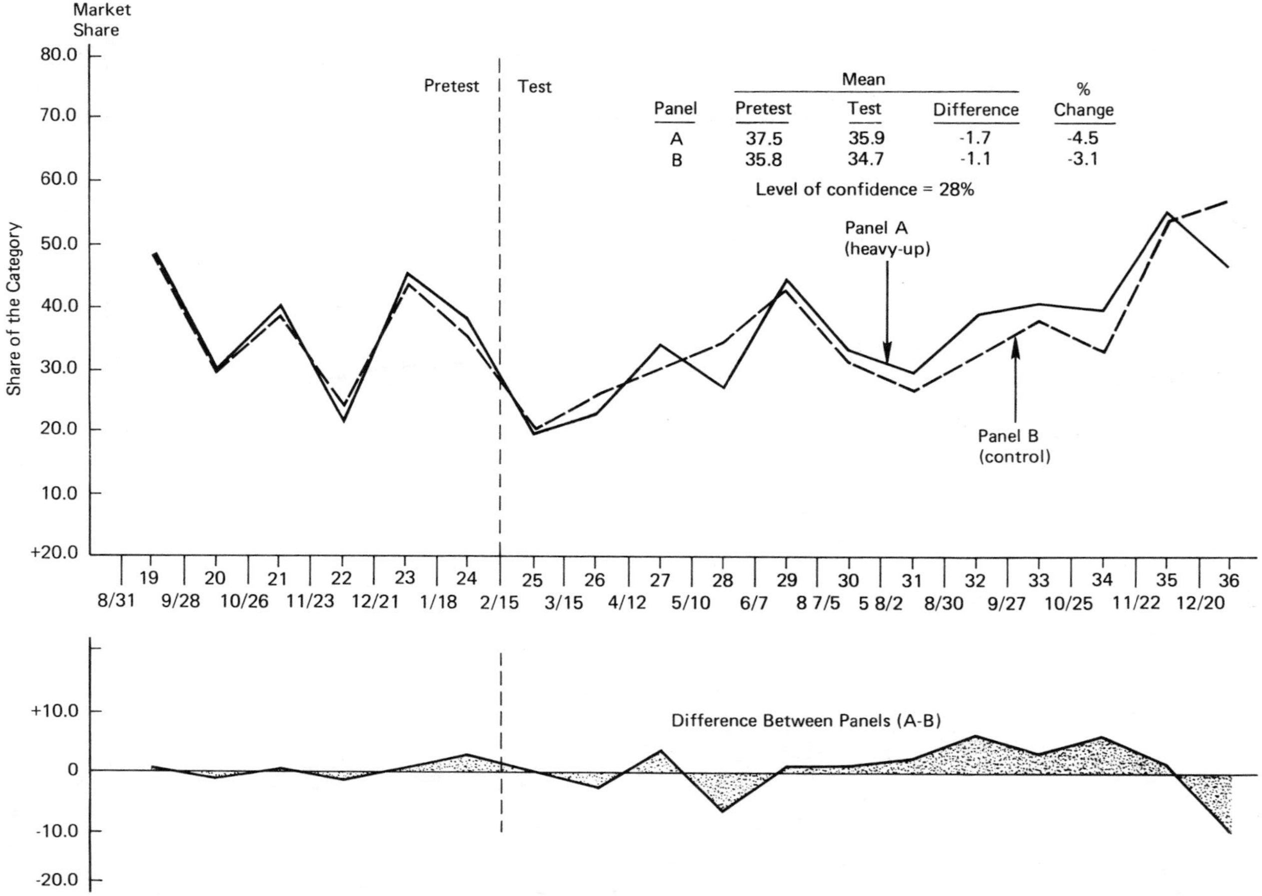

[1]One equivalent unit equals 12.0 ounces.

Exhibit 3
AdTel Ltd.

Category Volume Per Reporting Panel Family
(equivalent units basis)[1]

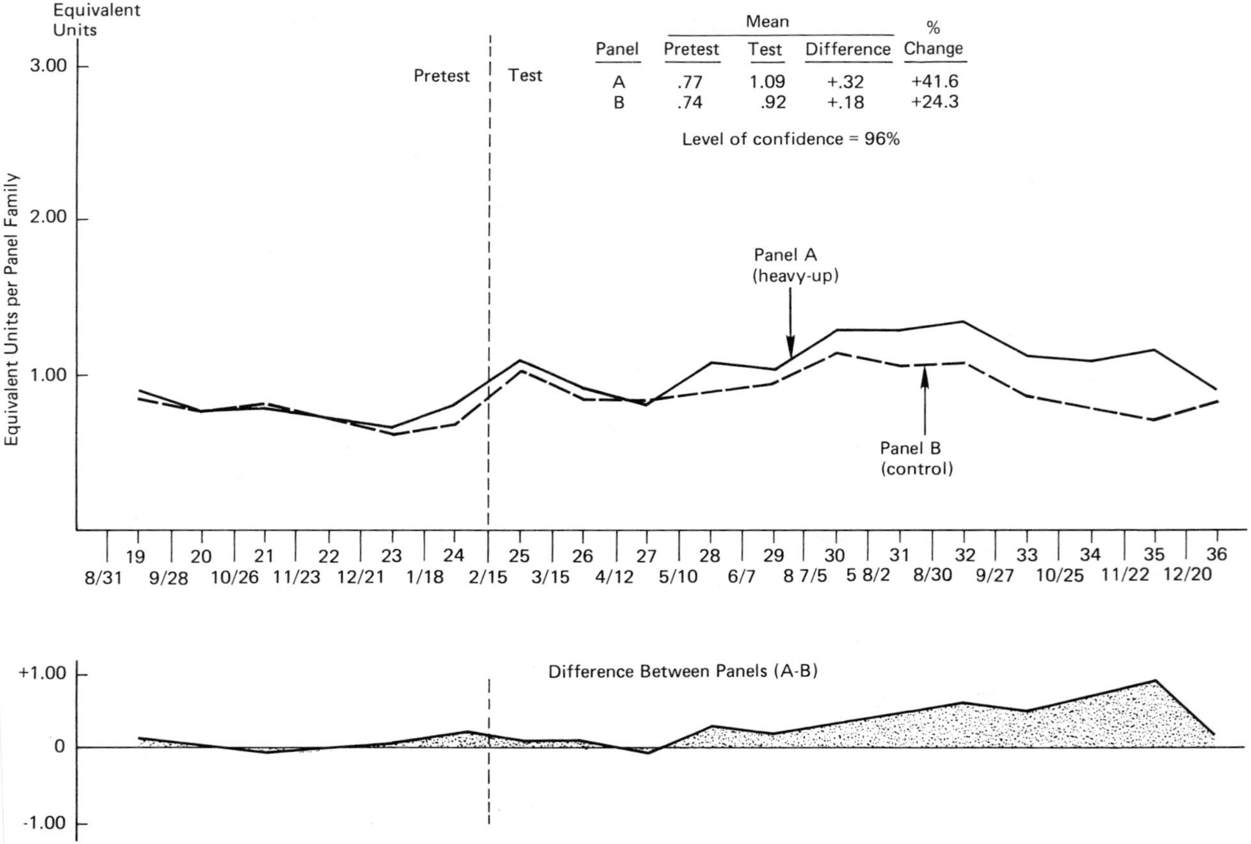

Panel	Mean: Pretest	Mean: Test	Mean: Difference	% Change
A	.77	1.09	+.32	+41.6
B	.74	.92	+.18	+24.3

Level of confidence = 96%

[1]One equivalent unit equals 12.0 ounces.

Exhibit 4
Adtel Ltd.

Mullen's Volume Per Reporting Panel Family
(equivalent units basis)[1]

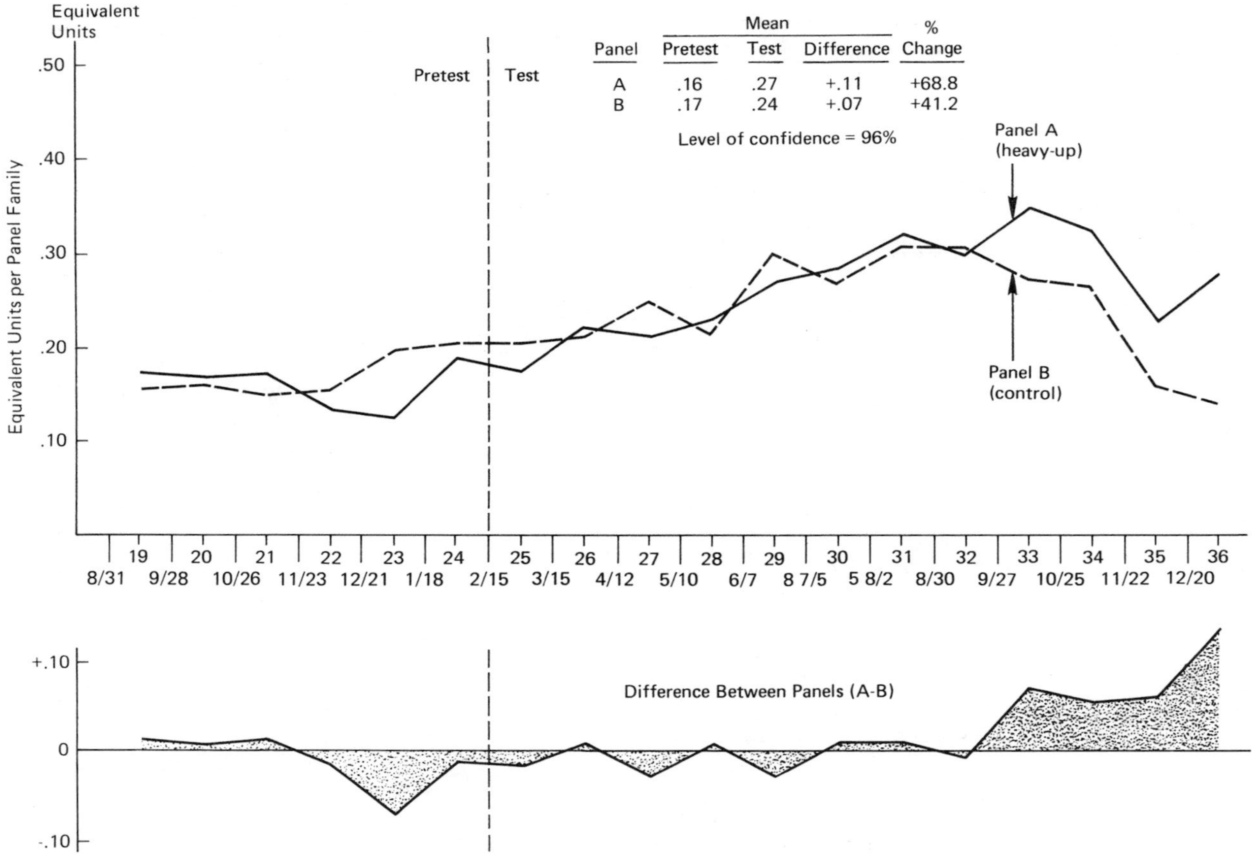

[1]One equivalent unit equals 12.0 ounces.

Exhibit 5
AdTel Ltd.

Price Brand Volume Per Reporting Panel Family
(equivalent units basis)[1]

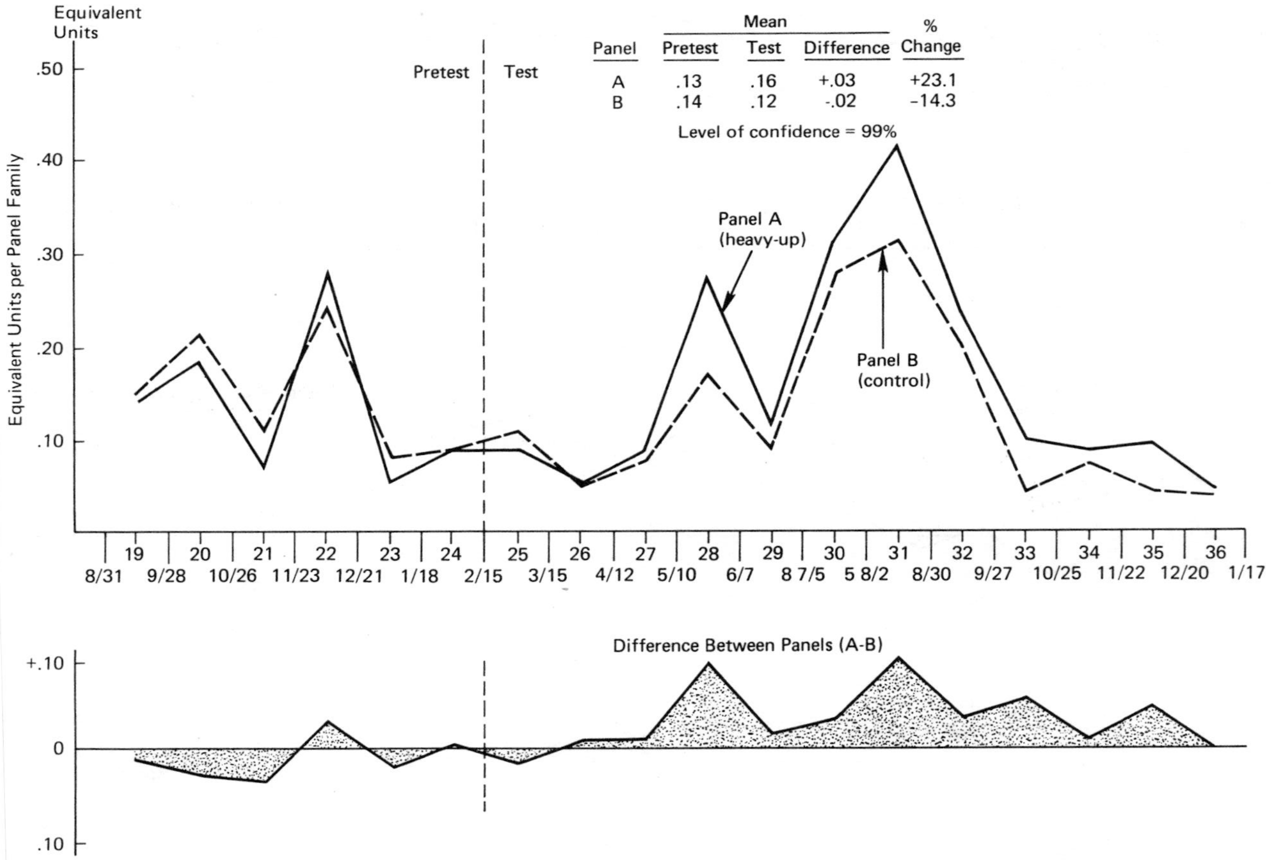

[1]One equivalent unit equals 12.0 ounces.

Exhibit 6
AdTel Ltd.

Private-label Volume Per Reporting Panel Family
(equivalent units basis)[1]

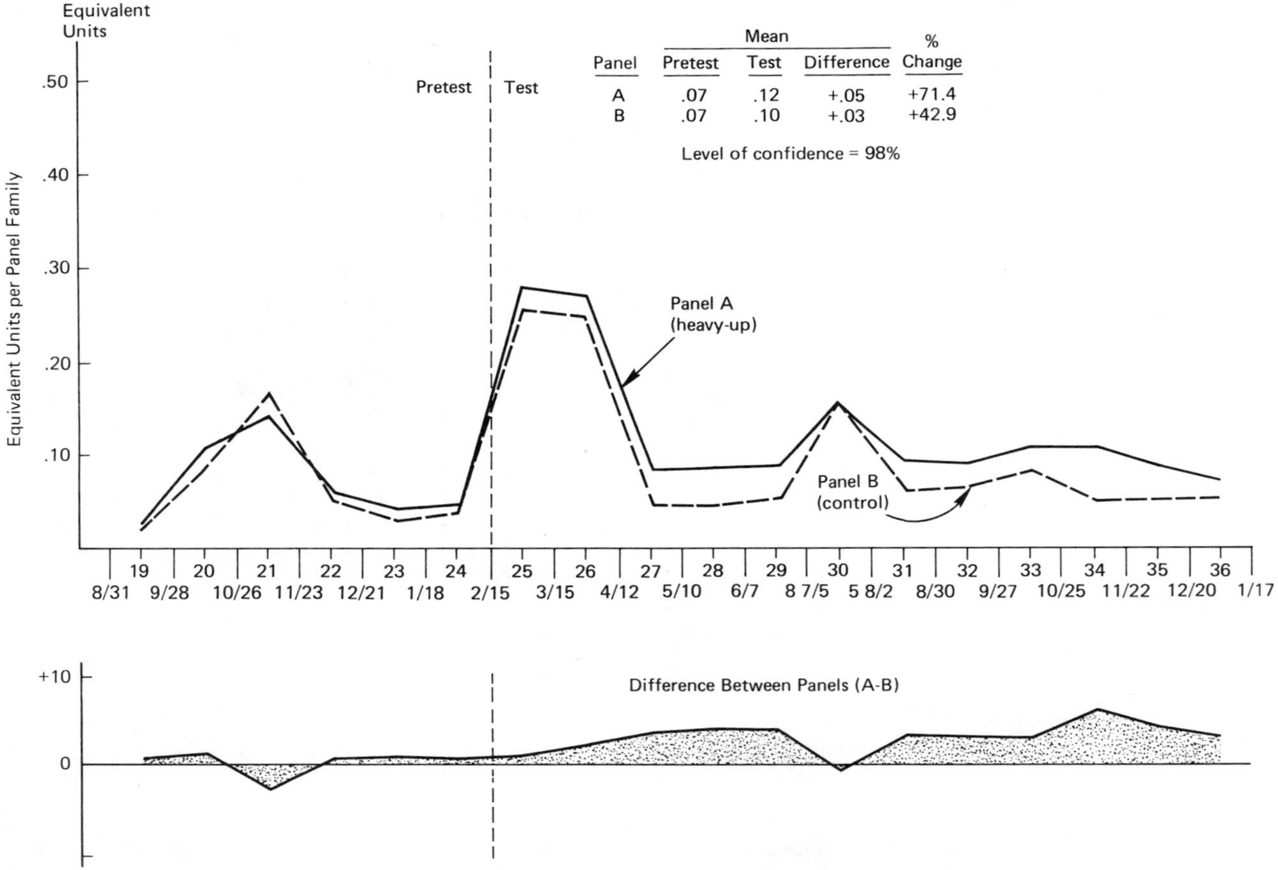

Panel	Mean: Pretest	Mean: Test	Mean: Difference	% Change
A	.07	.12	+.05	+71.4
B	.07	.10	+.03	+42.9

Level of confidence = 98%

[1]One equivalent unit equals 12.0 ounces.

Exhibit 7
AdTel Ltd.

Average Market Share by Brand During the Pretest and Test Period
(equivalent units basis)[1]

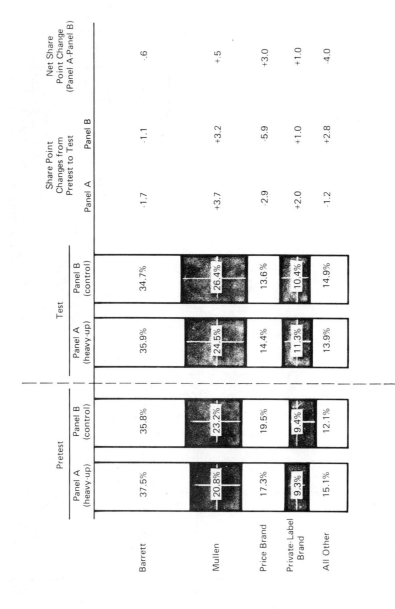

	Pretest		Test		Share Point Changes from Pretest to Test		Net Share Point Change (Panel A-Panel B)
	Panel A (heavy-up)	Panel B (control)	Panel A (heavy-up)	Panel B (control)	Panel A	Panel B	
Barrett	37.5%	35.8%	35.9%	34.7%	-1.7	-1.1	-.6
Mullen	20.8%	23.2%	24.5%	26.4%	+3.7	+3.2	+.5
Price Brand	17.3%	19.5%	14.4%	13.6%	-2.9	-5.9	+3.0
Private-Label Brand	9.3%	9.4%	11.3%	10.4%	+2.0	+1.0	+1.0
All Other	15.1%	12.1%	13.9%	14.9%	-1.2	+2.8	-4.0

[1]One equivalent unit equals 12.0 ounces.

Exhibit 8
AdTel Ltd.

Percentage of Reporting Panel Families Purchasing Barrett

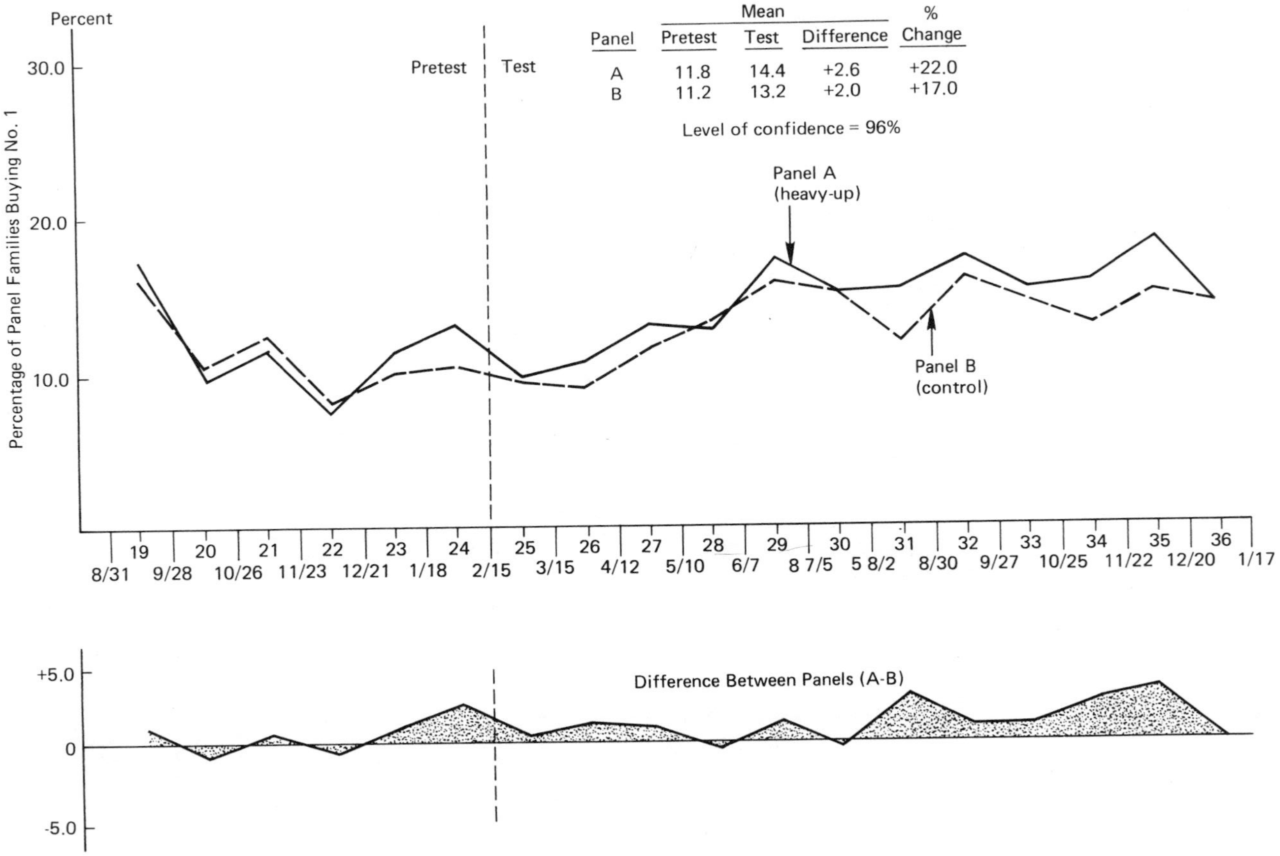

Panel	Mean Pretest	Mean Test	Mean Difference	% Change
A	11.8	14.4	+2.6	+22.0
B	11.2	13.2	+2.0	+17.0

Level of confidence = 96%

Exhibit 9
AdTel Ltd.

Barrett Volume Per Barrett Buyer
(equivalent units basis)[1]

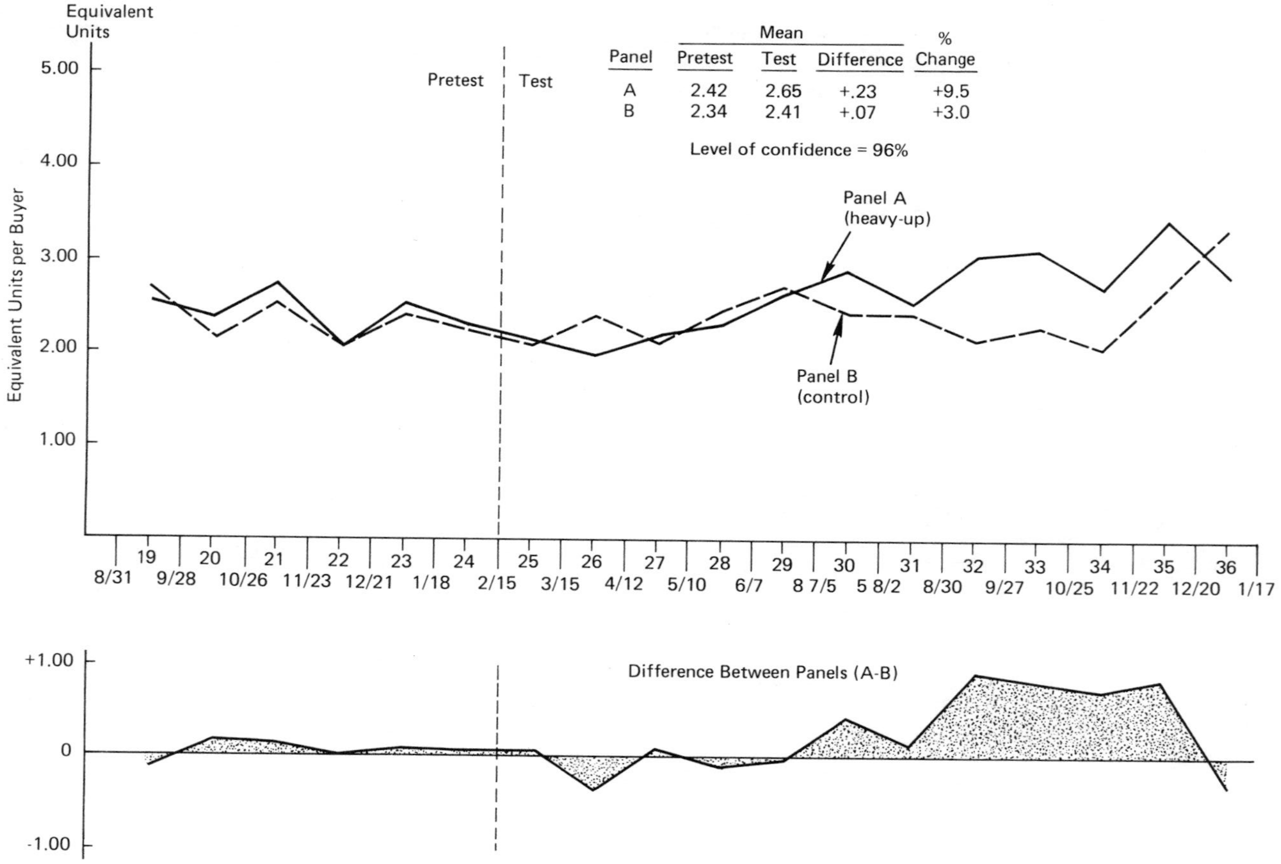

[1]One equivalent unit equals 12.0 ounces.

Exhibit 10
AdTel Ltd.

Percentage of Reporting Panel Families Purchasing Category

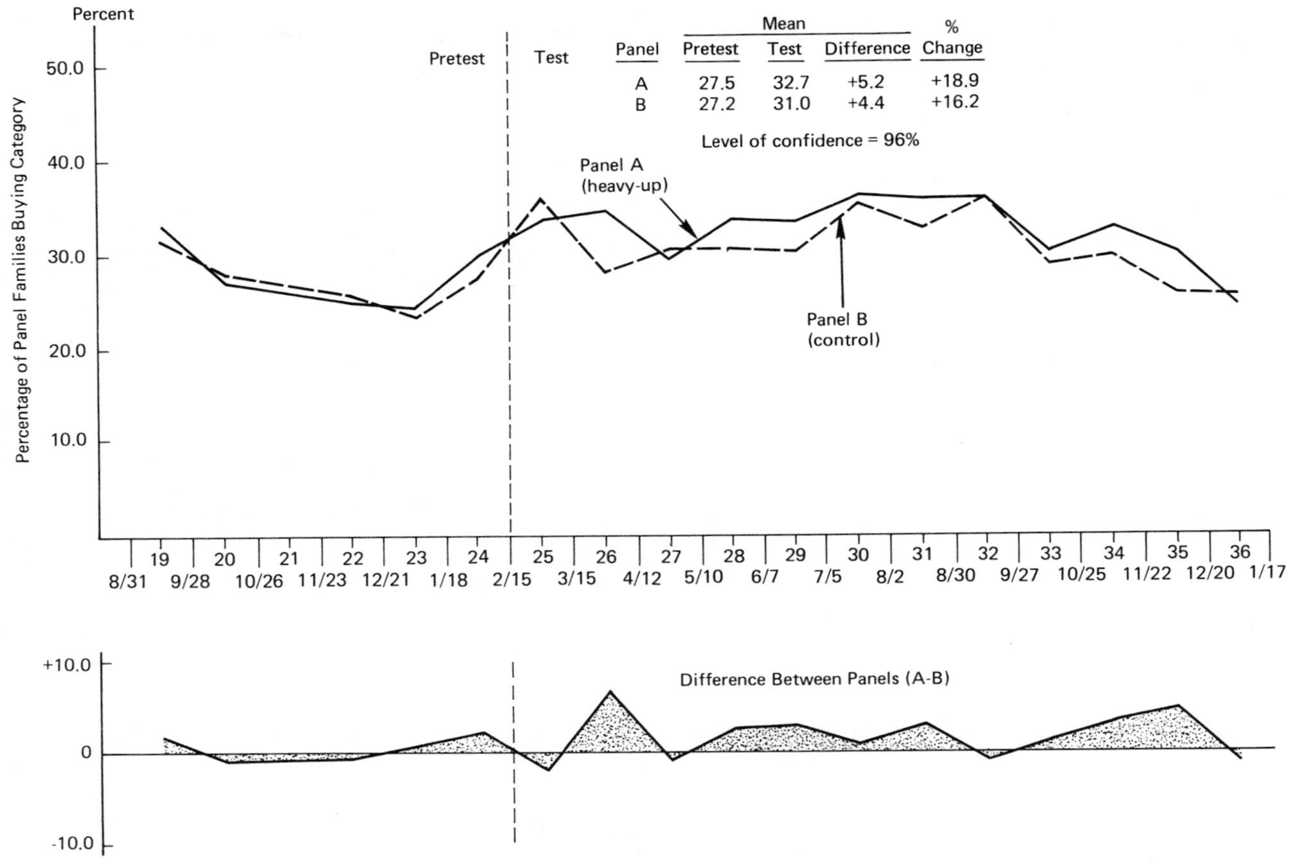

Panel	Mean Pretest	Mean Test	Mean Difference	% Change
A	27.5	32.7	+5.2	+18.9
B	27.2	31.0	+4.4	+16.2

Level of confidence = 96%

Exhibit 11
AdTel Ltd.

Total Category Volume Per Category Buyer
(equivalent units basis)[1]

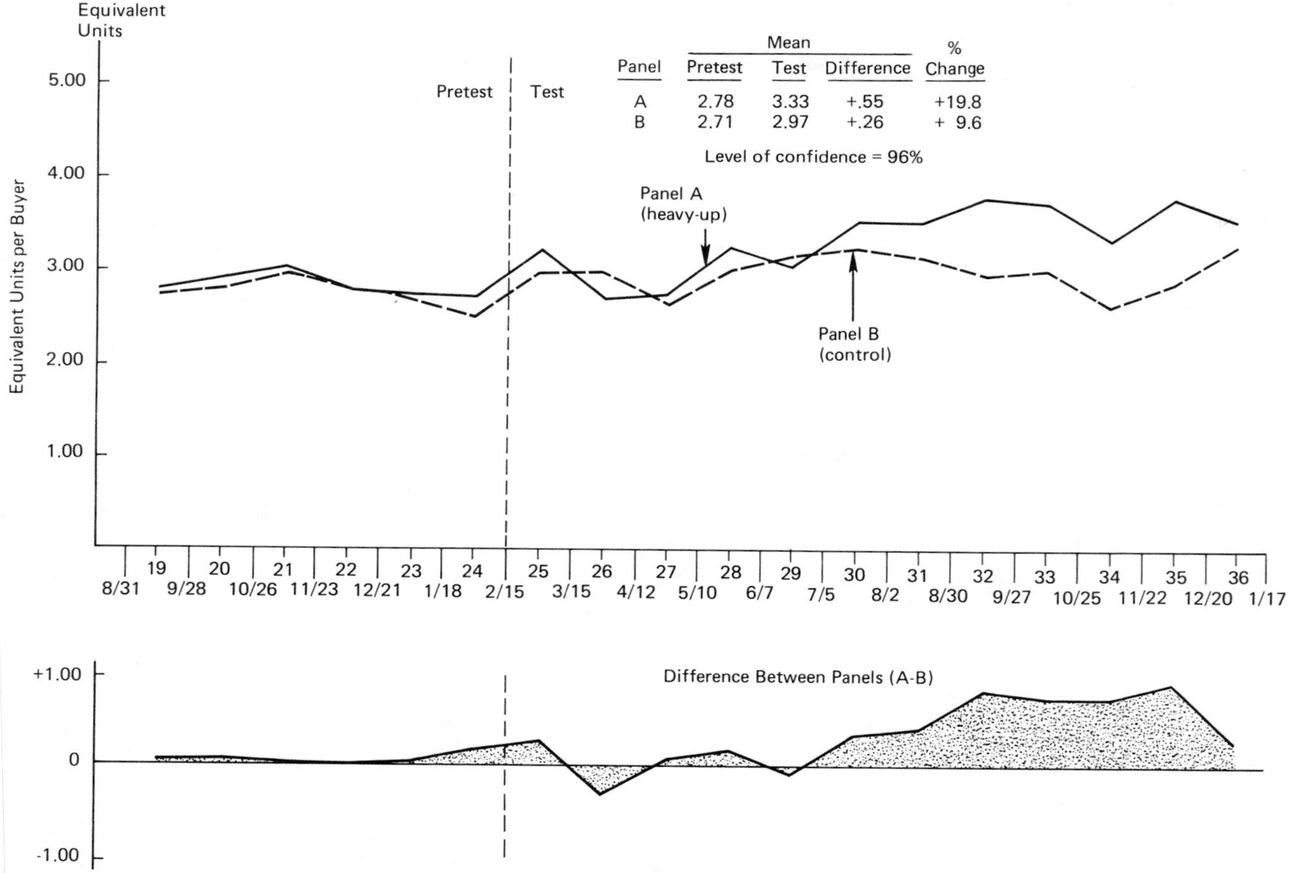

[1]One equivalent unit equals 12.0 ounces.

Exhibit 12
AdTel Ltd.

Percentage of Barrett Volume Purchased on a Consumer Recognized Deal
(equivalent units basis)[1]

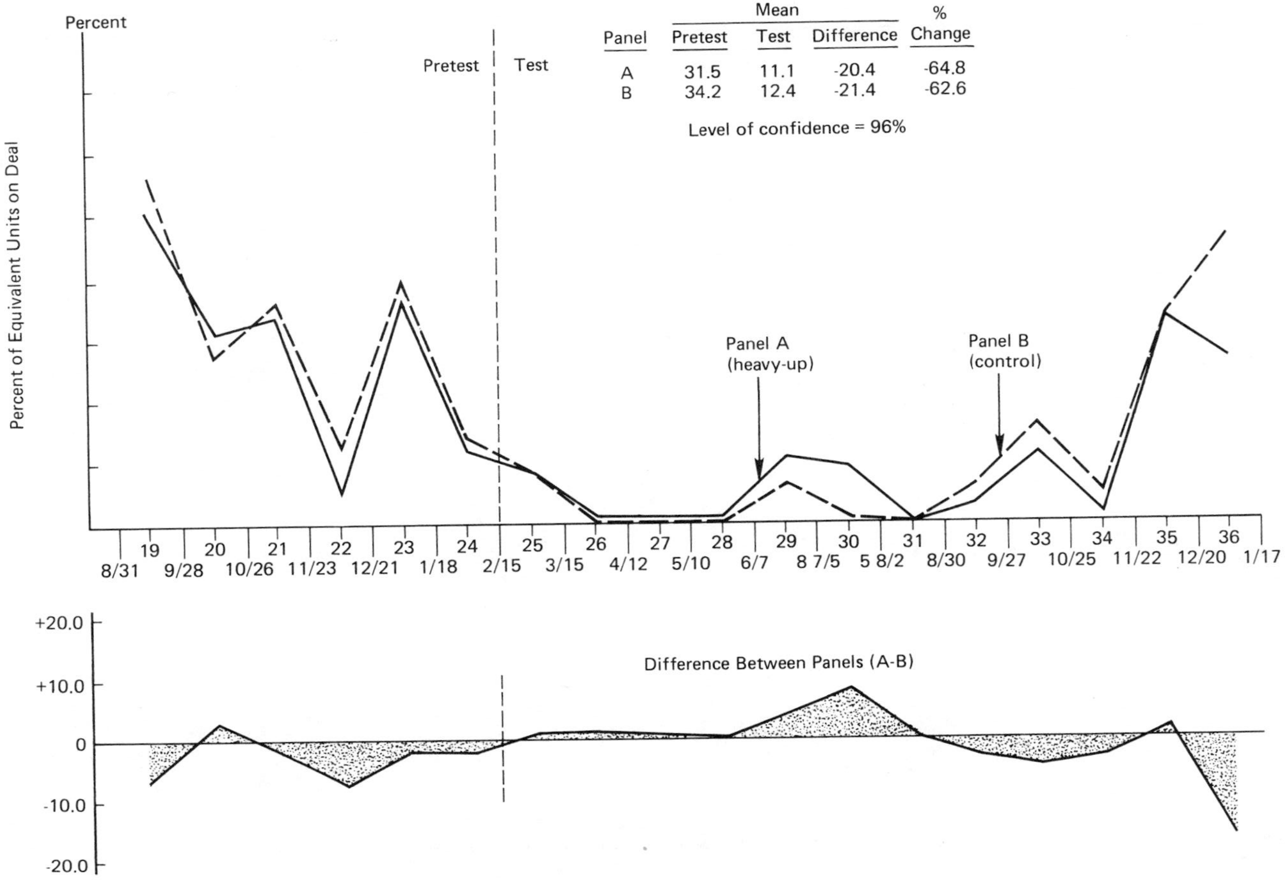

Panel	Mean: Pretest	Mean: Test	Mean: Difference	% Change
A	31.5	11.1	-20.4	-64.8
B	34.2	12.4	-21.4	-62.6

Level of confidence = 96%

[1]One equivalent unit equals 12.0 ounces.

Exhibit 13
AdTel Ltd.

Percentage of Category Volume Purchased on a Consumer Recognized Deal
(equivalent units basis)[1]

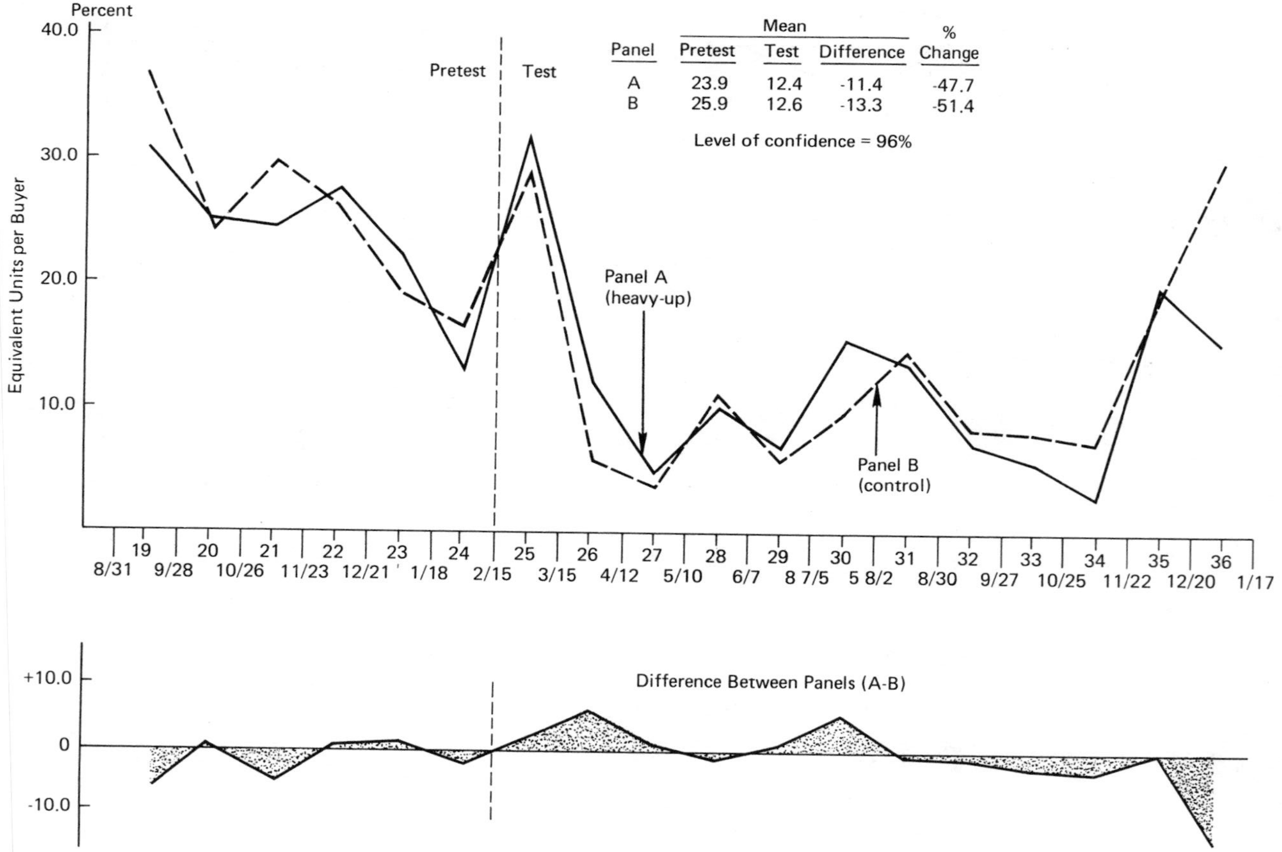

Panel	Mean Pretest	Mean Test	Mean Difference	% Change
A	23.9	12.4	-11.4	-47.7
B	25.9	12.6	-13.3	-51.4

Level of confidence = 96%

[1]One equivalent unit equals 12.0 ounces.

Exhibit 14
AdTel Ltd.

The New York Times, Sunday, November 9, 1969

Advertising:

Testing TV Marketing in the Laboratory

By PHILIP H. DOUGHERTY

There are research services that will find out for an advertiser if his ads are noticed or if consumer attitudes toward his product have changed. But what the manufacturer really wants to know is, "Is my advertising selling goods?"

With the amount of money riding on TV commercial production and time these days, the answer is vital.

John Adler, a pleasant, 42-year-old Dartmouth graduate with a ready smile and thinning hair, thinks he can get that answer. His quest for a way to deliver hasn't been easy and the charge for it is high.

AdTel is the tool and its president said of it, "This is the first time marketing has gotten close to the physical sciences in terms of having a real-life laboratory with rigidly controlled experiments."

That laboratory is a city and the 12,000 of its people who subscribe to Community Antenna Television.

Advertisers on any or all of the three television networks, through AdTel, half of whose subscribers are on one cable and half on another, can substitute other spots in the time they have bought from the networks.

•

They can discover which commercial is more effective, how many spots are needed over a given time to produce the best results, if 30-second commercials are as effective as 60-second spots, which audience (mothers or children, for example) to go for, and whether daytime or evening advertising best moves the product.

They get the answers from 2,400 subscribers to CATV who are members of a consumer panel that each week fills out and mails a diary of that week's package goods purchases.

Half of the panel is hooked into one cable and half to another and both halves are balanced as to habits and backgrounds. They know they are cooperating in some great marketing research activity and are rewarded with little goodies, but they don't know about the doctored television reception.

Mr. Adler would consent to an interview only with the understanding that the identity of his laboratory city would be kept secret. Can't blame him, really, since it's so important for him to keep the reactions of the panelists as natural as possible. A lot of time, trouble and money went into finding this town, this microcosm of America, which he now chooses to call the nation's advertising research capital or AdTel City.

•

More than 2,000 cities were screened and 25 visited before the last two or three finalists and the winner was picked. The requirements were strict. The population had to be over 50,000 and it had to be "typical of the United States," have only one affiliate of each of the three networks and no existing CATV, since putting in a second cable would in the long run be more expensive than laying the two at once.

Now, Mr. Adler knew all about what had to be done because it was he as a consultant

Fabian Bachrach

John Adler

who had done the feasibility study for the Advertising Research Foundation for setting up such a project. When the foundation was unable to get the necessary financial support they allowed him to go ahead with it privately.

The split cable idea isn't new. It's been going on in Milwaukee for years and was done also in Port Jervis, N.Y., a couple of years back. But it hasn't been done before on such an independent or grand scale.

The grandness is reflected in some of the client names - Procter & Gamble, Lever, Colgate-Palmolive, General Foods, General Mills, Campbell Soup, Warner-Lambert and Miles Laboratories.

"The first year we sold on hope," Mr. Adler said. "The second year I'm selling on results."

•

Every client pays $60,000 for each product category for which he gets unlimited cut-ins (on his own network time only), product exclusivity, the purchase reports from the panelists and attitude and awareness studies made among the nonpanelist subscribers.

"We are measuring through sales for the first time, but as a little icing on the cake we give them attitudes as they relate to sales," the president said. What the heck, for $60,000 you're entitled to a little icing.

Just how does a young man who grew up in Westchester and not only graduated from Dartmouth but its Amos Tuck School as well, find himself deeply involved in research for the nation's top package goods people?

Well, in 1949 right after Tuck he joined the training squad at Gimbels for a quick $40 a week and stayed with them for 10 years, leaving as assistant general manager and along the way serving as corporate research director. From there he went to Booz, Allen & Hamilton,* the consulting firm, where he spent four years and ended up in charge of acquisitions, mergers, liquidations and such stuff. Next stop, and this a brief one of a year and a half, was at Audits & Surveys where he was a vice president for corporate development and after that he began John Adler & Associates, a consulting firm that still exists.

"I picked the marketing-communications area because I felt there was more leverage on the profit dollar. Most manufacturing is cut and dried but I felt that if you can improve the effectiveness of advertising that had to be worth something."

"The old saying," he said, bringing up an old saying, "'Find a need and fill it.'"

So in 1965 for an information group of agency research men known (appropriately) as the Agency Research Committee he did a feasibility study on setting up a consolidated interviewing force.

He was "paid peanuts," he recalls, but he made friends with important advertising researchers.

•

Time went by and the young man gained in the wisdom and learning of the marketplace and then one day the late Sherwood Dodge, president of the A.R.F., asked for a feasibility study for a thing called the Field Audit and Completion Test. Mr. Adler again worked cheaply. So when the big one came along, the split cable bit, he was once again called on.

When the A.R.F. turned the project over to him it was William Eldridge, son of Clarence, the marketing great, who helped raise the $2-million to start the project. Now he's chairman of AdTel and the rest of it is marketing history.

And, somewhere in the great land of free enterprise, at this very moment, there are homeowners watching the same channels but different commercials than their neighbors. And probably wishing they were watching different programs, too.

*AdTel was merged into Booz, Allen & Hamilton in June 1972.

Exhibit 14 (continued)

AdTel Ltd.

Journal of Advertising Research, October 1975

Dr. Albert C. Rohloff
Guest Contributor

AdTel: Optimizing the Timing of Exposure Frequency

AdTel's last two JAR ads (October and December 1975) presented some of the findings from a pilot analysis of the sales impact of brand frequency and competitive brand frequency of television commercial exposure on purchase behavior. This study, which was presented at the last ARF Annual Conference, was analyzed in large part by Dr. Albert C. Rohloff, Vice President of Market Science Associates. Al, who has made many substantial contributions to the market research industry, is making another with the observations contained in this article.

Three exposures may be enough (for a time) against no competitive exposures but not against ninety. AdTel's analyses have shown that merely relating an individual's frequency of television exposure to the individual's purchase behavior is a weak research approach. Important variables beyond reach and frequency are needed to understand the sales effects of brand advertising:

- brand share of relevant category exposures (share of voice)
- level of competitive exposures (noise)
- pre-disposition towards the brand (targeting)

AdTel dual-cable tests have demonstrated that two different schedules, each with the same copy and the same media cost, can produce a significantly different sales response. These differences cannot be explained only in terms of reach and frequency. Consequently, in studying the effect of frequency of exposure it is valuable to concentrate on the question: When does the same frequency of exposure deliver a different sales response?

This question leads beyond consideration of frequency alone, to an understanding of how frequency interacts with who is being exposed and the competitive environment; most importantly, the interaction with competitive commercials. This type of analysis can develop scheduling strategies aimed at controlling who is being exposed, with what timing, and in what competitive environment. AdTel has back data -- both purchase and viewing -- available on more than 100 product categories for clients who want to work with it to develop more effective scheduling strategies.

One such strategy, **Impact Scheduling** (as it has recently come to be called) was a common practice in the early years of television. Impact scheduling aims for multiple exposure of brand commercials within a short time, usually within the same show. In the early years of television a brand was frequently advertised on the same show for several years. A number of advertisers are now reconsidering impact scheduling, using AdTel to determine whether impact scheduling does deliver more sales.

As television costs increased substantially over the years, less emphasis was placed on the **sales effectiveness** of advertising scheduling alternatives, and more emphasis was put on **efficiency** -- buying at a lower cost per thousand. Some of the results were a shift from 60's to 30's...and more reliance on **Scatter Plans.** The scatter plan became one way for a brand manager to avoid the risk of buying into a low-rated show for a season. Major advertisers made administrative decisions to remove the risk for each individual brand by using a scatter plan for scheduling brands over the company's network buys. Targeting became secondary to equalizing risk.

A scatter plan and an impact schedule can have nearly identical reach-frequency distributions, and yet have substantially different commercial exposure **density distributions.** (The closer multiple exposures are in time, the greater the density.) Typically, an impact schedule has higher density than a scatter plan. Flighting advertising is also a way of getting more density than a typical scatter plan provides.

In summary, reach and frequency alone are insufficient for distinguishing between different types of schedules such as scatter plan, flighting, impact, etc. However, the reach-frequency analyses at the **individual household level** now being done with AdTel data enable clients to determine the density distribution of a schedule for various groups and relate density along with frequency to changes in buying behavior.

For more information on how AdTel can work with you on developing and testing more effective television scheduling strategies, please contact:

Bill McKenna, President or Steve Grove, Western Region Manager

AdTel, Ltd.
135 South LaSalle Street
Chicago, Illinois 60603

(312) 782-3437

Reg Rhodes, Vice President or Bob McCann, Eastern Region Manager

AdTel, Ltd.
245 Park Avenue
New York, New York 10017

(212) 661-2890

ADTEL

A Subsidiary of Booz, Allen & Hamilton, Inc.

As seen in the February 1976 issue of the JOURNAL OF ADVERTISING RESEARCH

AdTel Ltd.

Journal of Advertising Research, February 1976

Tang Instant Breakfast Drink (A)

One day late in 1972, Dick Jackson, product manager of General Foods' Tang Instant Breakfast Drink,[1] sat down to resolve a problem which had both strategic and tactical consequences. In preparation for the next year's annual business plan, he had to decide what total budget amount to recommend for Tang advertising and promotional (cents-off deals, coupons, etc.) activities.[2] Within that total budget amount, he also had to recommend what proportion to allocate to advertising and what proportion to promotion.

Jackson's decisions was made more difficult because all members of his product group were not yet in complete agreement about the strategic thrust of the brand's activities. Some believed that Tang was still viable after 14 years as a long-run growth vehicle. This would justify investment spending on such marketing activities as advertising and promotion to build future sales, while meeting some satisfactory profitability goals for next year. Others were of the belief that Tang business was peaking and could not support further marketing investment in the long run, which would dictate a strategy which concentrated primarily on short-term profits. Jackson felt that he must present a spending plan which delivered substantial profitability next year and assured sufficient long-run sales volume for Tang.

As inputs to his decision, Jackson had before him the results and recommendations generated by two mathematical models developed to help analyze the advertising and promotion spending decision. One was built inhouse by the division's Operations Research Group. The other was developed by the Management Science Department at Young & Rubicam, the brand's advertising agency. The output of each model was in slightly different

[1]Tang is a concentrated, instant beverage formulation. A small amount (⅔ cup) is added to a larger amount of water (1 quart) to make over 1 quart of beverage. Tang was described by its package label as "A natural tasting orange flavor breakfast drink. It contains more Vitamin C and A than like amounts of orange, grapefruit, or tomato juice. Tang is not a juice, juice product, or a soft drink mix. Tang is a nutritious instant breakfast drink."

[2]Dollar and unit figures used in this case are disguised.

form. The conclusions from the two models were also somewhat in conflict. Jackson thought that this was due to the differing structure and assumptions upon which each model was built. However, the direction of the conclusions was the same: both models seemed to recommend spending levels which were a good deal higher than Tang was presently employing, and both seemed to recommend an advertising/promotion balance weighted more heavily toward advertising than Tang had used.

BACKGROUND

General Foods Corporation (GF) was a leading manufacturer and marketer of grocery products, chiefly convenience foods. Its brands were among the best selling products nationally in a variety of categories: coffee, frozen foods, gelatin desserts, puddings, soft drink mixes, syrups, semimoist and dry dog food, and cereals. Going into the last quarter of fiscal 1973, sales were expected to be over $2.5 billion and net profit over $100 million for the year.[3] The company's long-term strength was built on large consumer franchises for its 400 products and some 30 of the food industry's best-known brand names, including Maxwell House coffee, Bird's-Eye frozen foods, Post cereals, Jell-O desserts, Gaines pet foods, and Tang Instant Breakfast Drink.

In the early 1970s, the company experienced some pressure on sales and profits. In 1970 the company's net income dropped for the first time in 20 years due to an after-tax extraordinary loss of $11 million resulting from the U.S. government's decision that year to restrict sales of food and beverage products containing the artificial sweetener cyclamate. Although some of GF's and its competitors' products suffered from this decision, the Tang business was not adversely affected because its sweetening agent was sugar.[4]

In 1972 General Foods' net income dropped again due primarily to a $47 million after-tax write-off resulting from the firm's decision to dramatically write down its fast food restaurant operations.

In terms of General Foods' marketing organization, a product manager worked within a product group, which in turn worked within a strategic business unit, designated an SBU. Until very recently, the company's marketing activities had been organized by products produced by similar technologies or by products that had developed as line extensions of a single brand. In the early 1970s, when the company was experiencing pressure upon sales and profits in the highly competitive convenience food markets, a major reorganization took place in the marketing structure.

Individual products and brands were placed into groups according to the SBU concept. This meant that all products, regardless of brand name or technology, which would be viewed in the same competitive framework by the consumer in the marketplace, were grouped and managed together, so that General Foods could concentrate on strategic markets as well as on individual products. For example, all dessert products, whether Bird's-Eye frozen desserts or Jell-O gelatins, were placed in the dessert SBU. All main meal dishes, whether Bird's-Eye frozen vegetables or Minute Rice or Shake'n Bake seasoned coating mixes, were placed in the main meal SBU. Tang was included in the beverage SBU, along with frozen beverage products (frozen orange juice concentrate and Orange Plus), other breakfast beverages (Start and Postum), and refreshment beverages (Kool-Aid products).

[3]Fiscal years begin April 1; fiscal 1973, for example, began on April 1, 1972, and ended on March 31, 1973.

[4]Other ingredients, in descending order of weight, are citric acid (for tartness), calcium phosphates (to regulate tartness and prevent caking), gum arabic (vegetable gum to provide body), natural flavor, potassium citrate (to regulate tartness), vitamin C, cellulose gum (vegetable gum), hydrogenated coconut oil, artificial flavor, artificial color, vitamin A, and BHA (a preservative).

The SBU managers reported to the president of one of the company's major divisions. Tang belonged to the Beverage and Breakfast Division. In addition, there were other divisions which marketed pet foods, grocery products (dessert and main meal SBUs), coffee, and institutional food products. Each division also had support staff personnel (staffs for finance, production, technical R&D, and a field sales force) to service its SBUs. Division presidents then reported to General Foods' top corporate management, which included the president, executive and group vice presidents, and support staffs at that level which provided service to all of the divisions—chief among them a financial staff and the corporation's Market Research Group. An organization chart sketching these relationships is shown in Exhibit 1.

Each product manager at GF acted as both a marketing and business manager for his brand. On the marketing side, he had the mission of planning and executing all advertising, promotion, pricing, and merchandising strategies for the brand. More generally, he had to compete for an coordinate all his division's functional resources as they impinged upon his product: technical inputs, marketing research, sales force activities, processing, packaging, and so on. On the operations side, he was responsible for the brand's financial contribution through volume attainment, marketing spending, and pricing decisions. On the planning side, he worked with GF top management in the development of current fiscal year objectives and longer-range objectives.

Dick Jackson, Tang's product manager, was assisted by an associate product manager and an assistant product manager (as were the product managers of other major brands in the SBU). They were supported by product development personnel and promotional (merchandising) personnel within the SBU. Jackson reported to Bill King. the product group manager with responsibility for Tang, Start, and Postum breakfast beverages. King in turn reported to the beverage SBU manager.

TANG'S HISTORY

Tang powdered instant breakfast drink was introduced nationally in 1958. After its introduction, Tang volume grew slowly but steadily. Volume seemed to plateau as the product matured about 1962, so marketing spending was stepped up and new copy devised. Jackson indicated that this gave the product a "shot in the arm," and sales improved through 1968, when stagnation began again. Accordingly, marketing efforts again intensified in fiscal 1969. The product was significantly improved, and sampling efforts, advertising, and promotional spending were increased. The brand's media copy program, which tied the product to America's space exploration efforts, was effective as the Apollo program became very active, providing frequent opportunities for media saturation during the televised Apollo flights. Tang sales were up 29% for fiscal 1969 over fiscal 1968.

In fiscal 1970, this approach continued and sales gained. Even when its price was raised, instead of depressing sales, volume continued strong due in part to the government's ban on cyclamates and Tang's immediate response with advertising noting that it used no artificial sweeteners. Sales were up 31% for the year.

In fiscal 1971, the Apollo program became less active, and a new Tang copy theme was presented. Sales continued to rise but at a slower rate, up only 19% for the year. In fiscal 1972, sales growth continued to slow. Tang prices had been increased to maintain profit margins close to historical levels, although some margin erosion had occurred as additional advertising and promotion funds were invested in the business. A flavor extension,

Grape Tang, was introduced and advertising and promotion funds to support it were diverted from the original Orange Tang. Another flavor extension, Grapefruit Tang, was introduced, with further diversion of funds. Finally, competitive powdered breakfast drinks began to appear. One firm introduced a product which offered more ounces in a package with the same price as Tang. Store private-label brands appeared with packages the same size as Tang, but costing 40% less. Estimates of competitive prices versus Tang and competitive advertising are listed in Exhibit 2. Orange Tang sales for fiscal 1972 were up only 3%.

At about this time, General Foods began implementing a portfolio approach to its many businesses modeled after the Boston Consulting Group's terminology. Products were classified as "stars," which justified investment spending with the objective of high volume and market share growth; "cash cows," which had less growth potential but could provide positive cash flow which could be channeled to the stars and should be managed for the objective of market share stability and positive cash flow; and "dogs," which should be dropped.

Early in fiscal 1973 (spring, summer, and fall of calendar 1972), sales began to fall precipitously—as much as a 13% drop in some bimonthly periods versus previous year figures—and the product group became increasingly concerned over the issues of advertising copy and marketing spending. Exhibit 3 shows Orange Tang sales and marketing spending figures from fiscal 1968 through mid-fiscal 1973, as well as competing powdered orange beverage product sales and price differences between Tang and frozen orange juice concentrate (FOJC).

Jackson felt that a serious reassessment of Tang's marketing plans was necessary if Tang were to continue to justify its star classification in the GF portfolio. Early in fiscal 1973 he could see volume shrinking and could see that Tang would not meet its goal set in the company's 1973 annual business plan of $7 million contribution after marketing costs. Tang's gross margin was approximately $3.15 per 10½ pound unit; marketing costs were primarily the amounts spent on advertising and promotion.

Jackson felt that a further price increase to deliver profits was infeasible. Product line extension (new flavors) to increase volume were no longer favored by the product group. No copy alternatives to the NASA theme had been developed and tested. The primary area of leverage seemed to be marketing spending, but where spending levels should be set to deliver sufficient profits next year *and* assure sustained sales growth was not clear to Jackson. Also, the proportions of funds that should be spent for advertising and for promotion were equally unclear. Historically, the spending balance for Tang had been roughly 50–60% for advertising, 40–50% for promotions in prior years. But there was uncertainty that these historical spending patterns were best given the current status of the brand.

To meet fiscal 1973's financial goals while the regrouping was taking place, planned advertising spending was reduced to a yearly rate below $3.0 million, whereas $4.0–4.5 million had been planned and current advertising themes were pulled off the air. Promotional spending for immediate sales impact was increased by $800,000. Media choices were examined and revised. Development and testing started on new advertising copy based on authority identity figures; for example, a female with a doctorate degree in nutrition, who was also a mother, who fed her family Tang. Product improvement programs were started.

Finally, the product group accelerated two related research projects which were begun late in fiscal 1972 to determine via statistical methods how Tang's marketing budget should be determined and allocated.

THE PLANNING MODELS: BACKGROUND

Early in 1972 at the request of King, two models had been put into development. The purpose of these models was to aid the product group in analyzing the problem and in making decisions regarding optimal total marketing spending and advertising/promotion split. Although not initiated expressly because of the present sales slump, the impetus for hastening development of these models came directly from the brand's depressed performance. In particular, King wanted both present diagnostic analysis and future planning put on a more quantitative basis. He felt sure that his market research support staff could help in finding relationships between advertising and promotional spending could help in finding relationships between advertising and promotional spending on the one hand and both short-run and long-run sales and profitability on the other. King and Jackson wanted the models to answer some specific questions:

1. What would sales and profit response be to varying levels of total advertising and promotional spending?
2. Within those levels, what advertising/promotion split would be most efficient?
3. Building up to the above, what is more efficient in each of Tang's geographical sales districts:[5] allocating all TV advertising dollars to national network TV or putting varying amounts into each district via the use of (more expensive) spot TV?
4. Again building up to the above, what were the optimal amounts of advertising and promotion to allocate to each district—the amounts that would lead to the most sales and profits in each district?

[5]The field sales force handling Tang and the division's other products was organized, at that time, into 21 geographical districts which roughly corresponded to TV media ADIs (areas of dominant influence). Thus the sales reporting and control system, as well as advertising and promotional execution, were done in terms of these geographic sales districts.

The last two questions were important in their own right. General Foods had moved from the allocation of total funds to sales districts based on only the district BDI (brand development index, or the ratio of sales per household in that district to sales per household nationally), thereby spending more where penetration was better, to an allocation that took into account not only BDI but the media costs in each district. But King and Jackson reasoned that each district could have a unique responsiveness to spending in the form of increased sales per ad dollar or increased sales per promotion dollar. If they could estimate these district response levels, they could allocate funds based on responsiveness, as well as cost and BDI, and achieve even greater spending efficiency. They could also make a major contribution to the corporation if this method of analysis could be applied to other products.

To aid in analyzing and making these decisions, Jackson decided that two separate and distinct models should be built and their results compared. One was to be built in house by Mike Goldberg, who was a marketing information services' operations research specialist assigned to work with the Tang and other product groups. Goldberg was a recent MBA graduate who had joined the company late that spring as a marketing research analyst. Although he had had limited quantitative experience prior to his MBA training, he was interested in operations research and his assignment upon joining General Foods was to aid in applying quantitative methods to brand management functions. The Tang model was the first major assignment that he undertook as a member of the marketing research staff. The second model would be developed by the management science group of Tang's advertising agency, Young & Rubicam.

Jackson gave several reasons for the parallel research efforts. He said he had full confidence in the in-house OR Group, but the OR Group had had to take on assignments for many other products as well. Jackson, therefore, wanted a cross check on the group's work. He also wanted the agency group to participate in the study so that the agency would be tied into at least some of the conclusions and thus work better with the product group to implement those conclusions. The cost of each model was minimal—the in-house model was charged to Tang's existing research budget and the agency model cost less than $15,000. Jackson said he truly desired alternate views so as to make the best possible decisions about spending recommendations. Finally, Jackson knew that the backing of two models to justify his recommendation would carry more weight. His hope, of course, was that the two models developed independently would generate parallel results and reach the same conclusions.

In commissioning the models to be developed, Jackson wanted the models to incorporate both short-run and long-run time frames so that the brand group could answer the larger question of investment spending (star status) versus short-run profitability (cash cow status) for the brand, and so could justify its recommendations on that issue to GF's top management.

Prime data sources were in-house shipment and spending information, Nielsen store-audit data on Tang and competitive retail sales, and advertising agency data on costs of network and spot TV for each district. Putting this data in usable form presented some problems. TV advertising dollars, both network and spot, had to be compiled from past years' data. Because of different TV delivery costs in different areas, any attempt to relate sales to advertising would not only have to input advertising dollars spent, but also a measure of how much consumer impact these dollars had. Thus advertising dollars were converted to gross rating points or GRPs (100 gross rating points equaled one impression per TV household per time period). Promotional dollars spent in past years had to be compiled for consumer promotion and trade promotion categories. Sales of competitive products in aggregate and by brand had to be compiled from sparse data. All this data for the geographical districts had to be rearranged into consistent time frames and consistent geographical areas.

Examples of national data used as input to the models are found in Exhibit 3. Examples of geographical data by district used as input are found in Exhibit 4.

Once the data were in hand, the agency and in-house model building efforts proceeded independently, and though the research strategies chosen by each group were similar in their overview of the problem, they differed substantially in the execution of their respective analyses. The two groups' approaches were similar in that both framed the problem in two parts, the first part being an estimation of sales response to advertising expenditures and a second part being a resource allocation procedure that used the response estimates to suggest how marketing budgets should be set and apportioned among advertising, promotion, and geographic areas. In the response estimation phase, the research approaches diverged with respect to how they attempted to account for a variety of intervening market variables and in their treatment of temporal and geographic effects. In the resource allocation phase, the research approaches used conventional marginal cost-benefit analysis methods and differed only with respect to the underlying estimated response functions.

ESTIMATING SALES RESPONSES TO ADVERTISING AND PROMOTION

The in-house response estimation procedure was the more straightforward of the two and was based on a regression equation of the following form:

Flow of questions to determine level of prompting required to stimulate recall

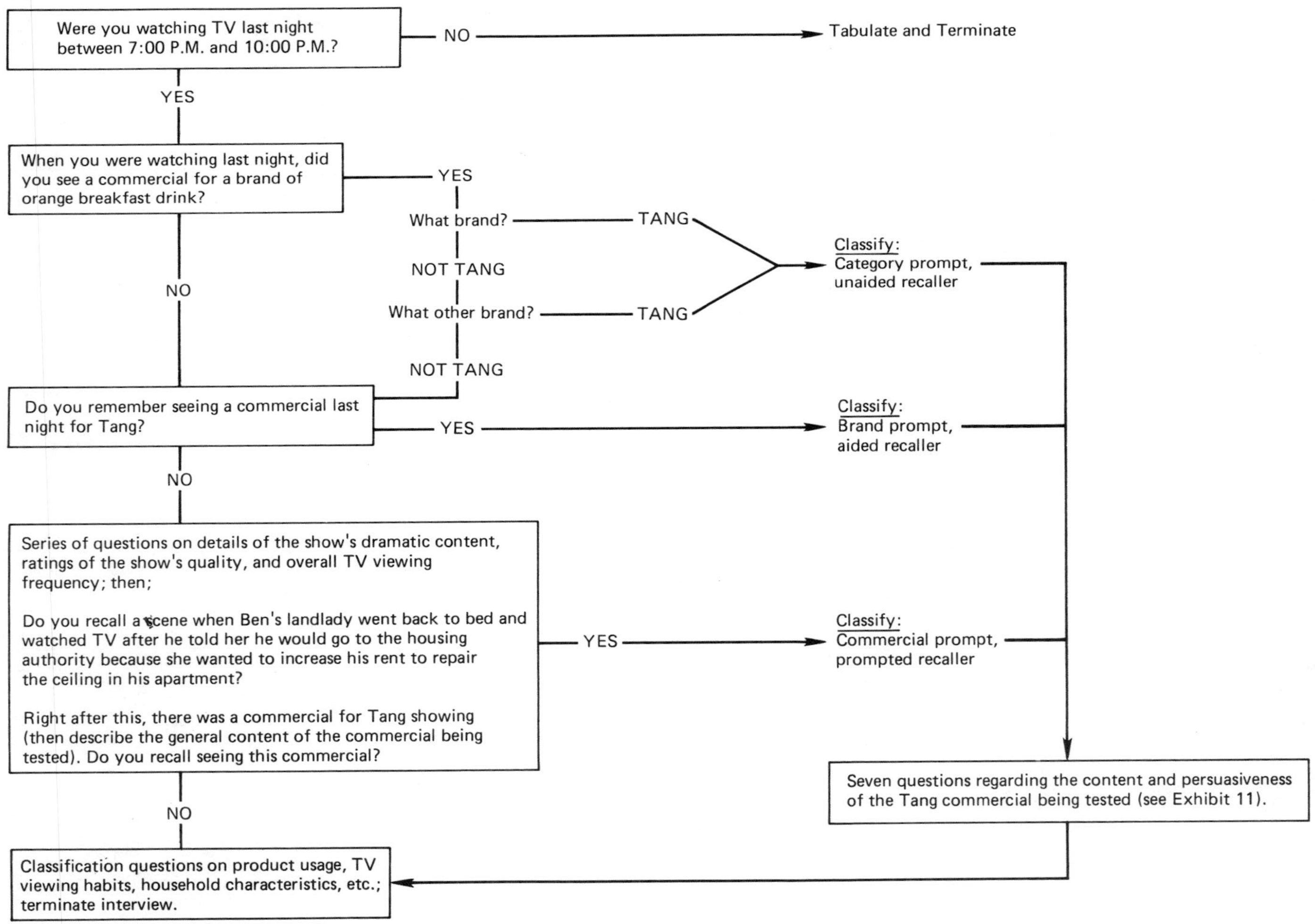

Were you watching TV last night between 7:00 P.M. and 10:00 P.M.?
NO
Tabulate and Terminate
YES
When you were watching last night, did you see a commercial for a brand of orange breakfast drink?
YES
What brand?
TANG
NOT TANG
What other brand?
TANG
NOT TANG
Classify: Category prompt, unaided recaller
NO
Do you remember seeing a commercial last night for Tang?
YES
Classify: Brand prompt, aided recaller
NO
Series of questions on details of the show's dramatic content, ratings of the show's quality, and overall TV viewing frequency; then;
Do you recall a scene when Ben's landlady went back to bed and watched TV after he told her he would go to the housing authority because she wanted to increase his rent to repair the ceiling in his apartment?
Right after this, there was a commercial for Tang showing (then describe the general content of the commercial being tested). Do you recall seeing this commercial?
YES
Classify: Commercial prompt, prompted recaller
Seven questions regarding the content and persuasiveness of the Tang commercial being tested (see Exhibit 11).
NO
Classification questions on product usage, TV viewing habits, household characteristics, etc.; terminate interview.

$$S_{i,t} = a_{0,i} + a_{1,i}A_{i,t} + a_{2,i}P_{i,t} + a_{3,i}D_{i,t} \qquad (1)$$

where

S_i = estimated sales in the ith territory in time period t,

$A_{i,t}$ = number of GRPs impacting in territory i in time period t,

$P_{i,t}$ = number of promotion dollars impacting in territory i in time period t,

$D_{i,t}$ = is the percentage of retail outlets carry Orange Tang in all package sizes in territory i in time period t,

and $a_{0,i}$, $a_{1,i}$, $a_{2,i}$, $a_{3,i}$ are response coefficients estimated by the regression analysis.

Goldberg had decided to include the distribution variable $D_{i,t}$ when he found that it improved the equation's "fit" with the data summarized in Exhibit 4 for any particular territory. In an attempt to adjust the equation to show the diminishing effects of advertising over time, Goldberg modified the variable $A_{i,t}$ so that it would reflect the cumulative effects of both present and past period's advertising. The modification he made was of the form

$$A_{i,t} = A_{i,t} + \sum_{m=1}^{M} R^m A_{i,t-m}$$

where R was a number less than 1 which indicated what proportion of a given period's advertising was thought to have impact in the succeeding period and M was the number of prior periods for which these carryover effects were to be accounted. The NASA-based message strategy, in an independent prior study, had indicated that R, when defined as a form of advertising retention rate, was found to be 0.80. This was assumed to be a practical maximum, and the message quality of other Tang campaigns would be adjusted in the model by judgmentally lowering the value of R. Since only three years of quarterly data were available, Goldberg let $M = 12$ throughout the response estimation part of the study. As an example using these assumptions, the carryover effect from one prior period was $.8^1(A_{t-1})$ and from these prior periods would be $.8^1(A_{i,t-1}) + .8^2(A_{i,t-2}) + .8^3(A_{i,t-3})$. Obviously, higher powers of R approached zero; thus estimated carryover effects diminished relatively quickly.

Since the response coefficient $a_{i,1}$ described an upwardly sloped straight line, it implied that increased values of $A_{i,t}$ would yield sales returns without limit at the same rate as long as advertising expenditures were increased. Although this was known to be unrealistic, the linear model fit the data better than did any curvilinear models that Goldberg had tried. The model was made to conform to expected practice by assuming that the true response curves were really S-shaped and that the values of $a_{i,1}$ described Tang's recent responses along the linear portion of the curve. Goldberg and the product group worked together to determine judgmentally where the upper and lower tails of the assumed response curves should be set on one hand so that increased spending would indicate no further sales increases and, on the other hand, so that threshold spending levels necessary to have any effect on sales would also be specified. Figure 1 illustrates the in-house model's relationship between sales and advertising.

The response coefficients of the in-house model were estimated on a territory-by-territory basis using the 12 quarterly observations of sales, advertising GRPs, promotion dollars, and distribution percentages from fiscal 1970, 1971, and 1972. When the territorial response coefficients had been determined and when they were applied to the actual data from the fiscal 1973 spending plan for each of the 26 territories, they predicted 1973 nationwide sales of 4.5 million units. Taking into account results through late fall of calendar 1972 (almost three quarters into fiscal 1973), the brand group's best estimate of full fiscal year

Figure 1

General Form of the In-house Models Advertising Response Function

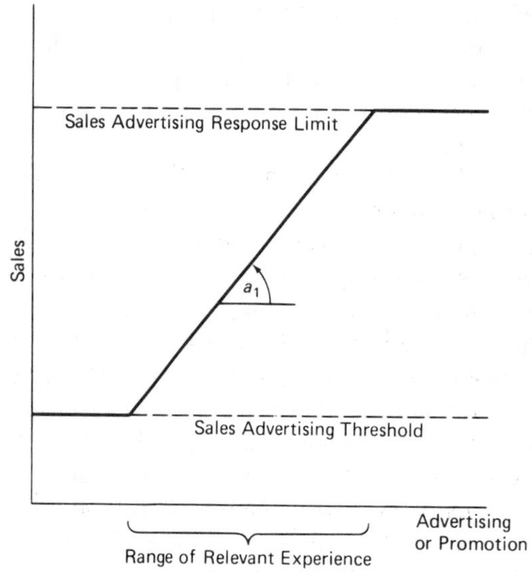

1973 volume was about 4.3 million units. Considering that the model's inputs took into account little or no competitive experience, the model's prediction appeared to be quite accurate. The model's 26 separate advertising response coefficients and 26 promotion response coefficients, along with the judgmentally determined thresholds and upper response limits, were the essential inputs to a resource allocation model.

The Young & Rubicam response estimation model used the same information required by the in-house model and also utilized demographic data from each territory. Probably the most significant difference was in the structure of the regression analysis used by the agency model, which used regression analysis rather than judgment to estimate curvilinear responses to advertising and promotion. The agency model used a different procedure for accounting for territorial differences. Finally, the agency model treated the entire country as a single universe, rather than treating each sales territory independently. This last point was important, since the data were broken down into 26 territories and 12 quarters. The data base for the agency regression analyses was 312 observations instead of the 12 observations for an individual district. As a result, the agency model could handle more independent variables with greater statistical reliability.

The agency response estimation model was built in two steps. The first step was to show how *changes* in sales occurred as functions of advertising GRPs and promotion dollars. The second step was to determine and demonstrate how the direct sales-advertising-promotion relationships should be modified due to interactions with distribution by package size, price differentials with competition, existing sales levels, demographic factors and seasonality. (For example, if improved distribution tended to increase sales, what effect, if any, would improved distribution have on the ability of advertising to generate sales?)

The agency model's structure was evolved from the following regression equation:

$$S_t - S_{t-1} = a_0 + a_1A_t + a_2P_t \qquad (2)$$

where S_t and S_{t-1} are the sales (per capita) of a given district at periods t and $t - 1$, respectively, A_t is the (per capita) advertising in time period t, P_t is the (per capita) promotion in time period t, and a_0, a_1, a_2 are coefficients estimated by regression analysis.

The agency director of Management Sciences described the next steps in the model building procedure as follows:

> We hypothesized that the sales response to advertising would display a pattern of diminishing marginal return. To test that hypothesis, the advertising variable was expressed as a quadratic function. In other words, in addition to regressing S_t against A_t and P_t, we also regressed S_t against a quadratic function of S_t and A_t and against a lagged sales variable, S_{t-1}, forming a measure

of sales retention. The resulting equation had the following form:

$$S_t = a_0 + a_1A_t + a_2A_t^2 + a_3P_t + a_4P_t^2 + a_5S_{t-1} \quad (3)$$

When this was done, the signs of a_1 and a_3 were positive and the signs of a_2 and a_4 were negative, which meant, of course, that the partial derivative of S_t with respect to A_t (the sales increase with an increase in advertising) was smaller as A_t grew larger. In other words, the sales relation to advertising exhibited a diminishing marginal return.

At this point an exponential fitting program was used to build a new equation for purposes of extrapolation since equation 3 when used for purposes of extrapolation resulted in sales values that approached minus infinity when carried forward over many time periods. The extrapolation equation, which was consistent with the diminishing, curvilinear marginal returns concept supported by equation 3, was of the following form:

$$S_t = a_0 + a_1 [1 - e^{-bA}t] + a_2P_t + a_3S_{t-1} \quad (4)$$

Equation 4 recast the advertising variable, A_t, into an exponential form of e, the base of natural logarithms; b was a coefficient estimated by means of a least squares exponential fitting program. Structuring the advertising variable in this manner resulted in a relationship between S_t and A_t that was curvilinear, with a size and rate of change that are indicated by a_1 and b as illustrated in Figure 2, and showed diminishing returns from larger expenditures. Equation 4 also permitted the estimation of the sales asymptote with increased advertising, which was interpreted as the maximum "advertising leverage."

The second step of the agency's response model building was to determine whether certain potentially interactive factors should be accounted for explicitly in the model of equation 4. The procedure involved searching via some rather complex estimation procedures for values to include in L, a modifier of the coefficient a_1, which altered equation 4 as follows:

$$S_t = a_0 + a_1L [1 - e^{-bA}t] + a_2P_t + a_3 S_{t-1} \quad (5)$$

As the value of L changed, the estimate of advertising leverage would also change, in response to whatever variables were included in the definition of L. For example, Figure 3 shows the type of relationship that was found to exist between sales and the level of distribution at various advertising spending levels. At any level of advertising, higher levels of distribution were associated with higher estimated sales. Furthermore, the incremental sales growth between \$2 million and \$3 million advertising spending was everywhere greater than the incremental sales growth estimated between \$3 million and \$4 million advertising

Figure 2

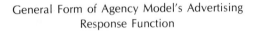

General Form of Agency Model's Advertising Response Function

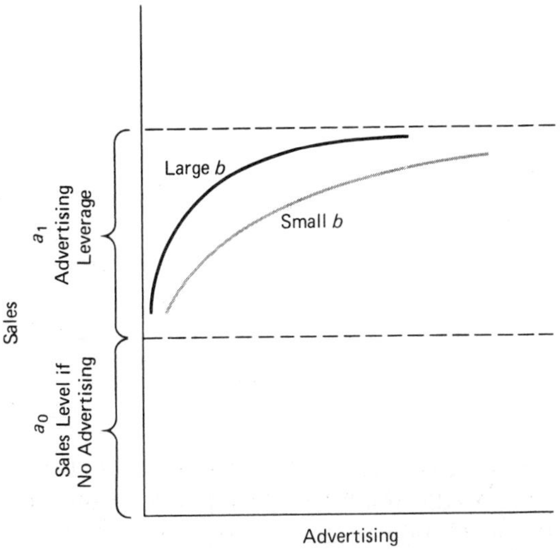

Notes: Under conditions where all other factors are constant, a_1, the coefficient of $(1e^{-bAt})$, denotes the sales difference between no advertising and unlimited advertising, a quantity called "advertising leverage"; b, the coefficient of A_t, indicates the rate at which incremental advertising taps the remaining sales potential due to advertising leverage.

Figure 3

Estimated Orange Tang Sales Growth Under Different Levels of Distribution and Advertising Spending

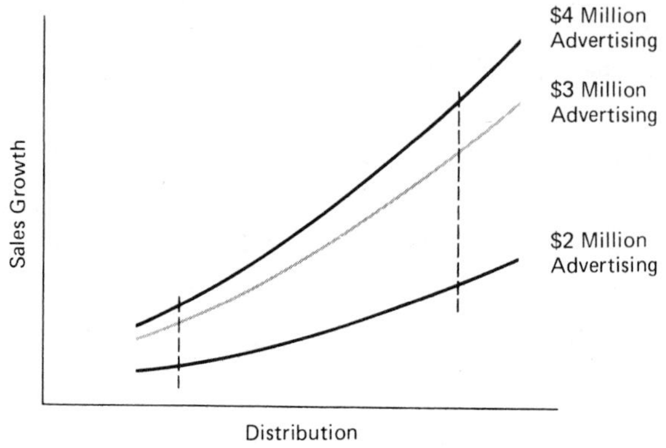

spending, as was suggested earlier in Figure 2. Finally, the difference in sales between any two levels of spending was greater as the level of distribution became larger. In short, advertising leverage was found to be related to the level of distribution.

In this situation, L was set equal to $D^{c}{}_{1}$, where D was the distribution level in a territory and c_1 was a coefficient estimated via exponential least squares estimation procedures. L eventually came to be defined as

$$L = D^{c}{}_{1}\, M^{c}{}_{2}\, S^{c}{}_{3}$$

where M was a demographic measure of the population in a sales territory, S was measure of the existing sales level, and c_1, c_2, and c_3 were coefficients found by the analysis. L was thus a composite coefficient that adjusted advertising leverage according to distribution, demographics, and existing sales levels in a territory. An examination of the advertising interactive effects of seasonality, package size distributions, promotion, and price differentials with competition were found *not* to be sufficiently significant to retain in the computation of L. One measure of the improvement that L contributed to equation 5 was that it improved the t value of a_1 from about 8.0 to about 20.0, indicating a large increase in the association between advertising and sales when interactively weighted by intervening market and marketing factors. L became the measure of a sales territory's advertising leverage and hence advertising effectiveness. The sales territory advertising effectiveness figures were found to range between 0.8 and 1.5 times the national average by the agency model.

To estimate the long-term effects of advertising and promotion, the agency used a model which showed the extent to which cumulative advertising or promotion expenditures were related to a present period's sales level. The model was of the form

$$S_t = a_0 = a_1(A_t + A_{t-1} + \cdot \cdot \cdot + A_{t-n}) \quad (6)$$

when n was the number of preceding periods for which the estimated cumulative advertising effects were desired. The value of a_1, which was determined by the regression analysis, was an indicator of the effects of the sum of each previous period's advertising on current sales, for any number of time periods for which data existed. A similar model was constructed using prior periods' promotional expenditures

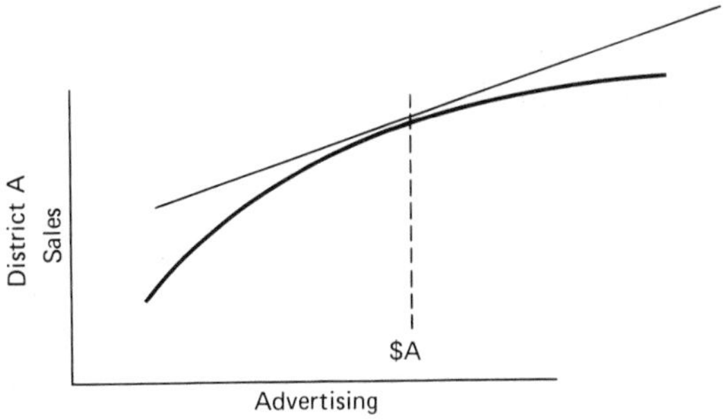

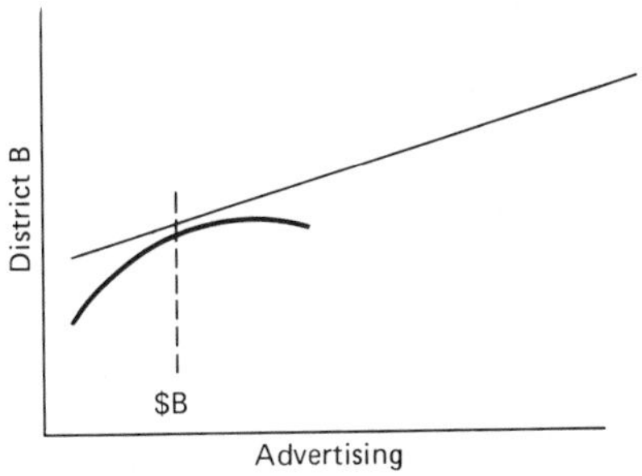

as the independent variable and b as the estimate of long-term carryover effects of promotion:

$$S_t = b_0 + b_1 (P_t + P_{t-1} + \cdot \cdot \cdot + P_{t-n}) \quad (7)$$

Using equations 6 and 7, it was possible to estimate the long-term carryover effects of both advertising and promotion up to n time periods. The agency found that the carryover effects for promotion expenditures were substantially lower than were those for advertising. The agency later applied the carryover estimates to alternative advertising plans and showed the expected future incremental sales over n periods from a present advertising schedule. The incremental contribution resulting from those sales were then evaluated in terms of their net present value to the advertiser using a 15% cost of capital.

ALLOCATING MARKETING RESOURCES

With the results of their respective procedures for estimating how sales responded to advertising and promotion in hand, the in-house group and the agency group followed similar procedures for evaluating alternative spending strategies. For decisions that involved choosing between competing sales territories and for choosing between advertising and promotion programs, the allocation procedure employed a marginal cost/marginal revenue framework. For example, assuming a fixed media budget and two sales territories with different sales response curves, the allocation procedure divided funds between the groups, such that the total budget was consumed and each territory's budget was set at that point on the sales response curve where the respective slopes were equal. District A, shown here, would receive *$A* and District B would receive *$B*, and both districts would show the same marginal rate of return, although their budgets might differ significantly.

In the case of the linear in-house models, funds were allocated only up to the judgmentally determined upper limit of territory responsiveness or to the equivalent of 2,250 GRPs, depending on which was lower.

Since each group had 26 advertising response functions and 26 promotion response functions, both the agency and the in-house allocation procedures could either apportion a fixed budget or show an optimal budget, given relaxation of budget constraints. Furthermore, by using estimated carryover effects, each group could adopt either long-run or short-run planning horizons and demonstrate the temporal implications of a given spending strategy.

The expected contributions from a given media program were expressed by both allocation methods net of media costs, and this led to a different interpretation of implications for media scheduling between the in-house and agency groups. The in-house sales response model showed response curves of apparently sufficient slope to justify use of more expensive spot TV. Spot TV costs per GRP were roughly 60% higher than that of networks in many areas. The agency sales response model did not justify the use of spot TV, and the agency recommended the use of spot TV only in the event that competition in the powdered orange beverage category increased in certain districts.

With respect to competitive factors, the agency allocation model modified its Tang sales and profit projections based on assumed competing sales of 1.0 million, 1.5 million, and 2.0 million annual units. The model assumed that only 40% of competitive sales would come from market expansion, while the rest would come from taking sales away from Tang. The in-house model made no explicit adjustment for anticipated competitive sales.

RESULTS OF THE MODELING PROCESS

The GF operations group used the findings of the response estimation research and the allocation model to write a computer simulation program that facilitated trial of many alternative advertising strategies.

The user of the program could specify the advertising retention rate, the number of periods in the planning horizon, the product's estimated VGP (variable gross profit) per unit, and the program option desired: program calculates optimal budget or program allocates given budget. The program then produced sales and profit forecasts and recommended budget allocations to network TV, spot TV, and promotions by sales territory.

After running the model many times using varying budgets and examining the resulting sales and profit projections, the operations research group presented a report on the model's implications to Tang brand management. The report contained the following conclusions:

1. A minimum of $4 million per year in advertising expenditure is necessary to maintain volume at current levels. Any expenditures above this amount will lead to volume growth. Expenditures below this amount will result in erosion of the franchise. For maximum long-term sales growth and profitability, advertising levels in excess of $6–7 million per year seem necessary.
2. Promotional spending does not affect long-term growth, only short-run sales volume. However, some minimal level of promotions probably have become part of the cost of doing business because of the expectations of the user franchise.
3. Tang definitely appears to be a star brand today because of its responsiveness to marketing spending and reluctant profitability. The amount of advertising support that it receives in the near future will in large part determines how long it remains a star.

The model's results for several proposed budget allocations with corresponding sales and profit forecasts are listed in Exhibit 5. Most of the in-house media allocations recommended that about one-fifth of the media budget be placed in spot TV.

The agency's Management Science Department's report presented its conclusions in terms of short-term and long-term implications. Because of the significant advertising carryover effects which the agency found in its research, adopting a long-term time frame argued for higher advertising spending levels than if a one-year time frame were assumed. Assuming either a four-year or a six-year time horizon, the agency model suggested that a sustained media spending level of $6.9 million was most profitable; assuming a one-year time frame media spending level of $4.0 million was suggested with the caveat that it would not sustain long-term sales volume. The one-year forecasts under ten alternative advertising and promotion budgets are listed in Exhibit 6. Long-term forecasts for sales and profits at the ends of two, four, and six years, assuming competitive sales increases of 0.5 million units per year of which 25% are claimed from Tang's franchise, are listed in Exhibit 7. The agency's media recommendations included no spot TV allocations, except for the Denver territory where spot TV was relatively low cost and for other territories only as competing products might exhibit rapid growth.

USING THE MODELS

Although Jackson had not reached a final evaluation of the models and had not concluded whether the in-house model or the agency model might be the superior candidate for use and further development, he had used the models on three separate occasions in late calendar 1972. First, with the approval of the beverage SBU manager, he used the models to show that Tang had advertising response rates that were historically higher than several other beverage products, justifying shifts in marketing funds to Tang.

Second, as the final quarter of fiscal 1973 approached, he found that the models were helpful in supporting divisional requests for an additional marketing spending infusion of $260,000 in the last quarter of fiscal 1973 to help Tang achieve its fiscal 1973 sales and profit targets. The targets were in grave danger of not being met due to large advertising and promotion reductions midway through the year. In his request, Mr. Jackson had written that

> The incremental $260,000 advertising and promotion spending should generate an incremental 18,750 units, or $60,000 variable gross profit for the quarter. Additionally, the $260,000 should pay back within one year. These conclusions are based upon mathematical analyses by both GF Operations Research and Young & Rubicam of the past three years of the Tang business. In brief, both analyses indicate that at current spending levels, Orange Tang marketing spending is generating approximately a 180%+ return on advertising and promotional dollars within one year. Projections from the models are

Incremental funds: $260,000 in next quarter

	Time Period	
Analyses	*Next Quarter*	*Next Four Quarters*
Young & Rubicam		
Incremental volume[1]	45,000 units	130,000 units
Adjusted volume[2]	45,000 units	65,000 units
Net contribution	$70,000	$205,000
In-house		
Incremental volume[1]	33,000 units	140,000 units
Adjusted volume[2]	16,000 units	70,000 units
Net contribution	$50,500	$220,000

[1]Incremental volume is the increase versus latest estimate of volumes under the current spending plan.
[2]Adjusted volumes assume that (1) advertising retention rate is average, not the high rate used in the models, and (2) competitive developments reduce incremental volume impact by 50%.

Finally, in December 1972, Jackson was considering using the models to renegotiate the volume objectives of the fiscal 1974 annual business plan. Midway through the 1973 fiscal year and before the models were available, Jackson had submitted a preliminary business plan for fiscal 1974. Management had responded by asking Jackson to try to find ways to increase fiscal 1974 target volumes by 225,000 units and target profits by $270,000, by increasing marketing funds only slightly. When the models became available, he prepared projections that showed that his original plan was consistent with the models' forecasts, but that the revised targets proposed by corporate management were infeasible according to the models. In making these fiscal 1974 projections, Jackson used corporate average advertising retention rates of .7 per quarter rather than the NASA .8 per quarter campaign retention rates; assumed a competitive cannibalization of 50% of projected Tang growth, and assumed a competitive volume of 2.5 million units in fiscal 1974.

As he prepared his final draft of his proposed 1974 annual business plan, he summarized the situation as follows in this table:

	Jackson's Initial Proposal for Fiscal 1974	*Management's Counterproposal for Fiscal 1974*
Advertising and promotion budget (millions)	$7.9	$8.4
Judgmental volume target, units (000)	3,900	4,125
Agency model projected volume, units (000)	3,800	3,860
In-house model projected volume, units (000)	3,924	3,990

Jackson knew that the long-term recommendations of the models called for advertising spending to be increased from the present annual rate of about $4 million to about $7 million, while reducing the promotional spending from about $3.5 million to less than $2 million. He wondered whether this was the time to initiate a major change in advertising and promotion strategy for Tang, and, if so, how he should justify those changes to division and corporate management.

Exhibit 1
Tang Instant Breakfast Drink (A)

General Foods Marketing Organization

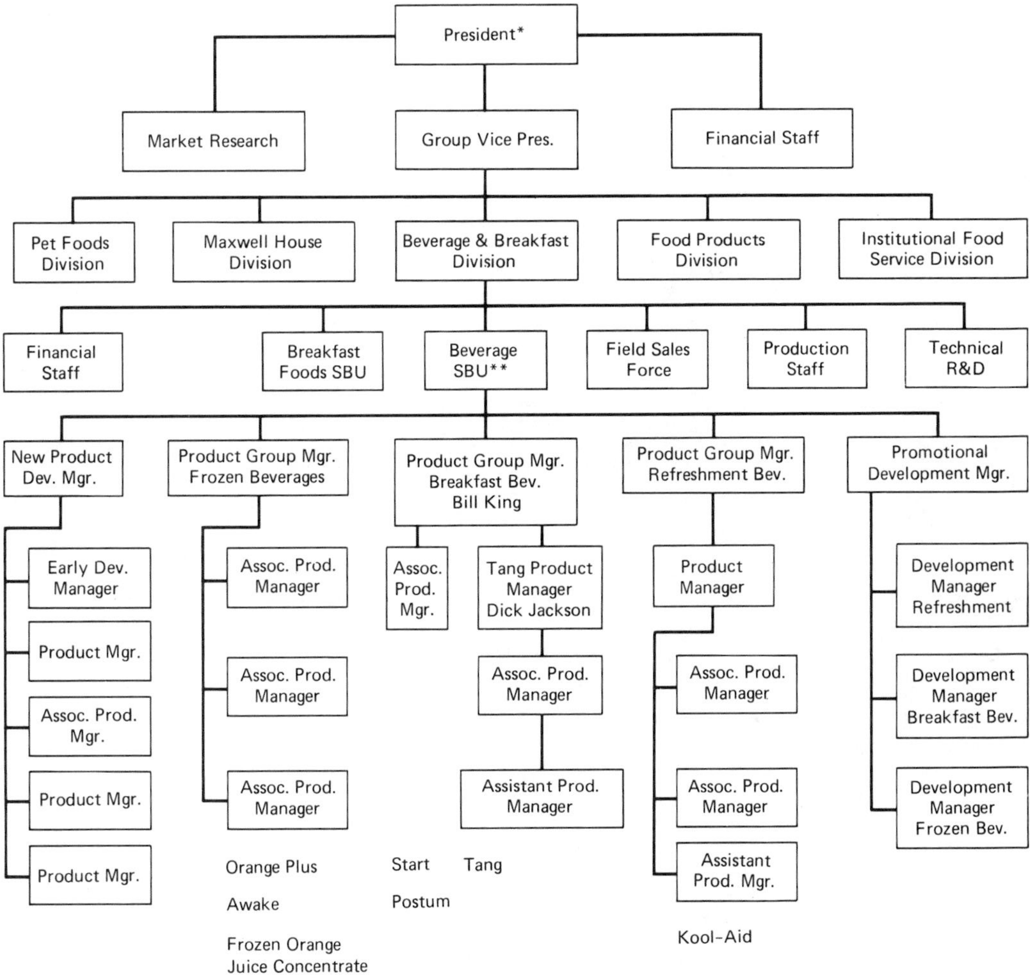

[1]Also attached to the president's office were support staffs for legal, purchasing, and so on.
[2]The SBU manager also had a staff supporting him with functions similar to the divisional staffs.

Exhibit 2
Tang Instant Breakfast Drink (A)

Recent Competitive Efforts

1. Tang price/unit over time (10½-pound units) at retail:

Fiscal 1967	$8.42
Fiscal 1968	8.41
Fiscal 1969	8.38
Fiscal 1970	8.71
Fiscal 1971	8.70
Fiscal 1972	9.03
Fiscal 1973 (first half)	9.08

2. Competitive price estimates (10½-pound units) at retail:

Fiscal 1972	$7.49
Fiscal 1973 (first half)	7.53

3. Competitive advertising (000):

	Borden	*Lipton*
Fiscal 1972	$ 59	—
Fiscal 1973 (first half)	278	$630

Exhibit 3

Tang Instant Breakfast Drink (A)

National Data Available to Modelers

Period: Fiscal Year	Period: Quarter	Orange Tang Sales of 10½-pound Units (000)	Advertising (000)	Promotion (000)	Competitive Sales of 10½-Pound Units (000)	Price Difference: FOJC–Tang (cents per 24 ounces)
1968	1	530	$ 365	$ 289	0	−0.5¢
	2	511	435	338	0	0.1
	3	514	303	330	0	1.4
	4	545	188	190	0	2.2
	Total	2,100	$1,291	$1,147	0	
1969	1	579	437	1,006	0	3.3
	2	615	331	51	0	3.8
	3	664	570	129	0	4.7
	4	850	1,176	471	0	6.0
	Total	2,708	$2,514	$1,657	0	
1970	1	801	992	254	0	6.3
	2	853	771	356	0	5.1
	3	872	802	128	0	4.8
	4	1,029	988	448	0	4.0
	Total	3,555	$3,553	$1,186	0	
1971	1	1,019	1,400	710	0	3.4
	2	1,002	806	549	0	3.2
	3	1,024	843	1,011	0	2.5
	4	1,197	1,110	684	0	2.1
	Total	4,242	$4,159	$2,954	0	
1972	1	1,088	883	339	0	3.4
	2	1,070	769	1,070	22	4.8
	3	1,052	864	1,006	50	5.1
	4	1,142	430	763	89	8.0
	Total	4,352	$2,946	$3,718	161	
1973	1	1,044	884	576	200	7.9
	2	965	363	851	271	7.9

Exhibit 4
Tang Instant Breakfast Drink (A)

Orange Tang Annual Sales, Advertising and Promotion Data by Sales District

District	*Fiscal Year*	*Orange Tang Sales of 10½-pound Units per 1,000 Persons*	*Orange Tang Advertising (000) (of gross rating points)*	*Orange Tang Promotions Dollars per 1,000 Households*	*Spot Media TV Costs Dollars per 1,000 Household Impressions*
1. Boston	1970	38.38	3.64	17.31	
	1971	43.58	6.92	35.10	
	1972	46.75	2.56	34.62	3.02
2. New York	1970	39.52	3.99	19.45	
	1971	46.92	5.21	37.22	
	1972	46.98	2.35	50.50	1.63
3. Syracuse	1970	55.31	3.58	21.74	
	1971	69.70	7.23	50.72	
	1972	69.25	3.11	54.73	3.26
4. Philadelphia	1970	62.46	3.79	24.78	
	1971	75.95	5.51	53.55	
	1972	72.27	2.69	69.21	2.59
5. Youngstown	1970	72.80	4.01	21.54	
	1971	88.27	6.71	49.12	
	1972	88.84	3.42	83.27	1.87
6. Washington, D.C.	1970	54.68	3.92	15.12	
	1971	63.74	6.26	43.95	
	1972	65.98	2.83	48.23	2.71
7. Charlotte	1970	55.80	3.51	13.29	
	1971	69.65	5.86	37.36	
	1972	73.06	3.03	31.65	2.52
8. Jacksonville	1970	34.38	3.15	9.07	
	1971	43.73	4.56	26.54	
	1972	47.32	2.73	21.17	2.76
9. Atlanta	1970	50.97	3.59	10.84	
	1971	55.11	6.32	27.63	
	1972	50.38	2.83	27.63	2.43

10. Memphis	1970	56.57	3.89	14.62	
	1971	57.84	6.57	37.73	
	1972	58.63	2.97	29.50	1.78
11. Detroit	1970	73.66	4.23	19.37	
	1971	91.35	7.18	62.19	
	1972	95.87	2.98	66.56	2.15
12. Indianapolis	1970	89.41	3.66	23.10	
	1971	92.43	5.75	65.71	
	1972	85.12	3.05	71.86	1.99
13. Cincinnati	1970	71.29	3.48	27.68	
	1971	91.75	5.93	56.21	
	1972	86.93	3.07	62.43	2.15
14. Chicago	1970	62.95	3.37	19.65	
	1971	81.58	6.09	57.69	
	1972	82.30	2.74	71.55	1.63
15. Milwaukee	1970	85.05	3.40	16.78	
	1971	97.58	7.53	57.44	
	1972	107.10	3.32	23.38	2.46
16. Minneapolis	1970	80.88	3.59	36.04	
	1971	95.60	5.52	78.60	
	1972	96.84	3.24	80.10	2.46
17. Omaha	1970	67.61	2.72	34.63	
	1971	97.16	4.27	71.93	
	1972	97.93	3.22	53.95	2.24
18. St. Louis	1970	65.48	3.99	24.61	
	1971	71.45	5.39	52.30	
	1972	72.95	3.07	53.52	2.20
19. Kansas City	1970	59.18	3.52	27.22	
	1971	68.41	5.05	58.23	
	1972	69.44	2.70	52.35	2.20
20. Dallas	1970	57.06	3.63	21.45	
	1971	62.85	6.45	49.41	
	1972	65.26	2.80	44.21	1.77
21. Houston	1970	47.35	3.69	16.88	
	1971	53.52	5.67	46.78	
	1972	58.14	2.93	32.79	1.77
22. Phoenix	1970	90.11	3.54	22.62	
	1971	114.24	5.12	80.82	
	1972	118.46	3.11	87.28	2.52

Exhibit 4, continued

Tang Instant Breakfast Drink (A)

Orange Tang Annual Sales, Advertising and Promotion Data by Sales District

District	*Fiscal Year*	*Orange Tang Sales of 10½-pound Units per 1,000 Persons*	*Orange Tang Advertising (000) (of gross rating points)*	*Orange Tang Promotions Dollars per 1,000 Households*	*Spot Media TV Costs Dollars per 1,000 Household Impressions*
23. Denver	1970	85.11	3.61	24.57	
	1971	114.33	5.50	78.62	
	1972	128.70	2.81	69.71	1.52
24. Portland	1970	72.22	3.29	18.52	
	1971	86.06	5.98	70.63	
	1972	96.11	2.87	59.44	1.98
25. San Francisco	1970	55.14	1.59	21.11	
	1971	68.72	5.35	45.50	
	1972	61.25	2.36	52.04	3.40
26. Los Angeles	1970	56.06	3.98	16.32	
	1971	63.24	5.88	48.40	
	1972	71.42	2.39	56.93	2.45
National	1970	59.16	3.68	19.78	
	1971	70.58	5.96	49.16	(Network)
	1972	72.41	2.81	52.88	1.41

Exhibit 5

Tang Instant Breakfast Drink (A)

Finding of the In-House Model[1]

Yearly Budget (millions)	*Advertising/ Promotion Split (millions)*	*First-Year Unit Volume (millions)*	*First Year Net Contribution[2] (millions)*	*Years to Peak[3]*	*Peak-Year Unit Volume (millions)*	*Peak-Year Net Contribution (millions)*
$ 7.0	$5.0 Ad 2.0 Promo	4.76	$8.0	3	5.15	$9.2
7.0	4.0 Ad 3.0 Promo	4.50	7.2	1	4.50	7.2
7.0	3.0 Ad 4.0 Promo	4.29	6.5	0	Will Not Sustain Current Volume	—
7.0	6.5 Ad 0.5 Promo	4.81	8.1	4	5.38	9.9
8.0	7.0 Ad 1.0 Promo	5.41	9.0	3	5.79	10.2
5.0	4.75 Ad 0.25 Promo	4.20	8.2	4	4.50	9.2
10.0	8.0 Ad 2.0 Promo	5.82	8.3	2	6.09	9.2

[1]This table summarizes the results of running the resource allocation system on the Tang model.
[2]Net contribution equals sales in units times variable gross profit of $3.15 per unit minus ad and promo costs.
[3]Peak year is the year in which Tang volume fails to grow significantly (starting with the given budget level and repeating it each year thereafter).

Exhibit 6

Tang Instant Breakfast Drink (A)

Tang One-Year Forecasts Estimated by Agency Model[1]

Yearly Budget (millions)	Advertising/ Promotion Split (millions)	If Competition Sells 1.0 Million Units		If Competition Sells 1.5 Million Units		If Competition Sells 2.0 Million Units	
		Unit Sales (millions)	*Net[2] (millions)*	*Unit Sales (millions)*	*Net (millions)*	*Unit Sales (millions)*	*Net (millions)*
$ 5.0	$ 2.5 Ad 2.5 Promo	3.68	$6.60	3.46	$5.90	3.23	$5.18
5.5	2.5 Ad 3.0 Promo	3.72	6.22	3.50	5.52	3.27	4.79
6.25	3.75 Ad 2.5 Promo	4.28	7.23	4.06	6.54	3.83	5.81
6.5	3.75 Ad 2.75 Promo	4.31	7.07	4.08	6.35	3.86	5.65
7.0	4.5 Ad 2.5 Promo	4.39	6.61	4.17	6.13	3.94	5.41
7.5	4.5 Ad 3.0 Promo	4.42	6.42	4.20	5.73	3.97	5.01
8.0	5.5 Ad 2.5 Promo	4.48	6.11	4.25	5.23	4.03	4.69
8.5	5.5 Ad 3.0 Promo	4.50	5.67	4.27	4.95	4.05	4.26
9.5	7.0 Ad 2.5 Promo	4.57	4.89	4.34	4.17	4.12	3.47
10.0	7.0 Ad 3.0 Promo	4.59	4.45	4.36	3.73	4.14	3.04

[1]Assumes 40% of competitive sales come from market expansion, 60% from Tang's franchise.
[2]Net equals unit sales time unit contribution of $3.15 minus advertising and promotion costs.

Exhibit 7
Tang Instant Breakfast Drink (A)

Tang Long-Term Forecasts Estimated by Agency Model[1]

Yearly Budget (millions)	Advertising/ Promotion Split (millions)	Year 2		Year 4		Year 6	
		Sales Unit (millions)	Net[2] (millions)	Sales Unit (millions)	Net (millions)	Sales Unit (millions)	Net (millions)
$ 6.5	$4.5 Ad 2.0 Promo	5.58	$11.1	5.68	$11.4	5.71	$11.5
7.0	4.5 Ad 2.5 Promo	5.63	10.7	5.76	11.1	5.79	11.2
7.5	4.5 Ad 3.0 Promo	5.70	10.5	5.83	10.9	5.85	10.9
8.0	6.0 Ad 2.0 Promo	5.75	10.1	6.48	12.4	6.55	12.6
8.5	6.0 Ad 2.5 Promo	5.83	9.9	6.56	12.2	6.62	12.3
9.0	6.0 Ad 3.0 Promo	5.89	9.6	6.62	11.9	6.69	12.1
9.5	7.5 Ad 2.0 Promo	5.86	8.9	6.91	12.3	7.00	12.6
10.0	7.5 Ad 2.5 Promo	5.94	8.7	6.99	12.0	7.08	12.3
10.5	7.5 Ad 3.0 Promo	6.01	8.4	7.06	11.7	7.15	12.1

[1]Assumes competitive sales increases of 500,000 units per year and 75% of competitive sales come from market expansion, 25% from Tang's franchise.
[2]Tang net equals sales in units times unit contribution of $3.15 minus advertising and promotion costs.

Tang Instant Breakfast Drink (B)

Bill King, product group manager of the Breakfast Beverage Product Group at General Foods, was faced with a most pressing and difficult decision. Sales of Orange Tang Instant Breakfast Drink[1] had been dropping significantly, and this decline was attributed to declining effectiveness of the brand's present advertising.[2]

To reverse the downward trend, the brand's product group management and its advertising agency, Young & Rubicam, had prepared new advertising approaches. The new approaches, which had been prepared over the summer of 1972, took the form of four 30-second TV commercials. Young & Rubicam had just completed the final phase of testing for the four commercials, and Frank Thomas, the Y&R account executive for the Tang account, had just completed his presentation of the findings. Thomas and Sharon Wolf, the Tang assistant product manager, had argued for the selection of one of the four candidates on the basis of qualitative research findings. Dick Jackson, the Tang product manager, disagreed with their choice on the basis of his interpretation of quantitative measures of brand-related recall. He argued instead for the selection of a different commercial based on his interpretation of the research results.

Having had the benefit of hearing Thomas, Jackson, and Wolf make and defend their choices, King had to make the final decision and defend it to his strategic business unit manager. It seemed that further copy development work was inadvisable, given the sales record of Tang over the recent weeks.

 This case was prepared by Harvey Singer and Gary Garrasi, under the supervision of F. Stewart DeBruicker.

[1]Tang is a trademark of the General Foods Corporation. A small amount of Tang, a dry crystalline powder, added to a larger quantity of water made a beverage described by the Tang package label as "A natural tasting orange flavor breakfast drink. It contains more Vitamin C and A than like amounts of orange, grapefruit, or tomato juice. Tang is not a juice, juice product, or soft drink mix. Tang is a nutritious instant breakfast drink."

[2]Dollar and unit figures in this case are disguised.

BACKGROUND

General Foods Corporation (GF) was a leading manufacturer and marketer of grocery products, chiefly processed foods. Its brands were among the best selling products nationally in a variety of categories: coffee, frozen foods, gelatin desserts, puddings, soft drink mixes, syrups, semimoist and dry dog food, and cereals. Going into the last quarter of fiscal 1973, sales were expected to be over $2.5 billion and net profit over $100 million for the year.[3]

The company's long-term strength was built on large consumer franchises for its 400 products and some 30 of the food industry's best known brand names, including Maxwell House coffee, Bird's-Eye frozen foods. Post cereals, Jell-O desserts, Gaines pet foods, and Tang Instant Breakfast Drink.

In terms of GF's marketing organization, a product manager worked within a product group, which in turn was part of a strategic business unit, or SBU. Until very recently the company's marketing activities had been organized by products produced by similar technologies or by products that had developed as line extensions of a single brand. In the early 1970s, pressure on sales and profits in the highly competitive convenience foods and fast-food restaurant markets led to a major reorganization in the company's marketing organization. Individual products and brands were placed into groups according to the strategic business unit concept. This meant that all products, regardless of brand name or production technology, which would be viewed in the same competitive framework by consumers in the marketplace, were grouped and managed together. The goal was to encourage managers to concentrate their efforts on strategic markets as well as individual products. For example, all dessert products, whether Bird's-Eye frozen desserts or Jell-O gelatins, were placed in the dessert SBU. All main meal dishes, whether Bird's-Eye frozen vegetables or Minute Rice or Shake 'n Bake seasoned coating mixes, were placed in the main meal SBU. Tang was included in the beverage SBU, along with frozen beverage products (frozen orange juice concentrate, Orange Plus, and Awake), other breakfast beverages (Start and Postum), and refreshment beverages (Kool-Aid brand products).

The SBU managers reported to the president of one of the company's major divisions. Tang was grouped in the Beverage and Breakfast Division. Each division also had support staff personnel (staffs for finance, production, technical R&D, and a field sales force) to service its SBUs. Division presidents then reported to General Foods' top corporate management, which included the president, executive and group vice presidents, and support staffs at that level which provided service to all of the divisions—chief among them a financial staff and a market research group. An organization chart sketching these relationships is shown in Exhibit 1.

Product managers at GF acted as both marketing and business managers for their brands. On the marketing side, they had the mission of planning and executing all advertising, promotion, pricing, and merchandising strategies for their brands. More generally, they had to compete for and coordinate all their division's functional resources for their respective brands, which included technical inputs, marketing research, sales force programs, processing, and packaging. On the operations side, they were responsible for their brands' financial contribution through volume attainment, marketing spending, and pricing decisions. On the planning side, they worked with top management on setting current fis-

[3]Fiscal years begin on April 1. Fiscal 1973, for example, began on April 1, 1972, and ended March 31, 1973. Operating quarters are named for the months in which they ended: June, September, December, and March.

cal objectives and longer-range expectations (five-year strategic plans).

Dick Jackson, Tang product manager, was assisted by an associate product manager and an assistant product manager, Sharon Wolf. They were supported by product development personnel and promotional merchandising personnel within the SBU. Jackson reported to Bill King, the product group manager with responsibility for Tang, Start, and Postum breakfast beverages. King in turn reported to the beverage SBU manager.

TANG HISTORY

Tang powdered instant breakfast drink was introduced nationally in 1958. Tang's ingredients, in descending order of weight were sugar, citric acid (for tartness), calcium phosphates (to regulate tartness and prevent caking), gum arabic (vegetable gum to provide body), natural flavor, potassium citrate (to regulate tartness), vitamin C, cellulose gum (vegetable gum), hydrogenated coconut oil, artificial flavor, artificial color, vitamin A, and BHA, a preservative. After its national introduction in 1958, Tang's volume grew slowly but steadily. Volume seemed to plateau as the product matured by about 1962, so marketing spending was stepped up and new copy was devised. Jackson indicated that this gave the product a "shot in the arm," and sales improved through 1968, when stagnation began again. Accordingly, marketing efforts were intensified in fiscal 1969. The product was significantly improved and sampling efforts, advertising, and promotion spending were all increased. The brand's media copy program featured association with the U.S. space program through the National Aeronautics and Space Administration (NASA). This association proved successful as Tang sales increased 20% in fiscal 1969 over fiscal 1968.

In fiscal 1970, this approach continued and sales gained. Even when its price was raised, volume continued to grow, due in part to the government's ban on cyclamates and the quick response of Tang advertising noting that it used no artificial sweeteners. Sales were up 31% for the year.

In fiscal 1971 the Apollo program became less active, so a new Tang campaign was introduced which was designed to enlighten and excite consumers about the "future" in space. This continued the Tang overall strategy of being associated with NASA and space, but shifted the campaign from actual space flights to potential space programs made feasible by the Apollo program.

Sales continued to rise but at a slower rate, up only 19% for the year. In fiscal 1972, sales growth again slowed. Tang prices had been increased to maintain profit margins close to historical levels, although some margin erosion occurred as additional advertising was invested in support of both Orange Tang and a new grapefruit flavor extension. In fiscal 1972, competing products began to appear. One firm introduced a product offering more ounces in a package priced the same as Tang, and some store label brands appeared which were priced as much as 40 percent below equivalent Tang packages. Estimates of competitors' prices and media spending are listed in Exhibit 2. Orange Tang sales for fiscal 1972 were up only 3%.

It was about this time that Sharon Wolf began to question the efficacy of the existing copy themes. She contended that both the client and the agency might be putting too much faith in the campaigns which were so closely associated with the hardware and mechanics of the space program. Though the overall strategy of the space theme was never in question, she believed that the brand group should consider alternative or backup campaigns.

Also about this time, General Foods

began implementing a portfolio approach to its many businesses modeled after the Boston Consulting Group's terminology. Products were classified as "stars" which justified investment spending with the objective of high volume and market share growth; "cash cows," which had less growth potential but could provide positive cash flow which could be channeled to the stars and should be managed for the objective of market share stability and positive cash flow; and "dogs," which should be dropped.

Early in fiscal 1973 sales began to drop precipitously—as much as 13% in some bimonthly periods versus previous year figures—and the product group became increasingly concerned over the issues of advertising copy and marketing spending. Jackson was concerned that Tang would not meet its goal of a $7 million contribution after marketing costs, as specified in GF's 1973 annual business plan. Exhibit 3 shows Orange Tang sales and marketing spending figures from fiscal 1968 through mid-fiscal 1973, as well as competing powdered orange beverage product sales and price differences between Tang and frozen orange juice concentrate (FOJC).

The Tang gross margin was about $3.15 per 10½-pound unit. Marketing costs were primarily the amounts spent on advertising and promotion. Jackson felt that a further price increase to deliver profits was infeasible. Product line extension (new flavors) to increase volume were no longer favored by the product group. Only one alternative to the NASA theme had been developed and tested.

The Client-Agency Relationship

There was a corresponding management hierarchy for the Tang account at Y&R. Walter Roberts was the senior management supervisor on the Tang account and for a variety of others accounts handled by Y&R. Reporting to him were Jack Kelso, account supervisor, and Frank Thomas, account executive. Thomas was responsible for planning and directing the Y&R support staffs for creative, media, and research and for supervising the activities of two assistant account executives. Thomas and his staff were in regular contact with the members of the Tang product management group. It was not unusual for the agency and client management teams to meet daily when engaged in strategic planning activities. During these meetings, the agency and client managers functioned as a team, with the agency personnel often taking strong advocacy positions for points of view with which the client might disagree. Final responsibility for decision making rested with the client, however. At meetings between the agency and client, it was customary for the most junior members of the agency and client staffs to offer their analyses and recommendations first, with other participants joining the discussion in order of increasing management responsibility.

The relationship between the GF product management group and the agency group was unusually strong. Since Tang was one of Y&R's largest clients in terms of billings, both the agency and the product group viewed themselves as partners in the Tang business. In this regard, the agency's responsibilities encompassed not only developing advertising strategies and creating and producing copy executions, but providing marketing research and merchandising consulting services too.

A number of people from the agency's account management group and creative department had worked on the Tang account for several years. Some had become very successful as a result of Tang performance. In fact, one of the agency's executive vice presidents had risen to his present position as a result of Tang success. Additionally, members of the agency groups and the GF product group had had continuous professional contact with each other over the years on accounts other than

Tang. This continuity of service on the part of both groups was considered to be one of the Tang marketing program's major strengths.

Orange Tang Positioning and Message Strategy

Since the Tang introduction in 1958, the product group and agency representatives had gone to great lengths to design strategy and copy that would portray Tang as a highly nutritional and flavorful breakfast drink substitute for fresh frozen orange juice concentrate. Over the years the product had been upgraded by increasing its vitamin content and improving its flavor. The issue of Tang legitimacy as a substitute for frozen orange juice concentrate had been of continuous concern to both the product group and the agency.

The NASA testimonials used in the Tang media strategy throughout the late 1960s had provided a strong sense of legitimacy to the product, differentiating it from children's beverage mixes. Studies conducted by both GF and Y&R had confirmed that Tang consumers felt that, if the product was nutritional enough to be selected by NASA to be included in the Apollo astronauts' diets when they traveled to the moon, then it must be nutritional enough to serve to their families.

Although sales in the fourth quarter of fiscal 1972 had declined compared with those in the same period one year earlier, the Tang basic message strategy was confirmed in an April 1972 meeting of the brand management team and members of the account team from Y&R. The product would continue to be positioned against fresh and concentrated frozen orange juice; private-label and "me-too" competition would not be discussed in any way. The target audience would continue to be married women between the ages of 18 and 44, with two or more children, and with at least a high school education. The copy development guidelines were that the nutritional story would continue to receive the major emphasis and that secondary emphasis on flavor and the brand's NASA connection would be continued.

There was to be one noteworthy change in the copy strategy. While the NASA themes had always associated the brand with the space program, the management group felt that the space theme was too "sterile" an environment to be realistic for many present users of the product. Therefore, the agency sought to develop thematic approaches that placed the product in more conventional consumption environments. Until satisfactory new copy approaches were developed, Jackson decided, with the approval of both King and the SBU manager, that the planned annual media spending on Tang would be reduced for the remainder of fiscal 1973 from $4.5 million to $3.0 million, and that consumer promotional expenditures would be increased by $800,000.

Sales in the first quarter of fiscal 1973 declined slightly from the level of the same period in 1972, but as the second quarter began, sales declines of over 10% from the previous year's levels were becoming evident nationwide. To hasten new advertising copy development, some of the normal procedures were suspended, and a major econometric analysis of the historic sales effects of advertising and promotion spending was begun. The agency forwarded a creative work plan to Jackson which described a so-called "authority strategy" aimed at further legitimatizing Tang.

Jackson approved the work plan, which is presented in Exhibit 4. In late June, Jackson decided to cancel the September quarter's planned advertising until more effective copy could be developed, thus vividly demonstrating to the agency the product group's dissatisfaction with the performance of the then available advertising copy. This cancellation was approved by the SBU manager.

The Search for New Copy Executions

Ordinarily, the typical advertising creative process involved the creation of a large number of copy executions by the agency's creative teams, with the executions then being reviewed by the agency's creative supervisor. The executions would then be forwarded to Y&R's associate creative director, who would either send the copy back to the creative supervisor for reworking by the creative teams or, if he was satisfied with the executions, would present them to Carol Alexander, the agency creative director, for inspection. If Alexander approved the copy, she would authorize the associate creative director to forward the executions to the account executive, Frank Thomas. Thomas would examine the copy executions closely for consistency with the product's strategy and, if the executions were satisfactory to him, would present them to Dick Jackson at GF.

The product manager would examine the copy executions with the account executive and would often request that revisions be made by the agency's creative team. After the revisions had been made, the account executive would review the executions with the product manager, who would then present the executions to Bill King, the product group manager. King usually requested further revisions, and when they had been made to his satisfaction, he would present them to the SBU manager for final approval. Normally six to eight executions, in rough storyboard form, survived at this point in the process.

After the SBU manager was satisfied with the copy executions, the agency and product management groups would meet and decide which executions should be rough produced on 16 mm film. The rough commercials would be tested for their intrusiveness (i.e., recall or memorability) and sales point communication. On the basis of test results and agency recommendations, the product management group would select one or more of the commercials for finished production using 35 mm film or videotape. Spot and/or network TV time would then be purchased, and the commercial would be televised nationally.

Both the agency and the client viewed this stepwise development process as an opportunity to provide the more junior members of their organizations with a valuable learning experience regarding the preparation of a product for market and the mechanics and intricacies of the agency-client relationship. The severity of the present situation did not permit the luxury of the normal procedures, however. It was decided that the number of formal copy presentations would be reduced and that the initial presentations would be made to Dick Jackson and Sharon Wolf so that the product manager and his assistant could comment on the copy and begin winnowing out some of the weaker executions immediately. In the summer of 1972 the Tang associate product manager was on special assignment elsewhere at GF and was not a part of the decision-making process.

By the end of June 1972, the agency had produced 16 storyboard executions for the product manager's consideration. At the initial presentation of the copy executions at the agency, the product manager and his assistant made several suggestions regarding copy content. The agency quickly revised the copy according to the client's suggestions and made a second presentation at the agency to Jackson and Wolf. This time only eight of the executions were selected for further development. A third presentation was convened, this time at GF's White Plains, New York, offices during the first week of July. This presentation was attended by the entire product management group as well as the agency account management group. The agency presented six copy executions to the product group (two others had been eliminated since the second presentation) and recommended that the product group produce executions entitled "Andromeda," which was the agency creative director's favorite, "Food Selection," and "Packing."

After some discussion of the agency's copy analyses and recommendations, the product group management authorized the agency to produce those three executions. The client group also requested that the agency produce "Lady Ph.D." as well. Sharon Wolf argued for this inclusion rather persuasively, even though no research had been conducted on any of the executions. Wolf contended that there was something about a real mother with an authentic scientific background serving her children Orange Tang for breakfast. It seemed to overcome the legitimacy obstacle while depicting a situation to which the target audience could relate readily.

At the conclusion of this meeting, the client authorized the agency to go directly to 35 mm production of the choices. This was a rather expensive procedure since the services of both professional production crews and professional actors and actresses had to be contracted. The cost of 35 mm production was likewise charged directly to the client. Due to the urgency of the present situation, Dick Jackson considered the cost of 35 mm production of all four executions to be a necessary and unavoidable expense. Filming of the four commercials was contracted out to independent production companies and was completed at the end of July. Photoscripts of the completed commercials are presented in Exhibits 5 through 8.

Copy Strategy Research

The commercials were immediately put into a program of research designed to develop data to help management choose the most effective execution for use in the fall media period and to use as a basis for developing more refined executions of the winning concept later in the fall. The commercials were tested using focus group interviews and sample surveys of recall of televised commercials in test markets. The focus group interviews were conducted by the agency in several shopping malls in early August. In the interviews, small groups of women typical of the target audience were invited to an informal screening of several commercials, and then interviewed in groups to determine their feelings as to the commercials' intentions and effectivness. The results of the interviews provided qualitative guidance, but due to their subjective nature, they were considered only one ingredient in the mix of data and judgments used to make final decisions on a set of executions.

Thomas, the account executive, noted that most of the respondents did not seem to like the spokesperson used in the Lady Ph.D. commercial, but they did seem to respect her judgment in matters of choosing nutritious foods for her family. He believed, however, that, unless that element of respect could be demonstrated in the sample surveys used in the TV recall testing procedures, he would have a difficult time selling the Lady Ph.D. execution to management. Interview summaries for Lady Ph.D. and Food Selection are presented in Exhibits 9 and 10.

The TV recall tests were designed to develop quantitative data on large samples of viewers of the four commercials in a realistic, in-home setting. These tests were conducted by GF's corporate marketing research group using standardized procedures that had been used to test past Tang advertisements. The procedures involved "cutting in" each of the four candidate commercials into the normal network commercial period on a nationally televised program. Next-day telephone interviews were then conducted in some market areas within 24 hours of the airing of the test commercials and questions were asked to determine their memorability and copy-point playback performance. The commercial that achieved the highest level of memorability over the historic Tang norm and that best communicated the strategic copy points, would be selected for airing. Arrangements were made for the commercials to be inserted into the 9:24 P.M. slot in the CBS Thursday Night Movie, "Night Gallery," on September 7, 1972, in the following cities:

Execution	*Length*	*Cities*
Andromeda	:30	Atlanta, Hartford, Sacramento
Food Selection	:30	Buffalo, Indianapolis, San Diego
Lady Ph.D.	:30	Cincinnati, Denver, Omaha, Syracuse
Packing	:30	Minneapolis, Phoenix, Portland, Youngstown

The cost of the TV recall studies was approximately $14,000 in out-of-pocket charges to the Tang budget.

The recall measurement procedure was a standard GF methodology that involved asking a hierarchy of questions to determine whether or not the respondent had in fact seen the commercial being tested and, if so, what level of awareness the commercial had generated for the respondent. Two measures, not necessarily independent of one another, were used to classify respondents into a hierarchical order that was roughly equivalent to the commercial's ability to promote accurate retention of intended copy points. The first measure was related to the level of cueing, or prompting, that was necessary to stimulate the respondent's memory of having seen (or not seen) the commercial.

As described in Exhibit 10, a flow diagram of the questionning procedure, three levels of prompting were employed: the first level was the category prompt in which only the product category—orange breakfast drink—was used as a memory cue. The second level was the brand prompt, in which the respondent was asked directly whether or not he/she saw a Tang commercial last night on TV. The final level was the commercial prompt in which the respondent who claimed to have seen the program in which the commercial was shown, but couldn't recall the commercial, was cued by prompts drawn from the dramatic storyline of the program before and after the airing to the Tang commercial. This was called the commercial prompt. The hierarchy of cues then, was

Level of Prompting	*Type of Prompt*
Unaided	Category: "Did you see a commercial for a brand of orange breakfast drink?"
Aided	Brand: "Do you remember seeing a commercial for Tang last night?"
Prompted	Commercial: "Right after this scene, there was a commercial for Tang. Do you recall seeing this commercial?"

The second measure of the quality of awareness which each commercial promoted was based on the verbatim responses of the respondents when questioned directly about the commercials which they claimed they had seen. Seven questions, listed in Exhibit 11, were asked of each person claiming to have seen the commercial being tested. Based on whether or not the verbatim responses described the actual content of the commercial, respondents were classified as falling into one of the three categories: "proven" recallers had the highest levels of recall with respect to the message and format of presentation of the commercial; "related" recallers showed a grasp of the basic content of the commercial though they were often less certain of the details of presentation; "incorrect" recallers were those respondents who claimed to have seen the

	Percentage of Commercial Audience (unaided and aided)				
Measure	Tang Norm	Andromeda	Food Selection	Lady Ph.D.	Packing
Proven recall	11%	7%	19%	7%	18%
Related recall	8	3	9	12	3
Combined	19%	10%	28%	19%	21%

commercial, but whose verbatim descriptions of the commercial's content were highly inaccurate. "Incorrect" recallers were usually eliminated from the tabulations of results prepared in management summary form by the GF marketing research department, while "proven" and "related" recallers were reported both separately and in the aggregate.

The verbatim responses to the seven questions regarding the test commercial's content were coded by specific copy points and reported in the quantitative summary of the test. Finally, the verbatim responses were reported in a qualitative supplement to each test commercial's research report, and were often used by management to enrich its insight into the commercial's audience impact.

The GF marketing research department summarized the results of the TV recall tests in a brief memo that accompanied the four separate reports, each numbering about 18 pages of tabulated findings and about a like number of pages of verbatim transcripts. In the management summary, the research department concluded that "The total proven and related recall was above the Tang norm for 'Food Selection' and 'Packing,' at the norm for 'Lady Ph.D.,' and below the norm for 'Andromeda' ". Additional recall tabulations are reported in Exhibit 12.

The marketing research summary went on to report that "Playback of all major copy points was below norm for 'Andromeda.' 'Food Selection' had superior playback on taste/flavor and convenience. 'Lady Ph.D.' had superior playback on space association, vitamins and taste/flavor. 'Packing' had superior playback on vitamins and convenience and average playback on nutrition."

The research department's summary concluded that "Responses to special questions directed to recallers of 'Lady Ph.D.' to elicit attitudes toward the presenter were generally positive and indicated that she was believable, convincing and seemed to lend an air of authority to the message. Responses to special questions to recallers of 'Andromeda' to elicit attitudes toward the unique execution were generally negative."

The copy testing studies were completed

	Percentage of Commercial Audience (unaided, aided, and prompted)				
Copy Point	Tang Norm	Andromeda	Food Selection	Lady Ph.D.	Packing
Space association	63%	46%	59%	66%	55%
Vitamins	53	23	43	66	74
Nutrition	29	8	20	24	29
Taste/flavor	49	23	70	55	23
Convenience	37	15	48	34	45

in about half the normal time, and by mid-September the findings had been reported to both the brand group and to the agency. Thomas, as the head of the administrative center for the copy development program, had prepared an analysis of the findings and with his colleagues from the creative and account groups. He went to what was to be the final decision-making meeting in White Plains in September.

At this meeting the agency group first presented and discussed the results of the TV recall scores and verbatims, followed by a qualitative analysis of the strengths and weaknesses of each of the four commercial copy executions. Frank Thomas concluded his presentation with a recommendation that the client use the Lady Ph.D. commercial to launch the new advertising campaign. Thomas explained that, although Food Selection scored highest on the TV recall tests, Lady Ph.D. seemed to be communicating the sales message better as indicated by the quality of the verbatim responses associated with this particular commercial. The verbatim reports of the individual telephone interviews of Lady Ph.D. and Food Selection covered over 54 pages of material and are not reproduced here for reasons of length. The subjective content of the verbatims is conveyed imperfectly, but adequately, by the focus group interview summaries listed in Exhibit 9 and 10.

Dick Jackson, the product manager, disagreed with the line of reasoning at the meeting by contending that the quality of the verbatim responses should not be given so much weight in this particular instance as it normally would because of the rather large margin in recall scores in favor of Food Selection. The product manager argued that, although the Lady Ph.D. verbatims were indeed richer qualitatively than those of Food Selection, the latter's recall scores were nearly one and a half times greater than those of Lady Ph.D. Further, Jackson stated that the quality of the Lady Ph.D. verbatims would mean very little if consumers were unable to recall that Lady Ph.D. was specifically associated with Orange Tang.

At that point of apparent impasse between the assistant product manager and the account executive on one hand and the product manager on the other, Bill King, the product group manager began his review of the situation. Everyone in the meeting was well aware that the shipments of Tang in the second quarter of fiscal 1973 had dropped well below the previous year's level and that further declines seemed likely in the absence of effective, fresh advertising copy.

Exhibit 1

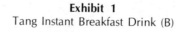

Tang Instant Breakfast Drink (B)

General Foods Marketing Organization

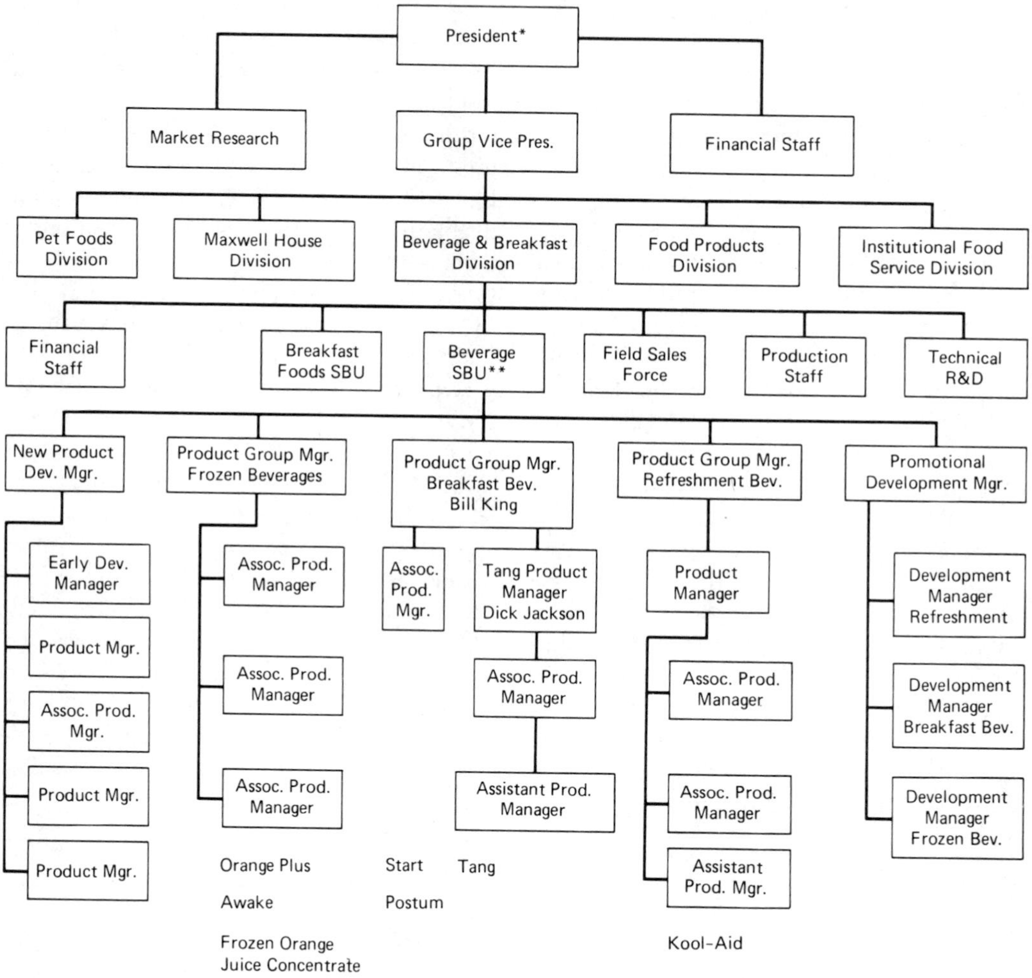

[1]Also attached to the president's office were support staffs for legal, purchasing, and so on.
[2]The SBU manager also had a staff supporting him with functions similar to the divisional staffs.

Exhibit 2
Tang Instant Breakfast Drink (B)

Recent Competitive Efforts

1. Tang price/unit first half 1967–1973 (10½-pound units) at retail:

Fiscal 1967	$8.42
Fiscal 1968	8.41
Fiscal 1969	8.38
Fiscal 1970	8.71
Fiscal 1971	8.70
Fiscal 1972	9.03
Fiscal 1973 (first half)	9.08

2. Competitive price estimates (10½-pound units) at retail:

Fiscal 1972	$7.49
Fiscal 1973 (first half)	7.53

3. Competitive advertising (000):

	Borden	*Lipton*
Fiscal 1972	$ 59	—
Fiscal 1973 (first half)	278	$630

Exhibit 3
Tang Instant Breakfast Drink (B)

Tang Sales and Marketing Expenditures

Period: Fiscal Year	Period: Quarter	Orange Tang Sales of 10½-pound Units (000)	Advertising (000)	Promotion (000)	Competitive Sales of 10½-Pound Units (000)	Price Difference: FOJC–Tang (cents per 24 ounces)
1968	1	530	$ 365	$ 289	0	−0.5¢
	2	511	435	338	0	0.1
	3	514	303	330	0	1.4
	4	545	188	190	0	2.2
	Total	2,100	$1,291	$1,147	0	
1969	1	579	437	1,006	0	3.3
	2	615	331	51	0	3.8
	3	664	570	129	0	4.7
	4	850	1,176	471	0	6.0
	Total	2,708	$2,514	$1,657	0	
1970	1	801	992	254	0	6.3
	2	853	771	356	0	5.1
	3	872	802	128	0	4.8
	4	1,029	988	448	0	4.0
	Total	3,555	$3,553	$1,186	0	
1971	1	1,019	1,400	710	0	3.4
	2	1,002	806	549	0	3.2
	3	1,024	843	1,011	0	2.5
	4	1,197	1,110	684	0	2.1
	Total	4,242	$4,159	$2,954	0	
1972	1	1,088	883	339	0	3.4
	2	1,070	769	1,070	22	4.8
	3	1,052	864	1,006	50	5.1
	4	1,142	430	763	89	8.0
	Total	4,352	$2,946	$3,718	161	
1973	1	1,044	884	576	200	7.9
	2	965	363	851	271	7.9

Exhibit 4
Tang Instant Breakfast Drink (B)
Creative Work Plan: "authority Strategy"

Key Fact

Orange Tang prime prospects, both regular and infrequent users, reflect a positive interest in the brand, yet are concerned about its legitimacy as a food product due to its powdered form.

Problems Advertising Must Solve

Due to OT's powdered form, most people do not believe it to be a legitimate substitute for FOJC at breakfast, and, therefore, not as "healthy" and "good" for their families.

Advertising Objective

To reassure current users and convince infrequent users that OT is a legitimate substitute for FOJC and, consequently, is good for their families at breakfast.

Prospect Definition

Women who are characterized as mothers aged 18–44 with two plus children under 12 years of age with incomes of $10,000 plus living in A&B counties and users of FOJC and/or instant breakfast drink (IBD). Attitudinally, these women are somewhat self-indulgent and have respect for authority. They are concerned with the well-being of their families and try to provide (not necessarily feed) them with a nutritionally adequate diet.

Principal Competition

FOJC is considered OT's primary competition and major source of volume. Lower priced IBD's are OT's secondary competition.

Promise

OT is a good-tasting, legitimate food product that helps you fulfill your role as the supplier of nutrition and health to your family by serving it at breakfast.

Reasons Why

1. Nutritious OT has a full day's supply of vitamin C plus vitamin A.
2. OT has a taste that can be enjoyed by the entire family and is especially liked by kids.
3. OT has been selected for use by the NASA astronauts.

Tone and Manner

The advertising must establish a sense of authority in support of the posture that Tang is a legitimate, serious food product. It must be consistent with the stature relationship between Tang and NASA.

Constraint Agreement

A consent agreement between GF and the Federal Trade Commission prohibits statements "disparaging" to any natural fruit juices.

Exhibit 5

Tang Instant Breakfast Drink (B)

Andromeda Photoscript

YOUNG & RUBICAM INTERNATIONAL, INC.

CLIENT: GENERAL FOODS CORP.
PRODUCT: ORANGE TANG
TITLE: "ANDROMEDA"

LENGTH: 30 SECONDS
COMM. NO. GFOT2518

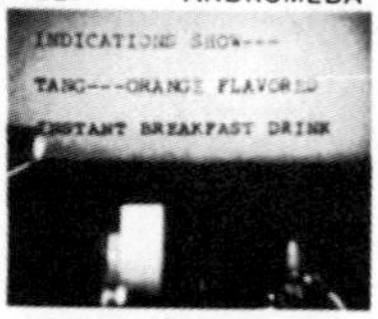

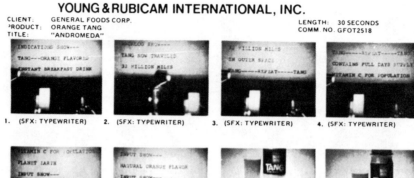

1. (SFX: TYPEWRITER)

2. (SFX: TYPEWRITER)

3. (SFX: TYPEWRITER)

4. (SFX: TYPEWRITER)

5. (SFX: TYPEWRITER)

6. (SFX: TYPEWRITER)

7. (SFX: TYPEWRITER)

8. (SFX: TYPEWRITER)

9. (SFX: TYPEWRITER)

10. (SFX: TYPEWRITER)

Exhibit 6
Tang Instant Breakfast Drink (B)

Food Selection Photoscript

YOUNG & RUBICAM INTERNATIONAL, INC.

CLIENT: GENERAL FOODS CORP.
PRODUCT: ORANGE TANG
TITLE: "FOOD SELECTION"

LENGTH: 30 SECONDS
COMM. NO. GFOT2517

1. (MUSIC THROUGH-OUT)

2. ANNCR: (VO) The Nutrition Team at the NASA Space Center

3. worked long and hard to come up with breakfast for outer space.

4. They looked at 28 versions of the scrambled egg ...

5. Spent months getting bacon crispy ...

6. Then they decided on an orange-flavored instant breakfast drink

7. straight from the super-market...

8. Tang. With a full day's supply of Vitamin C.

9. Good, nutritious Tang.

10. It passed the test.

Exhibit 7
Tang Instant Breakfast Drink (B)

Packing Photoscript

YOUNG & RUBICAM INTERNATIONAL, INC.

CLIENT: GENERAL FOODS CORP.
PRODUCT: ORANGE TANG
TITLE: "PACKING"

LENGTH: 30 SECONDS
COMM. NO. GFOT2516

1. (MUSIC THROUGHOUT) WOMAN: (VO) If you were leaving for a day on the moon,

2. you'd have to pack a little differently.

3. You'd need a helmet, so you could breathe...

4. an extra-vehicular suit...

5. something special in the way of footwear...

6. and protective gloves.

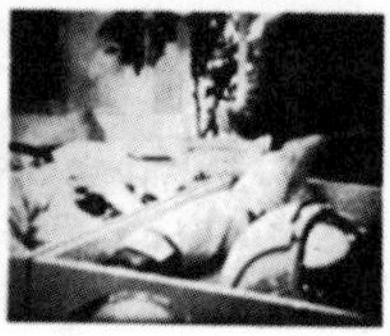

7. But there's one scientific miracle that you could pack right from your kitchen table...

8. Tang. The orange-flavored instant breakfast drink

9. with a full day's supply of Vitamin C.

10. Tang. Good no matter where you're having breakfast.

Exhibit 8
Tang Instant Breakfast Drink (B)

Lady Ph.D. Photoscript

YOUNG & RUBICAM INTERNATIONAL, INC.

CLIENT:	GENERAL FOODS CORP.	LENGTH:	30 SECONDS
PRODUCT:	ORANGE TANG	COMM. NO.	GFOT2520
TITLE:	"LADY P.H.D."		

1. MARY ETHIMION: I'm a mother of two children.
2. And I have a PHD in biological science.
3. You know a woman involved with science
4. wants to be sure her family gets their breakfast vitamins.

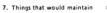

5. I know the astronauts use Tang,
6. and I am sure NASA took a lot of time and trouble to find good things for them.
7. Things that would maintain
8. their vitamin supply.

9. And Tang is a good source of Vitamin C and A.
10. We drink it all the time.
11. Mm. It really tastes
12. great.

Exhibit 9

Tang Instant Breakfast Drink (B)

Lady Ph.D. Group Interview Summary

COMMUNICATION OF PRODUCT MESSAGES

In both sessions, it was quite clear that virtually all the respondents seemed to understand what was being said in the Lady Ph.D. commercial and that all the women played back the messages that Tang is "good for you" because of its vitamin content. In addition to pointing out that Tang is rich in vitamins C and A, the women came away with the impression that Tang is a "well-researched product" that is scientifically accepted as being nutritious. The NASA reference seemed to be picked up by many of the women too, and the women seemed to realize that, if Tang is being sent to the moon with the astronauts, it must be a nutritionally superior product. Consequently, the NASA reference, plus the presence of a Ph.D. degree holder endorsing the product, seemed to convey the intended claim that Tang is a "good product" for spacemen and earth families.

REACTIONS TO THE COMMERCIAL

In reacting to the commercials and its messages, there was a mixed response, with users of Tang, interestingly enough, being particularly inclined to react favorably to the Ph.D. theme and to the idea that this knowledgeable "authority" was endorsing the product (which, incidentally, is a product they themselves use). These women seemed to accept the commercial as being both believable and convincing in conveying the idea that Tang is nutritionally "good for you." Spontaneously, several volunteered that Tang has apparently been well researched by scientists and many of the women seemed to be impressed with the idea that a "mother with her doctorate in science" believed in the product enough to integrate it into her family's diet. It is important to note that, in the course of discussing this commercial, several of the women latched onto the "mother/scientist" role of the presenter and the respondents reacted positively to the fact that this woman thinks enough of Tang, from a professional vantage point, to use the product in her home. As one woman remarked, "her children are first in her mind and she wants to take good care of them." Virtually all users in the session, as well as several nonusers of the product, spontaneously commented that a scientist obviously has more "authority" and "knowledge" about the product than the average housewife and yet, at the same time, she is a mother of two children who naturally wants the best for her family. In a sense, the women seemed to feel that the commercial combined "the business and home life together."

A number of these women went on to describe the person in Lady Ph.D. as being a "capable" woman whose first concern is her children's health and well-being. The respondents seemed to feel that she was "happy and healthy" looking, "neat and attractive," and "realistic" in that she is not the typical model type but rather an ordinary housewife who is the mother of two children. A few of the respondents volunteered that they could "relate to her" on a personal level because of her age and her appearance. In total, it should be recognized that the differences in the reactions of users and nonusers can possibly be attributed to the fact that the Ph.D. mother, speaking for the product, seemed to reinforce for the users the idea that they are "good mothers" in that they are concerned about their children's health and diet and, at the same time, to offer them additional rebuttal for the reservations they themselves might have had about the product.

Among the nonusers, however, the reactions to the commercial were somewhat different. While some of the women seemed to respect the opinion of a "mother/scientist" as being an authority on nutrition, others in the session, upon being probed directly, indicated that they couldn't really relate to or identify with "Ph.D." in spite of the fact that they respect her educational background. On a more personal level, they seemed to perceive the woman as being "cold," "stiff," and somewhat "distant." One or two of the respondents commented that she didn't seem like a "homey" person but, rather, like an "efficient" person who is more "executive" than motherly.

Yet, despite their tendency to disassociate themselves from the presenter, the nonusers also agreed that her education makes her a qualified person to speak about the nutritious elements of Tang and, at least on an intellectual level, they too were able to take away the essential "nutrition" message of the commercial.

Exhibit 10

Tang Instant Breakfast Drink (B)

Food Selection Group Interview Summary

COMMUNICATION OF PRODUCT MESSAGES

In both the sessions with users and nonusers, there seemed to be some confusion on the part of the respondents as to what the Food Selection commercial was saying about the product. Those who seemed to understand the commercial played back the idea that the astronauts' menu is planned and selected carefully and that Orange Tang has been chosen over other orange drink products because of its superior taste and nutritional value. The women, who seemed to grasp the idea that selectivity has gone into making Tang the drink of the astronauts, pointed out that nutritionists have sampled and evaluated many foods and came up with Tang as the best in the orange drink category. The nutritional quality of the product, rich in vitamin C, was played back frequently by these respondents and the astronaut association seemed to confirm the fact that Tang must be nutritious. Several of the women seemed to say, "If it is good enough for the spacemen, then it should be good enough for us."

Others in the session were baffled as to what point the commercial was trying to make. Some of the women were confused as to why the eggs and bacon were being rejected. Interestingly enough, because of their lack of understanding, they played back the message that Tang is a complete breakfast drink . . . "a product that can replace bacon and eggs." These respondents failed to understand the intended idea that NASA is highly selective in choosing food that is suitable for the astronauts and, consequently, they got the impression that Tang will take the place of a full-course breakfast.

Interestingly enough, some of the respondents found the commercial confusing because they could not understand the purpose of showing bacon and eggs. A few of the women added that Tang contains vitamins whereas bacon and eggs are protein foods and they could not see the connection or purpose for showing both kinds of foods. Thus, it was apparent that a number of the women were confused about what the commercial was trying to say about Tang.

REACTIONS TO THE COMMERCIAL

On the whole, the respondents in both Denver as well as St. Louis seemed to react negatively to the way in which this commercial was presented. In fact, it appeared that the Food Selection commercial seemed to antagonize many of the consumers interviewed, which, in effect, caused many of the respondents to disbelieve the product claims.

A number of the respondents specifically commented that they were "turned off" by the actors in the commercial who were portraying the researchers. As one woman put it, "I would expect my little boy to react this way over eggs but not an adult." Others also seemed to disapprove of the way in which NASA was represented in the commercial, and here too, the women commented that "researchers would never look or act like the people in the film." Furthermore, because the women seemed to perceive the commercial as being "cartoonlike" and "spoofish," it was difficult for them to relate to the product messages as being real and credulous. In a sense, science and research seem to be a matter taken more seriously by the respondents and they seemed to resent the way in which it was portrayed in the commercial. By parodying NASA in a "Mickey Mouse" way, many of the women immediately seemed to discredit what was being said.

In light of this objection to the commercial, the respondents went on to object to the hard-sell approach of the commercial. These consumers from the midwestern states complained that the pace of the commercial was "too fast" and "pushy." One woman in particular objected to the "driving tempo" that was constant throughout the commercial. Several women in each of the sessions mentioned that they resent being told to use a product because "the astronauts use it," and these women went on to say that they feel quite qualified to judge for themselves whether a product is good or not. In a sense, they seemed to feel "put down" by the commercial and tended to feel that it was "stupid" and "insulting."

Consequently, in spite of the fact that some of the women were getting the message that Tang is a nutritious orange drink, the claim itself seemed to be ignored in light of the presentation. Surprisingly, even those women who were using Tang commented that a commercial such as Food Selection would never motivate them to buy the product.

Exhibit 11

Tang Instant Breakfast Drink (B)

Open-ended questions used to determine whether viewer was proven recaller, related recaller, or inaccurate recaller

1. Please tell me anything at all you remember about the Tang commercial you saw last night? (probe for detail, record verbatim)
2. In addition to what you already told me, what did the commercial look like? What did you see in the Tang commercial last night? (probe, record verbatim)
3. What (else) did they say about Tang in last night's commercial? (probe, record verbatim)
4. What ideas about Tang were brought out in the commercial last night? What other ideas were brought out? (probe, record verbatim)
5. Advertising generally tries to tell you what is good about a product and tries to convince you to buy it. What did the advertising for Tang tell you in order to convince you that it is good or that you should buy it? (probe, record verbatim)
6. Did the commercial make Tang seem different from other brands? (If yes, in what ways did it make it seem different?) (probe, record verbatim)
7. Have you ever seen this very same commercial before?

Exhibit 12
Tang Instant Breakfast Drink (B)

Results of Recall Test

	Andromeda		*Food Selection*		*Lady Ph.D.*		*Packing*	
Number of contacts	2,266		4,048		3,745		3,470	
Number of program viewers	170		249		206		214	
Size of commercial audience	128		160		148		146	
Proven recallers								
Unaided (category prompt)	9	7%	34	15%	6	4%	11	8%
Aided (brand prompt)	2	2	7	4	1	1	15	10
Prompted (commercial prompt)	0	0	1	1	3	2	8	5
Total	11	9%	32	20%	10	7%	34	23%
Related recallers								
Unaided (category prompt)	3	2%	5	3%	3	2%	2	1%
Aided (brand prompt)	1	1	8	5	16	11	3	2
Prompted (commercial prompt)	1	1	6	4	7	5	5	3
Total	5	4%	19	12%	26	18%	10	7%
Incorrect recallers								
Unaided (category prompt)	5	4%	7	4%	5	3%	2	1%
Aided (brand prompt)	4	3	8	5	6	4	4	3
Prompted (commercial prompt)	3	2	3	2	2	1	1	—
Total	12	9%	18	11%	13	9%	7	5%
No claimed recall	100	78%	91	57%	99	67%	95	65%
Total	128	100%	160	100%	148	100%	146	100%

6

Market Testing of Comprehensive Marketing Programs

"Daisy" (D)

DESIGNING A TEST MARKET OVERVIEW

By May 1974, the Gillette Safety Razor Division had, according to Bryan Dwyer, product manager for Daisy, "a great product, a super package, great displays, and fabulous advertising." The product was Daisy, a lightweight, disposable shaver with a permanently locked-on Trac II cartridge. The polystyrene handle was curved near the shaver's head to provide better visibility and easier access to hard-to-reach areas. Daisy was produced in two colors—lavender and rose. (See Exhibit 1 for a picture of Daisy.)

Daisy was packaged in what looked like two cups placed together. The top cup was transparent, exposing the two shavers inside. In designing the package, the task force had worked on several concepts and, in consultation with some consumers, had narrowed the choices to the cup package and a blister package. About 250 women were then interviewed in a shopping center and asked which package they preferred. Seventy-nine percent chose the cup. According to Dwyer, the Daisy package looked very feminine, provided good visibility of the shavers, provided easy and safe disposability, and was reusable. (See Exhibit 2 for a picture of the Daisy package.)

The Daisy package did not fit onto a regular pegboard display as did most SRD packages, but it was designed to be displayed in health and beauty aids departments. (Flicker had initially been displayed in health and beauty aids departments along with other feminine grooming products, and it had made the transition to regular pegboard displays without any serious decline in sales.) Three systems were designed for Daisy—a floor boutique display, which held 72 Daisy packages; a counter carousel display, which held 36 Daisy packages; and a shelf extender, which held 12 Daisy packages. (See Exhibit 3 for pictures of the various displays.)

The Daisy task force felt that selling two

disposable shavers at a retail price of around $1.00 would generate high consumer interest and that consumer interest would produce enthusiastic trade support because of the sales potential associated with a fast-selling product. They estimated that, on the average, a woman would buy five Daisy packages a year, substantially more than any other woman's wet shaver or razor on the market. The theme, "Wouldn't Hurt a Thigh," had been adopted, and the J. Walter Thompson Company had created advertisements for TV, magazines, and newspapers. (See Exhibit 4 for sample advertisements.)

SRD's management concurred with the task force's recommendation to test market Daisy to determine its real sales and profit potential prior to launching the product nationally. They felt that the test should continue for a full year so that the product's seasonality could be assessed adequately, but they also pointed out that, if after six months the test market was proving successful, SRD could proceed with a national rollout while the test market was still running. They were especially concerned with the following questions:

1. How should Daisy be priced?
2. What would be the effect of different advertising levels on sales and total market?
3. Exactly what sales and market share levels could Daisy expect?
4. How much and what type of both consumer and trade promotions were needed?
5. What would the trade's reaction to Daisy be? Would they buy it? Would they give it the display it needed? Would they keep the displays stocked?
6. What would be the reaction of the SRD sales force?

In discussions with SRD's Marketing Research and Sales departments, the Daisy task force decided that testing Daisy in four markets in different geographical regions would allow them to test different variables and to average out regional idiosyncrasies but would keep the test small enough for the team to monitor carefully exactly what was going on in each market. The designated marketing areas (DMAs)[1] they selected were Memphis, Tennessee; Dayton, Ohio; Seattle, Washington; and Milwaukee, Wisconsin. These metropolitan areas had a combined population of 8,321,300 or 4.04% of the total U.S. population. The population by DMA was as follows:

Designated Marketing Area	*Population*	*% of Total U.S. Population*
Memphis	2,435,100	1.18%
Dayton	1,521,300	.74
Seattle	1,723,400	.84
Milwaukee	2,641,500	1.28
	8,321,300	4.04%

See Exhibit 5 for data about each of these cities.

After selecting the test market cities, the members of the task force had to determine exactly what they were going to test and where they were going to test it. One member argued that, since they had four cities, they should test four key variables: price, advertising levels, consumer and trade promotions, and support and incentives required by the SRD sales force. Another member thought that they should pair the cities somehow and test one or two key variables in each pair. Still another member felt that they should hold all variables constant in all four markets. "The more we start tinkering with different pricing structures or offering different terms to the trade in different cities, the less conclusive our data is going to be because it will be based on too small a sample," she said. "We'd be better off

[1]A designated marketing area was defined in terms of the reach of TV stations. That is, a DMA consisted of an area within which the local stations achieved the largest share of the 9:00 A.M. to 12:00 midnight of average quarter-hour household audience or one station acheived a larger share of the 9:00 A.M. to 12:00 midnight average quarter-hour household audience than any station outside the DMA.

to hold everything constant and try to generalize from 4.04% of the population rather than to try to test a lot of different variables and generalize from less than 1% of the population." "Obviously we can't test everything we'd like to," Dwyer said. "Let's look carefully at each of our questions and see what trade-offs we're going to have to make."

PRICE

In an attempt to determine the appropriate price point for Daisy, the members of the task force were considering two retail prices, $.99 and $1.19. SRD's pricing structure for direct buying retailers and wholesalers would then be as follows:

Price Category[1]	*I*	*II*
Retail price per package	$.99	$1.19
Regular invoice price to direct-buying retailers and wholesalers	.594	.714
Introductory special deal invoice price to direct-buying retailers and wholesalers	*	*
Regular invoice price to retail accounts being serviced by wholesalers	.713	.857
Introductory special deal invoice price to retail accounts being serviced by wholesalers	*	*

[1]The task force defined these terms as follows. The retail price per package was the price at which SRD *recommended* retailers sell the product. In reality, SRD had no control over this price, and large retail outlets frequently discounted the price. The regular invoice price to direct-buying retailers and wholesalers was the price SRD charged its immediate customers. The introductory special deal invoice price to direct-buying retailers and wholesalers was the price SRD charged its immediate customers after various trade allowances were deducted. The regular invoice price to retailers being serviced by wholesalers was the price at which wholesalers sold the product to their customers. The introductory special-deal invoice price to retail accounts being serviced by wholesalers took into account any special offers wholesalers wished to make to their customers. SRD had no control over this price.
*To be decided.

The task force suspected that some discounting would probably occur, especially in the markets where Daisy retailed for $1.19. Nevertheless, they thought that these prices, once introductory trade allowances were taken into account, would be very helpful in gaining distribution for Daisy in health and beauty aids departments of supermarkets, mass merchandise outlets, and large drugstores where gross margins averaged about 40%. At that time, Lady Sure Touch, Lady Trac II, and Flicker were retailing for the following prices:

Model	*Manufacturer's Suggested Retail Price*	*Actual Retail Price Range*
Lady Sure Touch	$1.29	$1.10–1.50
Lady Trac II	2.95	2.59–3.25
Flicker	1.49	1.29–1.69

MEDIA ADVERTISING LEVEL

In developing a TV commercial for Daisy, the J. Walter Thompson researchers created three different commercials, which they showed to about 500 women over a three-day period. Each day, about 165 women were shown what they were told was a pilot program for a new TV series. A Daisy commercial was inserted at an appropriate point in the program. After the viewing, focus groups were held in which the women were asked their opinions of the Daisy commercial as well as their opinions of the program that was the professed object of the survey.

To test the effects of different levels of advertising, Dwyer and the task force thought that they might test at least two levels. Some markets would receive relatively low expenditures, whereas others would receive relatively high expenditures. The data with which they would determine exactly what "high" and "low" would be were sketchy. They knew that in 1973 Flicker had spent $1,450,500 on media advertising in the 65 markets in which it was distributed throughout the United States, and that Memphis, Seattle, Dayton, and Milwaukee were included in these markets. (See Exhibit 6 for Flicker's media advertising expenditures.) On Lady Sure Touch, SRD had spent approximately $846,000 nationally in 1973, mainly on national TV and magazines. It had not done any media advertising of Lady Trac II. In contrast to the small amount spent on the products for women, SRD had spent about $9 million on media advertising plus another $4.5 million on samples for the launch of the man's Trac II in 1972.

SALES AND MARKET SHARE

The product manager and his team suspected that the sales and market share Daisy could get would largely be a function of the amount of advertising and promotion with which SRD supported it. Nevertheless, they had to establish some realistic, profitable objectives based on the current size of the markets, their projections about how these markets might expand as a result of increased advertising and promotion by SRD, the position of competitive products, Daisy's performance in shave tests, and some estimates of what trial and repurchases Daisy could get. Earlier they had estimated that, on the average, a woman would buy five Daisy packages a year, substantially more than any other woman's wet shaver or razor on the market.

Since Daisy was a disposable product more comparable to blades than to razors, the members of the task force planned to base their estimates on the total blade market (i.e., blades purchased for both men and women), which they thought would consist of approximately 2.372 billion blades throughout the United States in 1974. To estimate the size of the markets in each of their test cities, they multiplied the total blade market by the percentage of the U.S. population in each DMA. Since they had fairly accurate estimates of the sales of Lady Sure Touch and Flicker, they could calculate market share data. However, they could not compare the position of Lady Trac II with that of Flicker and Lady Sure Touch because Lady Trac II was considered part of the razor market. (See Exhibit 7 for market shares of these products.)

In "shave tests" where SRD researchers asked several people to compare the performance of Daisy with that of Flicker, Lady Sure Touch, and Lady Trac II, Daisy ranked well above the other products. On a scale where 100 was the highest possible score, Daisy scored 92 points, Lady Trac II scored 84 points, Lady Sure Touch scored 73 points, and Flicker scored 68 points. Moreover Dwyer knew that, even with limited marketing support, Lady Sure Touch had been tried by about 6% of the women who shaved in the United States and 55% of those who tried it had repurchased it.

TRADE PROMOTIONS

To get strong support at the retail level and to achieve desired levels of distribution, the task force felt that SRD had to offer the trade very substantial promotional deals. American Safety Razor (ASR) had used four types of trade promotions to introduce Flicker and to secure display space in health and beauty aids departments. The first trade promotion was an 8⅓% off-invoice allowance; that is, the manufacturer's invoice price was reduced by 8⅓%, regardless of the amount of the product the customer ordered.[2] ASR's second type of trade promotion was the cooperative advertising allowance. After a retailer ran an advertisement

[2]Off-invoice allowances were sometimes escalated—a manufacturer might offer 2.5% off each case if a retailer purchased, say, 25 cases, 5% off if he purchased 50 cases, and so on. While the escalated buying allowance usually did increase the initial orders of a product, many retailers opposed it because they felt it constituted unusual and unwarranted pressure from a supplier.

which included a picture of Flicker, he sent a tear sheet of the ad to ASR, and ASR paid him \$1.50 for every counter display and \$3.25 for every floor stand he had purchased. (Sometimes wholesalers ran ads for several of their customers, in which case they too were eligible for cooperative advertising allowances.) ASR's third program was the display allowance. Under it, ASR paid its direct-buying retail customers \$.50 for every counter display and \$1.25 for every floor stand they purchased. ASR's final introductory trade promotion consisted of placement money. In this program, ASR paid \$1.00 to wholesaler salespeople for every 24-unit counter display they sold and \$2.00 for every 54-unit floor stand they sold.

When SRD first introduced Lady Sure Touch, it offered a 16⅔% off-invoice allowance and a 30¢ display allowance for every 12-unit display placed in retail outlets. When it began to sell Lady Sure Touch nationally, its trade promotions consisted of a 10% off-invoice allowance, a cooperative advertising allowance which consisted of 50¢ per 12-unit carton purchased, and a 75¢ display allowance for each special display set up in a retail outlet. By May 1974, SRD was offering no trade promotions on Lady Sure Touch. The introductory trade promotions for Lady Trac II had consisted of a 16⅔% off-invoice allowance plus 3,500,000 samples distributed to the trade. By May 1974, SRD offered only a 10% off-invoice allowance.

For Daisy's introduction, the task force was considering a 16⅔% off-invoice allowance, an 8% cooperative advertising allowance, and 4% placement money. When the task force's representative from SRD's sales department asked the district managers their opinions of this trade promotion structure, most agreed that it would probably be adequate. However, the manager of the Dayton district thought that it might be better to reduce the cooperative advertising allowance and add an additional display allowance for chains. He stated further that placement money should be \$1.00 per counter display because wholesaler salespeople would not be interested in anything less. The manager of the Milwaukee district felt strongly that a larger off-invoice allowance would be more effective. He thought a 25% off-invoice coupled with a 5% cooperative advertising allowance would be the optimum trade promotion. He felt that placement money was not a useful promotion because, while it did increase the initial sell-in, it sometimes led to overloading the trade. Since SRD accepted merchandise returns, he thought that placement money might simply result in customers' ordering large quantities initially but returning a lot if it did not move very quickly.

CONSUMER PROMOTIONS

When ASR introduced Flicker, it did not run any consumer promotions. On one occasion since the introduction, it had run a self-liquidating promotion whereby a customer could purchase two pairs of pantyhose for \$1.50 if she mailed in a coupon which was printed on the Flicker package. Coupons were also often included in newspaper ads.

SRD had run only one consumer promotion with Lady Sure Touch. It consisted of a coupon on the Lady Sure Touch package which allowed the customer to purchase ten pieces of elegant stationery for \$1.00.

SRD had run three consumer promotions with Lady Trac II. The first was a coupon placed in Lady Trac II packages for 50¢ off on the purchase of Soft and Dry antiperspirant. The second and most successful was a coupon in Lady Trac II packages for a free pair of pantyhose. This promotion doubled Lady Trac II's market share. The third was a vial of Sea and Ski Sun Cream placed on each Lady Trac II package. The total cost of these promotions, including the premium item, trade discounts, and various other expenses, generally ranged between 15 and 30% of sales.

Daisy's task force members were considering two types of consumer promotions for Daisy. First, they wanted to distribute samples to as many women in the 18 to 24 age group as they could afford. These samples would consist of a single Daisy shaver in a blister pack with a 10¢-off coupon that could be applied to the purchase of a regular Daisy package. Two relatively inexpensive ways were found to distribute these samples. The first was through a company which had arrangements with various movie theaters whereby women who attended one of those theaters during a specified time period received a free sample of a particular product. The theaters often ran special ads stating that the product was being given away, gave passes to the manufacturer's salespeople and their major accounts, and displayed posters promoting the product in their lobbies. It was felt that up to 8 million women (throughout the United States) could be reached through this program, at a cost (not including the samples themselves) of approximately $78 per thousand samples distributed. It was estimated that each sample would cost about 17¢.

Another method by which Daisy might be sampled was the Superbox program, a program whereby various manufacturers gave samples of their products to a company which then assembled "Superboxes" containing the products and sold them to university bookstores. These stores in turn either sold or gave away the Superboxes to their customers. SRD might be able to reach as many as 1.5 million women (throughout the United States) via this program, at a cost of $55 per thousand women, not including the samples themselves.

Both programs were available in all four test cities, and the task force estimated that through them SRD would be able to reach approximately the following number of women in each city:

Region	*Movie Theaters*	*Superboxes*
Memphis	94,000	18,000
Seattle	59,000	11,000
Dayton	67,000	13,000
Milwaukee	102,000	19,000
	322,000	61,000

The second type of consumer promotion Daisy's team wanted to consider was widescale couponing. The coupons would be placed inside sample packages of Daisy and in print ads in newspapers and magazines. When presented for redemption at a retail store, a coupon would entitle the bearer to 10¢ off the listed retail price of Daisy. The retailer would then send the coupon to the manufacturer for reimbursement plus handling fee, usually about 5¢ for each redeemed coupon.

DISTRIBUTION

One of the task force's most difficult problems was determining distribution objectives for Daisy. The members wanted to make projections for Daisy's initial sell-in before the advertising programs started and for three and six months after the program had been inaugurated. They had substantial data on the number of accounts, number of stores, and SRD's sales by different types of customers. (See Exhibit 8.) Moreover, the Marketing Research Department had supplied national trends in food and drugstores for the major women's shaving products, and they were fairly certain the same distribution patterns would be applicable to Daisy's four test market cities. They felt that these data should be used only as general indicators, however, because the sample of stores checked was relatively small and because the Research Department did not generate data on distribution of specific Gillette products in mass merchandise outlets. (See Exhibit 9.)

In assessing what the reactions of different types of customers probably would be, the task force relied heavily on its representative from the sales department, Steve Tandy. Currently SRD's director of sales planning, Tandy had considerable experience in field sales and now served as liaison between sales and marketing. Tandy stated that about half of SRD's blade business went through food stores, where the blades were purchased by women for their husbands. However, food stores had never been good outlets for razors, and only about 18% of SRD's razor sales went through food stores. (The men's Trac II had achieved over 75% distribution in food stores, but this was considered highly unusual.) While SRD considered Daisy as part of the blade market, food stores would view it more as a razor because of the amount of space it required. If it did not generate substantially more purchases than did most razors, it would be unprofitable for a food store to carry it. Tandy suspected, however, that the favorable experience many food stores recently had with Flicker would actually make these customers more willing to try Daisy.

Tandy felt that Daisy would be more readily accepted in drugstores than in food stores. Small drugstores and drug chains accounted for a substantial amount of SRD's razor sales, and these outlets usually reacted favorably to products for women. The only problem might be that drug wholesalers, who were responsible for selling and servicing small drugstores, were often skeptical about new products for women.

Mass merchandisers, Tandy felt, would be Daisy's most avid customers. SRD enjoyed very favorable relations with most of them, and they were usually not averse to trying new products for women, especially when the products offered them good margins. Toiletry merchandisers ran such diverse businesses that Tandy could not readily assess their probable acceptance of Daisy. Moreover, he thought that SRD should count on virtually no business for Daisy from food wholesalers and tobacco jobbers.

Tandy also pointed out significant features of each of the test market cities. Memphis, he thought, would be a tough test town. It had five food chains, three of which were not headquartered in Memphis. He described SRD's relationships with two of these chains as "touchy," and he said a third chain was not interested in nonfood items. He also foresaw a couple of problems with drug chains. Again, very few of them were headquartered in Memphis. In one drug chain, the relationship between SRD's headquarters salesperson and the chain headquarters, where the decision about Daisy would be made, was very strong, but the SRD salesperson who handled the Memphis stores would not get credit for selling Daisy, and he was expected to react quite adversely since he would be expected to service the stores that carried the product. In another chain, the district manager for Memphis had considerable influence over product selection, and the salesperson who dealt with him was quite certain he would not be interested in Daisy. SRD's relation with local mass merchandisers was excellent, but those headquartered elsewhere posed problems. Tandy stated that Memphis' major strengths as a test market were that (1) it was an "average" American city in income levels, family size, cars per family, TV viewing, and so forth; (2) it was fairly isolated geographically so that the people who comprised the market were pretty clearly defined; (3) the reach of the local media was fairly well defined, and TV stations and newspapers from outlying areas were not major factors in the market; and (4) most of the stores of SRD's major accounts were located within Memphis' designated marketing area.

Tandy stated that Seattle had all the strengths of Memphis as a test market, plus it was located in SRD's smallest district. The district manager who had been in the area for about eight years supervised only four or five men, so that he himself had excellent rapport with SRD's major accounts. Since SRD's district office was located in Seattle, the district manager knew all the relevant people in the Seattle area.

Tandy felt that the Milwaukee area was an excellent test market because it had virtually no outside influence except for Zayre's and the Walgreen drugstore chain. The Zayre influence consisted of five "Shopper City" stores which Zayre had acquired but which still retained their old name and had a fair degree of autonomy. Another plus for Milwaukee was that the district manager was considered an exceptionally competent administrator who could easily handle the thousands of details necessary to make the test market work.

Tandy stated that Dayton was a fairly good test market for SRD in that SRD had a career salesperson with about 15 years of experience selling SRD products, who could practically guarantee distribution in all his major accounts. However, Dayton posed some problems in that it was not as isolated geographically as were the three other markets. The influence of Cincinnati and Columbus were felt in both TV and print media.

REACTION OF THE SRD SALES FORCE

In all, about 15 SRD salespeople would be involved in the test market. They were considered to be highly motivated, professional salespeople, most of whom enjoyed good relations with their customers. While they had had substantial experience with new products, products for women had always posed special problems for them. Both they and their customers knew that SRD had never before made a serious commitment to the women's shaving market.

Test markets also posed special problems for the sales force. In addition to convincing customers to buy the new product, the salespeople had to make extra calls on retail outlets to be sure that the product was adequately stocked and properly displayed. In the case of Daisy, they even had to convince customers to put the product in health and beauty aids departments and therefore increase the total space they were devoting to SRD products.

To generate enthusiasm for the Daisy test market, the task force members thought that they would hold a two-day sales meeting at the Nordic Hills Inn in Chicago. At this meeting, extensive promotional material about Daisy which the salespeople would later use with their customers was to be distributed. The total cost of this material would be about $22,000. In addition, Dwyer thought he would offer an AM/FM radio to all salespeople who met their quotas, but he thought that the cost of this sales promotion would not exceed $2,000. He did not want to offer special monetary incentives to the salespeople, but some members of his team thought that would be the only way to get the salespeople to give Daisy the support it needed.

MERCHANDISING VEHICLES

While special merchandising vehicles had been designed for Daisy, the task force had not yet decided whether to order permanent metal displays or temporary cardboard displays for the test markets. As was the custom in the trade, SRD would cover the cost of these displays. The initial cost of permanent displays was substantially greater than that of temporary displays:

Display Type	Temporary (per unit)	Permanent (per unit)
Floor boutiques (72 Daisy packages)	$7.00	$17.00
Counter carousels (36 Daisy packages)	2.25	4.50
Shelf extenders (12 Daisy packages)	1.10	2.50

However, Dwyer was certain that all the temporary displays would be thrown away, probably as soon as they became stocked out, and he knew that retailers also often threw away "permanent" displays. He estimated that, under optimum conditions, retailers would retain about 75% of the permanent displays after the test market. "Not only do we have to consider the initial cost of the displays," he told his team, "we also have to estimate what we think the retention rate of the permanent displays will be."

Some of these merchandising vehicles were obviously more suitable for certain retail outlets than for others. To determine the number of each type of display that was needed, the task force had to rely on the estimates of the four regional managers involved. Their early estimates were as follows:

	Floor Boutiques		*Counter Carousels*		*Shelf Extenders*	
Region	*Permanent*	*Temporary*	*Permanent*	*Temporary*	*Permanent*	*Temporary*
Memphis	150–200	263	250–300	525	60–75	130
Seattle	120	187–300	60	75–200	15	40–50
Dayton	155	250	130	350	30	80
Milwaukee	100–150	225	195	375	50	90
Total	525–625	925–1,038	635–685	1,425–1,450	155–170	340–350

MISCELLANEOUS FINANCIAL CONSIDERATIONS

Gillette's cost accounting department estimated that capital equipment expenditures for Daisy's test market would be about $525,000. This would include the handle mold, packaging tooling, developmental costs, and assembly line setup. If the decision was made not to go national with Daisy, the total capital equipment of $525,000 would have to be written off.

The cost accounting department had also determined that manufacturing costs for the test market would be 30.8¢ per package. Adding freight costs resulted in an estimated costs of 33.8¢ per package. The direct costs of the sample packages which contained only one shaver and which were blister packed on cardboard amounted to 17¢ per package, including freight.

Exhibit 1
"Daisy" (D)

Picture of Daisy

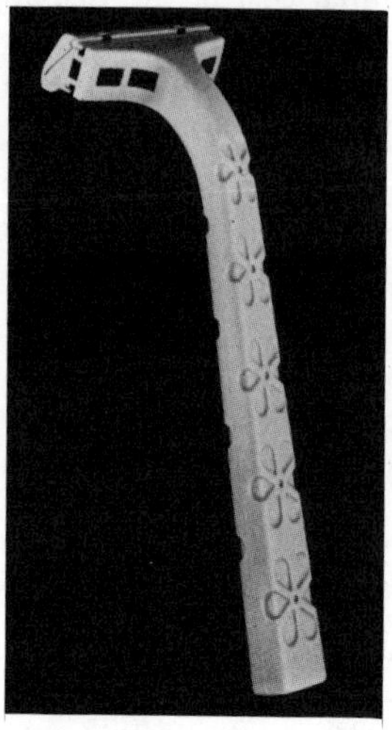

Exhibit 2
"Daisy" (D)

The Daisy Package

Exhibit 3
"Daisy" (D)

The Display Vehicles

Floor Boutique

Counter Carousel

Shelf Extender

Exhibit 4
"Daisy" (D)

Sample Daisy Advertisements
Magazine Advertisement

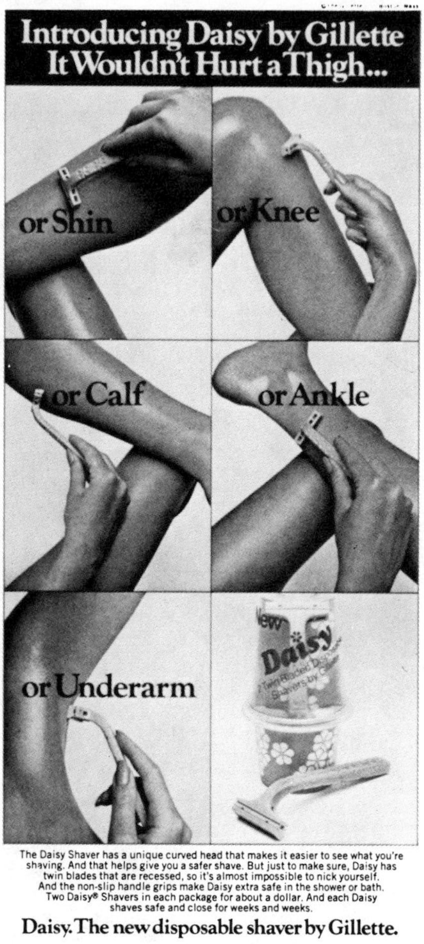

TV Storyboard

The Daisy Shaver by **Gillette**

"Wouldn't Hurt A Thigh" Commercial

ANNCR (VO): Introducing Daisy by Gillette.

The new woman's shaver that's curved,

so it wouldn't hurt a thigh.

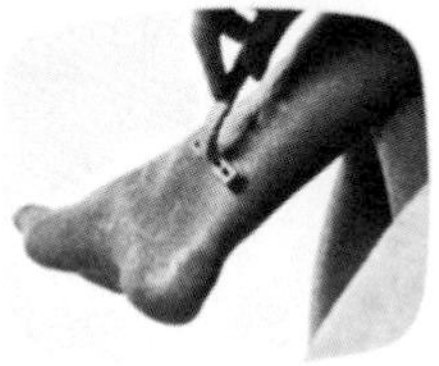

Or ankle.

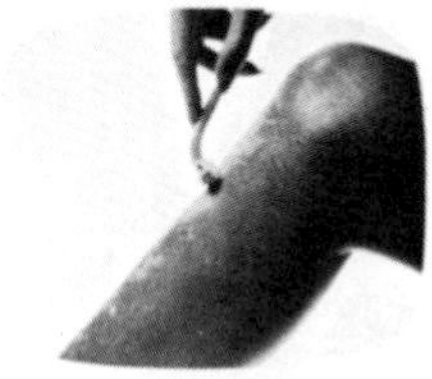

Or shin.

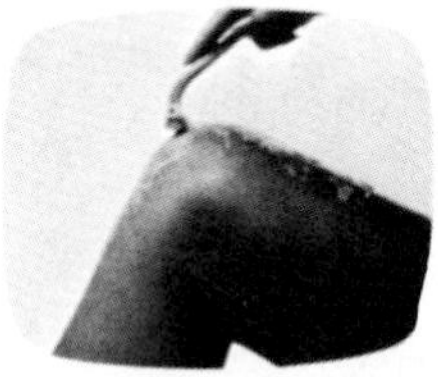

Or knee.

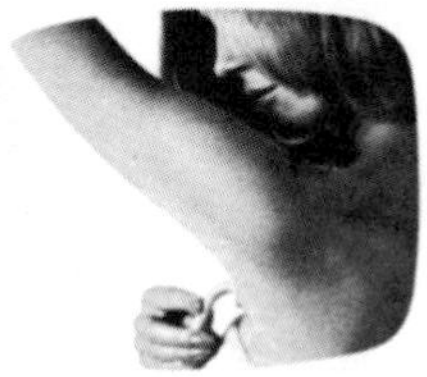

Or underarm.

The Daisy has twin blades, recessed and permanently locked in at a safe angle,

so you won't hurt yourself.

Then after weeks of close, safe shaving it's disposable. Throw it away and pick the other Daisy.

Two for only a $1.19.

The Daisy Shaver. It wouldn't hurt a thigh.

Exhibit 5
"Daisy" (D)

Data regarding the four test market cities

	Memphis	*Seattle*	*Dayton*	*Milwaukee*
Time zone	Central	Pacific	Eastern	Central
Rank by households	16	26	32	14
Population and households, 1972				
Total population (000)	2,435.1	1,723.4	1,521.3	2,641.5
% of U.S.	1.18%	.84%	.74%	1.28%
Total households (000)	777.9	600.6	490.9	840.1
% of U.S.	1.16%	.89%	.73%	1.25%
TV households (000)	753.7	572.0	480.4	814.0
% of U.S.	1.16%	.88%	.74%	1.25%
Effective buying income (millions)	$8,248.4	$5,942.9	$5,210.3	$8,908.2
Effective buying income per household	$10,603	$9,895	$10,614	$10,608
TV market profile, February–March 1973 (% household)				
UHF penetration	68%	NA	59%	65%
Color TV ownership	59	67%	68	69
Multiset households	44	37	48	38
CATV penetration	7	11	7	8
Daypart average quarter-hour households reached by total local stations (000), February–March 1973				
Mon.–Fri., 9:00 A.M.–noon	130	108	111	113
Mon.–Fri., noon–4:30 P.M.	210	129	150	175
Mon.–Fri., 4:30 P.M.–7:30 P.M.	390	305	242	340
Mon.–Fri., 11:00 P.M.–11:30 P.M.	260	134	197	280
Mon.–Fri., 11:30 P.M.–1:00 A.M.	95	61	102	100
Sat.–Sun., 9:00 A.M.–midnight	280	202	202	285
Sat.–Sun., 7:30–11:00 P.M.	458	334	327	425

NA – Not available.

Advertising costs by medium in test market cities

TV spot advertising
(1 spot is a 30-second commercial)

Region	Prime Time[1] (per spot)	Daytime and Fringe Evening (per spot)
Memphis	$803	$80
Dayton	416	80
Milwaukee	597	87
Seattle	491	58

[1]7:00–11:00 P.M. Eastern Standard Time or 7:00–10:00 P.M. Central Standard Time.

Insertions in newspaper supplements

Region	Cost per Insertion
Memphis	$3,600
Dayton	3,850
Milwaukee	3,850
Seattle	3,600

Regional issues of magazines

Magazine/Region	Cost per Insertion
Family Circle	
Memphis	$ 975
Dayton	1,151
Milwaukee	2,175
Seattle	1,750
Good Housekeeping	
Memphis	747
Dayton	550
Milwaukee	1,024
Seattle	576
McCall's	
Memphis	1,520
Dayton	1,066
Milwaukee	2,304
Seattle	1,095
Woman's Day	
Memphis	540
Dayton	666
Milwaukee	1,090
Seattle	665

Exhibit 6
"Daisy" (D)

Flicker Advertising Expenditures by Medium, by Quarter (000)

	1972		*1973*				*1974*
Medium	*III*	*IV*	*I*	*II*	*III*	*IV*	*Q-I*
Day network TV	—	—	—	$ 42	$148	—	$309
Night network TV	—	—	—	112	321	$171	—
Spot TV	—	—	$ 9	10	—	—	—
Magazines and supplements	—	—	115	244	—	—	—
Newspaper	$33	$147	126	150	—	—	—
Network radio	—	—	—	—	—	—	—
Total							
By quarter	$33	$147	$250	$558	$469	$171	$309
By year	$180			$1,448			

Exhibit 7
"Daisy" (D)

1973 Unit Sales and Unit Share of Lady Sure Touch, Lady Trac II, and Flicker in Daisy's Test Market

	Lady Sure Touch		*Lady Trac II*	*Flicker*		*Total Sales (units)*	
Region	*Units*	*Share*	*Units*	*Units*	*Share*	*Razors*	*Blades*
Memphis	26,098	.09%	15,038	307,950	1.1%	375,960	27,995,000
Seattle	22,323	.11	16,692	358,722	1.8	417,300	19,929,000
Dayton	21,746	.12	13,195	438,912	2.5	329,810	17,556,000
Milwaukee	51,682	.17	25,147	576,992	1.9	628,680	30,368,000

Exhibit 8
"Daisy" (D)

SRD Business in Test Market Cities, 1973

Region	Number of Headquarters	Number of Retail Outlets	1973 Sales of Lady Sure Touch	1973 Sales of Lady Trac II
Milwaukee				
Drug chains	5	51	$ 8,715	$ 9,570
Food chains	2	92	912	—
Discount merchandisers	12	124	10,331	17,769
Toiletry merchandisers	11	1,440	3,623	2,896
Drug wholesalers	8	982	11,190	9,523
Food wholesalers	3	280	913	—
Miscellaneous other wholesalers	10	2,680	929	592
Total	51	5,649	$36,613	$40,350
Dayton				
Drug chains	2	64	$ 6,357	$ 6,903
Food chains	3	163	652	—
Discount merchandisers	2	13	2,941	2,873
Toiletry merchandisers	2	273	434	2,273
Drug wholesalers	3	300	2,688	4,777
Food wholesalers	3	1,300	1,956	3,562
Miscellaneous other wholesalers	5	675	377	800
Total	20	2,788	$15,405	$21,188
Memphis				
Drug chains	7	25	$ 4,165	$ 5,415
Food chains	5	203	2,095	2,725
Discount merchandisers	1	60	9,235	12,055
Toiletry merchandisers	8	675	1,100	1,430
Drug wholesalers	4	1,170	900	1,170
Food wholesalers	11	960	800	973
Miscellaneous other wholesalers	11	3,000	200	354
Total	47	6,093	$18,495	$24,122
Seattle				
Drug chains	3	37	$ 8,884	$17,517
Food chains	2	109	552	1,201
Discount merchandisers	1	36	464	—
Toiletry merchandisers	7	73	3,723	5,205
Drug wholesalers	3	425	1,856	2,852
Food wholesalers	0	0	—	—
Miscellaneous other wholesalers	2	67	221	—
Total	18	747	$15,700	$26,775

Exhibit 9
"Daisy" (D)

Distribution of Women's Shaving Products in Drug and Food Stores[1]

	Gillette Lady Trac II		*Schick Super II for Women*		*Lady Gillette*		*Gillette Lady Techmatic*		*Lady Sure Touch*		*Flicker*	
	Drug	*Food*	*Drug*	*Food*	*Drug*	*Food*	*Drug*	*Food*	*Drug*	*Food*	*Drug*	*Food*
June '72	—	—	—	—	37%	6%	21%	6%	—	—	10%	3%
Jan. '73	—	—	—	—	35	2	21	10	8	8	29	25
June '73	22%	10%	8%	7%	36	2	23	6	32	15	46	35
Jan. '74	25	13	11	5	33	2	19	4	29	14	54	45

[1]The numbers indicate the percentage distribution in the drug and food stores which SRD researchers monitored regularly.

"Daisy" (E)

DESIGNING A NATIONAL MARKETING PROGRAM OVERVIEW

By January 1975, SRD's test market of Daisy had been running for six months, and SRD had gathered considerable data about the product's performance in the four test market cities. SRD management had decided to keep the test running through June 1975, but it was generally felt that SRD should proceed with its national rollout while the test was going on. If SRD did not do so, many executives felt, competitors would copy the product and distribute it nationally immediately.

DAISY'S TEST MARKET

The Daisy task force had established the following general marketing objectives for Daisy:

 This case was prepared by Nancy J. Davis under the supervision of Steven H. Star.

1. To generate incremental profit for SRD by aggressively marketing Daisy to the potential 65 million women shavers in the United States.
2. To expand the current $75 million female wet shaving market by informing women that Daisy will provide the ultimate in a close, safe shave.
3. To establish SRD as the leader in the women's wet shaving market by drawing more women into the Gillette wet shaving franchise by trading women up to the Daisy shaving system.
4. To convince women of the advantages of using a disposable twin-bladed shaving system, designed exclusively to satisfy a woman's shaving needs.
5. To preempt competition from further inroads into the women's disposable wet shaving market, thereby protecting SRD's current position in the twin-bladed shaving field.
6. To generate enthusiastic trade support by introducing a female- shaver which will generate a high level of profitability due to its rapid turnover.

In designing the test market, the task force members had decided to pair the cities and to test what they considered the most important variable—different advertising levels By putting Memphis and Seattle together and Dayton and Milwaukee together, they had two units, each of which represented 2.02% of the total U.S. population. They had settled on a suggested retail price of $1.10 per package. Trying to test for other items such as different promotion strategies would only complicate the test to the point that the results might be inconclusive, they thought.

The specific objectives which the team had established for Daisy's test market were as follows:

1. To achieve a 1.4% share of the entire blade market in the Dayton and Milwaukee designated marketing areas and a 2.0% share of the blade market in the Memphis and Seattle designated marketing areas within Daisy's first product year.
2. To test the impact of two different advertising levels upon the share development in each pair of the test markets. Milwaukee and Dayton would receive relatively low expenditures, while Memphis and Seattle would receive relatively high expenditures.
3. To generate the equivalent of $686,268 in full revenue sales (i.e., revenue before trade discounts) by selling 2,079,600 shavers (i.e., 1,039,800 packages) in Daisy's first product year in the test markets.
4. To achieve a 9–11% trial rate among the potential women shavers in the test market areas.
5. To achieve at least a 15% conversion rate among sample recipients.
6. To achieve an initial repurchase rate of 65%, followed by subsequent repurchase rates of 80%, then 90% ad infinitum.
7. To achieve the following levels of distribution:

Distributor	*Start of Advertising (Sept. 9, 1974)*	*By Jan. 1, 1975*	*By July 1, 1975*
Food	25%	40%	50%
Drug	40	65	70
Mass merchandiser	50	75	80

8. To obtain permanent placement of the Daisy displays in female-oriented shopping areas of the store, away from the traditional pegboard locations.
9. To determine the impact of Daisy share growth on Lady Trac II share levels as well as determine reaction of "one-time" Daisy purchasers.

The task force had established market share objectives by looking at the position of Lady Sure Touch, Lady Trac II, and Flicker in the various markets, considering Daisy's outstanding performance in shave tests, and estimating what the impact of the different advertising levels would be. They then calculated the sales requirements as follows:

Total U.S. blade market for 1974
× % U.S. population in test city DMAs
= Total blades sold in DMAs in 1 year
× Anticipated share levels
= Total consumer sales
+ Pipeline coverage @ 3 months

Total shipments

Dayton and Milwaukee (low media expenditures)	*Memphis and Seattle (high media expenditures)*
2.372 billion	2.372 billion
× 2.02%	× 2.02%
= 47.9 million	= 47.9 million
× 1.4%	× 2.0%
= 670,600	= 958,000
+ 191,000	+ 260,000
= 861,600 shavers (430,000 packages)	= 1,218,000 shavers (609,000 packages)

The test market got underway officially on July 1 and 2, 1974, when the Daisy task force met with the salespeople from the Memphis, Seattle, Dayton, and Milwaukee markets. These salespeople had already been told that a test market of a new product for women was scheduled for their areas, and many had been consulted about specific accounts as district managers and regional managers worked with the task force in setting distribution objectives. The salespeople began selling Daisy on July 8, and initial orders were shipped on July 15.

To guarantee that a substantial number of women would at least try Daisy, between 350,000 and 400,000 samples were distributed between August 26 and September 9. About 325,000 of these were distributed via movie theaters and 25,000 through the Superbox program on college campuses. The remainder were sent to beauty editors, various cosmeticians, stewardesses, and other women selected by the salespeople. Each sample package, which consisted of a single shaver blister packed on cardboard, contained a 10¢-off coupon to be applied to the purchase of a regular Daisy package.

To further stimulate trial and repurchases, SRD relied heavily on its advertising campains. Daisy's TV advertising began on September 9, its newspaper advertising on September 29, and its magazine advertising in November issues. The advertisements were targeted toward the 15- to 34-year-old age group and emphasized that Daisy would give a better, safer shave than other products because (1) its curved handle provided maximum visibility and control while the user shaved areas which were hard to see and reach; (2) it had the most advanced shaving head on the market—twin blades, set at precise angles to give a closer, safer shave than single-bladed razors provided; (3) the twin-blade cartridge was permanently locked into place to eliminate any need for blade handling, and, when the blade was finally used up, the entire shaver was discarded; (4) recessed grips in the shape of daisies were molded into the handle to facilitate steady handling of the shaver; and (5) a transparent safety cap provided protection for both travel and storage. The tone of Daisy's advertising was described as "exciting and of news value, implying this is a significant new product in female shaving." The product was presented in a contemporary, light manner, conveying that it was an impulse item easy to use, inexpensive to buy, and available everywhere. (See Exhibit 1 for sample advertisements.)

Daisy's introductory advertising used both TV and print media. In Memphis and Seattle, SRD's media expenditures for Daisy were equivalent to an annual national level of $5,500,000 while in Dayton and Milwaukee the comparable figure was $3,500,000. The actual expenditures in Memphis and Seattle totaled $133,320 for the first year; those in Dayton and Milwaukee amounted to $84,840. If these numbers were extrapolated nationally in direct proportion to the percentage of the national population contained in the cities, the national expenditures would have been substantially higher than they actually were because media costs per thousand people reached were substantially higher on a local or regional basis than on a national basis.

The specific objectives of the advertising programs were as follows:

Vehicle	Objective	Dayton and Milwaukee	Memphis and Seattle	Cost per Thousand	
				Target (age 15–34)	Women
Prime network	Maximize reach	38%	49%	$8.25	$2.80
Late fringe network	Obtain frequency against working women and upper-income groups	35	35	5.80	1.80
Selective magazines	Maximize exposure in beauty/grooming environment	19	11	4.75	2.00
Sunday supplements	Maximize trial and coupon	8	5	8.35	3.25
		100%	100%		
Summary					
Total TV		73%	84%		
Print		27	16		
Reach and frequency[1]					
Introduction		87%/3.9	90%/4.7		
Sustaining		32%/1.4	63%/2.6		

[1]This meant that, under its introductory advertising plans, SRD would reach 87% of the women in Dayton and Milwaukee an average of 3.9 times, whereas in Memphis and Seattle, it would reach 90% of the women an average of 4.7 times.

See Exhibit 2 for summaries of the media plans for the test markets.

The task force had worked very closely with SRD headquarters and field salespeople in establishing distribution objectives. "We looked at each of our accounts individually, determined which ones we could count on from the very beginning, which would probably purchase Daisy once it got established in other outlets and our advertising program got underway, and which would probably never touch Daisy," Tandy said later. The trade terms which the task force decided upon consisted of a 16⅔% off-invoice allowance, 4% placement money, and an 8% co-operative advertising allowance. With these terms, Daisy's cost structure was as follows:

Terms	Per Unit	72-Unit Floor Boutique	36-Unit Counter Carousel	12-Unit Shelf Extenders
Suggested retail	$1.10	$79.20	$39.60	$13.20
Regular invoice	.66	47.52	23.76	7.92
Deal invoice	.55	39.60	19.80	6.60
Regular wholesale	.79	57.02	28.51	9.48
Deal wholesale	.66	47.52	23.76	7.92

The Daisy task force was confident that these terms, plus the selling expertise of SRD's sales force, would enable Daisy to achieve desired distribution objectives, even in health and beauty aids departments.

TEST MARKET RESULTS

When SRD's salespeople started selling Daisy initially, most buyers responded with "Oh no, another lady's razor." However, once the salespeople completed their presentation, the buyers generally were impressed by the Daisy program and SRD's commitment to the product. They commented positively on the package, the shaver itself, the display concepts, and the promotional support. The salespeople used portable Fairchild projector audiovisual aids to tell the Daisy story, and this, many felt, greatly increased the professionalism of the presentation.

As had been anticipated, customers in some cities responded more favorably and more quickly than did those in other cities. In Milwaukee, all the local mass merchandisers, all the drug wholesalers, one of the two major food chains, and over half of the toiletry merchandisers had ordered Daisy by the end of July. In Dayton the major mass merchandisers, three of the four drug wholesalers, and all the tobacco jobbers ordered Daisy immediately. However, only one of the two major drug chains had placed an order by the end of July. Moreover, none of the food chains, toiletry merchandisers, or food wholesalers ordered Daisy during July although several had indicated that they were interested in the product and that their orders would soon be forthcoming. In Memphis, all drug chains, all drug wholesalers, half the food wholesalers, and half the tobacco jobbers placed orders during the first month. However, none of the five food chains and only 5 of the 15 mass merchandisers ordered Daisy in July. The buyer for the largest mass merchandiser ordered only token quantities, but said that, if Daisy moved well initially without advertising, he would purchase large quantities and run a two-packages-for-$1.00 special. In Seattle, all drug chains and drug wholesalers ordered Daisy immediately, as did two of the three food chains. Seattle mass merchandisers proved to be reluctant to purchase Daisy, as were food wholesalers and tobacco jobbers. In many instances throughout the test market cities, salespeople stated that many orders were expected to come through soon, but were being delayed because chain headquarters or wholesalers had to carefully survey the retail outlets they serviced to know better what quantities they could move.

As the test marketing progressed, several additional accounts were opened. Milwaukee attained the highest overall distribution and display, and Memphis still proved to be the most difficult market in spite of intensive efforts by SRD's sales force. By the end of August, 10 of SRD's 11 national accounts (2 drug chains, 8 mass merchandisers, and 1 drug wholesaler) had ordered generous quantities of Daisy for their stores in the four test cities. Also by this time, a few accounts had begun to reorder Daisy. Daisy's management team felt that this was especially encouraging because it indicated that retail movement was good even before the sampling and media advertising programs began.

Over the next few months, SRD salespeople periodically held intensive retail campaigns to secure display space for Daisy and keep the displays stocked. On the whole, they found that Daisy moved well if it was displayed well, but that there were frequent delays in getting the product from an account's warehouse into its retail stores. The 36-package counter carousel proved to be the most popular display vehicle, and Dwyer ordered

500 additional units. He was also considering ordering more boutiques because many were being discarded when their stock was depleted and reorders were draining SRD's supply.

As Dwyer had expected, Daisy was promoted heavily by many retailers. In fact, only a few independent food and drugstores charged the full suggested retail price of $1.10. Pricing in food and drug chains and mass merchandise outlets was usually under $1.00, often in the $.88 to $.99 range. When retailers advertised special price promotions, the results were often impressive. For example, Raleigh Drug Stores in Memphis sold virtually all their stock the first day of a heavily advertised promotion in which they sold Daisy for $.59 per package, and Super Discount Stores in Memphis sold 375 packages in the first three days of their two-packages-for-$1.00 promotion.

By January 1, 1975, SRD had shipped the following Daisy packages:

Region	*Shipments*
Seattle	172,288
Memphis	160,634
Milwaukee	220,685
Dayton	199,307
National accounts	8,978
	761,892 (1,523,784 shavers)

Dwyer was quite pleased with these sales, especially since most had occurred during winter months which were traditionally slow periods for women's shaving products.

The percentages of the different types of accounts which had purchased Daisy were as follows:

Distributors	*Memphis*	*Seattle*	*Dayton*	*Milwaukee*
Drug chains	66%	100%	100%	100%
Food chains	80	100	100	100
Mass merchandisers	73	100	100	100
Toiletry merchandisers	100	80	100	91
Drug wholesalers	100	100	100	100
Food wholesalers	70	0	50	66
Miscellaneous wholesalers, mainly tobacco jobbers	91	0	100	70

Throughout the months of the test, Daisy attained the following unit share[1] levels:

Region	*Sept.*	*Oct.*	*Nov.*	*Dec.*
Memphis/Seattle	.75%	3.0%	3.8%	4.1%
Dayton/Milwaukee	1.7	3.0	2.3	1.8

[1]The unit share data that follow are based on the *total* blade markets in the DMAs, not on the markets for women's products alone.

Daisy's product management team noted that, if Daisy could attain a 4.1% share nationally as it did in the Memphis/Seattle markets, it would be SRD's fourth best-selling blade, just behind Trac II 5's, Trac II 9's, and Super Stainless Steel 5's.

Since Flicker was currently the leading shaving product for women, Dwyer and his associates were extremely interested in Daisy's performance in relation to Flicker. In the drug and food stores which SRD monitored, distribution of the two products was as follows:

Region/Product	Aug.	Sept.	Oct.	Nov.	Dec.
High Advertising					
Drug					
Memphis					
Daisy	32%	47%	55%	63%	68%
Flicker	49	46	44	47	53
Seattle					
Daisy	17	22	43	48	52
Flicker	88	82	80	75	70
Food					
Memphis					
Daisy	—	—	42	38	50
Flicker	21	20	19	19	25
Seattle					
Daisy	—	11	37	37	31
Flicker	49	53	46	63	67
Low Advertising					
Drug					
Dayton					
Daisy	33	53	87	93	93
Flicker	78	83	80	87	87
Milwaukee					
Daisy	21	92	92	92	92
Flicker	95	98	100	92	92
Food					
Dayton					
Daisy	—	21	21	17	18
Flicker	49	53	57	50	50
Milwaukee					
Daisy	10	41	45	48	45
Flicker	61	62	64	62	64

In addition to showing that Daisy was achieving high levels of distribution, the test market results indicated that, on a unit basis, Daisy outsold Flicker by the following ratios:

Distributor	Memphis/ Seattle	Dayton/ Milwaukee
Food	4.2 to 1	1.5 to 1
Drug	3.4 to 1	1.2 to 1

Moreover, when Daisy and Flicker were promoted simultaneously, Daisy invariably outsold Flicker by a substantial margin. For example, a leading discount chain in Milwaukee promoted both products in October. During this period, Daisy's sales per store were 402 packages, whereas Flicker's were 231 packages. In November and December, when neither product was promoted, Daisy's and Flicker's per-store sales for this account were

Month	Daisy	Flicker
November	146	76
December	145	65

Dwyer's group felt Daisy's sales were especially impressive since Daisy had been on the market only six months whereas Flicker had been on the market two years. Dwyer thought that Daisy's sampling program had probably contributed substantially to the successful sales. The test results indicated that at least one of every three sample recipients later purchased a Daisy shaver.

The chief problems the test market had revealed centered on the merchandising vehicles. It was extremely difficult, for example, to keep them stocked adequately, and when they became stocked out, many retailers threw them away. Moreover, some retailers did not use the top card on the Daisy counter carousel either because it had been lost in original packing or because they thought it made the display too high. Some cosmeticians (i.e., saleswomen, usually in drugstores and mass merchandise outlets) felt that the Daisy floor boutique was not very feminine and they took it down. Particularly during the Christmas season, when retailers needed space for Christmas displays, many Daisy displays were removed, especially in food stores. Several retailers said that neither the boutique nor the carousel was durable, and they doubted that the vehicles would last as permanent display systems. Many felt that the boutique had too much open space and that it should be redesigned to hold larger quantities. In the first six months of the test market, SRD had sold 210 floor boutiques, 274 counter carousels, and 68 shelf extenders.

As a result of these complaints, Daisy's display vehicles were redesigned and two new ones were created. The counter carousel, which had consisted originally of four tiers, each of which contained 9 packages, was converted to a three-tier, 12-packages-per-tier display. This vehicle was considered most appropriate for drug wholesalers, some drug chains, some toiletry merchandisers, and some tobacco jobbers. The floor boutique, which consisted originally of six tiers, each of which held 12 packages, was converted to a five-tier display with each tier holding 18 packages. It was thought that products in this vehicle would be sold primarily to food chains, some drug chains, some toiletry merchandisers, and food wholesalers. Daisy's product management team thought that ideally the boutique would be located near the L'eggs pantyhose boutique or in the feminine care section in health and beauty aids departments.

Two new display vehicles, the Omni display and cut case displays were designed primarily for discount chains. The Omni was a six-tier display, each tier of which contained 30 packages. The cut case display was simply a cardboard carton in which 72 packages were shipped. Directions on the top and sides of the carton indicated how it should be cut open so that it could be used as a display vehicle. Finally, for toiletry merchandisers and tobacco jobbers who called on small accounts, the Adapta display was created. This unit contained 12 Daisy packages, and it could be fastened to pegboard, clamped to a shelf, or hooked onto any other display vehicle SRD would need for the national program. It was essentially a more versatile version of, and a replacement for, the shelf extender used in the test market. The unit cost, including freight, of each display vehicle was as follows:

Carousel	*$ 4.50*
Boutique	*17.00*
Omni	*28.60*
Adapta	*2.60*
Cut case	*1.40*

See Exhibit 3 for SRD accounts by headquarters and number of retail outlets.

The test market had also revealed that, while consumer "pick-up" of Daisy was strong, no permanent "home" had been established for the brand. Exactly how SRD could establish Daisy in the health and beauty aids sections of retail outlets was still a matter of much discussion. Dwyer noted that Towne-Oller, an organization that measured movement of about 6,100 items from warehouses into retail outlets, had reported that in 1974 U.S. blade and razor sales in a representative sample of food stores had totaled $29,063,074. If Daisy could capture a 4.1% unit share of this market, its dollar sales in food stores would be

$1,598,470, and it would rank 42 on the Towne-Oller list, behind such blade items as Trac II 5's (8) and Trac II 9's (12). It would also generate more dollars than all individual sizes of body talcs, hand lotions, and all leading depilatories.

Since the conversion rate of Daisy's sample recipients had been exceptionally high during the test markets, Dwyer felt that widespread sampling would be an important part of Daisy's national launch. He was "fairly certain" that product managers in Gillette's Personal Care Division were interested in a joint promotion of Daisy and Earthborn Shampoo, a "natural scent" shampoo which was considered very strong among women in the 18 to 34 age group. Introduced nationally in May 1974, Earthborn had captured a substantial share of the market and was then the fourth best-selling shampoo on the market. It was distributed through 75% of the food stores and 80% of the drugstores in the United States. Its advertising budget for 1975 was $9,700,000. Under the program currently being discussed, the Personal Care Division would pay SRD 17¢ per shaver, and a 10¢ in-pack coupon to be applied to the purchase of a regular Daisy package would be included. It was thought approximately 6 million shavers would be distributed through this program. Dwyer was also considering distributing 2 to 3 million samples via the theater sampling program, 1 million through the college Superbox program, and 500,000 to 750,000 through the mail. Moreover, he was discussing a tie-in promotion whereby 1 to 2 million Daisy shavers would be distributed in conjunction with L'eggs pantyhose.

FINANCIAL IMPLICATIONS

The task force was sure that Daisy would cannibalize sales of Lady Sure Touch, and the test market proved that this did, in fact, occur. It was not a matter of serious concern, however, because SRD was in the process of phasing out Lady Sure Touch. The group was concerned, however, about Daisy's effect on Lady Trac II. The test alleviated these concerns because it indicated that Daisy hardly affected Lady Trac II at all. It appeared that most of Daisy's customers were drawn from competitors or from women who normally shaved with their husband's used blades. Even if Daisy did cannibalize Lady Trac II's sales somewhat, its estimated profitability was greater than that of Lady Trac II.

The controller had calculated Daisy's cost per sample to be about 17¢ and its cost per package to be 33.8¢. He thought that the full selling price before any promotional offers would be 66¢ per package. An additional $350,000 would be required for capital tooling for the national launch.

CONCLUSION

As Dwyer and his associates reviewed Daisy's performance during the first six months of the test market, they were quite pleased with the results. They were anxious to get the national launch underway quickly so that Daisy would be well established in time for the busy summer selling season. In planning the national rollout, they first had to determine exactly what their sales objectives would be. Next, they had to decide what mixture of samples, advertising, and trade terms would most likely guarantee that they meet their objective. Finally, they had to estimate the probable demand for each of the different types of merchandising vehicles, and they had to formulate a plan whereby the sales force would be more successful than they were during the test market in getting retailers to keep the displays well stocked.

Exhibit 1
"Daisy" (E)

Sample Daisy Advertisement: Magazine

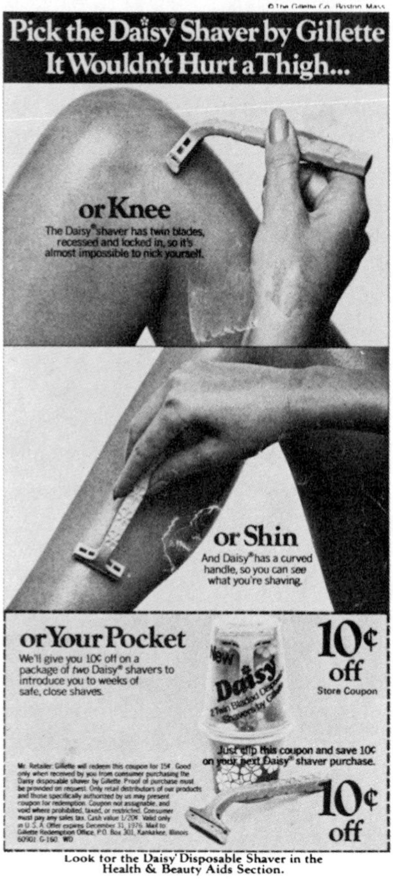

TV Storyboard

The Daisy Shaver by Gillette

"Wouldn't Hurt A Thigh" Commercial

ANNCR (VO): Introducing Daisy by Gillette.

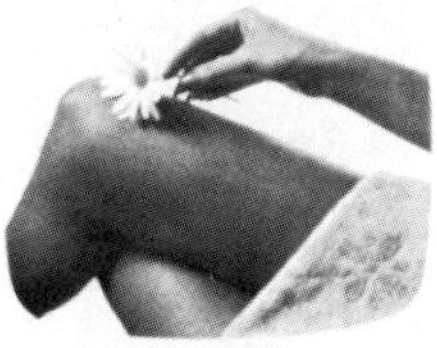

The new woman's shaver that's curved.

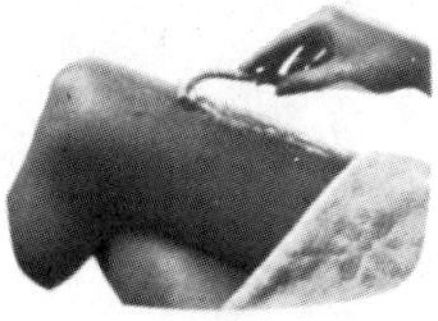

so it wouldn't hurt a thigh.

Or ankle.

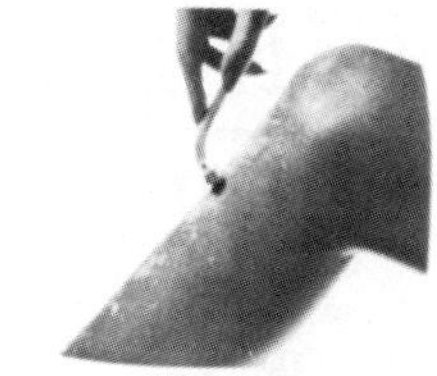

Or shin.

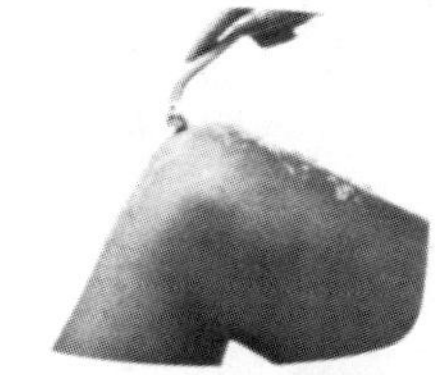

Or knee.

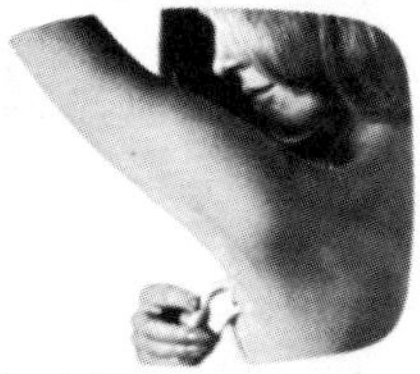

Or underarm.

The Daisy has twin blades, recessed and permanently locked in at a safe angle.

so you won't hurt yourself.

Then after weeks of close, safe shaving it's disposable. Throw it away and pick the other Daisy.

Two for only $1.10.

The Daisy Shaver. It wouldn't hurt a thigh.

Exhibit 1, continued

Newspaper

Exhibit 2

"Daisy" (E)

The Daisy Advertising Programs: Media Plan Summary
(six months)

Low-Expenditure Cities: Dayton/Milwaukee — *Equivalent National Cost: $1,750,000*

Television

A. Network prime
   1. Nine weeks of network prime time beginning in September 1974
   2. Impact: Averaging 44 GPRs[1] per week
   3. Frequency: Equivalent to 3 commercials per week
   4. Scheduling: Shows such as

ABC "Sunday Night Movie"	NBC "Emergency"
ABC "Tuesday Night Movie"	NBC "Friday Night Movie"
ABC "Marcus Welby"	NBC "Adam-12"
NBC "Sunday Night Movie"	NBC "Police Story"
NBC "Sanford and Son"	

B. Late fringe
   1. Duration: 14 weeks of late-fringe TV beginning in September 1974
   2. Impact: Averaging 33 GRPs per week
   3. Frequency: Equivalent to 4 commercials per week
   4. Scheduling: Shows like
      ABC "Wide World of Entertainment"
      CBS "Late Movie"
      NBC "Tonight Show"

Print

A. Newspapers
   Sunday supplements
   4-color advertisements
   10¢ in-store coupon adv.

B. Magazines
   4-color advertisements in
   Woman's Day
   McCall's
   Family Circle
   Ladies' Home Journal
   2–3 insertions per month

[1] A rating point is the percentage of TV or radio households which a station reaches with a program. The term "gross rating point" refers to the number of rating points a program bearing a commercial has on each station in an area, multiplied by the number of times it is run within a specified period, such as a week.

Exhibit 2, continued

High-Expenditure Cities: Memphis/Seattle	*Equivalent National Cost: $2,750,000*

Television
A. Network prime
 1. Duration: Twelve weeks of network prime time beginning in September 1974
 2. Impact: Averaging 66 GRPs per week
 3. Frequency: Equivalent to 4 commercials per week, total of 48 commercials
 4. Scheduling: Shows such as
  ABC "Sunday Night Movie"
  ABC "Tuesday Night Movie"
  ABC "Marcus Welby"
  NBC "Sunday Night Movie"
  NBC "Sanford and Son"
  NBC "Emergency"
  NBC "Friday Night Movie"
  NBC "Adam-12"
  NBC "Police Story"
B. Late fringe (after 11:30–10:30 Central)
 1. Duration: 22 weeks of late-fringe TV beginning in September 1974
 2. Impact: Averaging 40 GRPs per week
 3. Frequency: Equivalent to 5 commercials per week, total of 110 commercials
 4. Scheduling: Shows such as
  ABC "Wide World of Entertainment"
  CBS "Late Movie"
  NBC "Tonight Show"

Print
A. Newspapers
 Sunday supplements
 4-color advertisements
 10¢ in-store coupon adv.
B. Magazines
 4-color advertisements in
  Women's Day
  McCall's
  Family Circle
  Ladies' Home Journal
 2–3 insertions per month

Exhibit 3
"Daisy" (E)

SRD Customers and Approximate Number of Retail Outlets Serviced by Each

Customers	*No. of Headquarter Accounts*	*Approximate No. of Retail Outlets*
Drug chains	760	8,700
Food chains	230	17,100
Discount chains	510	8,200
Toiletry merchandise	370	100,700
Drug wholesalers	430	64,300
Food wholesalers	470	99,100
Miscellaneous other wholesalers	850	177,900
Total	3,620	476,000

L'eggs Products, Inc. (B)

Near the end of 1972, L'eggs Products, Inc.,[1] a subsidiary of the Hanes Corporation, had achieved distribution for its line of L'eggs branded hosiery products in over 75% of the United States. In looking forward to achieving fully national distribution late in 1973, Jack Ward, group product manager for L'eggs, had begun to plan for the product's first national promotion campaign which was scheduled for the fall 1973 selling season. Four alternative promotions involving different combinations of cents-off price discounting and special packaging were being considered. Because the national promotion would have to meet criteria of acceptability imposed by differing levels of market development, differing levels of L'eggs market penetration, and increasing levels of competitive activity, the choice among the four possibilities was not an easy one. Furthermore, the promotion finally selected would have to be implemented in a way that encouraged the support of drug and grocery chains. Finally, the promotion would have to encourage the desired balance of trial and repurchase behaviors among consumers.

The alternatives were a 25¢ coupon which would be mailed to prospective user households and redeemed for a discount at the time of purchase of one pair of pantyhose, a 25¢ price-off twin-pack, a 40¢-off twin-pack, and a 20¢-off single-pack. The last three promotions would be implemented in point-of-purchase displays placed in high-foot-traffic locations in drugstores and supermarkets. Although Ward had gained considerable experience by managing the promotions of L'eggs products as they were rolled out into individual new market territories, he had very few objective bases for judging between the alternatives for the planned national promotion.

 This case was prepared by Harvey Singer under the supervision of F. Stewart DeBruicker.

[1]Whenever the 20¢ single-pack promotion was implemented, field labor was required to change all existing L'eggs packs in the store to 20¢ off also to comply with fair trade laws. This was to be done by inserting flags specifying 20¢ off into all existing packs. For the other alternatives, the price-off promotional twin-packs could coexist in the stores with regular-priced single-packs without violating fair trade (because different quantity packages were involved). Thus, no field labor or flags were necessary for the twin-pack alternatives or for the 25¢ mailed coupon.

In choosing these alternatives to be tested, the product group had reasoned as follows about their likely effects: the 40¢ twin-pack probably would achieve the objective of loading the consumer in high L'eggs penetration areas best (for her next pair, the consumer would *have* the second pair of L'eggs in the twin-pack already and would have no need to go out and purchase, perhaps, a competitive brand). More product use and experience with the two pairs rather than one would, it was hoped, predispose the consumer more to purchase L'eggs again the next time she did need hosiery. However, Ward thought that the twin-pack might not be effective in low L'eggs penetration areas because with low trial and low market share in these areas, sufficient numbers of consumers may not purchase the twin-pack often enough to make the promotion effective. Besides, the objective here was to increase trial and the twin-pack might inhibit trial—the consumer, not a L'eggs user anyway, might balk at having to purchase two pairs to try L'eggs.

The 25¢-off twin-pack would presumably produce the same behavior against those objectives and would improve unit contributions considerably. The question in Ward's mind was whether the offer would be effective enough—whether 25¢ off on two pairs would induce sufficient incremental purchases to produce any results at all.

The mailed coupon worth 25¢ off on one pair was included as an alternative to be tested for comparative effectiveness, even though the brand group really wanted the fall promotion vehicle to be an in-store offer. The 25¢ mailed coupon had been reasonably effective when used in many rollout markets during introduction and was expected to aid in inducing trial among nonusers because it was to be mailed to all homes (thus coming to the attention of women who were nonusers, whereas these women may not have noted an in-store offer because they would not look for, or at, a L'eggs display). The coupon was not expected to be effective in inducing consumer loading or repurchase, however, because it could only be used to purchase one pair.

The 20¢ single-pack seemed to be somewhat effective against both objectives. In low-penetration areas, consumer takeaway for the promotion (the number of consumers purchasing) would presumably be higher because the new trier would not be forced to purchase two pairs. So the single-pack was assumed more effective in raising trial rates. In high-penetration areas, there was certainly nothing to prevent the consumer from buying two or more single packs, so the objective of consumer loading and thus raising repeat rates might just be satisfied. On the other hand, there was nothing to encourage the consumer (or force the consumer, as was the case of the twin-pack) to purchase more than one pair—and so the single-pack was judged somewhat less effective against consumer loading and increasing the total *number of pairs* purchased under the promotion. In addition, the single-pack was significantly more expensive to implement.

With considerable uncertainty, then, about the effectiveness of each of the alternatives against each of the objectives in each type of market, Ward turned to the L'eggs marketing research group to test the alternatives. It was hoped that these tests would provide information useful in resolving the problem.

MARKET RESEARCH AT L'EGGS

Just as L'eggs Products, Inc., differed considerably from the rest of the hosiery industry in its marketing and distribution strategies, it also took a radically different approach to marketing research. The original research policy adopted in 1970 had been continued and strengthened by Paul Fulton, L'eggs' president, and Bob Odear, L'eggs' marketing vice president. This policy, in effect, said that "any marketing decision, whether major or minor, must have justification based on marketing research data." Evidence that that policy was in effect could be taken from the marketing research budgets. From the original $400,000 that was spent through 1970 on consumer and channel research, funding had grown to include over $1 million for the development of L'eggs' on-line computer system for marketing information and sales tracking. In addition, over 1% of sales was spent for ongoing product and market research activity each year—an amount expected to exceed $1 million in 1973. This was considered very high for a company of L'eggs' size and was even more dramatic in comparison with the traditional hosiery industry approach to research which was described by Ward as, ". . . just have salesmen find out what the trade buyer wants."

The director of marketing research at L'eggs, Jerry Clawson, had a staff of two consumer research managers and two sales research managers working under him. Exhibit 1 describes the organization of the marketing and marketing research groups at L'eggs in the summer of 1973. The sales research group did all the analysis of the data supplied by the on-line sales tracking system.

The sales research managers' specific duties included

1. Routine sales tracking using the internal marketing information system.
2. Competitive sales tracking using syndicated Nielsen and MRCA data.
3. Forecasting using Nielsen, MRCA, and L'eggs' own data.
4. Tracking the sales effects of special advertising and promotional tests.

For consumer behavior research, the usual practice was to have the L'eggs market research personnel do all planning and research design themselves and make use of the advertising agency or independent outside suppliers to execute the research and make a preliminary analysis; then the consumer research analysts did their own data analysis and prepared conclusions for brand management.

The consumer researchers' specific duties included

1. Product tests—the company ran roughly ten major performance tests for each year on existing and new products.
2. Advertising research—concept tests, "ad labs," testing consumers for quantitative and qualitative impact of recognition and recall of advertising.
3. Consumer surveys—to measure cannibalization and proportions of sales purchased "on deal" versus regular price in a market.
4. "ATU" studies—the group ran frequent studies titled "Attitude, Trial, and Usage" in L'eggs markets to develop measures of brand awareness, product satisfaction, trial, and repeat rates.

The market research group had access to many techniques and data sources for information to support marketing decisions: product tests, concept tests, focus group interviews, Nielsen store audits, consumer surveys, trade research, and sales tracking data from L'eggs' own on-line marketing information system. But despite the large budget allocation and many sources of information the market research function at L'eggs had to cope with some severe problems in carrying out meaningful research. Primary among these was the short and complicated history of hosiery products in food and drug channels. Research projects were disrupted frequently by such events as the introduction of new product extensions, new advertising and promotion activities, and competitors' product introductions and promotions. Competitive events in markets could of course not be controlled.

THE MARKET TESTS

Using procedures developed as the research group had gained experience with the L'eggs product information system, Clawson developed a strategy for testing the four promotion alternatives. Each of the promotions would be implemented in a carefully chosen test market, and the results of each test market would be compared with similar data observed in an equally carefully selected control market. Sales data would be obtained from the on-line product information system, and consumer attitude and behavior data would be obtained via special consumer surveys to be conducted in each of the test markets.

Specially made up promotion packs in shipper displays were put into stores in the test markets as follows:

> Denver—20¢ single-pack (in Denver, flags were also put into regular boutique packs)[1]
> Syracuse—40¢ twin-pack
> Columbus—25¢ twin-pack

In the fourth test market, Cincinnati, coupons worth 25¢ off one pack were mailed to 50% of the households. The control market, which received no cents-off promotion and only normal L'eggs advertising, was Boise/Twin Falls/Pocatello (hereafter referred to as Boise). The testing period was set at four weeks, the same time period to be used for the impending fall promotion. In addition to the special packages and retail prices, each promotion was supported by point-of-sale and local newspaper advertising to simulate the national support program. No special attention was given to adusting the use of spot TV advertising, and, of course, it was impossible to simulate the effects of network TV advertising.

In earlier market tests, the technique used most often to evaluate sales performance in test markets was an experimental design which separated markets into test markets, which received the "treatments" consisting of different strategies or alternatives), and control markets, which were given no such treatment. Control markets were chosen to approximate closely the behavior of test markets before the treatments were given. Test market sales were compared with control market sales before, during, and after the testing period. This technique had been used with satisfactory results, but Jerry Clawson commented that good control markets were becoming harder to identify and that he was actively searching for better research methods.

In general, Clawson preferred control markets that had high measures of statistical correlation in pretest sales trends with the test markets, that roughly matched the test markets on the length of time L'eggs had been in distribution, that had minimal exogenous activities due to competitors' and L'eggs' other marketing developments, and that were roughly equivalent in seasonality effects of sales. For this test, the Boise ADI was the only candidate that met Clawson's criteria.

At weekly intervals, sales results in each test market were to be obtained from the online information system. For each test market, the research group would measure both absolute sales results and the variance or change in sales results over time from a "norm." This norm was defined as the expected sales in the test market if the test market had behaved in relation to the control market as it had before the alternatives were introduced. For example, if Denver sales were uniformly 1.45 times Boise sales before the test, then the Denver norm over the test period would be 1.45 times actual Boise results. Of course, the product group hoped for sustained sales increases over the expected norm in the winning test market or at least a sales increase sufficient to cover increased costs of the promotion.

Concurrent with sales tracking in each of the test markets, surveys were to be undertaken in each test market to determine consumer reactions and response to the promotional alternatives. The surveys would be used to break the sales figures down into estimates of new trials versus repurchases, which sales figures alone would not reveal. Given these two kinds of data, the brand group could then project test market results onto the national population and determine which promotion strategy best met the objectives of a national promotion program. Jerry Clawson sent a proposal to Jack Ward and to Bob Odear, L'eggs marketing vice president, which described the consumer survey project that the Market Research Department proposed to undertake. That proposal is included as Exhibit 2.

As in previous promotional tests, the market research group expected a pattern in each test market as follows. First, a period of sales increase, designated the "bump" period, was expected in the weeks immediately following introduction of the promotion. This would represent consumers purchasing their normal amount of purchases plus increased purchasing due to the promotion. Then, there would be several weeks of decreased purchases relative to the norm, designated the "loading" period, which would come about because regular purchasers had presumably "loaded up" on promotional packs during the bump period and would have no need to make their regular purchases. After the bump and loading periods, a period of sustained increase was hoped for which would be due to regular purchasers, new triers, and new repeaters making regular purchases after the promotion ended.

Clawson's proposal was accepted and the test market program was implemented during the spring of 1973.

Market Test Results: Sales Analysis[2]

The actual sales results from the market tests led the Sales Research group to conclude that each of the four promotions was somewhat effective in generating a short-term sales increase but that none of the alternatives was likely to result in significant long-term sales increases. They arrived at these conclusions by comparing sales results during and after the test in each test market with the expected norms for each market, derived from Boise control market sales. Results of the Syracuse test are presented below. Comparisons for each market were made in the same manner.

[2]Reported sales volume does not equal consumer (retail) sales exactly but is rather a total of retail sales plus new inventory shipped into stores—this method of reporting was common at L'eggs and usually served as a reliable surrogate measure of consumer sales. Sales units are in dozens of pairs.

Syracuse: two for 40¢ price off

	Units (dozens)	*Cumulative*
1. Increase (bump) period: Weeks 1–4		
Expected sales	10,000	10,000
Actual sales	19,000	19,000
Increase	9,000	9,000
% of increase	90%	90%
2. Loading period: Weeks 5–6		
Expected sales	5,000	15,000
Actual sales	4,000	23,000
Increase (decrease)	(1,000)	8,000
% of increase (decrease)	(20%)	53%
3. Postpromotion period: Weeks 7–16		
Expected sales	23,000	38,000
Actual sales	21,850	44,850
Increase (decrease)	(1,150)	6,850
% of increase (decrease)	(5%)	18%

In analyzing the unit sales for the four promotions, the sales research group noted that the sales increases or decreases might not be directly comparable between markets because of differing time periods for the bump and loading effects in each market. With this warning, they presented the following table summarizing the effects of the four alternatives:

Promotion	*2 for 40¢ Off*	*20¢ Price Off*	*2 for 25¢ Off*	*25¢ Coupon*
Market	Syracuse	Denver	Columbus	Cincinnati
Initial bump, increased sales	90%	30%	82%	3%
Loading period, decreased sales	−20%	−10%	−33%	−15%
Total cumulative short-term sales effect	53%	20%	−12%	−6%
Cumulative long-term sales effect	18% dropping	7% dropping	−12%	−6%
Number of weeks of promotional effect				
Bump	4	6	3	8
Loading	2	2	13	8
Long term	10	8	0	0
Total	16	16	16	16

Based on these findings, the sales research group concluded that

> The 2 for 40¢-off promotion (Syracuse) was the most effective, with a net short-term cumulative increase in sales of 53% felt over 6 weeks. The 20¢ price-off promotion (Denver) was the second most effective, with a net cumulative short-term increase of 20% felt over 8 weeks.
>
> The 2 for 25¢ price-off promotion (Columbus) had as high an initial increase in sales as the 2 for 40¢ price-off, but the market has not recovered from the loading period for 13 weeks afterward. Ten weeks after the start of the promotion, sales had returned to within the expected range of the norm. However, for the 6 weeks following that, the L'eggs sales group has reduced their sales calls to Columbus stores and therefore the possibility of ascertaining the exact loading period, all other things being equal, has been obscured.
>
> The 25¢-coupon promotion (Cincinnati) was the least effective promotion with a 3% short-term increase in sales felt over 8 weeks. From the eighth week forward, sales have fluctuated (which may be partially due to a wide swing in number of sales calls by the L'eggs sales personnel). The net effect has been an overall 6% cumulative decrease in sales over 16 weeks.

Market Test Results: Consumer Survey Research

The consumer survey research was supervised by the Market Research Department at the L'eggs advertising agency, Dancer-Fitzgerald-Sample (DFS) and carried out by Burke Marketing Research, Inc., an independent research company. After receiving the data from Burke, DFS personnel examined it and sent their report to the L'eggs consumer research group. Following that, L'eggs consumer research personnel examined the data and presented Mr. Ward with a report of their findings. Excerpts from the DFS report are included in Exhibit 3.

The L'eggs market research group interpreted the findings from the survey data. They reported that

The 25¢ coupon and 40¢ twin-pack created more awareness (respondents who remembered the promotion) among competitive brand users than did either of the alternatives. Promotional awareness among L'eggs' usual branders was highest for the coupon and lowest for the 25¢ twin-pack. The 25¢ coupon was most successful in obtaining involvement—i.e., purchase of L'eggs on promotion—among competitive branders. The price-offs did not show great differences, but the 25¢ twin-pack was the weakest. The 20¢ single-pack involved the greatest percentage of L'eggs usual branders. [These data are summarized in Exhibit 4.]

The promotions having the greatest retail value produced the greatest immediate sales effect. Very high percentages of those sales, however, were to customers who already considered L'eggs their usual brand. The coupon was the only one of the 4 promotions which sold more goods in total to competitive usual branders than to L'eggs usual branders—and it sold about as many total pairs, per thousand women exposed, as did the 25¢ twin-pack.

The following table illustrates this:

Pairs of L'eggs sold on promotion (per thousand wearers exposed to promotion)

	40¢ Twin		*20¢ Single*		*25¢ Twin*		*25¢ Coupon*	
Wearers	*No.*	*%*	*No.*	*%*	*No.*	*%*	*No.*	*%*
All respondents	338	100	382	100	201	100	199	100
L'eggs usual branders	238	70	322	84	151	75	63	32
Competitive usual branders	100	30	60	16	50	25	136	68

The 25¢ coupon was most successful in generating first-time trial among competitive usual branders. There was little difference among the price-offs on that measure, with the 20¢ single-pack having whatever edge did exist, as shown below:

Promotion purchase was the first time L'eggs ever purchased

	40¢ Twin	*20¢ Single*	*25¢ Twin*	*25¢ Coupon*
% of competitive usual branders	1%	2%	1%	6%

The 25¢ coupon was the most successful of the 4 promotions tested in involving numbers of competitive branders, inducing purchase by them, and obtaining first-time trial. It minimized the number of pairs sold on promotion to women who already considered L'eggs their usual brand. The price-off promotions generally produced more activity among L'eggs usual branders than among users of competitive brands. The 20¢ single-pack was most popular with L'eggs women. While the 40¢ twin-pack was also heavily weighted toward L'eggs users, it sold proportionally more units to competitive users than did the 20¢-off one promotion. The 25¢ twin-pack was the weakest promotion tested.

It is recommended that the 25¢ coupon be considered the most viable of the promotions tested for use in an *offensive* strategy designed to obtain involvement of competitive usual branders while holding to a minimum the promotional sale of L'eggs to women who already consider it their usual brand. The 20¢ single-pack and 40¢ twin-pack are recommended as defensive promotions when the strategy is to load L'eggs customers with product and have them less responsive to competitive promotions. It is recommended that the 25¢ twin-pack be dropped from further consideration at this time.

Ward requested the market research group to estimate how many of the pairs sold on promotion in each instance would not have been sold if there had been no promotions. Clawson's group attempted to determine this from the survey data. They reported that

None of these attempts produced results which seemed judgmentally reasonable. The

> basic difficulty is in obtaining a sound measure of the long-term effects of loading. For example, it is quite easy to see that many L'eggs usual branders loaded up on L'eggs when they saw the price-off promotions, and thereby purchased considerably more pairs than they otherwise would have during that period. But the question of how that affects the total number of pairs they buy over a longer period of time remains unanswerable from this particular research. Sales tracking of these promotion markets is being done, and hopefully will provide insight into this question.

The market research group had included questions in the survey designed to enable them to gauge switching from competitive brands to L'eggs in the consumer interviews, but found that "in these surveys, participation in the promotions by competitive usual branders was too low to provide usable basis for switching analyses."

CONFLICTING RESULTS

Given the results from the sales analysis and the consumer research in the test markets, Ward was still not sure of the implications of the marketing research for his decision. First, the results obtained seemed to disprove some of the preresearch reasoning (i.e., that the 20¢ single-pack would be more effective in inducing trial or purchase among competitive users, that the 40¢ twin-pack would be a more effective consumer loading vehicle among L'eggs usual branders, that the 25¢ coupon would not have as high an impact on either objective as the in-store alternatives, and that the winning alternative, at least, would generate significant long-term volume after the promotion).

In addition, some of the results of the consumer research were in direct conflict with the results of the sales tracking analysis. The most glaring example of this conflict was the 25¢ coupon's apparent effectiveness in the consumer survey versus its poor performance in the sales analysis.

Ward tried to sort out the effects of the research findings upon his analysis of each alternative. The 25¢ twin-pack might be dropped from consideration because of its poor showing on both tests (subject to perhaps a quick re-examination to see if the apparent poor showing was more than compensated for by its minimum margin loss, thereby looking more attractive on a cost-effectiveness basis).

The 25¢ coupon's poor showing in actual sales results might be due partially to the differences in test versus control markets. In the consumer research it received top awareness scores, top impact on number of competitive branders it influenced, fair results in terms of the number of pairs purchased, and the best effect on inducing new trial.

The real conflict came in evaluating the 40¢ twin-pack and 20¢ single-pack alternatives. Both seemed to be reasonably strong promotions in generating incremental sales through trial by nonusers and loading among users. The 20¢ single-pack involved more total people in the promotion. The sales analysis showed that it did seem to increase the permanent franchise slightly. Many users did indeed buy two or more promotion packs, so that alternative accomplished the loading objectives, in part. However the results showed that the 20¢ single-pack seemed to be even more effective against L'eggs users than the 40¢ twin-pack. Given that it would be the most expensive promotion to implement and in terms of reducing margins by 20¢ on every purchase, not only incremental purchases, he wondered whether to recommend its implementation.

The 40¢ twin-pack alternative also appeared to be a reasonably strong promotion. It involved L'eggs users heavily and sold more pairs to each L'eggs user who did purchase under promotion, thus accomplishing the loading objective. By substituting the second incremental pair in the pack for a possible other brand purchase, it would help to ensure users being repeaters. The sales tracking analysis confirmed that the twin-pack was most effective in terms of total actual sales gains. The alternative, however, was not quite as effective as the single-pack in generating purchase among numbers of competitive users (although it loaded them more when they did purchase) and in generating new trial.

More Tests

Due to new style introductions, the promotion was not needed immediately. Therefore, Ward made the decision to do some further testing. He was especially concerned about learning the effects of the 40¢ twin-pack and the 20¢ single-pack more clearly, since they were the two in-store promotions which had given the best indication of producing sustained sales increases. However, since the two differed considerably in costs and problems to implement, he wished to determine more clearly which one gave better results, and he wanted to ensure that the better alternative did in fact build long-run volume.

As a means of determining this information, he called on the market research group to re-test these two alternatives in several additional markets and to perform sales tracking analyses on the results. The methodology was to be the same as in the original market tests (each promotion to run for 4 weeks with ad and point-of-sale support), except that only the 40¢ twin-pack and the 20¢ single-pack alternatives were tested. Each of these was to be tested in high- and low-penetration markets. Sales results were to be measured but no consumer awareness surveys were planned for the retest.

The 40¢ twin-pack promotion was tested in Salt Lake City, Santa Barbara, Las Vegas, and Salinas, and the results were analyzed each week for 20 weeks after the start of the promotion. The respective control markets were Fresno, Green Bay, and Colorado Springs. The pre-test sales correlation between each pair of promotion and control markets was .98.

The 20¢ single-pack promotion was tested in Houston (low penetration) and Albany (high penetration). Again, sales tracking analysis was done each week for 20 weeks. The Dallas market was matched as a control market against Houston, and Davenport was matched as a control market against Albany.

Retest Results: 40¢ Twin-Pack

Figures for all four test markets in which the twin-pack was placed were reported in aggregate, rather than individually. The Market Research Group summarized their findings:

> During the first 5 weeks of the promotion, L'eggs sales increased 105% in these markets. During the next 5 weeks, it appears that only 10% of the sales gained in the first 5 weeks were lost because of consumer loading. During the most recent 10 weeks, L'eggs sales have increased relative to the control markets by 20%. This indicates that the promotion had a long-term positive effect on L'eggs sales in these markets.
>
> It appears that the promotion generated long-term incremental volume in these markets and increased the size of the L'eggs franchise. Long-term incremental cumulative volume has increased by 30% and is holding at that level.

Although test results were not broken out by individual markets, the market research group informed Ward that the 40¢-off twin-pack had apparently performed better in high-penetration areas (Salinas and Las Vegas) than in low-penetration areas (Santa Barbara and Salt Lake).

Retest Results: 20¢ Single-Pack

The market research group analyzed this retest by looking at sales results separately for each of the two markets which received the 20¢ single-pack in the retest. They reported to Ward that

> In Houston, the promotion appears to have generated a sizeable amount of long-term volume. After 23 weeks, L'eggs sales increased 11% relative to the control market—an incremental volume of 5,000 dozen. The 23 weeks following the start of the promotion are grouped into 3 periods:
>
> 1. First 6 weeks—During and immediately following the actual promotion, L'eggs sales increased 38% relative to the control market (increase of 4,200 dozen).
> 2. Next 8 weeks—During this period, L'eggs sales declined 5% (800 dozen) relative to the control market, indicating that 20% (800 divided by 4,200) of L'eggs incremental sales in the promotion period was lost because of the negative effect of consumer loading during the next 8 weeks.
> 3. Final 9 weeks—During this period, L'eggs sales increased 9% (1,600 dozen) relative to the control market. This suggests that the promotion has increased the size of the L'eggs franchise in Houston, although 9 weeks may not be long enough to tell exactly how much it has been increased.
>
> In this market test, no intervening factors on the scale of the sales call pattern switching in the original tests occurred. Within limits, the test proceeded as smoothly as could be expected in a generally volatile marketing environment.

For the Albany market test, the following results were reported:

> For the 16-week period following the start of the 20¢-off promotion in Albany, L'eggs sales increased 4% relative to the control market. The 20¢ single-pack appears to have gained volume for L'eggs for a 10-week period (the large decline during this initial period appears to be a function of the L'eggs Easter packages being placed earlier in the control marker than in Albany). During this 10-week period, L'eggs volume still increased 14% (3,200 dozen) relative to the control market.
>
> During the most recent 6 weeks, L'eggs sales in Albany declined 14% (1,700 dozen) relative to the control. At this time 53% (1,700 divided by 3,200) of the volume gained in the first 10 weeks have been lost due to consumer loading.
>
> We conclude that in Houston, for the 23-week period following the start of the promotion, the promotion appears to have increased L'eggs share of market among L'eggs users during the promotion period and/or attracted new or infrequnt L'eggs buyers. The promotion did not seem *only* to load up L'eggs customers with our goods and thus remove them from the market for awhile.
>
> In Albany, for the 16-week period following the start of the promotion, the 20¢ single-pack also appears to have achieved at least the objective of loading up L'eggs customers with our goods. It is too early to tell if the promotion will generate any incremental long-run volume in this market. If the Houston and Albany tests can be validly compared, it appears that the 20¢-off single-pack alternative performed better in a low penetration area (Houston) than in the high penetration area (Albany).

PAYOUT ANALYSIS ON A NATIONAL BASIS

Despite the fact that these additional tests of the 20¢ single-pack and 40¢ twin-pack alternatives still did not resolve all the issues surrounding the research, Ward knew that he must soon come to a final decision. Since the fall season was rapidly approaching and much work was needed to implement the chosen alternative, he felt that there was no time to perform any more market tests and that the decision would have to be based on analysis of the information he had at that point. As part of that analysis, Ward decided to structure payout projections for the single-pack and twin-pack promotions on a national basis, based on the costs of the alternatives and their assumed effectiveness shown in the market tests performed previously.

Some of the factors were known with relative certainty. Costs of packaging, sales materials, flags, and additional freight for shippers averaged out to 35¢ per dozen for the 20¢ single-pack and 38½¢ per dozen for the 40¢ twin-pack. The 20¢ single-pack would require a temporary labor force to put flags on the existing L'eggs boutiques, and the cost of that would be approximately $270,000. No temporary labor force would be required for the 40¢ twin-pack alternative.

Another factor which Ward could estimate, though with less precision, was the percentage of routine L'eggs purchases at normal prices that would be diverted to promotional-priced merchandise with a resulting loss in gross margin. From the market tests, he believed that 80% and 60%, respectively, of the 20¢ single- and 40¢ twin-pack promotions would represent diverted sales.[3] Since normal sales were running at the rate of about 3 million dozens of pairs over a 20-week period (the short-run payout analysis to be performed was done on the basis of a 20-week period, consistent with the market tests, even though the promotional packs would only be in the stores for 4 weeks), the losses in margin due to diversion could be estimated using these assumptions in the payout calculation.

The hardest factor to estimate was, of course, the effect of the promotion alternatives on incremental business. Based on his first interpretations of the test market results, Ward guessed that incremental sales of about 10% or more could be achieved through either promotion, at least for the 20-week period beginning with the start of the promotion.

Finally, there was the question of to what extent, if any, either promotion would foster incremental sales growth beyond the 20-week period used in the national payout projections. Ward estimated a step increase of 10% under the 20¢ single-pack promotion, but using the Syracuse results from the earlier test market, he assumed no long-term sales increase for the 40¢ twin-pack. He wondered whether other assumptions were better supported by the test market findings.

These assumptions resulted in the national payout projections listed in Exhibit 5. Over the 20-week period used in the near-term analysis, the 40¢ twin-pack appeared to be superior with a net payout of $216,000 versus a net loss of $198,000 for the 20¢ single-pack. The 20¢ single-pack, however, was expected to show a much better long-run payout. There were differences in implementation issues between the two promotions, but those seemed secondary to the question of which promotion met the objectives of the proposed national promotion, and which was likely to show the best return for the funds to be employed.

IMPLEMENTATION OF THE PROMOTIONS

In addition to the possible payouts for each alternative, Ward's decision would also be influenced by the nonquantifiable factors involved for each alternative. For example, there were the problems of trade resistance to promotions in general, and specific trade resistance to devoting additional floor space necessary for the promotional shippers. Ward wanted to choose the alternative which maximized the potential effect of sales and profit

[3] An 80% estimate for the 20¢ single-pack because of some stores not taking the promotion, lost flags, etc., and 60% for the 40¢ twin-pack because single pairs at regular prices would coexist in stores with twin pack promotions, and women who did not want two pairs might still buy a regular pack at normal prices.

gains while minimizing trade resistance, so that the alternative would actually be implemented in as many stores as possible.

A related question was whether L'eggs should advertise the promotion via national and local media. Given some trade resistance, advertising the deal would almost force all retailers to take the promotion, and would ensure more promotional awareness, thus increasing the chances of overall success. On the other hand, arguments could be made for using this advertising time and cost for other purposes and messages and for improving trade relations by giving retailers more flexibility to refuse the promotion. Again, the key seemed to be in choosing an alternative which would be palatable to the trade.

Ward reviewed the earlier implementation arguments. The 20¢ single-pack alternative could conceivably be accomplished solely via flagged boutique packs without the need for shippers and extra store floor space. However, because of the fair trade laws, virtually every pair sold during the promotion would be at reduced price (and reduced margin for the retailer). Thus L'eggs must convince the retailer, perhaps via the use of test market results, that the promotion would lead to significant numbers of increased purchases—or else the retailer would see his total dollar markup eroding. Such persuasion was crucial here, because in low-penetration markets where the 20¢ single-pack had shown the best results, L'eggs wanted *all* retailers to accept the promotion in order to get the increased trial effect and thus long-term sustained volume increases predicted by the test markets.

The 40¢ twin-pack alternative required shippers (and thus extra floor space) to implement. On the other hand, the retailer could not only be shown test market indications of higher volume, but also would be allowed to retain regular single boutique packs at regular prices (and margins) during the promotional period and thus could be shown that purchases made under the promotion were more likely to represent incremental volume rather than substitute volume. Again, the product group was anxious to get full cooperation for the twin-pack alternative. This was especially true in high-penetration areas and stores with heavy L'eggs sales volume, since market testing had shown that the twin-pack was a successful loading vehicle in high-penetration areas.

Finally, he had to consider implementation problems involved should a mixed strategy be chosen—with each alternative being implemented in specific markets, instead of using one national promotion vehicle across all markets. He thought he should give hard consideration to the mixed strategy because the market research studies did in fact seem to show that the 20¢ single-pack might lead to increased trial and some increased sustained volume in low-penetration markets, whereas the 40¢ twin-pack led to loading of customers in high-penetration markets and perhaps some increased sustained volume. Those were important factors when Ward considered the planned introductions of Activ and No Nonsense products into L'eggs markets that fall with a potentially unfavorable effect upon the L'eggs franchise in those markets.

However, implementing two alternatives rather than one posed serious problems, some of which were referred to earlier. Local rather than national network media would have to be used to advertise the promotion, at additional cost. Two sets of point-of-sale materials, packages, and shipper displays complicated production and distribution logistics. The mechanics of persuading retailers (especially national chains) to accept two different promotions would be difficult for L'eggs sales force to implement. Nevertheless, the option of two alternatives must be considered if choosing just one alternative did not seem to meet the promotional objectives in both types of markets—the long-run benefits of going with both might just be sufficient to offset the considerable difficulty and cost of doing so.

With all the information before him, Ward sat down to look once more at the results of the test markets and surveys. He would go through further analysis of the information presented by his market research department, and come to a decision.

Exhibit 1

L'eggs Products, Inc.

Organization Chart

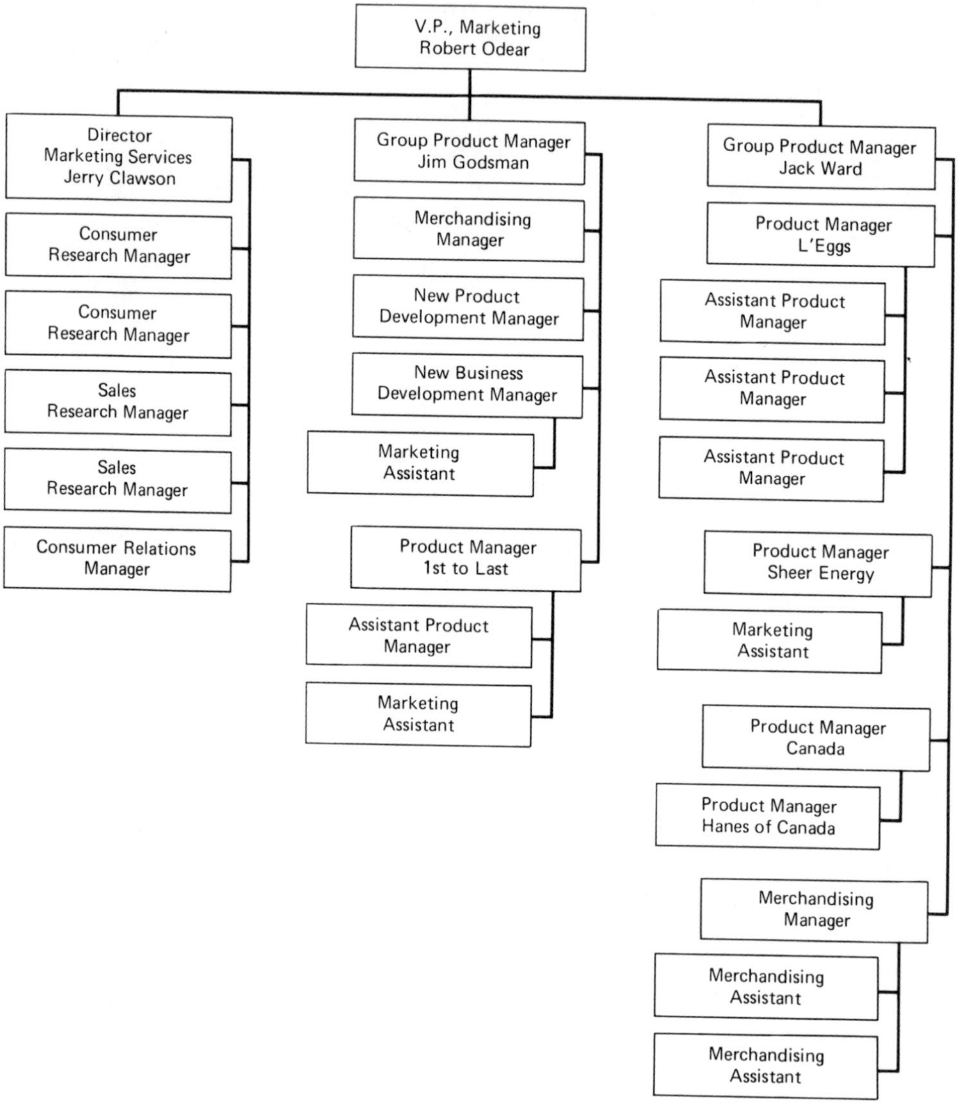

Exhibit 2
L'eggs Products, Inc.
Promotion Research Proposal

TITLE: L'eggs 25¢ Coupon and Price-Off Promotions Evaluation

PURPOSE: To determine the effectiveness of a 25¢ direct-mail coupon and three "price-off" promotions in inducing trial of and conversion to L'eggs among competitive brand users.

BACKGROUND: These are several promotional techniques being tested for possible national use in the fall of 1973. Alternatives to be market tested are a 20¢-off single-unit price pack, twin-pack price pack (buy 2, Save 40¢), twin-pack price pack (Buy 2, Save 25¢), and a 25¢-off one-pack coupon mailed to about 200,000 households. Each alternative will be placed in a different test market. Each test will involve the full pantyhose line. Point-of-purchase and newspaper advertising will support the promotion. The price packs will be on the boutiques for about four weeks, while the coupon mailings will be implemented in three mailing "flights" with approximately one week's time between each flight. Sales tracking will be done to monitor the effect on sales. This project is to help determine the types of consumer reactions which generate the sales.

EXPECTED USE OF RESULTS: Results will be used in helping to decide which, if any, of the promotions would be most promising for national program utilization.

METHODOLOGY: Five weeks after price packs are placed in stores, and five weeks after the second mailing flight of coupons, telephone interviewing will be done among pantyhose users. Data will be collected on usual pantyhose brand, awareness of the L'eggs coupon or price pack promotion, degree of participation in the promotion, any recent switching in usual pantyhose brand, and usual brand before switching.

NUMBER, LOCATION, AND DESCRIPTION OF RESPONDENTS:

	Pantyhose Users in General
Denver (20¢-off single unit)	400
Syracuse (40¢-off 2-pack)	400
Columbus (25¢-off 2-pack)	400
Cincinnati (25¢ mailed coupon)	300

TIMING:

Implementation—As soon as approval given to this proposal and promotional materials made up (approximately six weeks)

Interviewing—Approximately five weeks after implementation

Report—Approximately six weeks after interviews

ESTIMATED COST:

\$10,000—three price pack alternatives
6,000—coupon alternative

Note: This cost includes interviewing and report preparation. It does not include cost of promotional materials or margin loss from the promotional deals.

Submitted by Jerry Clawson

Exhibit 3

L'eggs Products, Inc.

Consumer Survey Research Findings from the Spring 1973 Test Markets—Excerpts from the DFS Report

I. Coupon awareness and purchase—Cincinnati

44% of respondents report awareness (remember receiving the coupon)
16% of respondents purchased under the promotion (redeemed coupon)
25% of coupon redeemers were new L'eggs customers

Respondents'	*Aware (remembered receiving coupon)*	*Purchase (redeemed coupon)*[1]	*Coupon Purchase Was First L'eggs Purchase*
All respondents[2] (sample size = 300)	44%	16%	4%
Respondents who were L'eggs usual branders	68	34	—
Respondents not L'eggs usual branders	40	13	6

[1]The large majority of those who redeemed the coupon (82%) purchased a single pair.
[2]Figures for "all respondents" in both reports should be interpreted as "figures for all respondents who were nonsupport pantyhose wearers."

In reporting results of the 25¢ coupon, all actual figures obtained were doubled to obtain the figures used in the reports. This was because only about half of the households in Cincinnati actually were sent the coupon. Therefore, when figures were obtained from the 300 interviews, they were treated as if those same figures were obtained from a base population of 150. For example, among all 300 consumers interviewed, 22% or 66 reported awareness of the promotion. Since only half the households in Cincinnati received the coupon, the base was cut to an estimated 150 and the percentage was therefore reported as 66/150 or 44%.

II. Price-off deals awareness and purchase—Denver, Syracuse, Columbus

More women responded to the 20¢-off single-pack (Denver) than to the other two promotions.

The 40¢-off twin-pack (Syracuse) ranked second and the 25¢-off twin-pack (Columbus) ranked a poor third.

Respondents	*Denver (20¢ single)*	*Syracuse (40¢ twin)*	*Columbus (25¢ twin)*
All respondents (sample size = 400)	22%	27%	20%
Respondents who were L'eggs usual branders	53	50	43
Respondents not L'eggs usual branders	13	22	14

The largest number of women who purchased L'eggs during the promotion were in Denver (20¢ single). Syracuse (40¢ twin) was second and Columbus (25¢ twin) was third. Promotion buyers were much more likely to be L'eggs regular branders than were non-L'eggs in all cases. In both

Columbus (25¢ twin) and Syracuse (40¢ twin), over 50% of purchasers bought two promotion packs (i.e., four pairs). In Denver, 30% bought a single-pack (pair) and 30% bought two packs (pairs).

	Denver (20¢ single)		*Syracuse (40¢ twin)*		*Columbus (25¢ twin)*	
Respondents	*Bought on Promotion*	*First L'eggs Purchase*	*Bought on Promotion*	*First L'eggs Purchase*	*Bought on Promotion*	*First L'eggs Purchase*
All respondents	13%	2%	10%	1%	6%	1%
Respondents who were L'eggs usual branders	43	—	33	—	23	—
Respondents not L'eggs usual branders	4	2	5	1	2	1

Exhibit 4
L'eggs Products, Inc.

Consumer Survey Results Presented by L'eggs Market Research

Respondents	*40¢ Twin-Pack*	*20¢ Single*	*25¢ Twin-Pack*	*25¢ Coupon*
Promotion awareness (respondents who remembered the promotion)				
All respondents	27%	22%	20%	44%
L'eggs usual branders	50	53	43	68
Competitive usual branders	22	13	14	39
Purchase of L'eggs on promotion				
% respondents purchasing on promotion				
All respondents	10%	13%	6%	16%
L'eggs usual branders	33	43	23	34
Competitive usual branders	5	4	2	13
Average no. pairs purchased by respondents who did purchase				
All respondents	3.4	2.9	3.2	1.2
L'eggs usual branders	4.0	3.4	3.4	1.1
Competitive usual branders	2.4	1.7	2.5	1.3

Exhibit 5

L'eggs Products, Inc.

Comparison of National Payout Projections

Item	*20¢ Single-Pack*	*40¢ Twin-Pack*
(1) Normal sales expected over 20 weeks (dozens of pairs)	3,000,000	3,000,000
(2) Sales increase over 20 weeks (%)	10–11%	10%
(3) Sales increase over 20 weeks (dozens) (line 1 × line 2)	320,000	300,000
(4) Incremental gross margin ($5/dozen)	$1,600,000	$1,500,000
(5) Normal sales over 4 weeks that promotional packs are in stores (dozens)	600,000	600,000
(6) Normal purchases made at reduced prices (%)	80%	60%
(7) "Regular" pairs bought on deal (dozens) (line 6 × line 7)	480,000	360,000
(8) Total pairs on which margin loss absorbed (dozens) (line 3 + line 7)	800,000	660,000
(9) Dollar margin loss (13¢/pair × 12 pair/dozen × line 8) For the 20¢ off each pair, L'eggs would absorb 13¢ and the retailer would absorb 7¢	($1,243,000)	($1,030,000)
(10) Costs of packaging, sales materials, freight, flags, etc. (per dozen)	$.350	$.385
(11) Total costs of packaging, sales materials, freight, flags, etc. (line 8 × line 10)	($280,000)	($254,000)
(12) Cost of temporary labor to flag boutique packs	($270,000)	0
(13) Total costs of promotion over 20 weeks (lines 9 + 10 + 12)	($1,798,000)	($1,284,000)
(14) Total payout over 20 weeks (line 4 − line 13)	($198,000)	$216,000
(15) Expected long-run weekly volume increase (%)	10%	0
(16) Expected weekly long-run gain ($5./dozen gross margin)	$75,000	0